AF174038

The United States in World War II

A Documentary History

The United States in World War II

A Documentary History

Edited, with an Introduction, by

Mark A. Stoler and Molly C. Michelmore

Hackett Publishing Company, Inc.
Indianapolis/Cambridge

Copyright © 2018 by Hackett Publishing Company, Inc.

All rights reserved
Printed in the United States of America

21 20 19 18   1 2 3 4 5 6 7

For further information, please address
   Hackett Publishing Company, Inc.
   P.O. Box 44937
   Indianapolis, Indiana 46244-0937

   www.hackettpublishing.com

Cover design by Rick Todhunter
Interior design by Elizabeth L. Wilson
Composition by Aptara, Inc.

Though every reasonable effort has been made to trace the owners of the copyrighted materials included in this book, in some instances this has proven impossible. The Publisher will be glad to receive information leading to a more complete understanding of the permissions required for this book and in the meantime extend their apologies for any omissions.

Library of Congress Cataloging-in-Publication Data
Names: Stoler, Mark A., editor. | Michelmore, Molly C., editor.
Title: The United States in World War II : a documentary history / edited, with
   an introduction, by Mark Stoler and Molly C. Michelmore.
Description: Indianapolis : Hackett Publishing Company, Inc., [2018] | Includes
   bibliographical references.
Identifiers: LCCN 2018008248| ISBN 9781624667473 (pbk.) | ISBN
   9781624667480 (cloth)
Subjects: LCSH: World War, 1939–1945—United States. | United States—
   History—1933–1945.
Classification: LCC D769 .U4958 2018 | DDC 940.53/73—dc23
LC record available at https://lccn.loc.gov/2018008248

The paper used in this publication meets the minimum requirements of American National Standard for Information Sciences—Permanence of Paper for Printed Library Materials, ANSI Z39.48–1984.

∞

CONTENTS

Preface   xiii

Introduction   xvii

    Estimated Military and Civilian Deaths Attributable to World War II   xviii
    Estimated Number of Deaths Attributable to World War II:
      Asia and the Pacific   xxxvi
    Estimated Number of Deaths Attributable to World War II: Europe   xxxvii

**Chapter 1: The Yanks Are Coming . . . Again: U.S. Entry into
World War II**   1

  1. The Neutrality Acts Seek to Avoid U.S. Participation in
     Another War, 1935–1939   5

  2. President Franklin D. Roosevelt Proposes a "Quarantine"
     of Aggressors, 1937   8

  3. President Roosevelt Denounces Isolationism and the
     Axis Powers, 1940   11

  4. President Roosevelt Proposes Lend-Lease Aid to Great Britain
     and the Four Freedoms, December 17 and 29, 1940,
     and January 6, 1941   14

  5. Charles A. Lindbergh Opposes Lend-Lease, February 6, 1941   20

  6. Americans Express Their Opinions on Aid to Britain and
     Entry into the War, 1940–1941   22

  7. Secretary of State Cordell Hull Responds to Japan's Final
     Proposal, November 26, 1941   24

  8. Japan Terminates Negotiations and Hull Replies Orally,
     December 7, 1941   27

  9. President Roosevelt Asks Congress for a Declaration of War,
     December 8, 1941   31

Chapter 2: Over Here: Mobilizing the American People for War   **33**

   1. Congress Institutes the Draft, 1940   36

   2. Conscientious Objectors Explain Their Reasons for
Refusing to Register for the Draft, 1941   39

   3. Representative Edith Nourse Rogers Introduces
the WAAC Bill, 1941   41

   4. Jobs Performed by White and African Americans in
the U.S. Army, 1942   43

   5. President Franklin D. Roosevelt Outlines a Blueprint
for Victory, January 6, 1942   44

   6. World War II and the American Economy   46

   7. African Americans Call for Victory at Home and Abroad, 1942   48

   8. The Bureau of Motion Pictures Enlists Hollywood in
the War Effort, 1942   49

   9. Rosie the Riveter Becomes the Image of
Patriotic Womanhood, 1943   52

  10. The U.S. Treasury Department Calls on All Americans to
Pay Their Taxes to Beat the Axis, 1945   53

**Chapter 3: Creating a Global Allied Strategy to
Defeat the Axis Powers**   **55**

   1. U.S. and British Military Officials Agree to a Germany-
First Strategy: Admiral Stark's Memorandum and the
ABC-1 Accord, November 1940 and March 1941   58

   2. Britain and the United States Reach Strategic Agreements
at the ARCADIA Conference, Washington, DC,
December 1941–January 1942   62

   3. Admiral Ernest J. King Calls for a Strategic Focus on Japan,
March 1942   66

   4. President Franklin D. Roosevelt "Promises" the
Soviets a Second Front, May–June 1942   68

   5. Churchill Vetoes Crossing the Channel in 1942 and
Proposes the North African Alternative, July 8, 1942   71

   6. Admiral Ernest J. King and General George C. Marshall
Respond with a Pacific-First Proposal, July 10, 1942   72

7. President Roosevelt Rejects the Pacific-First Alternative,
   July 14, 1942   73

8. Britain and the United States Agree on a Mediterranean
   Strategy for 1943 during the Casablanca Conference,
   January 1943   74

9. Stalin Angrily Responds to the Continued Delays in
   Establishing a Second Front, June 24, 1943   76

10. President Roosevelt, Churchill, and Stalin Debate and
    Decide Future Allied Strategy at the Tehran Conference,
    November 29–30, 1943   78

Chapter 4: Fighting and Defeating Nazi Germany   **83**

1. Army Ground versus Air Plans for the War against Germany:
   The "Victory Program" (with AWPD-1) of September 1941   85

2. The Naval and Air Campaigns against German U-Boats and
   Cities Receive High Priority at the Casablanca Conference,
   January 1943   88

3. A Mother Questions and General Henry H. "Hap"
   Arnold's Staff Defends the Bombing of German Cities   91

4. The Original Overlord Plan Proposes Landing on the
   Normandy Beaches and Explains the Problems to
   Be Overcome, July 27, 1943   93

5. Generals Eisenhower and Montgomery Debate Broad versus
   Narrow Front Strategies, September 1944   97

6. Generals Bradley and Patton Express Their Anger at
   Montgomery, April 1943 and December 1944   101

7. General Marshall Explains the Key Military Events in
   German Defeat as Perceived by Captured Members of
   the German High Command, September 1945   110

8. Tuskegee Airman Lieutenant Alexander Jefferson Recalls
   His Combat Missions and Internment, 1944   112

9. Sergeant Bernard Bellush Recalls D-Day on Omaha Beach,
   November 14, 1944, and March 16, 2000   119

10. Newspaper Columnist Ernie Pyle Depicts the Realities
    of War for Americans at Home, 1943   125

Chapter 5: The War against Japan—and the Japanese 129

    1. Public Opinion Favors a Japan-First Strategy, 1942–1943 132

    2. The Military Plans for the Defeat of Japan, May 21, 1943 133

    3. Army Nurse Lieutenant Juanita Redmond Describes a Japanese Air Attack on Bataan in the Philippines, April 1942 135

    4. Navy Pilot George Gay Survives the Battle of Midway, June 1942 138

    5. Marine Private E. B. Sledge Remembers the Hellish Battle of Okinawa, 1945 142

    6. Japanese Civilians Tomizawa and Kobayashi Hiroyasu Live through the Firebombing of Tokyo, 1945 145

    7. General Joseph Stilwell Bitterly Explains His Problems in China, 1944 148

    8. President Franklin D. Roosevelt Orders Japanese Relocation, 1942 150

    9. Japanese American Mikiso Hane Remembers His Wartime Internment 154

Chapter 6: For the Duration: Life and Society on the American Home Front 159

    1. War Jobs Trigger the Second Great Migration 162

    2. The NAACP Explains What Caused the Detroit Race Riots, 1943 164

    3. Mississippi Congressman John Rankin Attacks the "Zoot Suiters," 1943 170

    4. Wartime and Postwar Conditions Affect Marriage, Divorce, and Birthrates, 1930–1950 172

    5. *Ladies Home Journal* Tells You What to Do "If You're a War Bride," 1942 175

    6. Pinup Girls Remind American Soldiers Why They Fight 181

    7. The Office of War Information Warns American Men about Venereal Diseases 182

    8. An African American Woman Reflects on Her Experiences as a War Worker, 1943 183

    9. President Franklin D. Roosevelt Talks to the Nation about Economic Sacrifice, 1942 184

Chapter 7: The Manhattan Project and Beyond: The Role of Science, Medicine, and Technology in the American War Effort 189

1. Office of Scientific Research and Development Director Dr. Vannevar Bush Reports to the White House on the Importance of Science during and after the War 191

2. Mass-Produced Penicillin Saves Countless Lives 195

3. Advances in Medicine Save Soldiers from Disease and Death 196

4. Radar Helps the Allies to Victory 198

5. Physicist Leo Szilard Issues a Warning about the Atomic Bomb, 1939 199

6. Albert Einstein Informs President Franklin D. Roosevelt of the Potential for an Atomic Bomb, 1939 200

7. The Manhattan Project Spans the Country 202

8. Physicist J. Robert Oppenheimer Later Explains the Establishment of the Atomic Bomb Laboratory at Los Alamos, New Mexico, 1954 204

9. Manhattan Project Commanding General Leslie Groves Reports the Results of the Alamogordo Test, 1945 208

Chapter 8: The Intelligence War: Code Breaking, Cryptography, Intelligence Gathering, and Allied Victory 213

1. A Congressional Committee Assesses Blame for the Pearl Harbor Disaster, 1945 215

2. Bletchley Park Cryptologist and Historian Peter Calvocoressi Explains How Enigma Worked during the War 218

3. WRNS Tends the Colossus Code-Breaking Computer, 1943 223

4. Americans Decode and Translate a Japanese Encrypted Message, 1944 224

5. The Navajo Language Becomes an Unbreakable American Code, 1942 226

6. Office of Strategic Services Official Allen Dulles Explains His Wartime Intelligence Activities, 1941–1945 228

7. Historian and OSS Official William Langer Describes the Contribution of Scholars to the Intelligence War, 1943–1946 232

Chapter 9: The United States and the Holocaust   **235**

   1. The National Origins Act Restricts Immigration, 1924   237

   2. Henry Ford's *Dearborn Independent* Reveals
      American Anti-Semitism, 1921–1922   238

   3. The United States Supreme Court Finds the Sterilization of
      "Defectives" Constitutional, 1927   241

   4. Public Opinion Polls Reveal American Attitudes about
      Jews in Europe, Refugees, and Immigration, 1938–1945   244

   5. Jan Karski of the Polish Underground Gives an
      Eyewitness Account of the Final Solution, 1942–1944   248

   6. The State Department Receives and Suppresses
      News of the Final Solution, 1942   253

   7. The Moscow Declaration on War Crimes, 1943   257

   8. Secretary of the Treasury Henry Morgenthau Jr. Denounces
      State Department Behavior to President Franklin
      D. Roosevelt, 1944   258

   9. U.S. Soldier Clinton C. Gardner Remembers the Liberation
      of the Buchenwald Concentration Camp, 1945   260

Chapter 10: Planning and Preparing for the Peace at Home   **265**

   1. The National Resources Planning Board Looks Forward, 1943   267

   2. President Franklin D. Roosevelt Proposes an Economic
      Bill of Rights, 1945   272

   3. Robert A. Taft Lays Out the Republican Vision for the
      Postwar World, 1943   274

   4. Vice President Henry Wallace Plans for a Third New
      Deal, 1943   279

   5. Women Give Up Their War Jobs   284

   6. Americans Worry about Postwar Employment Prospects:
      The Gallup Poll, December 27, 1944   288

   7. President Roosevelt Promises Veterans a New Bill
      of Rights, 1944   290

   8. Black Veterans Debate the Impact of the GI Bill, 1945   292

Chapter 11: President Franklin D. Roosevelt and Allied Diplomacy for War and Peace 299

1. The Atlantic Charter States Allied War Aims, 1941 301

2. Josef Stalin Demands Territorial Settlements, 1941 302

3. The Allies Announce Formation of the Grand Alliance and Declare Their War Aims: The Declaration by the United Nations 307

4. President Roosevelt Enunciates the Unconditional Surrender Policy, 1943 308

5. The Allies Agree on Postwar Policies: The Moscow Declaration on General Security and the Cairo Declaration, 1943 309

6. President Roosevelt Informs His Allies of His Postwar Plans, 1942 and 1943 311

7. The Allies Agree to a Postwar International Organization: The Dumbarton Oaks Agreements, 1944 315

8. Churchill and Stalin Divide Eastern Europe, 1944 317

9. The Allies Reach Postwar Agreements at the Yalta Conference, 1945 318

10. President Roosevelt Sends Messages to Stalin and Churchill Just before His Death, 1945 324

Chapter 12: The Atomic Bomb and the End of World War II 327

1. Supreme Court Justice Felix Frankfurter Shares with President Franklin D. Roosevelt Physicist Niels Bohr's Suggestion That the Soviets Be Informed about the Atomic Bomb Project, 1944 330

2. Churchill and President Roosevelt Reject Informing the Soviets, 1944 331

3. Secretary of War Henry L. Stimson Informs President Harry Truman of the Atomic Bomb Project, April 25, 1945 332

4. The Franck Committee Warns of a Nuclear Arms Race and Calls for a Noncombat Demonstration of the Bomb, 1945 334

5. The Scientific Panel of the Interim Committee Recommends Combat Use of the Bomb against Japan, 1945 338

6. Conventional versus Nuclear Bomb Destruction:
   Dresden and Hiroshima, 1945   340

7. Public Opinion Polls Show Strong Support for
   the Atomic Bomb, August 1945   341

General Bibliography   **343**

PREFACE

Contrary to popular belief, history does not consist of the rote memorization of facts about the past. Rather, it involves the selecting, organizing, and interpreting of facts about specific events to form a coherent pattern. And in doing so, historians often disagree with each other in their interpretations of a specific event.

That is definitely the case with regard to the Second World War. While the basic facts about the war may be clear, their organization and meaning are subject to multiple interpretations. Furthermore, these interpretations have changed over time and often reflect to an extent the time period in which they were written.

Early interpretations of U.S. participation in World War II echoed the debates over intervention that had taken place within the United States before Pearl Harbor. Reflecting the American decision to remain deeply involved in international affairs once the war ended, most of these interpretations focused on the international as opposed to the domestic aspects of the war, sided with the interventionist point of view, and condemned the anti-interventionists. Diplomatic and military historians divided, however, in their assessments of U.S. foreign and military policies after Pearl Harbor. Heavily influenced by the Soviet-American Cold War then in its early stages, some condemned American policy makers for naivete during the war in regard to the Soviet Union and what they labeled an apolitical U.S. military strategy, both of which enabled the USSR to control Eastern Europe while its Communist allies triumphed in China against the American-supported government of Chiang Kai-shek. Other historians, however, defended wartime U.S. policies and strategies in light of the diplomatic and military realities of the time—most notably the need to defeat Nazi Germany and its Italian and Japanese allies and the critical importance of the Soviet war effort to achieve that goal.

New perspectives and interpretations began to emerge in the 1970s and 1980s as a result of major U.S. and British declassifications of wartime government documents as well as the impact of the Vietnam War, which deeply divided Americans and led many of those who opposed it to question previous interpretations of World War II and develop new ones. Some of these directly challenged the pro-internationalist interpretations of their predecessors, noting the numerous negative impacts (such as dramatically increased executive power) that the anti-interventionists had correctly predicted. Others challenged the prevailing orthodoxy regarding

Soviet responsibility for the Cold War, emphasizing its wartime origins in British and American actions and inactions, from not establishing a "second front" against the Germans in western Europe until 1944 to using the atomic bomb to affect Soviet behavior rather than end the war quickly as previous historians had claimed. Still others focused on the Anglo-American "special relationship" during the war, noting the numerous and serious wartime disagreements between the two nations.

As Vietnam affected these new interpretations, so the black civil rights movement and the women's rights movements of the 1960s and 1970s led to a new emphasis in World War II scholarship on the American home front and domestic aspects of the war. This emphasis was also the result of the new social history then developing throughout the historical profession, instead of the previous and traditional diplomatic, military, and political history of the conflict.

The result of all these events and factors was a major questioning of the then-popular and widely held view of World War II as the "good war" for the United States. On many issues, most notably but far from exclusively the use of the atomic bomb against Japan, the result was a very heated controversy between those supporting traditional views and those espousing very different and at times diametrically opposed ones.

This is actually a pattern quite familiar in all historical studies whereby early, traditional interpretations are eventually attacked by those labeled revisionist historians because they try to revise the standard approach, sometimes dramatically. And in this pattern, a synthesis eventually emerges. Such a synthesis has already begun to develop on some controversial wartime issues, though far from all of them.

The chapters in this volume have been selected and organized so as to present documents on some of the most controversial and debated historical issues regarding the U.S. participation in the war: how and why the United States entered the conflict, mobilized at home, developed a global and Allied strategy; fought the war in Europe and in the Pacific and Far East; experienced revolutionary changes in life at home; created and made use of major advances in technology, science, and medicine; failed for the most part to deal with German and Japanese wartime atrocities; planned for the postwar world, both at home and internationally; and ended the war against Japan with nuclear weapons. Each chapter consists of a general introduction that explains the key facts and interpretive controversies about the specific issue, followed by seven to ten documents with brief introductions.

Preceding these chapter introductions and documents is a general introduction that briefly describes the origins and causes of World War II; the military successes and ensuing expansion of German and Japanese territory and power before U.S. entry; how and why the United States and its allies were able by 1945 to totally defeat the Axis Powers; and the impact of the war on both the nation and international relations in general. The ensuing chapters are arranged both chronologically and topically, beginning with the road to U.S. entry into the war and ending with the atomic bomb and surrender of Japan. Both the chapter and the document introductions raise a series of questions to consider, many of which have divided and continue to divide World War II historians.

INTRODUCTION

World War II was the largest and most devastating conflict in recorded human history. The nations involved fought a total war on virtually every continent and ocean, in the air and underwater as well as on land and the seas. The war was fought against civilians as well as nations' uniformed armed forces. The result was a staggering and unprecedented death toll of approximately 60 million people. In the end, the war gave birth to a new international order that would survive into the twenty-first century. Equally important, the total war effort transformed the economy, politics, and culture of almost every society involved.

The United States emerged from the war as the most powerful nation the world had ever seen. Although the nation had suffered the greatest number of deaths for any war in its history save the 1861–1865 Civil War, that number (approximately 294,000 in combat and approximately 405,000 total deaths) was far lower both absolutely and as a percentage of the prewar population than the death toll for any of the other major powers involved (see Figure 1, as well as Figures 2 and 3 at the end of this Introduction). The United States was the only major combatant to suffer neither air attack[1] nor invasion. As a result, civilian casualties were minimal, while U.S. industrial power expanded enormously: by war's end fully half of the world's manufacturing capacity was American.

World War II began long before the United States officially entered the conflict in December of 1941. In Europe, it officially began on September 1, 1939, when Nazi Germany invaded Poland, and Britain and France responded with declarations of war. In the Far East the war began at least two years earlier, in 1937, when Japan began an undeclared war against China. Some date the start of World War II in Asia as early as 1931, when the Japanese army forcibly seized the Chinese province of Manchuria and established the puppet state of Manchukuo. But, the roots of the conflict reach back at least to the First World War of 1914–1918, and perhaps even further back to the long-term causes of that earlier conflict: the Industrial Revolution of the nineteenth century, and the rise of the new powers of Germany, Italy, and Japan as well as the United States who challenged the

---

1. When the Japanese military attacked the U.S. Naval Base at Pearl Harbor, Hawaii was not yet a state. First annexed by the United States in 1898, Hawaii gained statehood in 1959.

Estimated Military and Civilian Deaths Attributable to World War II

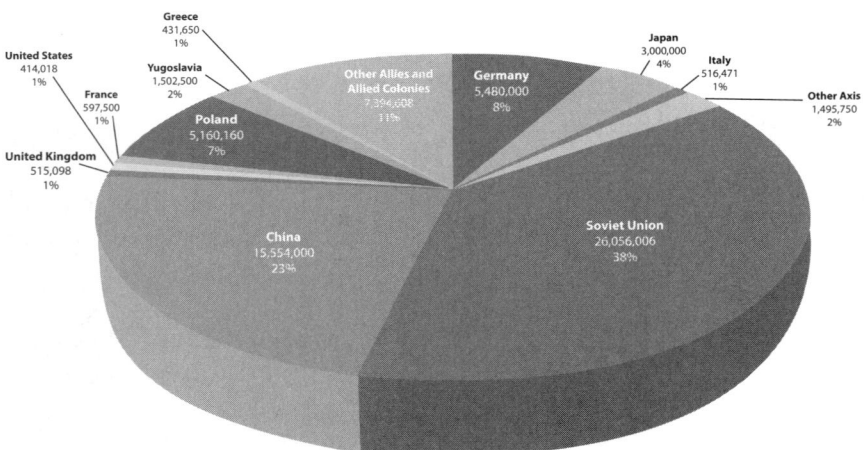

More than 400,000 Americans lost their lives in World War II. Indeed, the Second World War resulted in more American deaths than any other war in U.S. history except the Civil War. Yet, as Figure 1 illustrates, those American deaths constituted a very small percentage—less than 1 percent—of the total number who died in this global conflict. Determining exactly how many did die is extremely difficult, if not impossible. The figures for many countries are only estimates and, in many cases, these estimates vary widely. The chart reproduced here uses a median estimate of civilian and military deaths to illustrate the human cost of the war. The more detailed tables at the end of this Introduction provide both high and low estimates of civilian and military deaths for the Axis and Allied nations in the European and Pacific theaters. Both are based on figures calculated by historian Richard Frank for his forthcoming trilogy on the Pacific War, 1937–1945.

supremacy of Great Britain and upset the old European and global balance of power.

The result was the First World War, referred to at the time and for the next two decades as the Great War, in which the Allied powers of Britain, France, Italy, Japan, and Russia until 1917, when it left the war and the United States entered it, fought the Central powers of Germany, Austria-Hungary, and Ottoman Turkey. After four years of bloody military stalemate, Austria-Hungary and the Ottoman Empire collapsed and ceased to exist, while Germany was forced to sue for peace. The ensuing Treaty of Versailles officially ended the war. The treaty weakened and punished Germany by disarming it, depriving it of its overseas colonies and forcing it to cede territory to France and the reconstituted Poland. Perhaps most controversially, the treaty also required Germany to pay reparations to the Allied victors and accept responsibility for starting the war.

Many Germans were extremely embittered by this treaty. Likewise, Italy and Japan felt that they had not been treated fairly by their other allies. In the decade after the war, all three nations also suffered from serious domestic problems—problems that were only compounded by the Great Depression of the 1930s. Highly aggressive and militaristic regimes, commonly labeled Fascist, took advantage of these conditions to seize power in these nations as well as others and made clear their determination to overthrow by force the new international order that had been established by the Versailles treaty system.

In Italy, Benito Mussolini and his paramilitary Black Shirts took power as early as 1922, established a highly militarized dictatorship, and pursued an aggressive foreign policy designed to recapture the glory of the ancient Roman Empire. In 1935, Italian armies invaded and conquered the African nation of Ethiopia. In Japan, army officers took over the northernmost Chinese province of Manchuria without government sanction and established the puppet state of Manchukuo in the early thirties. Over the next few years, militarists gradually took control of the Japanese government from civilians and in 1937 invaded China proper. The Japanese also sought to expand their empire in the western Pacific and East Asia. In Germany, Adolf Hitler and his Nazi movement took power in 1933 with the avowed aim of overthrowing the entire Versailles treaty system and making Germany the dominant power in Europe—and the world. By 1936, Hitler had quit the League of Nations, as had Japan a few years earlier, and rearmed Germany while marching into the demilitarized Rhineland in direct violation of the Treaty of Versailles. In that same year, the three nations formed the Rome-Berlin-Tokyo Axis—and henceforth would be known as the Axis powers. Hitler and Mussolini also sent military forces to Spain to aid the pro-Fascist Nationalist forces led by General Francisco Franco in their civil war against the established republican government. Then in 1938 Hitler annexed Austria and set his sights on the acquisition of the Sudetenland in western Czechoslovakia—two states that had been established after the collapse of the Austro-Hungarian Empire at the end of World War I.

Germany and its Axis partners posed a potentially mortal threat to the two major democratic nations in Europe, Great Britain and France. Yet neither country was willing to challenge Axis aggression. Both had suffered devastating losses during World War I, losing virtually an entire generation to bloody trench warfare. As a result, many French and British citizens, as well as their leaders, believed that anything would be better than another world war. Many also believed that Germany had been unjustly treated in the Treaty of Versailles and was thus entitled to revision of that punitive peace settlement. In addition, neither power felt militarily prepared or sufficiently unified internally to begin another war. And any successful military opposition to Germany and its Axis partners would require alliance with the detested and feared Communist regime in the Soviet Union, a regime that during World War I had seized power in Russia, signed a separate peace with Germany, and both called for and supported similar Communist revolutions against all capitalist governments. During the 1930s dictator Josef Stalin had also launched a series of bloody purges within both the Communist Party and the Red Army, leading many to discount the Soviets' military strength.

Consequently, Britain and France followed a policy known as appeasement, whereby they acceded to Italian and Japanese military conquests in Africa and Asia, Italian and German military intervention in the Spanish Civil War, Hitler's violations of the terms of the Treaty of Versailles, and his ensuing territorial demands and annexations. At the notorious Munich Conference in September of 1938, France and Britain agreed to Hitler's annexation of the Sudetenland, a move that British Prime Minister Neville Chamberlain claimed would guarantee "peace in our time." Six months later, however, Hitler annexed the rest of Czechoslovakia and began to make territorial demands on Poland.

The refusal of the United States to involve itself in a meaningful way in any effort to deter the Axis powers also informed the Anglo-French policy of appeasement. In addition to being mired in the Great Depression and preoccupied with the New Deal measures of President Franklin D. Roosevelt, many Americans had come to believe that Germany had been unfairly treated in the Versailles peace settlement and that the United States' entry into the First World War had been a mistake. The result was the American policy often known as isolationism. Many historians now reject that label as inaccurate and misleading and prefer the term "noninterventionist." Nevertheless, scholars agree that in the 1930s the United States sought to avoid any political or military commitments in Europe that could involve the nation in another world war. As a result of these beliefs Congress passed a series of Neutrality Acts from 1935 to 1939, which outlawed the overseas travel, arms trade, loans, and involvement of American merchant ships that it believed had led to U.S. entry into the First World War. By removing the nation from any potential coalition against the Axis, American policy reinforced the British and French desire to appease rather than fight.

Hitler's annexation of the rest of Czechoslovakia in March of 1939 and ensuing territorial demands on Poland ended the obviously failed policy of appeasement and led to Anglo-French guarantees to Poland and an effort to obtain Soviet support against German aggression. But on August 23 Hitler struck an unexpected nonaggression pact of his own with the Soviet Union, his great racial and ideological enemy. The agreement, known as the Molotov-Ribbentrop Pact after the two countries' foreign ministers, also contained a secret section dividing Poland and the rest of Eastern Europe between the two powers. With the threat of a two-front war removed, Hitler invaded Poland on September 1. Two days later Britain and France declared war.

Using new and revolutionary military technology and tactics involving airpower and armor known as "*blitzkrieg,*" or "lightning war," German forces quickly conquered Poland in the fall of 1939 and divided it with the Soviet Union. Then in the spring of 1940 they just as rapidly conquered Denmark, Norway, Belgium, Luxembourg, the Netherlands, and France itself, with Italy joining the war on June 10, just in time to obtain some of the spoils. Only Britain, now under Winston S. Churchill, its new prime minister, stood between Hitler and total victory. And despite the dramatic and unexpected rescue of its army at Dunkirk during the Anglo-French military collapse, Britain's ill-equipped forces appeared incapable of preventing a successful German invasion and conquest of the British Isles.

Success in any such invasion required control of the air, however, and throughout the summer and fall of 1940 Hitler unsuccessfully attempted to obtain such control by destroying the outnumbered Royal Air Force in the so-called Battle of Britain. At the same time, Japan took advantage of French defeat and British preoccupation to move its armed forces into French Indochina and to pressure Britain into closing the Burma Road, a major supply route to Chinese leader Chiang Kai-shek's forces battling the Japanese army. Although the Germans inflicted great damage on the British, they proved unable to destroy the Royal Air Force. As a result, Hitler canceled his plans to invade Great Britain and instead turned his sights—and his military might—to the East. In April of 1941 Nazi forces invaded and conquered Yugoslavia and Greece. Three months later, in June, Hitler turned on his recent ally by launching a massive invasion of the Soviet Union, code-named Operation Barbarossa.

Throughout this time period Americans watched Axis conquests with growing alarm. The unexpected German successes in Western Europe led to a major reassessment of U.S. policies and a growing belief that British survival was essential to U.S. security. As a result, President Roosevelt and the U.S. Congress agreed to provide Britain with military aid—first via arms sales and then free of charge with the passage of the Lend-Lease bill in March of 1941. Public and congressional opinion was far from unified on this policy, however. Many Americans continued to believe that helping Britain would lead to a needless war that would destroy democracy and that the nation could and should instead maintain its traditional isolation from European wars. While these anti-interventionists were defeated in the Lend-Lease debate, they nevertheless constituted a formidable force that precluded actual U.S. entry into the war as Britain's ally. Anti-interventionist opposition, however, did not prevent Roosevelt from meeting with Churchill off the coast of Newfoundland in August where the two agreed to the Atlantic Charter, a broad statement of postwar aims. Nor could the anti-interventionists stop the president from extending Lend-Lease aid to the Soviet Union and to China, or from using his powers as commander in chief to effectively institute an undeclared naval war with German submarines in the Atlantic to ensure the arrival of Lend-Lease supplies in England. At the same time, Roosevelt sought to deter further Japanese expansion by moving the U.S. fleet to Pearl Harbor, by providing the Chinese government with aid, and by initiating economic sanctions against Tokyo.

In September 1940, Germany, Italy, and Japan had responded to these moves with the Tripartite Pact. By its terms each nation agreed to come to the defense of the others if any of them was attacked by a presently neutral nation. The pact was clearly aimed as a warning to the United States to stay out of the conflict, but the gambit backfired. Indeed, American aid to Britain and China increased after the Tripartite Pact was formalized. With Japan dependent on American oil and steel for its war in China and for expansion in Southeast Asia, Washington gradually applied stiffer and stiffer sanctions and, in the summer of 1941, instituted a de facto embargo by freezing all Japanese assets. Japan responded with a decision to obtain the resources it needed in Southeast Asia via attacks against and conquest of British, Dutch, and American possessions in the Far East, most notably British Malaya, the Dutch East Indies, and the Philippines. To neutralize the threat the U.S. fleet at Pearl Harbor posed to its expansionist agenda, Japanese naval aircraft launched a surprise attack against that fleet on December 7, 1941. The attack cost 2,403 Americans their lives; another 1,176 were wounded. Four days later Hitler declared war on the United States and the United States responded in kind, thereby linking the European and Far Eastern conflicts into one total and global war.

After the war ended, most historians sided with Roosevelt and the interventionists. A few, however, supported the anti-interventionist point of view and argued that formal, full-scale U.S. entry and participation in the European war could and should have been avoided—as could and should any war with Japan. Others have argued that however necessary war might have been with Germany and/or Japan, Roosevelt's behavior set dangerous precedents regarding the use of executive power in the future.

Once formally in the war, the United States mobilized its military, economy, society, and even culture for the war against the Axis powers. That mobilization had actually begun more than a year before Pearl Harbor with the first billion-dollar defense bills in the spring of 1940 and the initiation of the first peacetime draft in U.S. history. Later defense bills increased U.S. spending on military preparedness to more than $17 billion by October 1940. The passage of Lend-Lease the following March not only provided Britain and eventually other allies with military supplies, it also helped to transform the United States into what Roosevelt had memorably termed the "arsenal of democracy." And the ensuing economic mobilization jump-started the U.S. economy and finally put an end to the Great Depression; by December 1941, the nation was spending more than $75 million per day for defense. Defense spending increased further and dramatically once the United States became a full and formal belligerent.

The effects of mobilization on the American economy cannot be over-stated. The United States added 17 million new jobs over the course of the war. In combination with the economic effect of military mobilization, the war all but eliminated the scourge of unemployment. The war years also produced remarkable productivity gains, as companies experimented with new production techniques to meet extraordinary demand. New production models in shipbuilding, for example, reduced the average time it took to build a merchant ship from six months to twelve days! The tight labor market together with newly powerful labor unions produced real economic gains for the average worker. Between 1939 and 1944, wages and salaries increased by more than 100 percent. Labor contracts negotiated during the war had long-term implications for the American social compact. Government policy placed strict caps on wages, but did not limit nonsalary forms of compensation. To attract and retain workers, companies began offering benefits including pensions and health insurance. These perks became a hallmark of postwar labor contracts.

The war also set the pattern for the relationship between the public and private sectors. Although the federal government sometimes used coercion to achieve desired economic ends, most public policies relied instead on voluntarism, market incentives, and a variety of financial inducements to put the nation on a war footing. Business, which had seen its reputation collapse during the Great Depression, benefited materially from wartime mobilization. Annual after-tax corporate profits increased from $6.4 billion in 1940 to almost $11 billion four years later. Most military leaders regarded this as a feature rather than a bug. As Secretary of War Henry Stimson later wrote in his diary, "If you are going to go to war, or prepare for war in a capitalist country, you have got to let businesses make money out of the process, or businesses won't work." The biggest businesses benefited the most, receiving the vast majority of federal defense contracts. In fact, the nation's thirty-three largest firms accounted for more than 50 percent of all military contracting. This pattern of partnership between the public and private sectors survived the war, and became a defining feature of the postwar American state.

Equally important, the war permanently enlarged the size and power of the federal state and arguably inaugurated the era of "big government." The war brought more and more Americans into direct contact with the federal government. More than 85 million Americans—or some 65 percent of the total population—became war bond holders. Some 17 million men and women worked in war-related production jobs. Another 16 million men—and 200,000 women—served in the armed forces. Of particular significance for the long-term development of the American state was the transformation of the federal income tax from a "class tax"—paid by only the very wealthy minority—to a "mass tax" paid by the vast majority of American citizens. Sold as a "war tax" under the slogan "taxes to beat the Axis," this newly robust and broad-based tax system financed almost half the cost of the war and became the basis of the American fiscal state after the war.

The full American mobilization for total war was of course not limited to the home front. Victory over the Axis would require not only American supplies and military forces but also a coordinated global strategy between the United States and its major allies—most notably Britain and the Soviet Union. Although the United States and Great Britain fused their war efforts to an unprecedented degree, such coordination proved difficult to achieve—as had been the case in most previous coalition wars. Each power entered the war with its own history, interests, and preferred strategy, and compromising their differences proved extremely difficult and time consuming.

The Americans, British, and Soviets agreed that Germany had to be defeated before Japan (the Soviet Union was not even at war with Japan before 1945), but they disagreed sharply as to how this should be accomplished. The British favored an indirect, peripheral approach centering on North Africa and the Mediterranean, while both the Soviet Union and the United States favored a direct strategy that focused on crossing the English Channel in northern France to establish a "second front" that would force Hitler into a two-front war and relieve the pressure on the hard-pressed Red Army. In addition, despite their commitment to a "Germany first" global strategy, the Americans also wanted to devote substantial resources to first halting and then reversing the Japanese sweep through Southeast Asia and the Western Pacific that had followed the Pearl Harbor attack.

In 1942 and 1943, Anglo-American forces followed the British approach by invading first French North Africa, then Sicily, and then the Italian mainland, resulting in the overthrow of Mussolini in July of 1943, and an Italian surrender in September. But at the Tehran Conference in November of 1943, Roosevelt and Soviet leader Josef Stalin forced Churchill to agree finally to an invasion of northern France across the Channel, as well as southern France, in the spring of 1944.

Historians still argue over the relative merits of the British and American strategic approaches in the European theater, and over whether the war could have been won sooner by making different strategic decisions. On one side stand those who maintain that the Channel could and should have been crossed earlier than 1944, that the 1942–1943 operations in North Africa and the Mediterranean distracted from what should have been the main effort, and that the delays in crossing the Channel delayed final victory. These delays also embittered the Soviets, who saw them as deliberate, and increased their suspicions of their allies, thereby playing a role in the ensuing Cold War. On the other side stand those who maintain that the Channel could not have been successfully crossed any earlier than 1944, and that the 1942–1943 North African and Mediterranean campaigns were necessary to obtain and maintain public support for the overall Germany first strategy as well as show Stalin some Anglo-American ground operations: standing idle for two years was not an option. These campaigns also led to the surrender of Germany's Italian ally and opened the Mediterranean to Allied shipping as well as air attacks on Germany.

Defeating Germany required the air and naval as well as the ground forces and war materiel of all three major Allied powers. Anglo-American forces advanced in North Africa and the Mediterranean while the Soviets fought the bulk of the German army in the East, suffering enormous casualties and inflicting enormous casualties on the Germans. At the same time, British and American naval forces fought German U-boats for control of the Atlantic while Anglo-American air forces launched a combined and controversial bomber offensive against German cities, industries, and civilians whose effectiveness, cost in lives, and morality historians still debate. By 1944 the strategic bombing offensive also had as its major goal the destruction of the German air force so as to both lower the high casualty rate for British and American bombers and control the air over the forces now scheduled to cross the Channel in the spring of 1944. Success against the U-boats was achieved by the spring of 1943 and against the fighter aircraft of the Luftwaffe in early 1944. Both victories were critical to the success of the cross-Channel invasion, which was launched on June 6, 1944 and which succeeded in liberating France in the spring and summer of 1944.

During that campaign a new Anglo-American strategic argument erupted, this time over the "broad front" approach favored by the Supreme Allied Commander, U.S. General Dwight D. Eisenhower, and British General Bernard Montgomery, who favored a narrower and more concentrated thrust directly toward Berlin by the Anglo-American-Canadian forces under his command in the north. U.S. Generals Omar Bradley, George S. Patton, and Jacob Devers also favored a narrower and more concentrated thrust into Germany, but by their American and French forces in the center and south of the Allied line instead of Montgomery's in the north. Eisenhower maintained the broad front approach throughout the 1944 campaign, successfully held against a major and unexpected German counteroffensive in December (the so-called Battle of the Bulge), and then invaded Germany proper, meeting the advancing Soviet army in late April and together obtaining, after Hitler's late April suicide, a full and unconditional German surrender on May 8, 1945.

Just as historians debate the relative merits of the British peripheral versus U.S. direct strategy in the European theater, and the strategic bombing campaign against Germany, so too do they debate the relative merits of the broad versus narrow front approach on the European continent. Eisenhower's critics argue that the war could have been won in 1944 rather than 1945 had he agreed to Montgomery's more concentrated plan—or, for that matter, the similar plans of Bradley, Patton, and Devers farther south. Eisenhower's defenders counter that the Germans could easily have destroyed what he derisively labeled a "pencil thrust," delaying further if not endangering final victory. They also note that Eisenhower was an Allied commander and as such could not give all resources to the national forces of only one country and its leader; the broad front approach in this regard enabled him to maintain the coalition and make use of all his forces against the Germans.

In the Pacific, U.S. forces first halted the Japanese in the naval Battles of Coral Sea and Midway in May and June of 1942 and then launched their own counteroffensive two months later against the recently Japanese-occupied island of Guadalcanal in the Solomons. The resulting bloody campaign lasted six months. Simultaneously U.S. and Australian forces under the command of General Douglas MacArthur halted an attempted Japanese advance in New Guinea toward Australia.

In early 1942, U.S. military leaders had divided the huge Pacific theater into two separate areas: the Southwest Pacific (SWPA) under General MacArthur in Australia and the Pacific Ocean Areas (POA) under Admiral Chester W. Nimitz in Hawaii—a decision that prevented a major army–navy conflict over control of the Pacific war but also divided American forces and led to major conflicts over scarce resources. Despite these obstacles, and making use of techniques known as "island hopping" and "leap frogging," these forces advanced in 1943–1944 in the Solomons and along the northern coast of New Guinea in the SWPA, as well as in the Gilbert and Marshall Island chains in the POA's Central Pacific, bypassing and isolating numerous Japanese strongholds along the way. In 1944 U.S. forces invaded the Philippines and breached the inner ring of Japanese defenses in the Mariana Islands. In the process they all but destroyed the

Japanese naval air arm and then the Japanese surface fleet in the Battles of the Philippine Sea and Leyte Gulf. Now within air range of the Japanese home islands, the Americans also unleashed a major bombing campaign against Japanese cities.

Despite the hopelessness of their military situation, the Japanese continued to fight fiercely, launching major offensives against China and India in 1944 and inflicting huge casualties with new suicide tactics on the Americans in bloody battles for the Philippines and for the islands of Iwo Jima and Okinawa in 1945. In these as in previous Pacific battles, little quarter was asked or given by either side. The Japanese *bushido* warrior code, which considered surrender dishonorable and unacceptable, led the Japanese to fight to the last man and to mistreat Americans who did surrender in such episodes as the 1942 Bataan Death March. Such behavior only reinforced anti-Japanese racism on the American side. The result was what historian John Dower has aptly called a "war without mercy" in the Pacific and Asia.

The import of anti-Japanese racism can also be seen in the internment of the Japanese—including American citizens—in the United States. In the wake of the surprise attack on Pearl Harbor, Americans of all political stripes harbored deep—and deeply racist—suspicions of anyone of Japanese heritage. In February 1942, responding to public pressure, President Roosevelt issued Executive Order 9066, authorizing the internment of Japanese American citizens as a "menace which had to be dealt with." Under the auspices of the evacuation order, more than 100,000 Japanese Americans were "relocated" to internment camps, and forced to leave behind their homes, their businesses, and their possessions. In its 1944 decision in *Korematsu v. United States*, the U.S. Supreme Court upheld the constitutionality of the evacuation order. Despite widespread public support for the internment policy, Supreme Court Justice Frank Murphy, who dissented in the *Korematsu* case, was surely right when he called the policy the "legalization of racism."

African Americans likewise faced endemic racism throughout the war years. Some historians have discerned a new militancy among black Americans in this period. Black newspapers like the *Pittsburgh Courier* and the *New Amsterdam News* advocated for a "Double Victory" against racism at home and abroad. Civil rights organizations grew in size and power, and were sometimes able to leverage that power to open up new opportunities for black Americans. In 1941, for example, labor and civil rights leader A. Philip Randolph used the threat of a massive march on Washington to convince President Roosevelt to prohibit, via executive order, racial discrimination in war industries. Executive Order 8802, which also created the Fair Employment Practices Committee (FEPC), was the first time since Reconstruction that the federal government had moved explicitly to protect the rights of black Americans. Indeed, despite its reluctance to address the "long-range problems of racial and minority-majority antagonisms," the federal government did encourage civil rights protest, if only indirectly. The public relations campaign against the Axis, both before and after Pearl Harbor, stressed the importance of American democracy and the fight against "racial discrimination in any of its ugly forms." Indeed, Hitler's abhorrent racial politics did help to destabilize and undermine all kinds of racial regimes—from European imperialism to American segregation.

Notwithstanding these important challenges to Jim Crow and white supremacy, however, progress was slow and incomplete. The FEPC was relatively toothless. The Great Migration of African Americans to the industrial North, Midwest, and Far West offered the new migrants economic opportunity, but also produced an often violent backlash as black and white workers competed for jobs and, especially, housing. One of the worst "race riots" of the war years occurred in 1943 in Detroit, when violence cost thirty-three people their lives; twenty-five of the dead were black Americans. Such racial violence was not directed at black Americans alone. The so-called Zoot Suit Riots, which shook Los Angeles in 1943, exposed Anglo anxiety and antipathy toward Mexican and Mexican American Angelenos. Equally important, the armed forces were rigidly segregated for the duration of the war. Because the majority of training bases were built in the South, black soldiers—who served in segregated units under the command of white officers—often found themselves subject to the routine surveillance and extralegal violence intrinsic to Jim Crow. Black men also found it more difficult to join the armed forces, thanks to local control of draft boards, and when they did manage to join up, were often relegated to menial noncombat positions. Although the exigencies of war sometimes forced the integration of white and nonwhite troops, for the most part, the military resisted efforts to eliminate Jim Crow from the Armed Forces.

The war had similarly ambiguous consequences for American women. Mobilization dramatically reshaped public opinion about women's work outside the home. In the 1930s, with the nation mired in the Great Depression and as many as one in four Americans out of work, more than 80 percent of Americans believed that married women should not work for wages. The war changed these attitudes almost overnight. With more and more American men joining the armed forces, it was left to women to keep the economic engine running. In all, 6 million American women took jobs outside the home during the course of the war; the size of the female labor force increased by 57 percent. Not only did the number of women who worked for wages skyrocket, the demographics of the female labor force changed dramatically. Young, single women had long worked for wages, at least until they got married. The war brought older, married women into the labor force in significant numbers. Indeed, by the end of the war, there were almost as many married women in the labor force as single ones. These changes in attitude and behavior did not happen by themselves. The federal government actively worked to change public attitudes toward women's work.

Many of these changes in the lives and status of American women were more apparent than real, however. While the federal government and popular culture did encourage women to contribute to the war effort, both were clear that women's work outside the home was to be "for the duration" only. Sex discrimination continued unabated. Despite the popularity of the "Rosie the Riveter" image, most women did not work in heavy industry, but rather found employment in sex-segregated occupations where they received only a fraction of male wages. Childcare was hard to find, thanks to pervasive attitudes that valued women's domestic work over their paid labor. Indeed, throughout the war, government officials and cultural authorities worried that wartime dislocations might destabilize existing gender hierarchies and unleash a sexual revolution. Wartime "purity" campaigns, which aimed to stem the spread of sexually transmitted diseases, targeted and disciplined female sexuality. To calm fears that military service would render the 200,000 women who signed up to serve in military auxiliary units unfit for postwar life, leaders of the women's auxiliaries insisted enlisted women would be as likely as any to "make marriage their profession" after the war. The military also took a hard line against any kind of "sexual deviance" and treated homosexuality as a variety of personality disorder that made gay men and women unable to fight. Nevertheless, many gays and lesbians did serve in the military both during and after the war.

Black women did not experience the same gains during the war as either white women or black men. Indeed, while the number of black Americans employed in manufacturing increased by 135 percent, the number of black women in manufacturing jobs increased by only 59 percent. The FEPC did little to protect the employment rights of black women. Black women were much more likely than other groups to work temporary or seasonal jobs—a work pattern that made it difficult for them to accrue seniority or earn promotions or pay raises.

Anti-Semitism was also prevalent in the United States. It was, of course, far less intense than the "eliminationist" anti-Semitism in Germany and German-occupied Europe, where the Nazis tried to exterminate all the Jews of Europe. But American anti-Semitism clearly played a role in maintaining rigid immigration restrictions during the 1930s and the war years—restrictions that prevented most European Jews fleeing Nazi persecution from entering the United States. It also played a role in minimizing American efforts to rescue Jews during the war and to halt what is known today as the Holocaust. Numerous other factors also played key roles in American inaction. These included a desire to minimize immigration in general during a time of severe economic depression and unemployment; limits on what could be done once the Germans controlled all of Europe; bureaucratic inertia; a single-minded military focus on victory as quickly as possible and the consequent desire to avoid any military action—such as bombing extermination camps—that would detract from such a focus; and difficulty believing that the Germans were actually conducting mass extermination of millions of human beings. Historians still debate the relative importance of these factors in their efforts to explain why the United States did so little, as well as how much more the United States could have done given such constraints.

The war also stimulated significant advances in science, technology, and medicine. The Manhattan Project, the code name for the successful joint American and British effort to develop an atomic bomb, is only the best-known scientific endeavor of World War II. Radar, which uses radio waves to detect distant objects, proved useful in the Battle of Britain, and ultimately helped the Allies to win the Battle of the Atlantic. New advances in medicine, including blood transfusions, the discovery of a synthetic alternative to the antimalarial drug quinine, and the use of pesticides like DDT, reduced mortality rates significantly. Indeed, the Second World War was the first conflict in which more American soldiers died in battle than from nonbattle-related injuries or diseases. No medical advance was more consequential than the mass production of penicillin. Safer and more effective than sulfa drugs in treating infection and disease, penicillin was tricky to manufacture in quantities sufficient to meet military, much less civilian need. Nevertheless, by 1944, more than 20 American companies had begun to produce enough of the miracle drug to meet mounting demand. These advances not only improved the quality of life in the postwar period, they also helped the Allies to win the war.

Intelligence gathering also played a critical role in the outcome of the war. By the time war broke out, signals intelligence—the interception and interpretation of electronic communications—had become the most vital and important source of information about other nations. By the late 1930s, the Germans had manufactured more than 100,000 automatic enciphering devices known as Enigma machines. The Japanese likewise used encrypting machines to scramble diplomatic and military communiques. Though both Axis powers believed their ciphers to be unbreakable, the British and the Americans had begun to crack both codes as early as 1940. Success in codebreaking efforts not only proved a key to Allied victory, it also gave birth to the computer age. The Colossus machine, developed at the British Government Code and Cypher School to break the Lorenz cipher between 1943 and 1945, is considered the world's first programmable, electronic computer.

The war thus contained the seeds of the postwar order, both at home and abroad. Domestically, wartime mobilization revitalized the American economy and transformed American industry. By 1944, more than $20 billion had been invested in the country's industrial plant; the vast majority of this sum—$16 billion—came directly from the federal government in the form of military contracts. This spending not only expanded productive capacity but also improved and modernized it. But the dependence of the U.S. economy on military spending raised concerns about what would happen *after* the war. Could the United States sustain the economic activity of the war years when federal contracts dried up? Would the end of the war mean the return of unemployment and economic stagnation? How and when should the U.S. economy begin to move some of its industrial plant back to civilian production?

These questions of "reconversion" occupied federal policy makers, the public, and other interested parties as early as 1943. According to one study, by the end of the war, more than 150 organizations at the national level were directly interested in the problems posed by the return to peace. Reconversion also raised basic political questions and revealed partisan and ideological divisions. Some liberals hoped and planned for a "third New Deal" after the war. Led by Vice President Henry Wallace, who *Time* magazine had identified as the "intellectual leader and spokesman for administration postwar planning," these liberals hoped to expand the social safety net they had begun to build in the 1930s. While Roosevelt's 1944 promise of an "economic bill of rights" seemed to portend the kind of cradle-to-grave welfare state envisioned by many liberals—and described in the 1943 National Resources Planning Board's *Postwar Planning* report—these plans never materialized. Instead, congressional conservatives, ascendant since 1937, in concert with a newly influential business sector, contained rather than expanded the "social rights" of American citizens in the postwar years.

Veterans proved the exception to this rule. In 1944, Congress approved, with broad and bipartisan support, President Roosevelt's proposal for a new GI Bill of Rights. Formally known as the Servicemen's

Readjustment Act of 1944, the new law provided nearly all returning veterans with a robust set of housing, employment, and educational benefits. The GI Bill was in many respects a model social program. Costing $95 billion between 1944 and 1971, the law helped to build the American middle class and to underwrite the long postwar economic boom. According to President Bill Clinton, the law not only gave "generations of veterans a chance to get an education, to build strong families and good lives" but also unleashed a "prosperity never before known." Others, however, were less sanguine about the consequences of the GI Bill. Although formally race neutral, the law worked through—and thus not only condoned but subsidized—housing, education, and labor markets deeply divided by race. Indeed, according to some critics, the GI Bill exacerbated racial inequality by providing returning white veterans with meaningful social and economic benefits that black Americans simply could not access.

While Americans planned and prepared for what war's end would mean at home, they also planned and prepared for the postwar world— a world in which, according to President Roosevelt, the Axis powers would be forced to surrender unconditionally and the four major Allied powers—the United States, Britain, the Soviet Union, and China— would maintain the peace within the context of a new League of Nations, soon to be known as the United Nations. While his allies agreed with this plan in principle, they disagreed sharply on the specifics. Whereas the president opposed both territorial aggrandizement by the victors and the continuation of European colonialism, Stalin wanted to acquire territory and control in Eastern Europe while Churchill refused to agree to the end of the British or any of the other European colonial empires. At the 1945 Yalta Conference in the Crimea, the three leaders appeared to compromise their differences successfully. But the agreements broke down soon thereafter, and the result was Allied conflict and, once the war ended, a Cold War that pitted the Soviet Union against the United States and Great Britain.

Historians have long debated the reasons for the collapse of the wartime alliance and have disagreed in their assessments of Roosevelt's wartime policies and behavior toward the Soviet Union. His critics maintain that Roosevelt's naivete about the future menace Stalin posed led him to appease a dictator who, like Hitler, could not be appeased. Roosevelt's defenders counter that such criticism ignores the vital importance of the Soviet Union to the Allied war effort and the very real limits on what the president could realistically do. They note in this regard that by the time of the Yalta Conference the Red Army occupied most of Eastern Europe, that Roosevelt did not give up any territory Anglo-American forces occupied, and that had he lived longer he could and probably would have used the promise of economic aid as well as the threat of atomic weapons—which he agreed during the war would be an Anglo-American monopoly in the postwar world—to win concessions from Stalin.

Of course, Roosevelt did not live to see the dawn of the atomic age. The Manhattan Project—begun in 1942—finally bore fruit in the summer of 1945, more than three months after the president's death. On July 16, a group of scientists under the command of General Leslie Groves successfully exploded the world's first atomic device in the remote desert outside of Alamogordo, New Mexico. New President Harry Truman, in Germany attending the final "Big Three" conference of the war in the Berlin suburb of Potsdam, had learned of the atomic project only months earlier, when on Roosevelt's death and his becoming president in April he received an extensive briefing from Groves and Secretary of War Stimson. There was little debate within Truman's inner circle about whether to use the bomb against Japan. On July 25—only nine days after the so-called Trinity Test—Truman ordered the bomb dropped if Japan failed to surrender before August 3. A day later, the American, British, and Chinese Nationalist governments issued the Potsdam Declaration, demanding Japan surrender immediately or face "prompt and utter destruction."

The deadline passed. At 8:15 on the morning of August 6, Colonel Paul Tibbets and his crew dropped a five-ton uranium-fueled device nicknamed "Little Boy" on the unsuspecting citizens of Hiroshima. The bomb exploded with a force of 15,000 pounds of TNT, reducing the city to rubble and killing 100,000 almost immediately. Three days later, the United States dropped a second bomb, this time a plutonium model dubbed "Fat Man," on the city of Nagasaki, while the Soviet Union declared war on Japan and invaded Manchuria. Although the Nagasaki bomb was larger, its impact was muted by the city's topography. Even so, at least 75,000 people died within hours of the attack. Six days later, the Empire of Japan announced its decision to surrender to the Allies. The instrument of surrender was formally signed on September 2, 1945.

The bombings of Hiroshima and Nagasaki remain the only use of nuclear weapons for warfare in history and the decision to use the bomb has, understandably, generated a great deal of debate—both among the general public and among scholars. At the heart of the debate is a seemingly simple question: Was the bomb necessary to end the war in the Pacific on terms acceptable to the United States? Revisionist challenges to traditionalist histories of the bomb—which had accepted at face value the Truman administration's claims that the bomb had hastened the end of the war and saved countless American lives—posited a variety of alternative explanations for the bomb's use. Some argued that the bomb had been used not to achieve a military victory against the Japanese, but rather to score a diplomatic one against the Soviet Union. Others pointed to the role that race and revenge played in the decision to use the bomb. Still others pointed to domestic political considerations or even President Truman's psychological need to live up to the office he had only recently inherited, and, by his own admission, felt overwhelmed by.

More recent scholarship has called into question many of the revisionists' key claims. Perhaps most importantly, newer work—which relies not only on American but also on Japanese and Soviet archival material—undercuts one of the revisionists' key arguments: that Japan was on the verge of surrender when the first bomb was dropped. At the same time, these studies have destabilized some of the central tenets of the traditional interpretation, and have usefully pointed out that Truman did not face a categorical decision between a costly invasion of the Japanese home islands and using the bomb—as had long been maintained. It is certainly possible that the combination of Soviet entry into the war, the continued bombing of Japanese cities, and the worsening food and military supply crisis could have brought about a Japanese surrender without either a full-scale invasion or dropping the bomb. Of course, we will never be able to know if that indeed would have happened, or if Japanese—not to mention American, Soviet, and Chinese casualties—would have been less than those in Hiroshima and Nagasaki.

When Winston Churchill noted at the end of the World War II that the United States stood "at the summit of the world" he did not exaggerate. The war transformed American life at home and American power abroad. At home, mobilization ended the Great Depression. The postwar economic collapse so many feared never came, thanks in part to economic security policies put in place in the 1930s, to the GI Bill of Rights, and to Cold War military spending. Indeed, the U.S. economy emerged dominant from the war. With half of the world's total manufacturing, two-thirds of global gold stocks, and two times more petroleum reserves than the rest of the world combined—not to mention the world's largest merchant fleet; dominance in the electronics and aerospace industries; and a complete, if temporary, monopoly on atomic power—the United States had never been stronger.

American participation—and success—in what many Americans called "the good war" all but eliminated isolationism from American politics. The nation that had rejected the League of Nations in 1920 now took responsibility for global leadership and the creation of numerous new international institutions, including the United Nations, the International Monetary Fund, the World Bank, and by 1949 the North Atlantic Treaty Organization. The European Recovery Plan of 1948—better known as the Marshall Plan—provided Western Europe with $17 billion dollars and succeeded in rebuilding the economies of the nations involved. But Roosevelt's hopes for a peaceful postwar world dominated by the wartime victors were quickly dashed. Instead the postwar era witnessed the Cold War, a global Soviet-American conflict that divided Europe and lasted for more than four decades, that included bloody if undeclared wars such as Korea, Vietnam, and Afghanistan, and that brought the two nations to the brink of nuclear war and annihilation. Roosevelt's hopes for an end to colonialism did come to fruition, however, as the peoples of Asia and Africa succeeded in overthrowing European colonial rule. As a result, membership in the United Nations has quadrupled since 1945.

The war had also set in motion seismic changes in American society, culture, and politics. The war had sparked a second Great Migration of African Americans from the rural South to the industrial North and West that changed the geography of race in America and ultimately transformed both the Republican and Democratic Parties. The war also destabilized existing racial and gender hierarchies and sowed the seeds for the civil rights and second wave feminist movements—movements that ended legal segregation in the country and redefined the role and status of women in society. While many of the wartime "Rosies" embraced domesticity in the immediate aftermath of the war, their sons and daughters—the so-called baby boom generation—grew up to lead the cultural revolt of the 1960s.

The war also inaugurated an era of big government. Financed by a broad-based and sharply progressive income tax, the federal government assumed unprecedented responsibility for managing economic growth and providing at least a modicum of security for ordinary Americans. New agencies, notably the Federal Housing Administration and the Veterans Administration, effectively subsidized the construction of the postwar suburbs, and put the American dream of homeownership within the reach of the middle and working classes—or at least the *white* middle and working classes. The success of the Cold War economy seemed to confirm the experience of World War II that government spending could stimulate and sustain broad economic prosperity. But big government and the Cold War also led to an anti-Communist hysteria and attacks on civil liberties. What is more, the creation of what has been labeled the national security and surveillance states during this period can be seen as both causes and consequences of the United States' increasing commitments around the world. In these ways, and in so many more, the impact of World War II was so great that one can say without exaggeration that it created much of the nation and world in which we live today.

Figure 2: Estimated Number of Deaths Attributable to World War II: Asia and the Pacific		
Allied and Occupied Nations		
Nation	**Military Deaths**	**Civilian Deaths**
China	3,000,000	12,554,000
Indonesia	—	3,000,000
India	—	2,040,000
Indochina/Vietnam	—	1,000,000
Korea	131,955	400,000
Philippines	10,000	517,000
Burma	—	170,000
Thailand	—	120,000
Malaya/Singapore	—	100,000
Burma-Thailand Railroad	—	70,000
Australia	17,501	—
New Zealand	672	—
United Kingdom & Other Allied Soldiers	56,000	—
United States	106,000	—
Indonesian European Civilians	—	30,000
Soviet Union	21,806	—
Allied and Occupied Nations Total	*3,343,934*	*20,001,000*
Axis		
Nation	**Military Deaths**	**Civilian Deaths**
Japan	2,000,000	1,000,000
Axis Total	*2,000,000*	*1,000,000*

Figure 3: Estimated Number of Deaths Attributable to World War II: Europe		
Allies		
Nation	**Military Deaths**	**Civilian Deaths**
Soviet Union	8,668,400–11,000,000	15,000,000–17,400,000
Poland	123,000–597,320	4,000,000–5,600,000
Yugoslavia	300,000–305,000	1,000,000–1,400,000
France	245,000–250,000	350,000
Greece	88,300–430,000	20,000–325,000
United Kingdom	383,000–403,195	65,000–67,000
United States	302,018	6,000
Czechoslovakia	250,000	90,000–215,000
Netherlands	6,000–7,900	200,000–204,000
Belgium	10,000–22,651	76,000–78,000
Canada	37,000–42,666	—
New Zealand	10,000–13,081	2,000
South Africa	7,000–8,861	—
Denmark	6,400	—
Norway	2,000–3,000	7,000-8,000
Albania	28,000	2,000
Luxembourg	—	5,000
Total Allies	*10,465,718–13,670,092*	*20,810,100–25,662,000*
Axis		
Nation	**Military Deaths**	**Civilian Deaths**
Germany	3,250,000–4,500,000	1,210,000–2,000,000
Italy	380,000–400,000	100,000–152,941
Romania	300,000	200,000
Austria	230,000–280,000	144,000–170,000
Hungary	160,000–200,000	270,000–290,000
Finland	82,000–84,000	2,000–16,000
Bulgaria	18,500–32,000	3,000–10,000
Total Axis	*4,420,500–5,796,000*	*1,929,000–2,838,941*

In making these calculations, Richard Frank relied primarily on the statistics in *The Oxford Companion to World War II*, ed. I. C. B. Dear and M. R. D. Foot (New York: Oxford University Press, 1995), 290; and Michael Clodfelter, *Warfare and Armed Conflicts: A Statistical Reference to Casualty and Other Figures, 1500–2000*, 3rd ed. (Jefferson, NC: McFarland, 2008), 496, 560–61. He also used David Glantz and Jonathan House, *When Titans Clashed: How the Red Army Stopped Hitler* (Lawrence: University Press of Kansas, 1995 and 2015), 57, 285–86, 292, table A, for Soviet military deaths; the Commonwealth War Graves Commission website for the UK deaths; Werner Gruhl, *Imperial Japan's World War II 1931–1945* (New Brunswick and London: Transaction Publishers, 2007) 19, table 2.1; R. J. Rummel, *China's Bloody Century: Genocide and Mass Murder since 1900* (New Brunswick and London: Transaction Publishers, 2008) for the Pacific War; numerous additional works for other countries; and his own calculations.

CHAPTER 1

THE YANKS ARE COMING . . . AGAIN:
U.S. ENTRY INTO WORLD WAR II

By the 1930s, many if not most Americans had concluded that their country's entry into World War I had been a mistake. Clearly, it had not been the "war to end all wars" and had not "made the world safe for democracy," as President Woodrow Wilson had claimed. Instead it appeared to have simply set the stage for another war. As war clouds gathered in Europe and Asia, some historians, as well as a Senate investigating committee chaired by Senator Gerald P. Nye of North Dakota concluded that U.S. entry had resulted from loans and arms sales to the Allies (the so-called "merchants of death" thesis) as well as the shipment of these arms in American merchant vessels and passenger travel on belligerent ships. Consequently, the Congress passed and President Roosevelt signed a series of neutrality acts outlawing these actions in any future war. Non-arms trade with belligerents would be allowed, but only on a "cash and carry" basis whereby belligerents would have to pay cash for desired goods and carry them away on their own ships.

The rapid German conquest of Denmark, Norway, Belgium, Luxembourg, the Netherlands, and France in the spring of 1940 precipitated a revolution in American thinking and a major debate over the appropriate U.S. response. Internationalists, including the president himself, had become more and more convinced by this time that Nazi Germany and its Axis partners posed an unprecedented and existential threat to the United States. Perhaps convinced by Prime Minister Winston Churchill's warning that only Great Britain stood between the world and a "new Dark Age made more sinister and perhaps more protracted by the lights of a perverted science" and his assertion that Britain would fight on until "the New World, with all its power and might, steps forth to the rescue and the liberation of the old," some young American men volunteered to fly with the Royal Air Force. Simultaneously, others at home organized so as to mobilize congressional and public support for the military aid to Britain that Churchill was now requesting.

In this regard, the unexpected success of the German *blitzkrieg* shattered public complacency. Before 1940, most Americans had assumed that

1

France and Britain together could hold off Germany and that the result would be another bloody stalemate similar to the one that had occurred in the trenches of World War I. Hitler's quick conquest of Western Europe shattered such beliefs and led to a major reassessment of American foreign policy objectives as well as military posture. With triumphant German forces now on the Continent's Atlantic shores as well as the English Channel and poised to invade England, the Atlantic Ocean no longer appeared to be the impenetrable barrier to invasion that Americans had long assumed it was. Forming such organizations as the Committee to Defend America by Aiding the Allies (CDAAA) and the Fight for Freedom Committee, they argued that Britain's survival was essential to U.S. security, that it had in effect become America's first line of defense, and that the United States should therefore provide that nation with assistance.

President Roosevelt fully agreed. At the outbreak of war in 1939 he had convinced Congress to end the ban on arms sales so that the British and French could purchase U.S. war materiel. He had also initiated a private correspondence with Churchill, at that time First Lord of the Admiralty. Now in the spring and summer of 1940 he expanded that correspondence with the new British prime minister, pressed his army and navy chiefs to make scarce U.S. arms available for sale to the British, publicly denounced Germany and Italy, and replaced his non-interventionist secretaries of war and navy with pro-interventionist Republicans Henry L. Stimson and Frank Knox so as to prevent aid to Britain from becoming a partisan issue in a presidential election year. He also proposed the first billion-dollar defense bills in U.S. history and supported legislation to establish the first peacetime draft in U.S. history as necessary for American defense. Congress agreed to both. Then in September, by executive order he transferred fifty overage U.S. warships to Britain in exchange for ninety-nine-year leases on British base sites in the Western Hemisphere, arguing that this constituted a net strategic gain for the United States.

Beyond that Roosevelt would not go prior to the presidential election, in which he was running for an unprecedented third term. After his success in that race, however, he responded to Churchill's warning that Britain was running out of funds with which to buy U.S. war supplies with the dramatic proposal that the United States agree to lend or lease these supplies to Britain free of charge.

Far from all Americans agreed with the CDAAA and presidential assessment of the need to aid the British. In the early fall of 1940, as the Battle of Britain continued to rage, prominent non-interventionists came together to form the America First Committee. The new organization opposed any form of U.S. intervention in the European war on the grounds that it would endanger U.S. security and jeopardize American democracy at home. Its members also argued that Britain was doomed to defeat, that its defense was not vital to U.S. security, that the nation needed to build up its own defenses rather than provide military supplies to the British, and that a triumphant Germany need not be a threat to the United States. The America First Committee had prominent and powerful allies in Congress who continued to resist any attempt to aid Britain. Senator Burton K. Wheeler, a Democrat from Montana, went so far as to describe Roosevelt's Lend-Lease plan to provide economic aid to Great Britain free of charge as the "New Deal's Triple A foreign policy—it will plow under every fourth American boy."

While more and more Americans recognized the Axis threat, the majority continued to oppose sending U.S. troops into battle. By 1941, however, public support for responses to the Axis threat that stopped "short of war" had risen considerably. In March, after months of debate, both houses of Congress by large majorities finally passed the Lend-Lease bill, which authorized the president to order the production of "any defense article for the government of any country whose defense . . . [he deemed] vital to the defense of the United States." By year's end Roosevelt had included China and, after the German invasion, the Soviet Union, a Communist dictatorship he and Churchill nevertheless welcomed as an ally. If Hitler invaded hell, the staunchly anti-Communist British prime minister commented, he would at least make a favorable reference to the devil in the House of Commons. Throughout 1941 Roosevelt also took a series of additional executive actions to provide assistance to anti-Axis forces, including extension of the self-proclaimed hemispheric security zone so as to allow U.S. military occupation of first Greenland and then Iceland as well as de facto naval assistance to the British in the western Atlantic. In August, he met with Churchill of the coast of Newfoundland and issued the Atlantic Charter, a joint statement of idealistic war aims (see Chapter 11, Document 11.1)—despite the fact that the United States was not formally in the war. In September, he responded to a German submarine attack on the U.S. destroyer *Greer* with a publicly announced order to U.S. naval forces to "shoot on sight" when they encountered German U-boats (though he did not mention that the U.S. warship had been aiding British forces attacking that submarine). In the following month, he asked Congress to end the "crippling provisions" of the Neutrality Acts so that U.S. merchant ships could be armed and carry Lend-Lease supplies to Britain. As naval incidents mounted, Congress agreed. By November, the United States was thus engaged in a full-scale but undeclared naval war with Germany in the Atlantic.

War officially came as a result of events in Asia and the Pacific, however, as Japan sought to take advantage of French defeat and British preoccupation with Germany by expanding into Southeast Asia as well as China and the United States responded with economic sanctions, aid to China, and movement of the fleet from California to Hawaii. In September of 1940, the Axis powers had sought to warn the United States that it was risking a two-front war by signing the Tripartite Pact, by which they pledged to come to one another's assistance if any one of them was attacked by a presently neutral power. But that only convinced Americans that there was indeed a global Axis conspiracy against them and reinforced their determination to oppose the Axis powers and support their enemies. High-level negotiations in Washington failed to alleviate Japanese-American tensions, as the United States insisted that Japan withdraw its military forces from China and French Indochina while Japan insisted on a free hand in Asia, no further U.S. aid to China, and a full resumption of U.S. trade. In July, the United States responded to additional Japanese troop movements into French Indochina with a freeze on all Japanese assets, a move that in effect created an embargo on any trade with Japan. Cut off by this embargo from the oil and other raw materials it needed to continue the war in China, Japan decided to attack U.S., Dutch, and British possessions in Southeast Asia to obtain these resources and create a self-sufficient empire, and to use naval aircraft to attack the U.S. fleet in Pearl Harbor—the only force in the Pacific capable of stopping them. Simultaneously, they decided to continue negotiations with the United States in hopes of achieving a diplomatic settlement on their terms that would make war unnecessary.

The United States knew of the final Japanese proposals and the likelihood of war if those proposals were rejected because American cryptanalysts had broken the Japanese diplomatic code (MAGIC), but that code did not reveal where the Japanese would attack. The ensuing December 7 attack on Pearl Harbor thus came as a surprise that crippled the U.S. fleet, with the loss of over 2,400 servicemen. One day later, after a major address by Roosevelt, Congress declared that war existed by act of Japan. On December 11, Hitler declared war on the United States, thereby joining the European and Asia/Pacific wars into one global conflict.

As previously noted in the Introduction, most historians have sided with Roosevelt and the interventionists and have praised the president's behavior and leadership during this time period. A few anti-interventionist historians disagreed sharply, however, and maintained soon after victory that war could and should have been avoided with Germany and/or Japan. Some went so far as to accuse Roosevelt of allowing the Pearl Harbor attack to take place so as to have a "back door to war" with Germany. Others have argued that while war with Nazi Germany may have been justified, war with Japan was not; poor diplomacy by Roosevelt and Secretary of State Cordell Hull, they maintain, precluded a peaceful settlement that was quite possible. Still others focus on Roosevelt's enormous expansion of executive power at this time, an expansion they see as having set very dangerous precedents for the future.

The documents presented in this chapter focus on key events in the U.S. movement from neutrality to full involvement in World War II and, in the process, raise a series of important questions. Why did Congress pass and President Roosevelt sign the Neutrality Acts? Did Nazi Germany, Fascist Italy, and/or Imperial Japan constitute serious threats to American security? Why, or why not? What were the key issues in the debate between interventionists and non-interventionists in 1940–1941? How did President Roosevelt respond to the Axis Powers, and what were the immediate and the long-term consequences of his actions? What were the issues on which the United States and Japan disagreed, and why were the two nations unable to resolve their differences short of war?

* * * *

1.1 The Neutrality Acts Seek to Avoid U.S. Participation in Another War, 1935–1939[1]

The Neutrality Acts of 1935, 1936, 1937, and 1939 outlawed the practices that many Americans believed had led the United States into a needless war in 1917. Most notable in this regard, the acts prohibited arms sales and shipments, loans to belligerents, and travel on belligerent ships. Trade in items other than instruments of war was allowed, but only on a "cash and carry" basis whereby belligerents would have to pay cash for items purchased and transport such items in their own ships. Passed after the outbreak of war in Europe, the 1939 act repealed the arms embargo in the earlier acts and placed all trade with belligerents on this "cash and carry" basis. Taken as a whole, these acts illustrate the strength of antiwar sentiment, often labeled isolationist sentiment, in the 1930s.

The 1935 Neutrality Act

Resolved by the Senate and House of Representatives of the United States of America in Congress assembled, That upon the outbreak or during the

1. From *U.S. Statutes at Large,* 49 (1935–1936): 1081–85; 50 (1937): 121–27; 54 (1939–1941): 4–12.

progress of war between, or among, two or more foreign states, the President shall proclaim such fact, and it shall thereafter be unlawful to export arms, ammunition, or implements of war from any place in the United States, or possessions of the United States, to any port of such belligerent states, or to any neutral port for transshipment to, or for the use of, a belligerent country. . . .

Sec. 3. Whenever the President shall issue the proclamation provided for in section 1 of this Act, thereafter it shall be unlawful for any American vessel to carry any arms, ammunition, or implements of war to any port of the belligerent countries named in such proclamation as being at war, or to any neutral port for transshipment to, or for the use of, a belligerent country. . . .

Sec. 6. Whenever, during any war in which the United States is neutral, the President shall find that the maintenance of peace between the United States and foreign nations, or the protection of the lives of citizens of the United States, or the protection of the commercial interests of the United States and its citizens, or the security of the United States requires that the American citizens should refrain from traveling as passengers on the vessels of any belligerent nation, he shall so proclaim, and thereafter no citizen of the United States shall travel on any vessel of any belligerent nation except at his own risk, unless in accordance with such rules and regulations as the President shall prescribe. . . .

The 1937 Neutrality Act

Section 1. (a) Whenever the President shall find that there exists a state of war between, or among, two or more foreign states, the President shall proclaim such fact, and it shall thereafter be unlawful to export, or attempt to export, or cause to be exported, arms, ammunition, or implements of war from any place in the United States to any belligerent state named in such proclamation, or to any neutral state for transshipment to, or for the use of, any such belligerent state.

(b) The President shall, from time to time, by proclamation, extend such embargo upon the export of arms, ammunition, or implements of war to other states as and when they may become involved in such war.

(c) Whenever the President shall find that a state of civil strife exists in a foreign state and that such civil strife is of a magnitude or is being conducted under such conditions that the export of arms, ammunition, or implements of war from the United States to such foreign state would threaten or endanger the peace of the United States, the President shall proclaim such fact, and it shall thereafter be unlawful to export, or attempt to export, or cause to be exported arms, ammunition, or implements of war from any place in the United States to such foreign state, or to any neutral state for transshipment to, or for the use of, such foreign state. . . .

Sec. 2. (a) Whenever the President shall have issued a proclamation under the authority of section 1 of this Act and he shall thereafter find that the placing of restrictions on the shipment of certain articles or materials in addition to arms, ammunition, and implements of war from the United States to belligerent states, or to a state wherein civil strife exists, is necessary to promote the security or preserve the peace of the United States or to protect the lives of citizens of the United States, he shall so proclaim, and it shall thereafter be unlawful, except under such limitations and exceptions as the President may prescribe as to lakes, rivers, and inland waters bordering on the United States, and as to transportation on or over lands bordering on the United States, for any American vessel to carry such articles or materials to any belligerent state, or to any state wherein civil strife exists, named in such proclamation issued under the authority of section 1 of this Act, or to any neutral state for transshipment to, or for the use of, any such belligerent state or any such state wherein civil strife exists. The President shall by proclamation from time to time definitely enumerate the articles and materials which it shall be unlawful for American vessels to so transport. . . .

Sec. 3. (a) Whenever the President shall have issued a proclamation under the authority of section 1 of this Act, it shall thereafter be unlawful for any person within the United States to purchase, sell, or exchange bonds, securities, or other obligations of the government of any belligerent state or of any state wherein civil strife exists, named in such proclamation, or of any political subdivision of any such state, or of any person acting for or on behalf of the government of any such state, or of any faction or asserted government within any such state wherein civil strife exists, or of any person acting for or on behalf of any faction or asserted government within any such state wherein civil strife exists, issued after the date of such proclamation or to make any loan or extend any credit to any such government, political subdivision, faction, asserted government, or person, or to solicit or receive any contribution for any such government, political subdivision, faction, asserted government, or person. . . .

Sec. 6. (a) Whenever the President shall have issued a proclamation under the authority of section 1 of this Act, it shall thereafter be unlawful, until such proclamation is revoked, for any American vessel to carry any arms, ammunition, or implements of war to any belligerent state, or to any state wherein civil strife exists, named in such proclamation, or to any neutral state for transshipment to, or for the use of, any such belligerent state or any such state wherein civil strife exists. . . .

Sec. 10. Whenever the President shall have issued a proclamation under the authority of section 1, it shall thereafter be unlawful, until such proclamation is revoked, for any American vessel engaged in commerce with any belligerent state, or any state wherein civil strife exists, named in such proclamation, to be armed or to carry any armament, arms, ammunition, or implements of war, except small arms and ammunition therefor which the President may deem necessary and shall publicly designate for the preservation of discipline aboard such vessels.

The 1939 Neutrality Act

Sec. 2. (a) Whenever the President shall have issued a proclamation under the authority of section 1 (a) it shall thereafter be unlawful for any American vessel to carry any passengers or any articles or materials to any state named in such proclamation. . . .

(c) Whenever the President shall have issued a proclamation under the authority of section 1 (a) it shall thereafter be unlawful to export or transport, or attempt to export or transport, or cause to be exported or transported, from the United States to any state named in such proclamation, any articles or materials (except copyrighted articles or materials) until all right, title, and interest therein shall have been transferred to some foreign government, agency, institution, association, partnership, corporation, or national.

1.2 President Franklin D. Roosevelt Proposes a "Quarantine" of Aggressors, 1937[2]

Primarily concerned with obtaining congressional passage of his numerous New Deal measures to combat the Great Depression, President Roosevelt bowed to isolationist sentiment and signed the Neutrality Acts despite his dislike of them. His first public challenge to such sentiment occurred on October 5, 1937, when he suggested in Chicago that the United States join with other nations to "quarantine" aggressor states. He quickly retreated from this proposal, however, in the face of press criticism.

---

2. From U.S. Department of State, *Papers Relating to the Foreign Relations of the United States: Japan, 1931–1941*, vol. 1 (Washington, DC: U.S. Government Printing Office, 1943), 379–83.

Some 15 years ago the hopes of mankind for a continuing era of international peace were raised to great heights when more than 60 nations solemnly pledged themselves not to resort to arms in furtherance of their national aims and policies. The high aspirations expressed in the Briand-Kellogg Peace Pact and the hopes for peace thus raised have of late given way to a haunting fear of calamity. The present reign of terror and international lawlessness began a few years ago.

It began through unjustified interference in the internal affairs of other nations or the invasion of alien territory in violation of treaties and has now reached a stage where the very foundations of civilization are seriously threatened. The landmarks and traditions which have marked the progress of civilization toward a condition of law, order, and justice are being wiped away.

Without a declaration of war and without warning or justification of any kind, civilians, including women and children, are being ruthlessly murdered with bombs from the air. In times of so-called peace, ships are being attacked and sunk by submarines without cause or notice. Nations are fomenting and taking sides in civil warfare in nations that have never done them any harm. Nations claiming freedom for themselves deny it to others.

Innocent peoples and nations are being cruelly sacrificed to a greed for power and supremacy which is devoid of all sense of justice and humane consideration. . . .

[I]f we are to have a world in which we can breathe freely and live in amity without fear—the peace-loving nations must make a concerted effort to uphold laws and principles on which alone peace can rest secure.

The peace-loving nations must make a concerted effort in opposition to those violations of treaties and those ignorings of humane instincts which today are creating a state of international anarchy and instability from which there is no escape through mere isolation or neutrality.

Those who cherish their freedom and recognize and respect the equal right of their neighbors to be free and live in peace, must work together for the triumph of law and moral principles in order that peace, justice, and confidence may prevail in the world. There must be a return to a belief in the pledged word, in the value of a signed treaty. There must be recognition of the fact that national morality is as vital as private morality. . . .

There is a solidarity and interdependence about the modern world, both technically and morally, which makes it impossible for any nation completely to isolate itself from economic and political upheavals in the rest of the world, especially when such upheavals appear to be spreading and not declining. There can be no stability or peace either within nations or between nations except under laws and moral standards adhered to by all. International anarchy destroys every foundation for peace. It jeopardizes either the immediate or the future security of every nation, large or small. It is therefore, a matter of vital interest and concern to the people of the United States that the sanctity of international treaties and the maintenance of international morality be restored.

The overwhelming majority of the peoples and nations of the world today want to live in peace. They seek the removal of barriers against trade. They want to exert themselves in industry, in agriculture, and in business, that they may increase their wealth through the production of wealth-producing goods rather than striving to produce military planes and bombs and machine guns and cannon for the destruction of human lives and useful property.

In those nations of the world which seem to be piling armament on armament for purposes of aggression, and those other nations which fear acts of aggression against them and their security, a very high proportion of their national income is being spent directly for armaments. It runs from 30 to as high as 50 percent.

The proportion that we in the United States spend is far less—11 or 12 percent.

How happy we are that the circumstances of the moment permit us to put our money into bridges and boulevards, dams and reforestation, the conservation of our soil, and many other kinds of useful works rather than into huge standing armies and vast supplies of implements of war.

I am compelled and you are compelled, nevertheless, to look ahead. The peace, the freedom, and the security of 90 percent of the population of the world is being jeopardized by the remaining 10 percent, who are threatening a breakdown of all international order and law. Surely the 90 percent who want to live in peace under law and in accordance with moral standards that have received almost universal acceptance through the centuries, can and must find some way to make their will prevail.

The situation is definitely of universal concern. The questions involved relate not merely to violations of specific provisions of particular treaties; they are questions of war and of peace, of international law, and especially of principles of humanity. It is true that they involve definite violations of agreements, and especially of the Covenant of the League of Nations, the Briand-Kellogg Pact, and the Nine Power Treaty. But they also involve problems of world economy, world security, and world humanity.

It is true that the moral consciousness of the world must recognize the importance of removing injustices and well-founded grievances; but at the same time it must be aroused to the cardinal necessity of honoring sanctity of treaties, of respecting the rights and liberties of others, and of putting an end to acts of international aggression.

It seems to be unfortunately true that the epidemic of world lawlessness is spreading.

When an epidemic of physical disease starts to spread, the community approves and joins in a quarantine of the patients in order to protect the health of the community against the spread of the disease.

It is my determination to pursue a policy of peace and to adopt every practicable measure to avoid involvement in war. It ought to be inconceivable that in this modern era, and in the face of experience, any nation could be so foolish and ruthless as to run the risk of plunging the whole world into war by invading and violating in contravention of solemn treaties the territory of other nations that have done them no real harm and which are too weak to protect themselves adequately. Yet the peace of the world and the welfare and security of every nation is today being threatened by that very thing. . . .

War is a contagion, whether it be declared or undeclared. It can engulf states and peoples remote from the original scene of hostilities. We are determined to keep out of war, yet we cannot insure ourselves against the disastrous effects of war and the dangers of involvement. We are adopting such measures as will minimize our risk of involvement, but we cannot have complete protection in a world of disorder in which confidence and security have broken down.

If civilization is to survive the principles of the Prince of Peace must be restored. Shattered trust between nations must be revived.

Most important of all, the will for peace on the part of peace-loving nations must express itself to the end that nations that may be tempted to violate their agreements and the rights of others will resist from such a cause. There must be positive endeavors to preserve peace.

America hates war. America hopes for peace. Therefore, America actively engages in the search for peace.

1.3 President Roosevelt Denounces Isolationism and the Axis Powers, 1940[3]

When war broke out in Europe in September, 1939, Roosevelt declared American neutrality as required by law but made clear that the United States favored the democracies of France and Great Britain.

---

3. From Miller Center, University of Virginia, http://millercenter.org/president/fdroosevelt/speeches/speech-3317; also in Samuel I. Rosenman, ed., *The Public Papers and Addresses of Franklin D. Roosevelt* (New York: Random House; Harper, 1938–1950), 259–64.

Consequently he requested and obtained from Congress within the Neutrality Act of 1939 repeal of the arms embargo so that those nations could purchase war materiel as well as other items, albeit only on a "cash and carry" basis. All other provisions of the earlier Neutrality Acts—most notably the ban on U.S. loans and shipping as well as travel on belligerent ships—remained in effect.

Nazi Germany's stupendous military victories in the spring of 1940, culminating in French surrender on June 22, 1940, led many Americans to question the wisdom of this rigid neutrality. When Italy joined Germany by declaring war on France on June 10, Roosevelt in the speech at the University of Virginia in Charlottesville excerpted here responded with a public denunciation of the act and an attack on isolationist thinking.

. . . Again today the young men and the young women of America ask themselves with earnestness and with deep concern this same question "What is to become of the country we know?"

Now they ask it with even greater anxiety than before. They ask, not only what the future holds for this Republic, but what the future holds for all peoples and all nations that have been living under democratic forms of Government—under the free institutions of a free people.

It is understandable to all of us that they should ask this question. They read the words of those who are telling them that the ideal of individual liberty, the ideal of free franchise, the ideal of peace through justice, are decadent ideals. They read the word and hear the boast of those who say that a belief in force—force directed by self-chosen leaders—is the new and vigorous system which will overrun the earth. They have seen the ascendancy of this philosophy of force in nation after nation where free institutions and individual liberties were once maintained.

It is natural and understandable that the younger generation should first ask itself what the extension of the philosophy of force to all the world would lead to ultimately. We see today in stark reality some of the consequences of what we call the machine age.

Where control of machines has been retained in the hands of mankind as a whole, untold benefits have accrued to mankind. For mankind was then the master; and the machine was the servant.

But in this new system of force the mastery of machine is not in the hands of mankind. It is in the control of infinitely small groups of individuals who rule without a single one of the democratic sanctions that we have known. The machine in hands of irresponsible conquerors becomes the master; mankind is not only the servant; it is the victim, too. Such mastery abandons with deliberate contempt all the moral values to which even this young country for more than three hundred years has been accustomed and dedicated.

Surely the new philosophy proves from month to month that it could have no possible conception of the way of life or the way of thought of a nation whose origins go back to Jamestown and Plymouth Rock.

Conversely, neither those who spring from that ancient stock nor those who have come hither in later years can be indifferent to the destruction of freedom in their ancestral lands across the sea.

Perception of danger to our institutions may come slowly or it may come with a rush and a shock as it has to the people of the United States in the past few months. This perception of danger has come to us clearly and overwhelmingly; and we perceive the peril in a world-wide arena—an arena that may become so narrowed that only the Americas will retain the ancient faiths.

Some indeed still hold to the now somewhat obvious delusion that we of the United States can safely permit the United States to become a lone island, a lone island in a world dominated by the philosophy of force.

Such an island may be the dream of those who still talk and vote as isolationists. Such an island represents to me and to the overwhelming majority of Americans today a helpless nightmare of a people without freedom—the nightmare of a people lodged in prison, handcuffed, hungry, and fed through the bars from day to day by the contemptuous, unpitying masters of other continents.

It is natural also that we should ask ourselves how now we can prevent the building of that prison and the placing of ourselves in the midst of it.

Let us not hesitate—all of us—to proclaim certain truths. Overwhelmingly we, as a nation—and this applied to all the other American nations—are convinced that military and naval victory for the gods of force and hate would endanger the institutions of democracy in the western world, and that equally, therefore, the whole of our sympathies lies with those nations that are giving their life blood in combat against these forces.

The people and the Government of the United States have seen with the utmost regret and with grave disquiet the decision of the Italian Government to engage in the hostilities now raging in Europe. . . .

The Government of Italy has now chosen to preserve what it terms its "freedom of action" and to fulfill what it states are its promises to Germany. In so doing it has manifested disregard for the rights and security of other nations, disregard for the lives of the peoples of those nations which are directly threatened by this spread of the war; and has evidenced its unwillingness to find the means through pacific negotiations for the satisfaction of what it believes are its legitimate aspirations.

On this tenth day of June, nineteen hundred and forty, the hand that held the dagger has struck it into the back of its neighbor.

On this tenth day of June, nineteen hundred and forty, in this University founded by the first great American teacher of democracy, we send forth our prayers and our hopes to those beyond the seas who are maintaining with magnificent valor their battle for freedom.

In our American unity, we will pursue two obvious and simultaneous courses. We will extend to the opponents of force the material resources of this nation; and, at the same time, we will harness and speed up the use of those resources in order that we ourselves in the Americas may have equipment and training equal to the task of any emergency and every defense.

All roads leading to the accomplishment of these objectives must be kept clear of obstructions. We will not slow down or detour. Signs and signals call for speed—full speed ahead.

It is right that each new generation should ask questions. But in recent months the principal question has been somewhat simplified. Once more the future of the nation and of the American people is at stake.

We need not and we will not, in any way, abandon our continuing effort to make democracy work within our borders. We still insist on the need for vast improvements in our own social and economic life. But that is a component part of national defense itself.

The program unfolds swiftly and into that program will fit the responsibility and the opportunity of every man and woman in the land to preserve his and her heritage in days of peril.

I call for effort, courage, sacrifice, devotion. Granting the love of freedom, all of these are possible.

And the love of freedom is still fierce and steady in the nation today.

1.4 President Roosevelt Proposes Lend-Lease Aid to Great Britain and the Four Freedoms, December 17 and 29, 1940, and January 6, 1941[4]

In the weeks and months following his Charlottesville speech, Roosevelt would request and receive from Congress massive increases in defense spending and passage of the first peacetime draft in U.S. history. He would also form what was in effect a bipartisan cabinet by

---

4. From December 17 remarks in *Complete Presidential Press Conferences of Franklin D. Roosevelt*, vol. 15–16, 1940 (New York: De Capo Press, 1972), 353–55; December 29 Radio Address in State Department, *Bulletin* 4 (1941): 3–8; Four Freedoms in *Congressional Record*, 1941, vol. 87, pt. 1.

replacing his isolationist secretaries of war and navy with Henry L. Stimson and Frank Knox, senior Republicans who favored U.S. intervention to help a beleaguered Great Britain facing imminent German invasion. Then in early September, the president agreed to provide Britain with fifty overage U.S. warships in return for ninety-nine-year leases on British military base sites within the Western Hemisphere.

British success in the Battle of Britain then in progress in the skies halted German plans to invade, but in November Churchill informed Roosevelt that his nation was running out of the financial resources needed to purchase additional arms from the United States. Roosevelt dramatically responded by proposing in late December that Congress agree to lend war supplies to Britain via what become known as Lend-Lease, thereby bypassing the ban on loans in the Neutrality Acts and making the United States, in his December 29 words, the "arsenal of democracy." In his State of the Union address only a week later, the president formally requested from Congress the funds and authority for Lend-Lease. After reiterating many of the points he had made in the December 29 radio address, he moved beyond the immediate issues to the future goals of the United States in world affairs: the "Four Freedoms."

December 17, 1940, Press Conference

. . . Now, what I am trying to do is to eliminate the dollar sign, and that is something brand new in the thoughts of practically everybody in this room, I think—get rid of the silly, foolish old dollar sign. All right!

Well, let me give you an illustration: Suppose my neighbor's home catches fire, and I have got a length of garden hose four or five hundred feet away; but, my Heaven, if he can take my garden hose and connect it up with his hydrant, I may help him to put out his fire. Now what do I do? I don't say to him before that operation, "Neighbor, my garden hose cost me $15; you have got to pay me $15 for it." What is the transaction that goes on? I don't want $15—I want my garden hose back after the fire is over. All right. If it goes through the fire all right, intact, without any damage to it, he gives it back to me and thanks me very much for the use of it. But suppose it gets smashed up—holes in it—during the fire; we don't have to have too much formality about it, but I say to him, "I was glad to lend you that hose; I see I can't use it any more, it's all smashed up." He says, "How many feet of it were there?" I tell him, "there were 150 feet of it." He said, "All right, I will replace it." Now, if I get a nice garden hose back, I am in pretty good shape. In other words, if you lend certain munitions and get the munitions back at the end of the war, if they are intact—haven't been hurt—you are all right; if they have been damaged or deteriorated or lost completely, it seems to me you come out pretty well if you have them replaced by the fellow that you have lent them to. . . .

December 29, 1940, Radio Address

This is not a fireside chat on war. It is a talk on national security; because the nub of the whole purpose of your President is to keep you now, and your children later, and your grandchildren much later, out of a last-ditch war for the preservation of American independence and all of the things that American independence means to you and to me and to ours. . . .

Never before since Jamestown and Plymouth Rock has our American civilization been in such danger as now.

For, on September 27, 1940, by an agreement signed in Berlin, three powerful nations, two in Europe and one in Asia, joined themselves together in the threat that if the United States interfered with or blocked the expansion program of these three nations—a program aimed at world control—they would unite in ultimate action against the United States.

The Nazi masters of Germany have made it clear that they intend not only to dominate all life and thought in their own country, but also to enslave the whole of Europe, and then to use the resources of Europe to dominate the rest of the world. . . .

Some of our people like to believe that wars in Europe and in Asia are of no concern to us. But it is a matter of most vital concern to us that European and Asiatic war-makers should not gain control of the oceans which lead to this hemisphere. . . .

Does anyone seriously believe that we need to fear attack while a free Britain remains our most powerful naval neighbor in the Atlantic? Does anyone seriously believe, on the other hand, that we could rest easy if the Axis powers were our neighbor there?

If Great Britain goes down, the Axis powers will control the continents of Europe, Asia, Africa, Australasia, and the high seas—and they will be in a position to bring enormous military and naval resources against this hemisphere. It is no exaggeration to say that all of us in the Americas would be living at the point of a gun—a gun loaded with explosive bullets, economic as well as military.

We should enter upon a new and terrible era in which the whole world, our hemisphere included, would be run by threats of brute force. To survive in such a world, we would have to convert ourselves permanently into a militaristic power on the basis of war economy.

Some of us like to believe that even if Great Britain falls, we are still safe, because of the broad expanse of the Atlantic and of the Pacific.

But the width of these oceans is not what it was in the days of clipper ships. At one point between Africa and Brazil the distance is less than from Washington to Denver—five hours for the latest type of bomber. And at the north of the Pacific Ocean, America and Asia almost touch each other. . . .

There are those who say that the Axis powers would never have any desire to attack the Western Hemisphere. This is the same dangerous form of wishful thinking which has destroyed the powers of resistance of so many conquered peoples. The plain facts are that the Nazis have proclaimed, time and again, that all other races are their inferiors and therefore subject to their orders. And most important of all, the vast resources and wealth of this hemisphere constitute the most tempting loot in all the world. . . .

The experience of the past two years has proved beyond doubt that no nation can appease the Nazis. No man can tame a tiger into a kitten by stroking it. There can be no appeasement with ruthlessness. There can be no reasoning with an incendiary bomb. We know now that a nation can have peace with the Nazis only at the price of total surrender. . . .

The American appeasers ignore the warning to be found in the fate of Austria, Czechoslovakia, Poland, Norway, Belgium, the Netherlands, Denmark, and France. They tell you that the Axis powers are going to win anyway; that all this bloodshed in the world could be saved; and that the United States might just as well throw its influence into the scale of a dictated peace and get the best out of it that we can.

They call it a "negotiated peace." Nonsense! Is it a negotiated peace if a gang of outlaws surrounds your community and on threat of extermination makes you pay tribute to save your own skins?

Such a dictated peace would be no peace at all. It would be only another armistice, leading to the most gigantic armament race and the most devastating trade wars in history. And in these contests the Americas would offer the only real resistance to the Axis powers.

With all their vaunted efficiency and parade of pious purpose in this war, there are still in their background the concentration camp and the servants of God in chains.

The history of recent years proves that shootings and chains and concentration camps are not simply the transient tools but the very altars of modern dictatorships. They may talk of a "new order" in the world, but what they have in mind is but a revival of the oldest and the worst tyranny. In that there is no liberty, no religion, no hope.

The proposed "new order" is the very opposite of a United States of Europe, or a United States of Asia. It is not a government based upon the consent of the governed. It is not a union of ordinary, self-respecting men and women to protect themselves and their freedom and their dignity from oppression. It is an unholy alliance of power and pelf to dominate and enslave the human race.

The British people are conducting an active war against this unholy alliance. Our own future security is greatly dependent on the outcome of that fight. Our ability to "keep out of war" is going to be affected by that outcome.

Thinking in terms of today and tomorrow, I make the direct statement to the American people that there is far less chance of the United States getting into war if we do all we can now to support the nations defending themselves against attack by the Axis than if we acquiesce in their defeat, submit tamely to an Axis victory, and wait our turn to be the object of attack in another war later on.

If we are to be completely honest with ourselves, we must admit there is risk in *any* course we may take. But I deeply believe that the great majority of our people agree that the course that I advocate involves the least risk now and the greatest hope for world peace in the future.

The people of Europe who are defending themselves do not ask us to do their fighting. They ask us for the implements of war, the planes, the tanks, the guns, the freighters, which will enable them to fight for their liberty and our security. Emphatically we must get these weapons to them in sufficient volume and quickly enough, so that we and our children will be saved the agony and suffering of war which others have had to endure.

Let not defeatists tell us that it is too late. It will never be earlier. Tomorrow will be later than today.

Certain facts are self-evident.

In a military sense Great Britain and the British Empire are today the spearhead of resistance to world conquest. They are putting up a fight which will live forever in the story of human gallantry.

There is no demand for sending an American Expeditionary Force outside our own borders. There is no intention by any member of your Government to send such a force. You can, therefore, nail any talk about sending armies to Europe as deliberate untruth.

Our national policy is not directed toward war. Its sole purpose is to keep war away from our country and our people.

Democracy's fight against world conquest is being greatly aided, and must be more greatly aided, by the rearmament of the United States and by sending every ounce and every ton of munitions and supplies that we can possibly spare to help the defenders who are in the front lines. It is no more un-neutral for us to do that than it is for Sweden, Russia, and other nations near Germany to send steel and ore and oil and other war materials into Germany every day.

We are planning our own defense with the utmost urgency; and in its vast scale we must integrate the war needs of Britain and the other free nations resisting aggression. . . .

As planes and ships and guns and shells are produced, your Government, with its defense experts, can then determine how best to use them to defend this hemisphere. The decision as to how much shall be sent abroad and how much shall remain at home must be made the basis of our over-all military necessities.

We must be the great arsenal of democracy. For us this is an emergency as serious as war itself. We must apply ourselves to our task with the same resolution, the same sense of urgency, the same spirit of patriotism and sacrifice, as we would show were we at war. . . .

January 6, 1941, State of the Union Address

. . . In the future days, which we seek to make secure, we look forward to a world founded upon four essential human freedoms.

The first is freedom of speech and expression—everywhere in the world.

The second is freedom of every person to worship God in his own way—everywhere in the world.

The third is freedom from want, which, translated into world terms, means economic understandings which will secure to every nation a healthy peacetime life for its inhabitants—everywhere in the world.

The fourth is freedom from fear, which, translated into world terms, means a world-wide reduction of armaments to such a point and in such a thorough fashion that no nation will be in a position to commit an act of physical aggression against any neighbor—anywhere in the world.

That is no vision of a distant millennium. It is a definite basis for a kind of world attainable in our own time and generation. That kind of world is the very antithesis of the so-called "new order" of tyranny, which the dictators seek to create with the crash of a bomb.

To that new order we oppose the greater conception—the moral order. A good society is able to face schemes of world domination and foreign revolutions alike without fear.

Since the beginning of our American history we have been engaged in change, in a perpetual, peaceful revolution, a revolution which goes on steadily, quietly, adjusting itself to changing conditions without the concentration camp or the quicklime in the ditch. The world order which we seek is the cooperation of free countries, working together in a friendly, civilized society.

This nation has placed its destiny in the hands and heads and hearts of its millions of free men and women, and its faith in freedom under the guidance of God. Freedom means the supremacy of human rights everywhere. Our support goes to those who struggle to gain those rights and keep them. Our strength is our unity of purpose.

To that high concept there can be no end save victory.

1.5 Charles A. Lindbergh Opposes Lend-Lease, February 6, 1941[5]

Passage of the Lend-Lease bill would clearly make the United States an unofficial belligerent in the war against Nazi Germany, and it consequently led to a major public and congressional debate. Spearheading the opposition was the anti-interventionist America First Committee and one of its chief spokespersons, Charles A. Lindbergh. The famed aviator was also one of the most popular figures of the interwar era, and on February 6 he explained in this testimony before the Senate Foreign Relations Committee his reasons for opposing the Lend-Lease bill. What were those reasons, and do you find them convincing?

Mr. Chairman and gentlemen, in the hope that it will save time and add to clarity, I have attempted to outline briefly my reasons for opposition to this bill. In general, I have two. I oppose it, first, because I believe it is a step away from the system of government in which most of us in this country believe. Secondly, I oppose it because I think it represents a policy which will weaken rather than strengthen our Nation. . . .

. . . I would like to say that I have never taken the stand that it makes no difference to us who wins this war in Europe. It does make a difference to us, a great difference. But I do not believe that it is either possible or desirable for us in America to control the outcome of European wars. When I am asked which side I would like to have win, it would be very easy for me to say "the English." But, gentlemen, an English victory, if it were possible at all, would necessitate years of war and an invasion of the Continent of Europe. I believe this would create prostration, famine, and disease in Europe—and probably in America—such as the world has

---

5. From Senate Foreign Relations Committee Hearings, *To Promote the Defense of the United States*, 77th Cong., 1st sess. (January 3, 1941, through January 2, 1942) (Washington DC: U.S. Government Printing Office, 1941), 490–92.

never experienced before. This is why I say that I prefer a negotiated peace to a complete victory by either side.

This bill is obviously the most recent step in a policy which attempts to obtain security for America by controlling internal conditions in Europe. The policy of depleting our own forces to aid England is based upon the assumption that England will win this war. Personally, I do not believe that England is in a position to win the war. If she does not win, or unless our aid is used in negotiating a better peace than could otherwise be obtained, we will be responsible for futilely prolonging the war and adding to the bloodshed and devastation in Europe, particularly among the democracies. In that case, the only advantage we can gain by our action lies in whatever additional time we obtain to prepare ourselves for defense. But instead of consolidating our own defensive position in America, we are sending a large portion of our armament production abroad. In the case of aviation, for instance, we have sent most of it, yet our own air forces are in deplorable condition for lack of modern equipment. The majority of the planes we now have are obsolescent on the standards of modern warfare.

This bill even authorizes the transfer of the equipment that our air forces now possess. From the standpoint of aviation, at least, I believe this policy weakens our security in America rather than strengthens it. . . .

. . . I believe it is obvious that England cannot obtain an air strength equal to Germany's without great assistance from the United States; and my personal opinion is that, regardless of how much assistance we send, it will not be possible for American and British aviation concentrated in the small area of the British Isles, to equal the strength of German aviation, with unlimited bases throughout the Continent of Europe. We would have a disadvantageous geographical position from which to fight, and an ocean to cross with aircraft, men, fuel, and supplies, while our ships would be constantly subjected to the bombs and torpedoes of our enemy.

With this picture of Europe in mind, I now return to my statement that, from the standpoint of aviation, the attempt to gain supremacy of the air in Europe weakens our security in America. If we follow the policy represented by this bill, we will find ourselves with England as a bridgehead in Europe; and, one might say, with the American neck stretched clear across the Atlantic Ocean. . . .

It is also essential to take into consideration the fact that we have another island bridgehead in the Philippines; so that if we follow out the policy represented by this bill, we will have to maintain and protect supply lines which stretch two-thirds of the way around the earth, and which end in positions exposed to attack by the most powerful nations of both Europe and Asia.

This would be an audacious undertaking even if our nation were fully prepared for war. But we are not prepared for war, and the attempt to hold control of island positions off the coasts of Europe and Asia, at the same time, would necessitate depleting even the small defense forces that we now have, as the terms of this bill clearly show.

What we are doing in following our present policy, is giving up an ideal defensive position in America for a very precarious offensive position in Europe. I would be opposed to our entering the internal wars of Europe under any circumstances. But it is an established fact today, that our army and our air force are but poorly equipped on modern standards, and even our Navy is in urgent need of new equipment. It we deplete our forces still further, as this bill indicates we may, and if England should lose this war, then, gentlemen, I think we may be in danger of invasion, although I do not believe we are today. If we ever are invaded in America, the responsibility will lie upon those who send our arms abroad.

I advocate building strength in America because I believe we can be successful in this hemisphere. I oppose placing our security in an English victory because I believe that such a victory is extremely doubtful.

I am opposed to this bill because I believe it endorses a policy that will lead to failure in war, and to conditions in our own country as bad as or worse than those we now desire to overthrow in Nazi Germany.

I do not believe that the danger to America lies in an invasion from abroad. I believe it lies here at home in our own midst, and that it is exemplified by the terms of this bill—the placing of our security in the success of foreign armies, and the removal of power from the Representatives of the people in our own land.

1.6 Americans Express Their Opinions on Aid to Britain and Entry into the War, 1940–1941

These public opinion polls of the time clearly reveal the development in 1940–1941 of strong public support for aid to England—even at the risk of war. Reflecting this support, Congress in March 1941 passed the Lend-Lease bill by votes of 60–31 in the Senate and 317–71 in the House of Representatives.

At the same time, however, an overwhelming majority of those polled continued to oppose formal U.S. entry into the war against Germany. How do you explain these apparently contradictory public views? How did President Roosevelt deal with them?

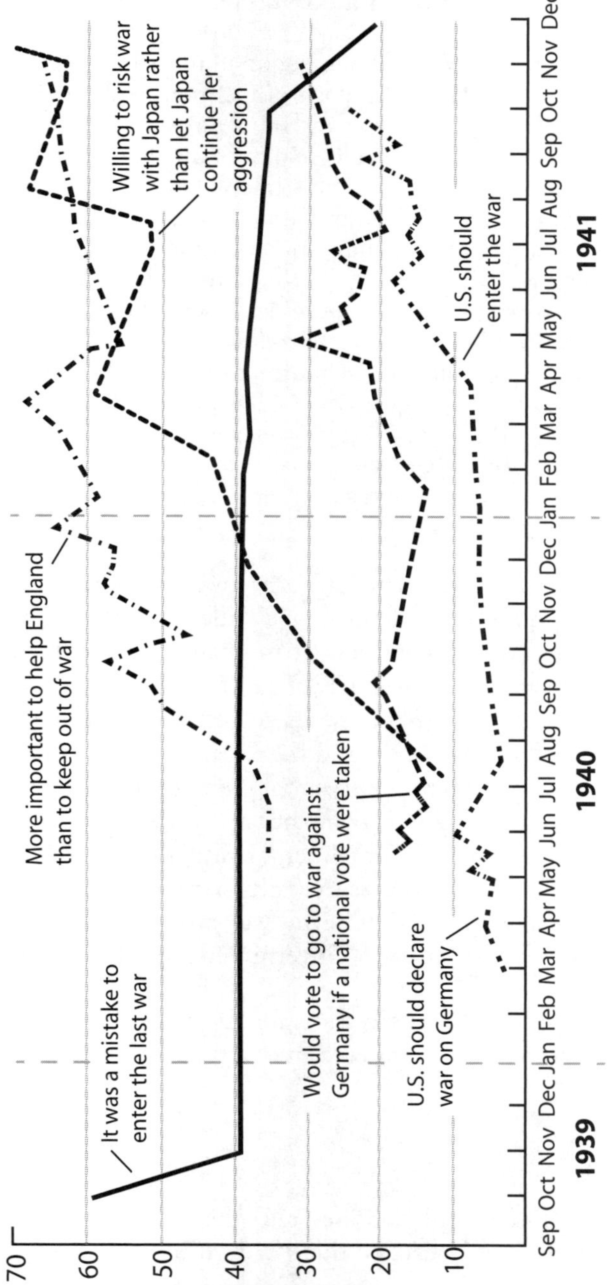

Percent of Total Vote

It was a mistake to enter the last war

More important to help England than to keep out of war

Willing to risk war with Japan rather than let Japan continue her aggression

Would vote to go to war against Germany if a national vote were taken

U.S. should declare war on Germany

U.S. should enter the war

70 — 60 — 50 — 40 — 30 — 20 — 10

Sep Oct Nov Dec Jan Feb Mar Apr May Jun Jul Aug Sep Oct Nov Dec Jan Feb Mar Apr May Jun Jul Aug Sep Oct Nov Dec

1939   **1940**   **1941**

From Hadley Cantril and Research Associates in the Office of Public Opinion Research, Princeton University, *Gauging Public Opinion* (Princeton, NJ: Princeton University Press, 1944; Port Washington, NY: Kennikat Press, 1972), 222.

1.7 Secretary of State Cordell Hull Responds to Japan's Final Proposal, November 26, 1941[6]

While the Sino-Japanese War that had begun in the 1930s continued, Japan sought in 1940 to take advantage of German military victories by expanding into French Indochina and other parts of Southeast Asia. Then in late September, it signed a formal military alliance with Germany and Italy, the Tripartite Pact. The United States responded with additional economic sanctions, culminating in a complete freeze on Japanese assets in July 1941. As the public opinion polls reproduced in the preceding document reveal, by this time a majority of those polled wished to oppose Japanese aggression even at the risk of war.

Throughout much of 1941, U.S. Secretary of State Cordell Hull engaged in negotiations with the Japanese ambassador to the United States in an effort to reach an agreement capable of avoiding a war that neither side wanted. On November 26, however, he rejected Japan's final offer and responded with what was, in effect, a statement of American principles. What were those principles, and what did he now propose?

[T]he Government of the United States offers for the consideration of the Japanese Government a plan of a broad but simple settlement covering the entire Pacific area as one practical exemplification of a program which this Government envisages as something to be worked out during our further conversations.

The plan therein suggested represents an effort to bridge the gap between our draft of June 21, 1941, and the Japanese draft of September 25 by making a new approach to the essential problems underlying a comprehensive Pacific settlement. This plan contains provisions dealing with the practical application of the fundamental principles which we have agreed in our conversations constitute the only sound basis for worthwhile international relations. We hope that in this way progress toward reaching a meeting of minds between our two Governments may be expedited.

Outline of Proposed Basis for Agreement
Between the United States and Japan

Section I

Draft Mutual Declaration of Policy

The Government of the United States and the Government of Japan both being solicitous for the peace of the Pacific affirm that their national

---

6. From U.S. Department of State, *Papers Relating to the Foreign Relations of the United States: Japan, 1931–1941*, vol. 2 (Washington, DC: U.S. Government Printing Office, 1943), 767–69.

policies are directed toward lasting and extensive peace throughout the Pacific area, that they have no territorial designs in that area, that they have no intention of threatening other countries or of using military force aggressively against any neighboring nation, and that, accordingly, in their national policies they will actively support and give practical application to the following fundamental principles upon which their relations with each other and with all other governments are based:

(1) The principle of inviolability of territorial integrity and sovereignty of each and all nations.

(2) The principle of non-interference in the internal affairs of other countries.

(3) The principle of equality, including equality of commercial opportunity and treatment.

(4) The principle of reliance upon international cooperation and conciliation for the prevention and pacific settlement of controversies and for improvement of international conditions by peaceful methods and processes.

The Government of Japan and the Government of the United States have agreed that toward eliminating chronic political instability, preventing recurrent economic collapse, and providing a basis for peace, they will actively support and practically apply the following principles in their economic relations with each other and with other nations and peoples:

(1) The principle of non-discrimination in international commercial relations.

(2) The principle of international economic cooperation and abolition of extreme nationalism as expressed in excessive trade restrictions.

(3) The principle of non-discriminatory access by all nations to raw material supplies.

(4) The principle of full protection of the interests of consuming countries and populations as regards the operation of international commodity agreements.

(5) The principle of establishment of such institutions and arrangements of international finance as may lend aid to the essential enterprises and the continuous development of all countries and may permit payments through processes of trade consonant with the welfare of all countries.

Section II

Steps to Be Taken by the Government of the United States and by the Government of Japan

The Government of the United States and the Government of Japan propose to take steps as follows:

1. The Government of the United States and the Government of Japan will endeavor to conclude a multilateral non-aggression pact among the British Empire, China, Japan, the Netherlands, the Soviet Union, Thailand and the United States.

2. Both Governments will endeavor to conclude among the American, British, Chinese, Japanese, the Netherland and Thai Governments an agreement whereunder each of the Governments would pledge itself to respect the territorial integrity of French Indochina and, in the event that there should develop a threat to the territorial integrity of Indochina, to enter into immediate consultation with a view to taking such measures as may be deemed necessary and advisable to meet the threat in question. Such agreement would provide also that each of the Governments party to the agreement would not seek or accept preferential treatment in its trade or economic relations with Indochina and would use its influence to obtain for each of the signatories equality of treatment in trade and commerce with French Indochina.

3. The Government of Japan will withdraw all military, naval, air and police forces from China and from Indochina.

4. The Government of the United States and the Government of Japan will not support—militarily, politically, economically—any government or regime in China other than the National Government of the Republic of China with capital temporarily at Chungking.

5. Both Governments will give up all extraterritorial rights in China, including rights and interests in and with regard to international settlements and concessions, and rights under the Boxer Protocol of 1901.

Both Governments will endeavor to obtain the agreement of the British and other governments to give up extraterritorial rights in China, including rights in international settlements and in concessions and under the Boxer Protocol of 1901.

6. The Government of the United States and the Government of Japan will enter into negotiations for the conclusion between the United States and Japan of a trade agreement, based upon reciprocal most-favored-nation treatment and reduction of trade barriers by both countries, including an undertaking by the United States to bind raw silk on the free list.

7. The Government of the United States and the Government of Japan will, respectively, remove the freezing restrictions on Japanese funds in the United States and on American funds in Japan.

8. Both Governments will agree upon a plan for the stabilization of the dollar-yen rate, with the allocation of funds adequate for this purpose, half to be supplied by Japan and half by the United States.

9. Both Governments will agree that no agreement which either has concluded with any third power or powers shall be interpreted by it in such a way as to conflict with the fundamental purpose of this agreement, the establishment and preservation of peace throughout the Pacific area.

10. Both Governments will use their influence to cause other governments to adhere to and to give practical application to the basic political and economic principles set forth in this agreement.

1.8 Japan Terminates Negotiations and Hull Replies Orally, December 7, 1941[7]

As expected, Japan rejected Hull's November 26 proposals and on December 7 responded not only with the attack on Pearl Harbor, but also with the following memorandum ending the talks and presenting the Japanese perspective on how and why negotiations had failed. Compare their perspective with that of the United States as presented by Hull in the preceding document.

Japan's memorandum was supposed to have been delivered by its negotiators at the same time the attack on Pearl Harbor commenced, but it was actually delivered nearly an hour and a half after that attack had begun, leading to Secretary Hull's emotional response.

Memorandum Handed by the Japanese Ambassador (Nomura) to the Secretary of State at 2:20 P.M. on December 7, 1941

. . .

2. It is the immutable policy of the Japanese Government to insure the stability of East Asia and to promote world peace and thereby to enable all nations to find each its proper place in the world.

Ever since [the] China Affair broke out owing to the failure on the part of China to comprehend Japan's true intentions, the Japanese Government has striven for the restoration of peace and it has consistently exerted its best efforts to prevent the extension of war-like disturbance. It was also to

---

7. From U.S. Department of State, *Papers Relating to the Foreign Relations of the United States: Japan, 1931–1941*, vol. 2 (Washington, DC: U.S. Government Printing Office, 1943), 787–92.

that end that in September last year Japan concluded the Tripartite Pact with Germany and Italy.

However, both the United States and Great Britain have resorted to every possible measure to assist the Chungking régime so as to obstruct the establishment of a general peace between Japan and China, interfering with Japan's constructive endeavours toward the stabilization of East Asia. Exerting pressure on the Netherlands East Indies, or menacing French Indo-China, they have attempted to frustrate Japan's aspiration to the ideal of common prosperity in cooperation with these regions. Furthermore, when Japan in accordance with its protocol with France took measures of joint defence of French Indo-China, both American and British Governments, willfully misinterpreting it as a threat to their own possessions, and inducing the Netherlands Government to follow suit, they enforced the assets freezing order, thus severing economic relations with Japan. While manifesting thus an obviously hostile attitude, these countries have strengthened their military preparations perfecting an encirclement of Japan, and have brought about a situation which endangers the very existence of the Empire. . . .

4. From the beginning of the present negotiation the Japanese Government has always maintained an attitude of fairness and moderation, and did its best to reach a settlement, for which it made all possible concessions often in spite of great difficulties. As for the China question which constituted an important subject of the negotiation, the Japanese Government showed a most conciliatory attitude. As for the principle of non-discrimination in international commerce, advocated by the American Government, the Japanese Government expressed its desire to see the said principle applied throughout the world, and declared that along with the actual practice of this principle in the world, the Japanese Government would endeavour to apply the same in the Pacific Area including China, and made it clear that Japan had no intention of excluding from China economic activities of third powers pursued on an equitable basis. Furthermore, as regards the question of withdrawing troops from French Indo-China, the Japanese Government even volunteered, as mentioned above, to carry out an immediate evacuation of troops from Southern French Indo-China as a measure of easing the situation. . . .

On the other hand, the American Government, always holding fast to theories in disregard of realities, and refusing to yield an inch on its impractical principles, caused undue delay in the negotiation. It is difficult to understand this attitude of the American Government and the Japanese Government desires to call the attention of the American Government especially to the following points:

1. The American Government advocates in the name of world peace those principles favorable to it and urges upon the Japanese Government the acceptance thereof. The peace of the world may be brought about only by discovering a mutually acceptable formula through recognition of the reality of the situation and mutual appreciation of one another's position. An attitude such as ignores realities and imposes one's selfish views upon others will scarcely serve the purpose of facilitating the consummation of negotiations.

Of the various principles put forward by the American Government as a basis of the Japanese-American Agreement, there are some which the Japanese Government is ready to accept in principle, but in view of the world's actual conditions, it seems only a utopian ideal on the part of the American Government to attempt to force their immediate adoption. . . .

2. The American proposal contained a stipulation which states—"Both Governments will agree that no agreement, which either has concluded with any third power or powers, shall be interpreted by it in such a way as to conflict with the fundamental purpose of this agreement, the establishment and preservation of peace throughout the Pacific area." It is presumed that the above provision has been proposed with a view to restrain Japan from fulfilling its obligations under the Tripartite Pact when the United States participates in the War in Europe, and, as such, it cannot be accepted by the Japanese Government.

The American Government, obsessed with its own views and opinions, may be said to be scheming for the extension of the war. While it seeks, on the one hand, to secure its rear by stabilizing the Pacific Area, it is engaged, on the other hand, in aiding Great Britain and preparing to attack, in the name of self-defense, Germany and Italy, two Powers that are striving to establish a new order in Europe. Such a policy is totally at variance with the many principles upon which the American Government proposes to found the stability of the Pacific Area through peaceful means.

3. Whereas the American Government, under the principles it rigidly upholds, objects to settle international issues through military pressure, it is exercising in conjunction with Great Britain and other nations pressure by economic power. Recourse to such pressure as a means of dealing with international relations should be condemned as it is at times more inhumane than military pressure.

4. It is impossible not to reach the conclusion that the American Government desires to maintain and strengthen, in coalition with Great Britain and other Powers, its dominant position it has hitherto occupied not only in China but in other areas of East Asia. It is a fact of history that the countries of East Asia for the past hundred years or more have been compelled to observe the *status quo* under the Anglo-American policy of imperialistic

exploitation and to sacrifice themselves to the prosperity of the two nations. The Japanese Government cannot tolerate the perpetuation of such a situation since it directly runs counter to Japan's fundamental policy to enable all nations to enjoy each its proper place in the world.

The stipulation proposed by the American Government relative to French Indo-China is a good exemplification of the above-mentioned American policy. . . .

5. All the items demanded of Japan by the American Government regarding China such as wholesale evacuation of troops or unconditional application of the principle of non-discrimination in international commerce ignored the actual conditions of China, and are calculated to destroy Japan's position as the stabilizing factor of East Asia. The attitude of the American Government in demanding Japan not to support militarily, politically or economically any régime other than the régime at Chungking, disregarding thereby the existence of the Nanking Government, shatters the very basis of the present negotiation. This demand of the American Government falling, as it does, in line with its above-mentioned refusal to cease from aiding the Chungking régime, demonstrates clearly the intention of the American Government to obstruct the restoration of normal relations between Japan and China and the return of peace to East Asia.

5. In brief, the American proposal contains certain acceptable items such as those concerning commerce, including the conclusion of a trade agreement, mutual removal of the freezing restrictions, and stabilization of yen and dollar exchange, or the abolition of extra-territorial rights in China. On the other hand, however, the proposal in question ignores Japan's sacrifices in the four years of the China Affair, menaces the Empire's existence itself and disparages its honour and prestige. Therefore, viewed in its entirety, the Japanese Government regrets that it cannot accept the proposal as a basis of negotiation. . . .

7. Obviously it is the intention of the American Government to conspire with Great Britain and other countries to obstruct Japan's efforts toward the establishment of peace through the creation of a new order in East Asia, and especially to preserve Anglo-American rights and interests by keeping Japan and China at war. This intention has been revealed clearly during the course of the present negotiation. Thus, the earnest hope of the Japanese Government to adjust Japanese-American relations and to preserve and promote the peace of the Pacific through cooperation with the American Government has finally been lost.

The Japanese Government regrets to have to notify hereby the American Government that in view of the attitude of the American Government it cannot but consider that it is impossible to reach an agreement through further negotiations. . . .

After the Secretary had read two or three pages he asked the Ambassador whether this document was presented under instructions of the Japanese government. The Ambassador replied that it was. The Secretary as soon as he had finished reading the document turned to the Japanese Ambassador and said,

> I must say that in all my conversations with you [the Japanese Ambassador] during the last nine months I have never uttered one word of untruth. This is borne out absolutely by the record. In all my fifty years of public service I have never seen a document that was more crowded with infamous falsehoods and distortions—infamous falsehoods and distortions on a scale so huge that I never imagined until today that any Government on this planet was capable of uttering them.

1.9 President Roosevelt Asks Congress for a Declaration of War, December 8, 1941[8]

Pearl Harbor was but one of many attacks the Japanese launched in the Pacific against British as well as American possessions. President Roosevelt, as infuriated as Hull by what they considered Japanese duplicity in planning war while continuing negotiations to maintain peace, informed Congress on December 8 of the multiple Japanese attacks and requested a declaration of war. Congress agreed the next day, and on December 11 Hitler declared war on the United States, thereby fusing what had been two very separate conflicts into a single war encompassing the entire world.

Yesterday, December 7, 1941—a date which will live in infamy—the United States of America was suddenly and deliberately attacked by naval and air forces of the Empire of Japan.

The United States was at peace with that Nation and, at the solicitation of Japan, was still in conversation with its Government and its Emperor looking toward the maintenance of peace in the Pacific. Indeed, one hour after Japanese air squadrons had commenced bombing in Oahu, the

---

8. From U.S. Department of State, *Papers Relating to the Foreign Relations of the United States: Japan, 1931–1941*, vol. 2 (Washington, DC: U.S. Government Printing Office, 1943), 793–94.

Japanese Ambassador to the United States and his colleague delivered to the Secretary of State a formal reply to a recent American message. While this reply stated that it seemed useless to continue the existing diplomatic negotiations, it contained no threat or hint of war or armed attack.

It will be recorded that the distance of Hawaii from Japan makes it obvious that the attack was deliberately planned many days or even weeks ago. During the intervening time the Japanese Government has deliberately sought to deceive the United States by false statements and expressions of hope for continued peace.

The attack yesterday on the Hawaiian Islands has caused severe damage to American naval and military forces. Very many American lives have been lost. In addition American ships have been reported torpedoed on the high seas between San Francisco and Honolulu.

Yesterday the Japanese Government also launched an attack against Malaya.

Last night Japanese forces attacked Hong Kong.

Last night Japanese forces attacked Guam.

Last night Japanese forces attacked the Philippine Islands.

Last night the Japanese attacked Wake Island.

This morning the Japanese attacked Midway Island.

Japan has, therefore, undertaken a surprise offensive extending throughout the Pacific area. The facts of yesterday speak for themselves. The people of the United States have already formed their opinions and well understand the implications to the very life and safety of our Nation.

As Commander-in-Chief of the Army and Navy I have directed that all measures be taken for our defense.

Always will we remember the character of the onslaught against us.

No matter how long it may take us to overcome this premeditated invasion, the American people in their righteous might will win through to absolute victory.

I believe I interpret the will of the Congress and of the people when I assert that we will not only defend ourselves to the uttermost but will make very certain that this form of treachery shall never endanger us again.

Hostilities exist. There is no blinking at the fact that our people, our territory, and our interests are in grave danger.

With confidence in our armed forces—with the unbounded determination of our people—we will gain the inevitable triumph—so help us God.

I ask that the Congress declare that since the unprovoked and dastardly attack by Japan on Sunday, December seventh, a state of war has existed between the United States and the Japanese Empire.

CHAPTER 2

OVER HERE: MOBILIZING THE AMERICAN PEOPLE FOR WAR

The United States was ill prepared to go to war when Nazi forces invaded Poland in September 1939. The American economy was still very much mired in the Great Depression. Many millions were unemployed, and American industry was producing at levels far below its total capacity. The American military was similarly unprepared. Decades of spending cuts—the product both of the Depression and widespread anti-interventionist sentiment—had seriously decimated the armed forces. The successful mobilization of both the American economy and the American military would prove critical to the outcome of the war.

At the end of the 1930s, the United States had a great reservoir of untapped industrial might, but harnessing that unused capacity proved politically difficult. The shadow of World War I hung over American politics. The majority of Americans believed that it had been a mistake to get involved in the First World War; many believed the war itself was a product of a conspiracy hatched by munitions manufacturers. Public antipathy toward the arms industry, in combination with public policies that made military production unprofitable, fatally wounded the American munitions industry. By the middle of the 1920s, that once formidable industry had all but disappeared. When it finally began to prepare for war in the late 1930s, the United States had to begin again from scratch.

Efforts to put the U.S. economy on a war footing began well before the United States entered the war in December of 1941. A raft of new agencies, from the Office of Price Administration to the War Production Board, endeavored to impose some order on the chaotic process. But these efforts were, by and large, poorly coordinated, particularly during the period of American neutrality. The task of mobilization was made easier by Pearl Harbor, but it was still beset by difficulties. Although the U.S. government sought to harness the instruments of public opinion—including the motion picture industry—to enlist the nation as a whole in the war effort, many Americans continued to resist the imperatives of war production.

By the end of 1942, however, the federal government had put into place a set of policies to put the economy on a war footing without relying overmuch on governmental coercion. Like the New Deal before it, wartime mobilization depended on cooperation between the public and private spheres to produce policy outcomes. Mobilization agencies rarely resorted to using policy "sticks," preferring instead to use the "carrots" of tax inducements, financial enticements, and other market mechanisms to encourage war production. Many businesses translated federal defense contracts into significant profits. Mobilization policy tended to enrich large manufacturers at the expense of smaller ones. More than two-thirds of all military contracts went to fewer than 100 companies; 33 corporations accounted for more than 50 percent of all war production.

Mobilization for the war injected new life into the American economy and ended the Great Depression. Wartime production, outlined in President Roosevelt's "blueprint for victory," all but eliminated unemployment and reversed the economic decline that had begun in 1929. Although many continued to worry that the Depression would return once the war emergency had ceased (see Chapter 10), low unemployment rates and economic growth continued well into the postwar period.

Economic mobilization complemented military mobilization. The U.S. military was unprepared to go to war with Nazi Germany or Imperial Japan, let alone both. Equipment and weapons were outmoded; ammunition was lacking for all types of weapons. The U.S. Army had only 280,000 men; the National Guard comprised another 250,000 poorly trained potential troops. American air power was in its infancy. The U.S. Navy, while in somewhat better shape, was nevertheless unprepared for the scale of the coming conflict.

The gathering storm in Europe in 1939 and 1940 helped to loosen the purse strings for military preparedness. In the spring of 1940, as Nazi forces smashed through Belgium, the Netherlands, and France, the nation's press began to call for massive increases in defense spending. On July 10, less than a month after the fall of France, Roosevelt called on Congress to spend billions of dollars for the "total defense" of the United States. In his third extraordinary defense message, the president called for more money to equip a two-ocean navy, to buy modern equipment, and to vastly improve American air power. It was not until 1942, however, that Congress modernized the federal tax system enough to pay for a large part of the war. The Revenue Act of 1942 transformed the federal income tax from a "class tax" paid by only the very wealthy minority, to a "mass tax" borne by the majority of American citizens. The modernization of the U.S. tax system is another lasting consequence of the Second World War.

Money was only part of the problem, however. The United States also had to figure out how to get more men into the armed forces. In his July 10 message, President Roosevelt had asked for an army of 1.2 million men, with another 800,000 in reserve. At the same time, Senator Edward Burke of Nebraska and Representative James W. Wadsworth of New York introduced a bill creating the nation's first peacetime draft. After months of contentious debate, Congress passed the Selective Training and Service Bill on September 14, 1940. Although World War II has since been dubbed "the good war," some 12,000 Americans nevertheless registered as "conscientious objectors" during the war; still others refused even to register and thus faced fines and jail time.

Racial discrimination pervaded the mobilization process. African Americans faced persistent labor market discrimination. Seventy-five percent of African Americans lived in the South, where they faced legal discrimination under Jim Crow laws and almost universal disfranchisement. The war, which was often depicted as a struggle for democratic values in official propaganda, provided the black community with an opportunity to achieve a "double victory" abroad and at home. Even before Pearl Harbor, black leaders organized to leverage the war emergency to achieve basic justice for their communities. In 1941, A. Philip Randolph, a black civil rights and labor leader, used the threat of a massive march on Washington to force Roosevelt to take action to eliminate racial discrimination in war production. Executive Order 8802, issued on June 25, 1941, also created the Fair Employment Practices Committee, a new federal agency charged with investigating complaints of racial discrimination in war work.

Ironically, at the same time as it took a stand against racial discrimination in war production, the federal government maintained racial discrimination in its own armed forces. African Americans were generally denied the right to serve on the front lines and were relegated to menial positions. Although the exigencies of war helped to break down the barriers of segregation on the battlefield, it was not until 1948 that the armed services were officially desegregated. The armed forces also discriminated against gay men and women and relied on the newly popular psychiatric sciences to designate these men and women as psychologically unfit for service. Despite this official policy, however, countless gay men and lesbians did serve during the war, and for some, the war offered new opportunities to "come out," at least in a limited sense.

The war also affected the role and status of women in American society. About 200,000 American women served in the military during the war, as part of special auxiliary units created by the navy, army, and coast guard. Women made even more significant inroads into the workforce. Desperate for new workers, U.S. industry tapped new sources of labor, including women. The federal government played an active role in recruiting women into war work, overseeing public relations campaigns designed to overcome what Roosevelt termed old "prejudices and practices." Yet if the war offered the nearly 2 million women who did work in defense plants an unprecedented opportunity, this period was less transformative than is often assumed. Women were only rarely employed in skilled or management positions, and were paid less than their male counterparts. Despite the attention given then and now to "Rosie the Riveter," few women moved into jobs once held by men, and even fewer kept them after the war.

The documents in this chapter encourage students to think about how the United States mobilized its economy and its military in the late 1930s and early 1940s. What obstacles did the mobilization process face? How might policy makers have overcome those obstacles? What changes did the mobilization make to the American economy and to American society in general? Did these changes outlast the war, or were they only "for the duration"? How did the public and private sectors interact in the mobilization effort? Why might this be important?

* * * *

2.1 Congress Institutes the Draft, 1940[1]

In September 1940, Congress passed the Selective Training and Service Act, which created the first peacetime conscription law in U.S. history. The new law required all men between the ages of twenty-one and thirty-six to register with local draft boards. Reflecting continued isolationist spirit in Congress and the country, the law specified that drafted soldiers had to remain in the Western Hemisphere or in American territories located in other parts of the world, and limited service to twelve months. The next summer, Congress approved a draft extension bill, extending the term of duty beyond twelve months, by a single vote. After the United States entered the war, Congress amended the draft law to allow more men to register and serve. By 1947, when the draft finally expired, more than 10 million had been inducted.

---

1. From U.S. House of Representatives, *Selective Training and Service Act of 1940: Conference Report*, 76th Cong., 2nd sess. (Washington, DC: U.S. Government Printing Office, 1940).

An Act

To provide for the common defense by increasing the personnel of the armed forces of the United States and providing for its training.

Be it enacted by the Senate and House of Representatives of the United States of America in Congress assembled, That (a) the Congress hereby declares that it is imperative to increase and train the personnel of the armed forces of the United States.

(b) The Congress further declares that in a free society the obligations and privileges of military training and service should be shared generally in accordance with a fair and just system of selective compulsory military training and service.

(c) The Congress further declares, in accordance with our traditional military policy as expressed in the National Defense Act of 1916, as amended, that it is essential that the strength and organization of the National Guard, as an integral part of the first-line defenses of this Nation, be at all times maintained and assured. To this end, it is the intent of the Congress that whenever the Congress shall determine that troops are needed for the national security in excess of those of the Regular Army and those in active training and service under section 3 (b), the National Guard of the United States, or such part thereof as may be necessary, shall be ordered to active Federal service and continued therein so long as such necessity exists.

Sec. 2. Except as otherwise provided in this Act, it shall be the duty of every male citizen of the United States, and of every male alien residing in the United States, who, on the day or days fixed for the first or any subsequent registration, is between the ages of twenty-one and thirty-six, to present himself for and submit to registration at such time or times and place or places, and in such manner and in such age group or groups, as shall be determined by rules and regulations prescribed hereunder.

Sec. 3. (a) . . . The President is authorized from time to time, whether or not a state of war exists, to select and induct into the land and naval forces of the United States for training and service, in the manner provided in this Act, such number of men as in his judgment is required for such forces in the national interest: . . . *Provided* . . . That except in time of war there shall not be in active training or service in the land forces of the United States at any one time under subsection (b) more than nine hundred thousand men inducted under the provisions of this Act. The men inducted into the land or naval forces for training and service under this Act shall be assigned to camps or units of such forces.

(b) Each man inducted under the provisions of subsection (a) shall serve for a training and service period of twelve consecutive months, unless sooner discharged, except that whenever the Congress has declared that the national interest is imperiled, such twelve-month period may be extended by the President to such time as may be necessary in the interests of national defense. . . .

Sec. 4. (a) The selection of men for training and service under section 3 (other than those who are voluntarily inducted pursuant to this Act) shall be made in an impartial manner, under such rules and regulations as the President may prescribe, from the men who are liable for such training and service and who at the time of selection are registered and classified but not deferred or exempted: *Provided*, That in the selection and training of men under this Act, and in the interpretation and execution of the provisions of this Act, there shall be no discrimination against any person on account of race or color. . . .

Sec. 5 (e) The President is authorized, under such rules and regulations as he may prescribe, to provide for the deferment from training and service under this Act in the land and naval forces of the United States of those men whose employment in industry, agriculture, or other occupations or employment, or whose activity in other endeavors, is found in accordance with section 10 (a) (2) to be necessary to the maintenance of the national health, safety, or interest. The President is also authorized, under such rules and regulations as he may prescribe, to provide for the deferment from training and service under this Act in the land and naval forces of the United States (1) of those men in a status with respect to persons dependent upon them for support which renders their deferment advisable, and (2) of those men found to be physically, mentally, or morally deficient or defective. No deferment from such training and service shall be made in the case of any individual except upon the basis of the status of such individual, and no such deferment shall be made of individuals by occupational groups or of groups of individuals in any plant or institution. . . .

(g) Nothing contained in this Act shall be construed to require any person to be subject to combatant training and service in the land or naval forces of the United States who, by reason of religious training and belief, is conscientiously opposed to participation in war in any form. Any such person claiming such exemption from combatant training and services because of such conscientious objections whose claim is sustained by the local board shall, if he is inducted into the land or naval forces under this Act, be assigned to noncombatant service as defined by the President, or shall, if he is found to be conscientiously opposed to participation in such noncombatant service, in lieu of such induction, be assigned to work of national importance under civilian direction. . . .

2.2 Conscientious Objectors Explain Their Reasons for Refusing to Register for the Draft, 1941[2]

The Selective Training and Service Act included provisions allowing those who "by reason of religious training or belief" were "conscientiously opposed to participation in war in any form" to refuse military service. The law expanded the definition of a conscientious objector beyond membership in the traditional "peace churches." Under the terms of the new draft law, conscientious objectors could be assigned to noncombatant service or "work of national importance under civilian direction." Some war resisters, however, refused even to register with their local draft boards on the grounds that to do so would make them "part of the act" of war itself.

It is impossible for us to think of the conscription law without at the same time thinking of the whole war system, because it is clear to us that conscription is definitely a part of the institution of war.

To us, the war system is an evil part of our social order, and we declare that we cannot cooperate with it in any way. War is an evil because it is in violation of the Way of Love as seen in God through Christ. It is a concentration and accentuation of all the evils of our society. War consists of mass murder, deliberate starvation, vandalism, and similar evils. Physical destruction and moral disintegration are the inevitable result. The war method perpetuates and compounds the evils it purports to overcome. It is impossible, as history reveals, to overcome evil with evil. The last World War is a notorious case of the failure of the war system, and there is no evidence to believe that this war will be any different. It is our positive proclamation as followers of Jesus Christ that we must overcome evil with good. We seek in our daily living to reconcile that separation of man from man and man from God which produces war.

We have also been led to our conclusion on the conscription law in the light of its totalitarian nature. It is a totalitarian move when our government insists that the manpower of the nation take a year of military training. It is a totalitarian move for the President of the nation to be able to

2. From "Joint Statement of Donald Benedict, Joseph J. Bevilavqua, Meredith Dallas, David Dellinger, George M. Houser, William H. Lovell, Howard E. Spragg, and Richard J. Wichlei," in *Why We Refused to Register* (New York: Fellowship of Reconciliation, Keep America Out of War Congress, National Council for Prevention of War, Youth Committee Against War, Young People's Socialist League, and War Resisters League, 1941); repr. in *Nonviolence in America: A Documentary History*, ed. Staughton Lynd (Indianapolis: Bobbs-Merrill, 1966): 269–99.

conscript industry to produce certain materials which are deemed necessary for national defense without considering the actual physical needs of the people. We believe, therefore, that by opposing the Selective Service law, we will be striking at the heart of totalitarianism as well as war. . . .

We feel a deep bond of unity with those who decide to register as conscientious objectors, but our own decision must be different for the following reasons:

If we register under the act, even as conscientious objectors, we are becoming part of the act. The fact that we as conscientious objectors may gain personal exemption from the most crassly un-Christian requirements of the act does not compensate for the fact that we are complying with it and accepting its protection. If a policeman (or group of vigilantes) stops us on the street, our possession of the government's card shows that we are "all right"—we have complied with the act for the militarization of America. If that does not hurt our Christian consciences, what will? If we try to rationalize on the theory that we must go along with the act in order to fight the fascism and militarism of which it is a part, it seems to us that we are doing that very thing which all pacifist Christians abhor: we are consciously employing bad means on the theory that to do so will contribute to a good end. . . .

In similar vein, it is urged that great concessions have been won for religious pacifists and that we endanger these by our refusal to accept them. Fascism, as it gradually supplanted democracy in Germany, was aided by the decision of Christians and leftists to accept a partial fascism rather than to endanger those democratic concessions which still remain. It is not alone for our own exemption from fighting that we work—it is for freedom of the American people from fascism and militarism.

Partial exemption of conscientious objectors has come about partly through the work of influential pacifists and partly through the open-mindedness of certain nonpacifists. But it has also been granted because of the fear of the government that, without such a provision, public opposition to war would be too great to handle. In particular, it seems to us that one of the reasons the government has granted exemption to ministers and theological students is to gain a religious sanction for its diabolical war. Where actual support could not be gained, it hoped to soothe their consciences so that they could provide no real opposition.

We do not contend that the American people maliciously choose the vicious instrument of war. In a very perplexing situation, they lack the imagination, the religious faith, and the precedents to respond in a different manner. This makes it all the more urgent to build in this country and throughout the world a group trained in the techniques of nonviolent opposition to the encroachments of militarism and fascism. Until we build such a movement, it will be impossible to stall the war machine at home. When we do build such a movement, we will have forged the only weapon which can ever give effective answer to foreign invasion. Thus, in learning to fight American Hitlerism, we will show an increasing group of war-disillusioned Americans how to resist foreign Hitlers as well.

For these reasons we hereby register our refusal to comply in any way with the Selective Training and Service Act. We do not expect to stem the war forces today; but we are helping to build the movement that will conquer in the future.

2.3 Representative Edith Nourse Rogers Introduces the WAAC Bill, 1941[3]

In May of 1941, Representative Edith Nourse Rogers, a Republican from Massachusetts, introduced a bill to create a Women's Army Auxiliary Corps (WAAC). Rogers' case for the new unit stressed both ideological and practical considerations. It was not until the next year, however, that Congress acted on the proposal. In 1943, the auxiliary corps became the Women's Army Corps (WAC). Some 150,000 women eventually served in the WAAC/WAC during the war, assuming such positions as switchboard operators, mechanics, postal clerks, and typists. They were the first women other than nurses to serve with the army.

Mr. Speaker, I introduced this bill with a view to having women enlist, not to be drafted, in the Women's Army Auxiliary Corps, for noncombatant service in the Army of the United States, for the purpose of making available to the national defense the knowledge, skill, and special training of the women of this Nation. I understand the War Department favors this bill. I am told that the Budget favors the bill with certain modifications. I know that the gentlemen of the Congress who have returned from England can testify as to the very splendid work done by the women in England. In the World War I saw the work of women with the British forces; some of them did work with our Army. Many men can be released for other duty. Women can take the place of cooks, waiters, telephone operators, and chauffeurs. They can take places as hostesses, librarians, in technical positions, in radio, in the Signal Corps, as dietitians, and physiotherapists. They can join the corps and thereby release men to go back to

---

3. From Representative Rogers, 77th Cong., 1st sess., *The Congressional Record* 89, pt. 9: 9747–49.

do vital defense work in industry. This bill will release men for work of vast importance in our national defense. There are many positions that women can fill, the Army believes, that will be of great benefit to the Army as the need arises. Many women have expressed eagerness to enlist in an auxiliary corps of this kind. The women of America are anxious to serve their country. They are intensely patriotic. . . .

This does not in any way interfere with volunteer work without pay, but it does allow a great group of women to enlist who could not afford to do patriotic national-defense work for nothing. Mr. Speaker, the women of America want to make every sacrifice; they want in every way to aid, in this war, the march to victory.

Be it enacted, etc., That the President is hereby authorized to establish a Women's Army Auxiliary Corps for noncombatant service with the Army of the United States for the purpose of making available to the national defense the knowledge, skill, and special training of the women of this Nation.

Sec. 2. . . . The Director shall receive a salary of $3,000 per annum, together with such other allowances as may be provided for hereinafter. . . .

Sec. 3. The Secretary is authorized to establish and maintain such number of schools as he may consider necessary for the purposes of training candidates for officers of the corps. . . . Candidates for such schools may be selected from women volunteers who are citizens of the United States and during their attendance at such schools shall be furnished living quarters, uniforms as hereinafter provided, medical and dental service, medicines, medical and hospital supplies, hospitalization, subsistence, texts, necessary school supplies, and pay at the rate of $50 per month. . . . *Provided,* That the whole number of officers so appointed initially shall not exceed 750, together with the Director and Assistant Directors; but the Secretary is authorized to increase this number when he deems such action necessary. The pay of officers so appointed shall be $2,000 per annum for each first officer, $1,575 per annum for each second officer, and $1,500 per annum for each third officer, together with such allowances as may be hereinafter provided. . . .

Sec. 5. The Secretary is authorized to have enrolled initially in the corps, in addition to the Director, Assistant Directors, and officers hereinabove provided for, by voluntary enrollment, not to exceed 25,000 women of excellent character in good physical health, between the ages of 21 and 45 years and citizens of the United States: *Provided,* That . . . [t]he pay of first leaders shall be $864 per annum, of leaders $720 per annum, of junior leaders $648 per annum, and for auxiliaries not otherwise classified $21 per month for the first 4 months of service and $30 per month thereafter.

Specialists of the first class shall be paid, in addition to their base pay, the sum of $15 per month, specialists of the second class shall similarly be paid $10 per month, and specialists of the third class shall similarly be paid $5 per month.

2.4 Jobs Performed by White and African Americans in the U.S. Army, 1942[4]

Between 1940 and 1945, over 1.2 million African Americans served in the armed forces. In the early years, most African Americans were assigned to noncombat units and relegated to service duties, such as supply, maintenance, and transportation. While these jobs were critical to the war effort, they were seen as low status and menial. As the war went on, however, troop losses forced the military to place more African American troops into combat positions. In late 1944, for example, General Eisenhower agreed to let African American volunteers fight in fifty-two all-black platoons under the command of white officers. World War II was the last conflict fought with a segregated military. In 1948, President Harry S. Truman issued Executive Order 9981, which desegregated all branches of the U.S. armed forces.

Type of Service	White	Negro	Percentage of All Negroes in Each Type of Service	Percentage of All Men in Army	
				Whites	Negroes
Army Total	4,532,117	467,883	10.3	100.0	100.0
Combat units	1,815,094	92,772	4.8	40.0	19.7
Service units	616,851	161,707	20.7	13.6	34.5
AAF and	1,190,363	109,637	8.4	26.4	23.5
ASWAAF[a]	363,820	65,880	15.3	8.0	14.1
Overhead[b]	238,500	27,500	10.3	5.3	5.9
ROTCs	72,200	800	1.1	1.5	0.2
OCS[c]	235,289	9,587	3.9	5.2	2.1

[a]Army Air Force and Arms and Services with Army Air Force.

[b]Overhead refers to administrative overhead, not qualified for overseas service, for such reasons as medical status, already completed tours, and instructors at training schools. This figure includes replacement depots and hospitals.

[c]Officer Candidate School.

---

4. From: Ulysses Lee, *The Employment of Negro Troops* (Washington, DC: U.S. Army Center of Military History, 2001; first printed 1963), 134, table 2.

2.5 President Franklin D. Roosevelt Outlines a Blueprint for Victory, January 6, 1942[5]

In his first State of the Union address since the attack on Pearl Harbor, President Franklin Roosevelt laid out an ambitious war production plan to ensure "victory for the institution of democracy." The plan aimed to transform the United States into what Roosevelt had called "the arsenal of democracy" two years earlier (see Chapter 1, Document 4). Recognizing that "victory requires the actual weapons of war and the means of transporting them," the president set out specific production goals: 60,000 aircraft in 1942, 125,000 more in 1943; 120,000 tanks in the same period; 55,000 antiaircraft guns; 16 million tons of merchant shipping. By fighting a "war of machines" based on the "crushing superiority" of American equipment, Roosevelt laid out a "blueprint for victory" that promised not only military victory, but also an end to the Great Depression.

. . . Victory requires the actual weapons of war and the means of transporting them to a dozen points of combat.

It will not be sufficient for us and the other United Nations to produce a slightly superior supply of munitions to that of Germany, Japan, Italy, and the stolen industries in the countries, which they have overrun.

The superiority of the United Nations in munitions and ships must be overwhelming—so overwhelming that the Axis Nations can never hope to catch up with it. And so, in order to attain this overwhelming superiority the United States must build planes and tanks and guns and ships to the utmost limit of our national capacity. We have the ability and capacity to produce arms not only for our own forces, but also for the armies, navies, and air forces fighting on our side.

And our overwhelming superiority of armament must be adequate to put weapons of war at the proper time into the hands of those men in the conquered Nations who stand ready to seize the first opportunity to revolt against their German and Japanese oppressors, and against the traitors in their own ranks, known by the already infamous name of "Quislings." And I think that it is a fair prophecy to say that, as we get guns to the patriots in those lands, they too will fire shots heard 'round the world.

This production of ours in the United States must be raised far above present levels, even though it will mean the dislocation of the lives and occupations of millions of our own people. We must raise our sights all

---

5. Franklin D. Roosevelt, "State of the Union Address," January 6, 1942. Online by Gerhard Peters and John T. Woolley, *The American Presidency Project*.

along the production line. Let no man say it cannot be done. It must be done—and we have undertaken to do it.

I have just sent a letter of directive to the appropriate departments and agencies of our Government, ordering that immediate steps be taken:

First, to increase our production rate of airplanes so rapidly that in this year, 1942, we shall produce 60,000 planes, 10,000 more than the goal that we set a year and a half ago. This includes 45,000 combat planes—bombers, dive bombers, pursuit planes. The rate of increase will be maintained and continued so that next year, 1943, we shall produce 125,000 airplanes, including 100,000 combat planes.

Second, to increase our production rate of tanks so rapidly that in this year, 1942, we shall produce 45,000 tanks; and to continue that increase so that next year, 1943, we shall produce 75,000 tanks.

Third, to increase our production rate of anti-aircraft guns so rapidly that in this year, 1942, we shall produce 20,000 of them; and to continue that increase so that next year, 1943, we shall produce 35,000 anti-aircraft guns.

And fourth, to increase our production rate of merchant ships so rapidly that in this year, 1942, we shall build 6,000,000 deadweight tons as compared with a 1941 completed production of 1,100,000. And finally, we shall continue that increase so that next year, 1943, we shall build 10,000,000 tons of shipping.

These figures and similar figures for a multitude of other implements of war will give the Japanese and the Nazis a little idea of just what they accomplished in the attack at Pearl Harbor.

And I rather hope that all these figures which I have given will become common knowledge in Germany and Japan.

Our task is hard—our task is unprecedented—and the time is short. We must strain every existing armament-producing facility to the utmost. We must convert every available plant and tool to war production. That goes all the way from the greatest plants to the smallest—from the huge automobile industry to the village machine shop.

Production for war is based on men and women—the human hands and brains which collectively we call Labor. Our workers stand ready to work long hours; to turn out more in a day's work; to keep the wheels turning and the fires burning twenty-four hours a day, and seven days a week. They realize well that on the speed and efficiency of their work depend the lives of their sons and their brothers on the fighting fronts.

Production for war is based on metals and raw materials—steel, copper, rubber, aluminum, zinc, tin. Greater and greater quantities of them will have to be diverted to war purposes. Civilian use of them will have to be cut further and still further—and, in many cases, completely eliminated.

War costs money. So far, we have hardly even begun to pay for it. We have devoted only 15 percent of our national income to national defense. As will appear in my Budget Message tomorrow, our war program for the coming fiscal year will cost 56 billion dollars or, in other words, more than half of the estimated annual national income. That means taxes and bonds and bonds and taxes. It means cutting luxuries and other non-essentials. In a word, it means an "all-out" war by individual effort and family effort in a united country.

Only this all-out scale of production will hasten the ultimate all-out victory. Speed will count. Lost ground can always be regained—lost time never. Speed will save lives; speed will save this Nation which is in peril; speed will save our freedom and our civilization—and slowness has never been an American characteristic.

. . . We are fighting today for security, for progress, and for peace, not only for ourselves but for all men, not only for one generation but for all generations. We are fighting to cleanse the world of ancient evils, ancient ills.

Our enemies are guided by brutal cynicism, by unholy contempt for the human race. We are inspired by a faith that goes back through all the years to the first chapter of the Book of Genesis: "God created man in His own image."

We on our side are striving to be true to that divine heritage. We are fighting, as our fathers have fought, to uphold the doctrine that all men are equal in the sight of God. Those on the other side are striving to destroy this deep belief and to create a world in their own image—a world of tyranny and cruelty and serfdom.

That is the conflict that day and night now pervades our lives. No compromise can end that conflict. There never has been—there never can be—successful compromise between good and evil. Only total victory can reward the champions of tolerance, and decency, and freedom, and faith.

2.6 World War II and the American Economy

The Second World War brought a decisive end to the Great Depression. Unemployment disappeared virtually overnight, and the size of the economy began to grow. Ordinary Americans experienced real improvements in their quality of life. Despite widespread fears of a crippling wage and price spiral created by a tight labor market, wartime shortages, and pent-up consumer demand, inflation was relatively mild. The war also permanently enlarged the size and power of the federal government. The federal government emerged from the war as a powerful economic actor, able to regulate economic activity and manage economic growth through tax and spending policy. While the war destroyed the economies of most of the major belligerents, the American economy was far more powerful in 1945 than it had been in 1941.

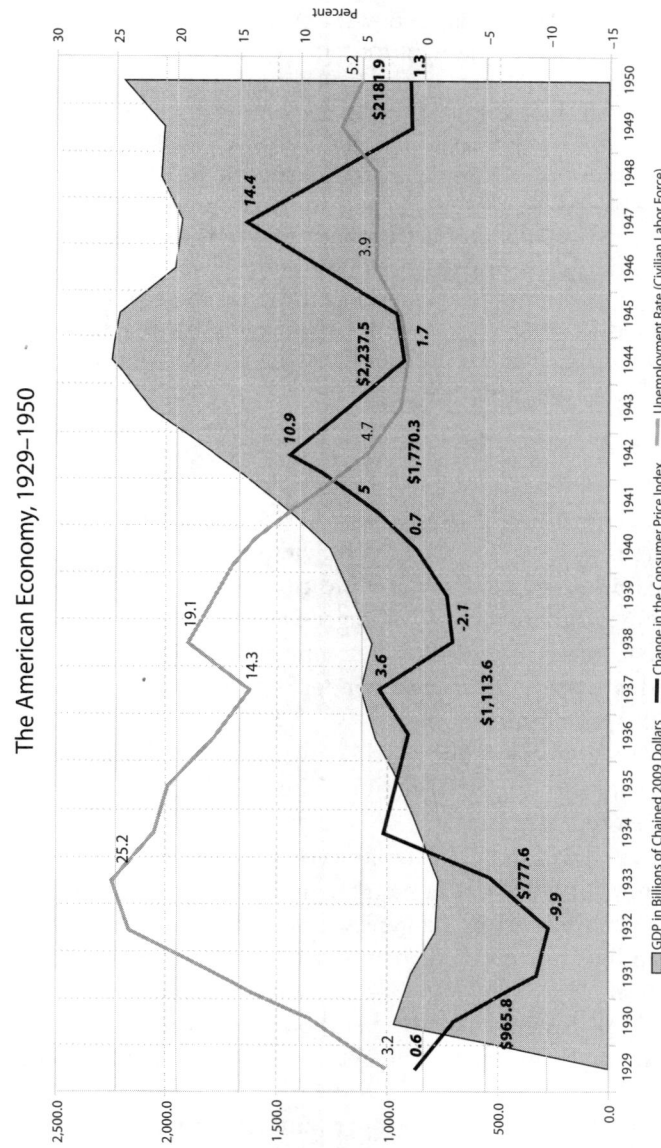

The American Economy, 1929–1950

From Bureau of Labor Statistics, Division of Consumer Prices and Price Indexes, *CPI Detailed Report, May 2014*, table 24, "Historical Consumer Price Index for All Urban Consumers (CPI-U); U.S. City Average, All Items Included," available at http://www.bls.gov/cpi/cpid1405.pdf (accessed June 18, 2014); Bureau of Economic Analysis, *Current Dollar and "Real Gross Domestic Product,"* available at http://www.bea.gov/national/xls/gdplev.xls; Department of Commerce, Bureau of the Census, *Historical Statistics of the United States, Colonial Times to 1970, Part 1* (Washington DC: U.S. Government Printing Office, 1975), Part D, Series D-1-10, Labor Force and Its Components: 1900–1947 and Series D 11-25, Labor Force Status of the Population, 1870–1970.

2.7 African Americans Call for Victory at Home and Abroad, 1942[6]

In the following letter to the editors of the *Pittsburgh Courier*, one of the nation's leading African American newspapers, a reader links the fight against fascism abroad to the fight for racial justice at home. The black community was well aware of the depth of racial inequality in all aspects of American life. While some black Americans felt alienated from the war effort, and affronted by the hypocrisy of a "war for democracy" in the context of American racial apartheid, others saw the war as an opportunity to achieve racial justice at home. In February 1942, the *Courier* inaugurated a national campaign that at once called on African Americans to participate fully in the war effort and demanded that the government make good on the promise of equal rights. This so-called Double V campaign galvanized African Americans and their liberal white allies, and set the stage for the civil rights movement of the 1950s and 1960s.

DEAR EDITOR:

Like all true Americans, my greatest desire at this time, this crucial point of our history; is a desire for a complete victory over the forces of evil, which threaten our existence today. Behind that desire is also a desire to serve, this, my country, in the most advantageous way. Most of our leaders are suggesting that we sacrifice every other ambition to the paramount one, victory. With this I agree; but I also wonder if another victory could not be achieved at the same time.

After all, the things that beset the world now are basically the same things which upset the equilibrium of nations internally, states, counties, cities, homes and even the individual.

Being an American of dark complexion and some 26 years, these questions flash through my mind: "Should I sacrifice my life to live half American?" "Will things be better for the next generation in the peace to follow?" "Would it be demanding too much to demand full citizenship rights in exchange for the sacrificing of my life." "Is the kind of America I know worth defending?" "Will America be a true and pure democracy after this war?" "Will colored Americans suffer still the indignities that have been heaped upon them in the past?"

These and other questions need answering; I want to know, and I believe every colored American, who is thinking, wants to know.

---

6. James G. Thompson, letter to the editor, *Pittsburgh Courier*, January 31, 1942; repr. April 11, 1942, 5; available at http://goo.gl/oSGnY9.

This may be the wrong time to broach such subjects, but haven't all good things obtained by men been secured through sacrifice during just such times of strife?

I suggest that while we keep defense and victory in the forefront that we don't loose sight of our fight for true democracy at home.

The "V for Victory" sign is being displayed prominently in all so-called democratic countries which are fighting for victory over aggression, slavery and tyranny. If this V sign means that to those now engaged in this great conflict then let colored Americans adopt the double VV for a double victory. The first V for victory over our enemies from without, the second V for victory over our enemies within. For surely those who perpetrate these ugly prejudices here are seeing to destroy our democratic form of government just as surely as the Axis forces.

This should not and would not lessen our efforts to bring this conflict to a successful conclusion; but should and would make us stronger to resist these evil forces which threaten us. America could become united as never before and become truly the home of democracy.

In way of an answer to the foregoing questions in a preceding paragraph, I might say that there is no doubt that this country is worth defending; things will be different for the next generation; colored Americans will come into their own, and America will eventually become the true democracy it was designed to be. These things will become a reality in time; but not through any relaxation of the efforts to secure them.

In conclusion let me say that though these questions often permeate my mind, I love America and am willing to die for the America I know will someday become a reality.

JAMES G. THOMPSON

2.8 The Bureau of Motion Pictures Enlists Hollywood in the War Effort, 1942[7]

After Pearl Harbor, Hollywood enlisted in the war effort. Many of the movies produced during the war years were patriotic rallying cries that affirmed a sense of national purpose. Combat films emphasized sacrifice and patriotism; home front films focused on the essential American values of democracy and freedom at stake in the war. Published in 1942,

---

7. Bureau of Motion Pictures and Office of War Information, *Government Information Manual for the Motion Picture Industry*, Record Group 208, Series 295 (Suitland, MD: National Archives and Records Service, General Services Administration, 1978).

the *Government Information Manual for the Motion Picture Industry* provided filmmakers with voluntary guidelines, and asked studios to consider the question "will this picture help to win the war" in making production decisions. During its existence, the bureau evaluated film scripts' depiction of war aims, American values, the American military, American enemies and allies, and the home front. In 1943, the responsibility for monitoring the film industry shifted to the Office of Censorship.

I. The Issues
Why We Fight. What Kind of Peace Will Follow Victory

If we are to win this war, Americans must be ready to sacrifice comforts, necessities, and life itself. Public opinion polls indicate that some confusion still exists as to the issues for which this war is being fought. Unless every American clearly understands how much he has at stake, the nation cannot gear itself to the all-out effort necessary for victory.

The motion picture should be the best medium for bringing to life the democratic idea. We practical-minded Americans can easily grasp such tangible programs as sugar-rationing or pooling of cars to save rubber. It is a challenge to the ingenuity of Hollywood to make equally real the democratic values which we take for granted. . . .

What Are We Fighting For?

1. We are fighting for survival as a nation. Some people do not realize that the actual existence of this nation as a politically independent state depends on winning the war. . . .
2. We are fighting for freedom and against slavery. For
   1) freedom of speech,
   2) freedom of religion,
   3) freedom from want,
   4) freedom from fear.

We must make the Four Freedoms live and breathe. They must not become mere trademarks. Each individual must know how these Four Freedoms affect his individual life, his everyday affairs. Few of our people have any real grasp of what life would mean to them as individuals if the Axis were to win.

The realization must be driven home that we cannot enjoy the Four Freedoms exclusively. They must be established on a world-wide basis—yes, even in Germany, Italy, and Japan—or they will always be in jeopardy in America. . . .

3. We are fighting for a New World. We are fighting for a more decent world—a world free from force and militarism. We are fighting not only to maintain for ourselves the gains we have made in the past, but also for the right to build a new and better life "for all people and for future generations." We are fighting for democracy among nations as among individuals, for a world community dedicated to the free flow of trade, ideas, and culture. . . .

Here are a few aspects of the war issues which need dramatization:

A) There are still groups in this country who are thinking only in terms of their particular group. Some citizens have not been made aware of the fact that this is a people's war, not a group war. For example, small segments of agriculture, labor and industry still think in terms of themselves. By all means, they are good Americans and want to win this war, but inevitably their own particular interest colors their thinking as to the way they want to fight this war. We must emphasize that this is a people's war, that we must hang together or we shall all hang separately. . . .

B) We must emphasize the American heritage, the historical development that has made us what we are. What is the American way of life? It is a 1942 version of 1776. We have developed into a complex socio-economic system, but it is all based on the framework of the doctrine that has lived since its promulgation in Independence Hall in Philadelphia. . . .

C) Some people may ask what the underprivileged, the uneducated, the oppressed minorities—even in this country—have to fight for. Can we not portray on the screen the fact that under the democratic process the underprivileged have become less underprivileged? For example, the Negroes have a real, a legal, and a permanent change for improvement of their status under democracy and no chance at all under a dictatorship. We are clearing our slums, we are establishing electric lines to out-of-the-way farmers, we are abolishing vicious tenant farming, we are improving the lot of minorities. . . .

D) We must emphasize that this country is a melting pot, a nation of many races and creeds, who have demonstrated that they can live together and progress. We must establish a genuine understanding of alien and minority groups and recognize their great contribution to the building of our nation. In this war for freedom they fight side by side with us. . . .

E) What then is our stake? It is liberation from fear and want, liberation from duress and force. We don't want to push anybody around, and we don't want anybody to push us around. The premium we must pay for this "life insurance" is to work, fight, and understand.

2.9 Rosie the Riveter Becomes the Image of Patriotic Womanhood, 1943

"We Can Do It" was produced by Pittsburgh artist J. Howard Miller for the Westinghouse War Production Coordinating Committee in 1943. Although Miller's image was little seen during the war, other, more widely circulated images of "Rosie" did try to recruit women to war work. The term "Rosie the Riveter" was first used in a 1942 song of the same name, written by John Jacob Loeb and Redd Evans and performed by Kay Keyser. The next year, she made her first appearance as a cover girl, in Norman Rockwell's cover for the *Saturday Evening Post*. While some historians have argued that the war had prompted a "revolution in the lives of women in America," others have insisted that the revolution was more apparent than real.

J. Howard Miller, "We Can Do It!" in Records of the Office for Emergency Management, War Production Board, RG 179, National Archives and Records Administration, available at https://catalog.archives.gov/id/535413.

2.10 The U.S. Treasury Department Calls on All Americans to Pay Their Taxes to Beat the Axis, 1945

In 1942, Congress passed the Revenue Act of 1942, which revolutionized American finance and created the modern income tax system. The new law lowered income tax exemptions and transformed the federal income tax from a "class tax" paid by only the wealthiest Americans to a "mass tax" borne by the majority of citizens. Indeed, between 1939 and 1945, the number of individual taxpayers increased from 3.9 million to almost 43 million. To "sell" the new tax to the American people, the Treasury Department enlisted A-list entertainers to enjoin everyone to pay their "taxes to beat the Axis." The government even commissioned a song from popular composer Irving Berlin and two short films from Walt Disney Studios featuring Donald Duck! With so many new taxpayers, the Bureau of Internal Revenue (BIR) also had to work hard to make sure Americans knew how and when to pay taxes. In the poster reprinted here, the BIR reminds every American with more than $500 in annual income to pay their taxes on time.

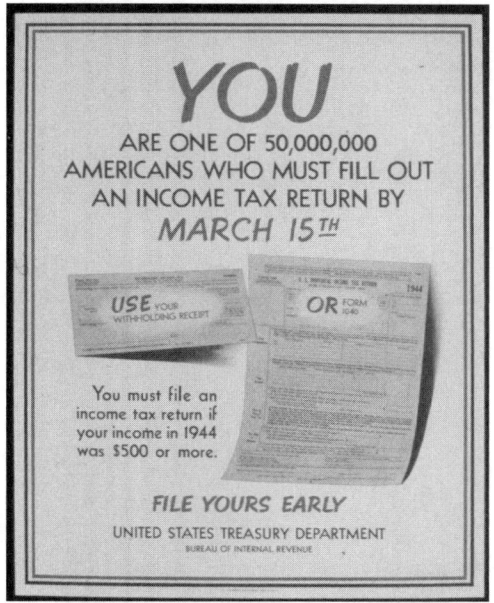

Poster from Office for Emergency Management, Office of War Information, Domestic Operations Branch, Bureau of Special Services, National Archives and Records Administration, Still Picture Records Section; available at Wikimedia Commons, https://upload. wikimedia.org/wikipedia/commons/d/d2/YOU_ARE_ONE_OF_50%2C000%2C000_ AMERICANS_WHO_MUST_FILL_OUT_AN_INCOME_TAX_RETURN_BY_ MARCH_15._FILE_YOURS_EARLY._-_NARA_-_516201.jpg.

CHAPTER 3

CREATING A GLOBAL ALLIED STRATEGY TO DEFEAT THE AXIS POWERS

The United States did not fight the Axis powers alone during World War II. It had numerous allies, who formally joined together on January 1, 1942 (see Document 11.3). Officially known as the United Nations and unofficially as the "Grand Alliance," this coalition was dominated by its three most powerful members: Great Britain, the Soviet Union, and the United States.

Together the Allies possessed the human and industrial resources necessary to defeat the Axis powers. But they could only do so if they agreed on a global and coordinated military strategy. This would prove extremely difficult, for each of the three major powers in the alliance favored a different strategy, one that reflected its own unique history, situation, and interests in the war. Further complicating matters was the fact that U.S. strategists and policy makers disagreed with each other as to the best strategic approach for the nation to follow. As a result, the years 1941–1943 witnessed a series of major disagreements over global strategy—both within the United States and among the Allies. This chapter examines those disagreements.

The three major Allied powers did agree that they had to concentrate first on the more powerful and dangerous German enemy in order to halt Hitler's numerous offensives in 1941–1942 and totally defeat him before refocusing on Japan. They also agreed that victory would require coordinated military operations. But they could not agree as to what those operations should be or where they should be launched.

Great Britain favored an indirect peripheral strategy for its own and U.S. forces that centered on a naval blockade of German-occupied Europe, bombing Germany's cities to destroy its industry and the morale of its people, encouraging and supporting indigenous European guerrilla forces to stretch and weaken Italian as well as German military forces, and ground campaigns in North Africa and the Mediterranean. These would be conducted primarily against the forces of Vichy France (a regime that collaborated with Nazi Germany) and Germany's weak Italian ally in order to, in Churchill's famous words, "close the ring" around Germany. He and his military advisers maintained that together such operations would force a German collapse at the cost of relatively few casualties—an issue of major concern because of the terrible losses Britain had suffered in the World War I trenches.

Such a strategy was also the only one possible for the British after their disastrous 1940 defeats and the surrender of France. By the end of 1941, however, they had two new allies who objected vehemently to a continuation of this strategy and who called instead for a more direct approach focusing on crossing the English Channel in order to establish a "second front" capable of confronting and defeating the German armies in Western Europe as quickly and decisively as possible.

The Soviets favored this approach because it would force Hitler to divert major forces from the Eastern Front and thereby relieve some of the pressure on the hard-pressed Red Army. They found existing British strategy unacceptable because it would not do so. Britain's approach would thus minimize Anglo-American casualties only by maximizing those of the Soviet Union, something Soviet leader Josef Stalin and his subordinates suspected to be a secret British aim. Letting the Germans and Russians bleed each other to death would enhance Britain's postwar position. So would placing British forces throughout the Mediterranean and the Middle East, areas of great imperial interest.

The United States would maintain an unprecedented level of military cooperation with the British during the war. In most theaters, for example, all British and U.S. ground, naval, and air forces would serve under a single commander, who would in turn report to the Combined Chiefs of Staff, a new organization composed of air, naval, and ground chiefs of staff of both nations and responsible only to Churchill and Roosevelt. Nevertheless, the American Joint Chiefs of Staff joined the Soviets in objecting to London's peripheral strategy and Mediterranean focus and in calling instead for an Anglo-American cross-Channel invasion of northern France as quickly as possible. American military planners believed Britain's approach would be militarily indecisive and that the only way to obtain victory was to confront the German armies in Western Europe while the Soviet armies did the same in the East, thereby forcing Hitler into a two-front war. They also feared that without the military assistance a second front would provide, the Soviet Union would either be defeated or be willing to sign a separate peace with Germany, either of which would, they argued, make total victory over Germany impossible as well as preclude a Soviet entry into the war against Japan that they deeply desired. Even if this worst-case scenario did not occur, Britain's indecisive and time-consuming strategy in the Mediterranean would delay victory over Germany and thereby delay the offensive operations against Japan being demanded by large segments of the public as well as the U.S. Navy; Southwest Pacific commander General Douglas MacArthur; and the Allied governments of China, Australia, and New Zealand.

This strategic debate dominated and seriously weakened Allied relations between 1941 and 1943. It also had a negative impact on U.S. civil-military relations, as Roosevelt in 1942 overruled his own chiefs of staff and supported the British insistence on invading French North Africa instead of northern France. In 1943, however, he shifted position to support the Joint Chiefs in calling for cross-Channel over Mediterranean operations. The final settlement of the debate in late 1943 set the stage for the highly successful and decisive Allied military victories of 1944 and 1945.

As previously noted, historians have continued these Allied strategic disagreements and arguments. Some insist that Anglo-American forces could and should have landed in northern France in 1942 or 1943 rather than being dispersed by operations in North Africa and the Mediterranean. Those operations, they argue, accomplished little militarily and delayed final victory. They also embittered the Russians, who interpreted the delay in crossing the Channel as a deliberate attempt to weaken them in the postwar era by leaving them to face the bulk of the German armed forces alone and to suffer enormous casualties. The delay thereby increased Stalin's preexisting suspicion of his Western allies and was a cause of the Cold War that followed German defeat. On the other side stand historians who insist that Anglo-American forces could not have successfully crossed the English Channel before 1944, that any attempt to do so would have led to disastrous military defeat, and that the North African and Mediterranean campaigns actually accomplished a great deal. Militarily they succeeded in knocking Italy out of the war, opening the Mediterranean to Allied shipping, providing new bases from which to bomb Germany, and dispersing German forces that otherwise would have been available for deployment in northern France and/or on the Eastern Front. Politically they played a major role in obtaining and maintaining public support for the Europe-first strategy as well as providing Stalin with some ground operations in 1942 and 1943; just standing idle until 1944 could have led to a separate Russo-German peace that would have made victory over Germany impossible.

This chapter focuses on the development of U.S. strategy and the strategic disagreements that took place within both the United States and the Grand Alliance as a whole. In examining these disagreements as presented in the chapter's documents, keep in mind the numerous, interrelated issues and questions that were involved. Why, for example, did U.S. military planners conclude more than a year before official U.S. entry into the war that they should concentrate on defeating Germany before Japan?

Why did they favor military coordination with the British but simultaneously oppose British strategy? Did Roosevelt "promise" the Soviets a second front in 1942 and, if so, why? Why did he then wind up supporting the British approach and rejecting the contrary proposals of his military chiefs in 1942, only to shift in 1943? What impact did this dispute have on Allied relations and the conduct of the war, and how was it finally resolved in late 1943?

* * *

3.1 U.S. and British Military Officials Agree to a Germany-First Strategy: Admiral Stark's Memorandum and the ABC-1 Accord, November 1940 and March 1941[1]

The first formal proposal that the United States ally with Great Britain and adopt a Germany-first strategy if it found itself at war with Japan as well as Germany and Italy came from U.S. Chief of Naval Operations Admiral Harold R. Stark in November 1940. Note the three alternative strategies Stark considered and rejected as well as the reasons he favored the fourth option "(D)." In line with Stark's concluding recommendation, secret staff talks between U.S. and British officers took place from January to March 1941 and resulted in agreement to this global strategy in the event both nations found themselves at war with all of the Axis powers.

The Stark Memorandum, November 1940

The strong wish of the American government and people at present seems to be to remain at peace. In spite of this, we must face the possibility that we may at any moment become involved in war. With war in prospect, I believe our every effort should be directed toward the prosecution of a national policy with mutually supporting diplomatic and military aspects, and having as its guiding feature a determination that any intervention we may undertake shall be such as will ultimately best promote our own national interests. We should see the best answer to the question: "Where should we fight the war, and for what objective?" . . .

---

1. From Stark Memorandum from Franklin D. Roosevelt Presidential Library; ABC-1 Accord from National Archives, Washington, DC; repr. in *American War Plans, 1919–1941*, ed. Steven D. Ross (New York: Garland, 1992), 3:225–50; 4:5–13.

... As I see affairs today, answers to the following broad questions will be most useful to the Navy:

(A) Shall our principal military effort be directed toward hemisphere defense, and include chiefly those activities within the Western Hemisphere which contribute directly to security against attack in either or both oceans? An affirmative answer would indicate that the United States, as seems now to be the hope of this country, would remain out of war unless pushed into it. If and when forced into war, the greater portion of our Fleet could remain for the time being in its threatening position in the Pacific, but no major effort would be exerted overseas either to the east or the west; the most that would be done for allies, besides providing material help, would be to send detachments to assist in their defense. It should be noted here that, were minor help to be given in one direction, public opinion might soon push us into giving it major support, as was the case in the World War.

Under this plan, our influence upon the outcome of the European War would be small.

(B) Shall we prepare for a full offensive against Japan, premised on assistance from the British and Dutch forces in the Far East, and remain on the strict defensive in the Atlantic? If this course is selected, we would be placing full trust in the British to hold their own indefinitely in the Atlantic, or, at least, until after we should have defeated Japan decisively, and thus had fully curbed her offensive power for the time being. Plans for augmenting the scale of our present material assistance to Great Britain would be adversely affected until Japan had been decisively defeated. The length of time required to defeat Japan would be very considerable.

If we enter the war against Japan and then if Great Britain loses, we probably would in any case have to reorient towards the Atlantic. There is no dissenting view on this point.

(C) Shall we plan for sending the strongest possible military assistance both to the British in Europe, and to the British, Dutch and Chinese in the Far East? The naval and air detachments we would send to the British Isles would possibly ensure their continued resistance, but would not increase British power to conduct a land offensive. The strength we could send to the Far East might be enough to check the southward spread of Japanese rule for the duration of the war. The strength of naval forces remaining in Hawaii for the defense of the Eastern Pacific, and the strength of the forces in the Western Atlantic for the defense of that area, would be reduced to that barely sufficient for executing their tasks. Should Great Britain finally lose, or should Malaysia fall to Japan, our naval strength might then be found to have been seriously reduced, relative to that of the Axis powers. It should be understood that, under this plan, we should be operating under handicap of fighting major wars on two fronts.

Should we adopt Plan (C), we must face the consequences that would ensue were we to start a war with one plan, and then, after becoming heavily engaged, be forced greatly to modify it or discard it altogether, as, for example, in case of a British fold up. On neither of these distant fronts would it be possible to execute a really major offensive. Strategically, the situation might become disastrous should our effort on either front fail.

(D) Shall we direct our efforts toward an eventual strong offensive in the Atlantic as an ally of the British, and a defensive in the Pacific? Any strength that we might send to the Far East would, by just so much, reduce the force of our blows against Germany and Italy. About the least that we would do for our ally would be to send strong naval light forces and aircraft to Great Britain and the Mediterranean. Probably we could not stop with a purely naval effort. The plan might ultimately require capture of the Portuguese and Spanish Islands and military and naval bases in Africa and possibly Europe; and thereafter even involve undertaking a full scale land offensive. In consideration of a course that would require landing large numbers of troops abroad, account must be taken of the possible unwillingness of the people of the United States to support land operations of this character, and to incur the risk of heavy loss should Great Britain collapse. Under Plan (D) we would be unable to exert strong pressure against Japan, and would necessarily gradually reorient our policy in the Far East. The full national offensive strength would be exerted in a single direction, rather than be expended in areas far distant from each other. At the conclusion of the war, even if Britain should finally collapse, we might still find ourselves possessed of bases in Africa suitable for assisting in the defense of South America.

. . . I believe that the continued existence of the British Empire, combined with building up a strong protection in our home areas, will do most to ensure the status quo in the Western Hemisphere, and to promote our principal national interests. As I have previously stated, I also believe that Great Britain requires from us very great help in the Atlantic, and possibly even on the continents of Europe or Africa, if she is to be enabled to survive. In my opinion Alternatives (A), (B), and (C) will most probably not provide the necessary degree of assistance, and, therefore, if we undertake war, that Alternative (D) is likely to be the most fruitful for the United States, particularly if we enter the war at an early date. . . . [S]hould we be forced into a war with Japan, we should, because of the prospect of war in the Atlantic also, definitely plan to avoid operations in the Far East or the Mid-Pacific that will prevent the Navy from promptly moving to the Atlantic forces fully adequate to safeguard our interests and policies in the event of a British collapse. We ought not now willingly engage in any war against Japan unless we are certain of aid from Great Britain and the Netherlands East Indies.

No important allied military decision should be reached without clear understanding between the nations involved as to the strength and extent of the participation which may be expected in any particular theater, and as to a proposed skeleton plan of operations.

Accordingly, I make the recommendation that, as a preliminary to possible entry of the United States into the conflict, the United States Army and Navy at once undertake secret staff talks on technical matters with the British military and naval authorities in London, with Canadian military authorities in Washington, and with British and Dutch authorities in Singapore and Batavia. The purpose would be to reach agreements and lay down plans for promoting unity of allied effort should the United States find it necessary to enter the war under any of the alternative eventualities considered in this memorandum.

United States–British Staff Conversations Report [ABC-1 Accord]

3. The purposes of the Staff Conference, as set out in the instructions to the two representative bodies, were as follows:

(a) To determine the best methods by which the armed forces of the United States and British Commonwealth, with its present Allies, could defeat Germany and the Powers allied with her, should the United States be compelled to resort to war.

(b) To coordinate, on broad lines, plans for the employment of the forces of the Associated Powers.

(c) To reach agreements concerning the methods and nature of Military Cooperation between the two nations, including the allocation of the principal areas of responsibility, the major lines of the Military strategy to be pursued by both nations, the strength of the forces which each may be able to commit, and the determination of satisfactory command arrangements, both as to supreme Military control, and as to unity of field command in cases of strategic or tactical joint operations. . . .

6. The High Command of the United States and United Kingdom will collaborate continuously in the formulation and execution of strategical

policies and plans which shall govern the conduct of the war. They and their respective commanders in the field, as may be appropriate, will similarly collaborate in the planning and execution of such operations as may be undertaken jointly by United States and British Forces. This arrangement will apply also to such plans and operations as may be undertaken separately, the extent of collaboration required in each particular plan or operation being agreed mutually when the general policy has been decided. . . .

13. . . .

(a) Since Germany is the predominant member of the Axis Powers, the Atlantic and European area is considered to be the decisive theatre. The principal United States Military effort will be exerted in that theatre, and operations of United States forces in other theatres will be conducted in such a manner as to facilitate that effort. . . .

15. To effect the collaboration outlined in paragraph 6, and to ensure the coordination of administrative action and command between the United States and British Military Services, the United States and United Kingdom will exchange Military Missions. These Missions will comprise one senior officer of each of the Military Services, with their appropriate staffs.

3.2 Britain and the United States Reach Strategic Agreements at the ARCADIA Conference, Washington, DC, December 1941–January 1942[2]

Soon after the official U.S. declaration of war on the Axis powers, British Prime Minister Winston Churchill and his advisers traveled to Washington to obtain American reaffirmation of the ABC-1 Germany-first strategy despite Pearl Harbor, and to establish additional strategic priorities as well as a basis for future Anglo-American military collaboration. The document reproduced here summarizes the most important of the agreements reached at this conference, code-named ARCADIA.

---

2. From U.S. Department of State, *Foreign Relations of the United States: The Conferences at Washington, 1941–1942, and Casablanca, 1943* (Washington, DC: U.S. Government Printing Office, 1968), 214–17, 232–34.

**Memorandum by the United States and British
Chiefs of Staff [December 31, 1941.]**

American-British Grand Strategy
I. Grand Strategy

1. At the A–B Staff conversations in February, 1941, it was agreed that Germany was the predominant member of the Axis Powers, and consequently the Atlantic and European area was considered to be the decisive theatre.

2. Much has happened since February last, but notwithstanding the entry of Japan into the War, our view remains that Germany is still the prime enemy and her defeat is the key to victory. Once Germany is defeated, the collapse of Italy and the defeat of Japan must follow.

3. In our considered opinion, therefore, it should be a cardinal principle of A–B strategy that only the minimum of force necessary for the safeguarding of vital interests in other theatres should be diverted from operations against Germany.

II. Essential Features of Our Strategy

The essential features of the above grand strategy are as follows. Each will be examined in greater detail later in this paper.

a. The realization of the victory programme of armaments, which first and foremost requires the security of the main areas of war industry.

b. The maintenance of essential communications.

c. Closing and tightening the ring around Germany.

d. Wearing down and undermining German resistance by air bombardment, blockade, subversive activities and propaganda.

e. The continuous development of offensive action against Germany.

f. Maintaining only such positions in the Eastern theatre as will safeguard vital interests (see paragraph 18) and denying to Japan access to raw materials vital to her continuous war effort while we are concentrating on the defeat of Germany.

III. Steps to Be Taken in 1942 to Put into
Effect the Above General Policy

The Security of Areas of War Production . . .
Maintenance of Communications . . .
Closing and Tightening the Ring around Germany

13. This ring may be defined as a line running roughly as follows:

Archangel—Black Sea—Anatolia—The Northern Seaboard of the Mediterranean—The Western Seaboard of Europe.

The main object will be to strengthen this ring, and close the gaps in it, by sustaining the Russian front, by arming and supporting Turkey, by increasing our strength in the Middle East, and by gaining possession of the whole North African coast.

14. If this ring can be closed, the blockade of Germany and Italy will be complete, and German eruptions, e.g., towards the Persian Gulf, or to the Atlantic seaboard of Africa, will be prevented. Furthermore, the seizing of the North African coast may open the Mediterranean to convoys, thus enormously shortening the route to the Middle East and saving considerable tonnage now employed in the long haul around the Cape.

The Undermining and Wearing Down of the German Resistance

15. In 1942 the main methods of wearing down Germany's resistance will be:

a. Ever-increasing air bombardment by British and American forces.

b. Assistance to Russia's offensive by all available means.

c. The blockade.

d. The maintenance of the spirit of revolt in the occupied countries, and the organization of subversive movements.

Development of Land Offensives on the Continent

16. It does not seem likely that in 1942 any large scale land offensive against Germany except on the Russian front will be possible. We must, however, be ready to take advantage of any opening that may result from the wearing down process referred to in paragraph 15 to conduct limited land offensives.

17. In 1943 the way may be clear for a return to the Continent, across the Mediterranean, from Turkey into the Balkans, or by landings in Western Europe. Such operations will be the prelude to the final assault on Germany itself, and the scope of the victory program should be such as to provide means by which they can be carried out.

The Safeguarding of Vital Interests in the Eastern Theatre

18. The security of Australia, New Zealand, and India must be maintained, and the Chinese war effort supported. Secondly, points of vantage

from which an offensive against Japan can eventually be developed must be secured. Our immediate object must therefore be to hold:

a. Hawaii and Alaska.

b. Singapore, the East Indies Barrier, and the Philippines.

c. Rangoon and the route to China.

d. The Maritime Provinces of Siberia.

The minimum forces required to hold the above will have to be a matter of mutual discussion.

Post-ARCADIA Collaboration [January 14, 1942]

1. In order to provide for the continuance of the necessary machinery to effect collaboration between the United Nations after the departure from Washington of the British Chiefs of Staff, the Combined Chief of Staffs . . . propose the broad principles and basic organization herein outlined.

2. To avoid confusion we suggest that hereafter the word "Joint" be applied to Inter-Service collaboration of one nation, and the word "Combined" to collaboration between two or more of the United Nations.

3. Definitions.—

a. The term "Combined Chiefs of Staff" is defined as the British Chiefs of Staff (or in their absence from Washington, their duly accredited representatives), and the United States opposite numbers of the British Chiefs of Staff.

b. The term "Combined Staff Planners" is defined as the body of officers duly appointed by the Combined Chiefs of Staff to make such studies, draft such plans, and perform such other work as may from time to time be placed on the "Combined Chiefs of Staff Agenda" by that Body, and duly delegated by them to the Combined Staff Planners.

c. The "Combined Secretariat" is defined as the body of officers duly appointed by the Combined Chiefs of Staff to maintain necessary records, prepare and distribute essential papers, and perform such other work as is delegated to them by the Combined Chiefs of Staff. . . .

5. The Combined Chiefs of Staff shall develop and submit recommendations as follows:

a. For the ABDA [American-British-Dutch-Australian Command] Area, specifically as set forth in the Directive, Annex 2 to U.S. ABC–4/5, British WW–6, dated January 5, 1942.

b. For other areas in which the United Nations may decide to act in concert, along the same general lines as in *a* above, modified as necessary to meet the particular circumstances.

6. The Combined Chiefs of Staff shall accordingly:

a. Recommend the broad program of requirements based on strategic considerations.
b. Submit general directives as to the policy governing the distribution of available weapons of war. (It is agreed that finished war equipment shall be allocated in accordance with strategical needs; to effectuate this principle, we recommend the utilization of appropriate bodies in London and Washington, under the authority of the Combined Chiefs of Staff.)
c. Settle the broad issues of priority of overseas military movements.

7. The question of the production and dissemination of complete Military Intelligence to serve the Combined Chiefs of Staff and Combined Staff Planners has been referred to the latter body for a report. Here also, it is contemplated that existing machinery will be largely continued.
8. It is planned that the Combined Chiefs of Staff will meet weekly, or more often if necessary; an agenda will be circulated before each meeting.

3.3 Admiral Ernest J. King Calls for a Strategic Focus on Japan, March 1942[3]

While the United States at the ARCADIA Conference agreed to maintain the Germany-first strategy despite Pearl Harbor, continued American defeats in the Pacific at the hands of the Japanese led to calls for at least a modification and perhaps abandonment of that global strategy. A major voice calling for such a shift was Admiral Ernest J. King, the wartime chief of naval operations and commander in chief of the U.S. fleet. In this March 5 memorandum to President Roosevelt, King explained why he favored such a strategic shift.

March 5, 1942

Memorandum for the President:
1. The delineation of general areas of responsibility for operations in the Pacific is now taking place, in which it appears that we—the U.S.—will take full charge of all operations conducted eastward of the Malay Peninsula and Sumatra.

---

3. From Ernest J. King Papers, Navy Historical Center and Franklin D. Roosevelt Presidential Library; repr. in Thomas B. Buell, *Master of Seapower: A Biography of Fleet Admiral Ernest J. King* (Boston: Little, Brown, 1980), 531–33.

2. You have expressed the view—concurred in by all of your chief military advisers—that we should determine on a *very few* lines of military endeavor and concentrate our efforts on these lines. It is to be recognized that the *very few* lines of U.S. military effort may require to be shifted in accordance with developments but the total number should be kept at a *very few*.

3. Consideration of what war activities we (U.S.) should undertake in the Pacific requires to be premised on some examination of our (U.S.) relationship with respect to world-wide war activities—the Pacific being one part of the larger whole.

4. Other than in the Pacific our principal allies—Great Britain and Russia—are already committed to certain lines of military effort, to which our (U.S.) chief contribution in the case of Russia will continue to be munitions in general.

5. As to Britain's lines of military effort:

(a) It is apparent that we (U.S.) must enable the British to hold the citadel and arsenal of Britain itself by means of the supply of munitions, raw materials and food—and to some extent by troops, when they will release British troops to other British military areas.

(b) The Middle East is a line of British military effort which they—and we—cannot afford to let go. This effort should continue to receive our (U.S.) munitions.

(c) The India-Burma-China line of British military effort is now demanding immediate attention on their part—and will absorb its proportion of our (U.S.) munitions—in addition to the munitions which we are committed to furnish to China.

6. The chief sources of munitions for the United Nations are Britain, the U.S. and, to some degree, Russia. The chief sources of manpower for the United Nations are China, Russia, the U.S., and to less degree, the British Commonwealth. The only mobile factors are those available to Britain and to the U.S., because of their use of sea power—navies and shipping.

7. Australia—and New Zealand—are "white man's countries" which it is essential that we shall not allow to be overrun by Japanese because of the repercussions among the non-white races of the world.

8. Reverting to the premise of paragraph 2—a *very few* lines of military endeavor—the general area that needs immediate attention—and is in our (U.S.) sphere of responsibility—is Australasia, which term is intended to include the Australian continent, its approaches from the northwest—modified ABDA [American-British-Dutch-Australian Command] area—and its approaches from the northeast and east—ANZAC [Australia-New Zealand Sea Command] area. These approaches require to be actively used—continuously—to hamper the enemy advance and/or consolidation of his advance bases.

9. Our primary concern in the Pacific is to hold Hawaii and its approaches (via Midway) from the westward and to maintain its communications with the West Coast. Our next care in the Pacific is to preserve Australasia (par. 8 above) which requires that its communications be maintained—via eastward of Samoa, Fiji and southward of New Caledonia.

10. We have now—or will soon have—"strong points" at Samoa, Suva (Fiji) and New Caledonia (also a defended fueling base at Bora Bora, Society Islands). A naval operating base is shortly to be set up in Tongatabu (Tonga Islands) to service our naval forces operating in the South Pacific. Efate (New Hebrides) and Funafuti (Ellice Islands) are projected additional "strong points."

11. When the foregoing 6 "strong points" are made reasonably secure, we shall not only be able to cover the line of communications—to Australia (and New Zealand) but—given the naval forces, air units, and amphibious troops—we can drive northwest from the New Hebrides into the Solomons and the Bismarck Archipelago after the same fashion of step-by-step advances that the Japanese used in the South China Sea. Such a line of operations will be offensive rather than passive—and will draw Japanese forces there to oppose it, thus relieving pressure elsewhere, whether in Hawaii, ABDA area, Alaska, or even India.

12. The foregoing outline (of U.S. participation in the war) points the way to useful lines in U.S. military endeavor in the Pacific, which may be summarized in an integrated, general plan of operations, namely:

Hold Hawaii

Support Australasia

Drive northwestward from New Hebrides.

3.4 President Franklin D. Roosevelt "Promises" the Soviets a Second Front, May–June 1942[4]

As noted in the chapter introduction, Army Chief of Staff General George C. Marshall countered Admiral King with a proposal from his staff for an immediate buildup of forces in the United Kingdom (Operation Bolero) for a cross-Channel attack to establish a second front in Western Europe on a large scale in 1943 (Operation Roundup) or on a smaller scale in 1942 (Operation Sledgehammer). Roosevelt quickly approved this proposal and, after obtaining limited British agreement, discussed it with visiting Soviet Foreign Minister Vyacheslav Molotov

---

4. From U.S. Department of State, *Foreign Relations of the United States, 1942*, vol. 3 (Washington, DC: U.S. Government Printing Office, 1961), 576–77, 582–83, 593–94.

in May and June of 1942. The document reproduced here contains a summary of their discussions on this matter, along with the press release Molotov desired and obtained.

May 30, 1942

Mr. Molotov thereupon remarked that, though the problem of the second front was both military and political, it was predominantly political. There was an essential difference between the situation in 1942 and what it might be in 1943. In 1942 Hitler was the master of all Europe save a few minor countries. He was the chief enemy of everyone. To be sure, as was devoutly to be hoped, the Russians might hold and fight on all through 1942. But it was only right to look at the darker side of the picture. On the basis of his continental dominance, Hitler might throw in such reinforcements in manpower and material that the Red Army might *not* be able to hold out against the Nazis. Such a development would produce a serious situation which we must face. The Soviet front would become secondary, the Red Army would be weakened, and Hitler's strength would be correspondingly greater, since he would have at his disposal not only more troops, but also the foodstuffs and raw materials of the Ukraine and the oil-wells of the Caucasus. In such circumstances the outlook would be much less favorable for all hands, and he would not pretend that such developments were all outside the range of possibility. . . .

Mr. Molotov therefore put this question frankly: could we undertake such offensive action as would draw off 40 German divisions which would be, to tell the truth, distinctly second-rate outfits? If the answer should be in the affirmative, the war would be decided in 1942. If negative, the Soviets would fight on alone, doing their best, and no man would expect more from them than that. He had not, Mr. Molotov added, received any positive answer in London. Mr. Churchill had proposed that he should return through London on his homeward journey from Washington, and had promised Mr. Molotov a more concrete answer on his second visit. Mr. Molotov admitted he realized that the British would have to bear the brunt of the action if a second front were created, but he also was cognizant of the role the United States plays and what influence this country exerts in questions of major strategy. Without in any way minimizing the risks entailed by a second front action this summer, Mr. Molotov declared his government wanted to know in frank terms what position we take on the question of a second front, and whether we were prepared to establish one. He requested a straight answer.

The difficulties, Mr. Molotov urged, would not be any less in 1943. The chances of success were actually better at present while the Russians still have a solid front. "If you postpone your decision," he said, "you will have eventually to bear the brunt of the war, and if Hitler becomes the undisputed master of the continent, next year will unquestionably be tougher than this one."

The President then put to General Marshall the query whether developments were clear enough so that we could say to Mr. Stalin that we are preparing a second front. "Yes," replied the General. The President then authorized Mr. Molotov to inform Mr. Stalin that we expect the formation of a second front this year. . . .

June 1, 1942

The President . . . went on to say that on the previous day he had discussed questions of tonnage and shipping with the Chiefs of Staff. Every week we were building up troop and plane concentrations in England with a view to getting at the Germans from there as quickly as possible. . . .

. . . The President . . . proposed that the Soviet Government consider reducing its lease-lend requirements from 4,100,000 tons to 2,000,000 tons. This reduction would release a large number of ships that we could divert to shipping to England munitions and equipment for the second front, and thus speed up the establishment of that front. . . .

The President repeated that we expected to set up a second front in 1942, but that every ship we could shift to the English run meant that the second front was so much the closer to being realized. After all, ships could not be in two places at once, and hence every ton we could save out of the total of 4,100,000 tons would be so much to the good. The Soviets could not eat their cake and have it too.

To this statement Mr. Molotov retorted with some emphasis that the second front would be stronger if the first front still stood fast, and inquired with what seemed deliberate sarcasm what would happen if the Soviets cut down their requirements and then no second front eventuated. Then, becoming still more insistent, he emphasized that he had brought the new treaty out of England. "What answer," he asked, "shall I take back to London and Moscow on the general question that has been raised? What is the President's answer with respect to the second front?"

To this direct question the President answered that Mr. Molotov could say in London that, after all, the British were even now in personal consultation with our staff-officers on questions of landing craft, food, etc. We expected to establish a second front. . . .

Press Release Issued by the White House, June 11, 1942

The People's Commissar of Foreign Affairs of the Union of Soviet Socialist Republics, Mr. V. M. Molotov, following the invitation of the President of the United States of America, arrived in Washington on May 29 and was for some time the President's guest. This visit to Washington afforded an opportunity for a friendly exchange of views between the President and his advisers on the one hand and Mr. Molotov and his party on the other. . . .

In the course of the conversations full understanding was reached with regard to the urgent tasks of creating a second front in Europe in 1942. In addition, the measures for increasing and speeding up the supplies of planes, tanks, and other kinds of war materials from the United States to the Soviet Union were discussed. Also discussed were the fundamental problems of cooperation of the Soviet Union and the United States in safeguarding peace and security to the freedom-loving peoples after the war. Both sides state with satisfaction the unity of their views on all these questions.

3.5 Churchill Vetoes Crossing the Channel in 1942 and Proposes the North African Alternative, July 8, 1942[5]

In early April the British had agreed "in principle" to the new U.S. plans for cross-Channel operations in 1942 or 1943, but within two months Churchill and his military advisers were voicing serious doubts about Sledgehammer, the 1942 operation—doubts he and the British chiefs of staff personally expressed to Roosevelt and the American chiefs during a June visit to Washington. Instead Churchill pressed for Operation Gymnast, the plan for an Anglo-American invasion of French North Africa. In this July 8 telegram to Roosevelt he forcefully expressed these views and pressed for American agreement.

July 8, 1942, 1:45 AM

From Former Naval Person to President. Personal and Secret.

1. No responsible British General, Admiral, or Air Marshal is prepared to recommend SLEDGEHAMMER as a practicable operation in 1942.

---

5. From Franklin D. Roosevelt Presidential Library, repr. in *Churchill & Roosevelt: The Complete Correspondence*, vol. 1, ed. Warren F. Kimball (Princeton: Princeton University Press, 1984), 520.

The Chiefs of the Staff have reported "The conditions which would make SLEDGEHAMMER a sound sensible enterprise are very unlikely to occur." They are now sending their paper to your Chiefs of Staff. . . .

3. In the event of a lodgement being effected and maintained it would have to be nourished and the bomber effort on Germany would have to be greatly curtailed. All our energies would be involved in defending the Bridgehead. The possibility of mounting a large scale operation in 1943 would be marred if not ruined. All our resources would be absorbed piecemeal on the very narrow front which alone is open. It may therefore be said that premature action in 1942 while probably ending in disaster would decisively injure the prospect of well organized large scale action in 1943.

4. I am sure myself that GYMNAST is by far the best chance for effective relief to the Russian front in 1942. This has all along been in harmony with your ideas. In fact it is your commanding idea. Here is the true second front in 1942. I have consulted cabinet and defence committee and we all agree. Here is the safest and most fruitful stroke that can be delivered this autumn.

3.6 Admiral Ernest J. King and General George C. Marshall Respond with a Pacific-First Proposal, July 10, 1942[6]

Strongly opposed to Churchill's proposed change in strategy and incensed by what they considered British duplicity in the matter, General Marshall and Admiral King responded with this formal proposal for an alternative Pacific-first strategy.

July 10, 1942

MEMORANDUM FOR THE PRESIDENT:

. . . Our view is that the execution of Gymnast, even if found practicable, means definitely no Bolero-Sledgehammer in 1942 and that it will definitely curtail if not make impossible the execution of Bolero-Roundup in the Spring of 1943. We are strongly of the opinion that Gymnast would be both indecisive and a heavy drain on our resources, and that if we undertake it, we would nowhere be acting decisively against the enemy and would definitely jeopardize our naval position in the Pacific. . . .

---

6. From National Archives and Franklin D. Roosevelt Presidential Library.

Neither Sledgehammer nor Roundup can be carried out without full and whole-hearted British support. They must of necessity furnish a large part of the forces. Giving up all possibility of Sledgehammer in 1942 not only voids our commitments to Russia, but either of the proposed diversions, namely Jupiter [invasion of Norway] and Gymnast, will definitely operate to delay and weaken readiness for Roundup in 1943. If the United States is to engage in any other operation than forceful, unswerving adherence to full Bolero plans, we are definitely of the opinion that we should turn to the Pacific and strike decisively against Japan; in other words assume a defensive attitude against Germany, except for air operations; and use all available means in the Pacific. Such action would not only be definite and decisive against one of our principal enemies, but would bring concrete aid to the Russians in case Japan attacks them.

It is most important that the final decision in this matter be made at the earliest possible moment.

3.7 President Roosevelt Rejects the Pacific-First Alternative, July 14, 1942[7]

Suspecting that the July 10 Marshall-King Pacific-first proposal might be a bluff designed to frighten the British into returning to cross-Channel operations, Roosevelt from his home in Hyde Park, New York, requested details. After receiving them on July 12, he rejected their proposal and ordered them to go to Britain with his close adviser Harry Hopkins to reach agreement on some 1942 operation in the European theater. If the British persisted in their refusal to cross the Channel in 1942, they were to agree to the North African alternative—which was renamed Operation Torch and successfully launched in November 1942.

Gen. Marshall

. . . I have carefully read your estimate of Sunday. My first impression is that it is exactly what Germany hoped the United States would do following Pearl Harbor. Secondly it does not in fact provide use of American troops in fighting except in a lot of islands whose occupation will not affect the world situation this year or next. Third it does not help Russia or the Near East.

---

7. From Franklin D. Roosevelt Presidential Library.

Therefore it is disapproved as of the present.

Roosevelt CinC
[Commander-in-Chief]

General Marshall:

I have definitely decided to send you, King and Harry [Hopkins] to London immediately. . . .

I want you to know now that I do not approve the Pacific proposal. Will see you in the morning. . . .

Roosevelt

3.8 Britain and the United States Agree on a Mediterranean Strategy for 1943 during the Casablanca Conference, January 1943[8]

On November 8, 1942, Anglo-American forces under General Dwight D. Eisenhower successfully landed along the coasts of French Algeria and Morocco in Operation Torch. While they soon obtained the surrender of Vichy French forces, they failed to take Tunisia from the Germans, who were soon reinforced by General Erwin Rommel's forces retreating from their October 23 defeat by the British at El Alamein. Eisenhower would not succeed in totally eliminating the Germans from Tunisia, thereby gaining control of the entire North African coast, until early May 1943.

In January, however, Churchill, Roosevelt, and their military advisers met in the captured Moroccan city of Casablanca to plan for additional 1943 operations. The American chiefs still favored crossing the Channel, but with major forces now committed to North Africa they were forced to agree to a continuation of British strategy in the Mediterranean, as the document here makes clear.

Memorandum by the Combined Chiefs of Staff

[Casablanca], January 19, 1943

---

8. From U.S. Department of State, *Foreign Relations of the United States: The Conferences at Washington, 1941–1942, and Casablanca, 1943* (Washington, DC: U.S. Government Printing Office, 1968), 774–75.

CONDUCT OF THE WAR IN 1943

The Combined Chiefs of Staff have agreed to submit the following recommendations for the conduct of the war in 1943.

1. *Security:*

The defeat of the U-boat must remain a first charge on the resources of the United Nations.

2. *Assistance to Russia:*

The Soviet forces must be sustained by the greatest volume of supplies that can be transported to Russia without prohibitive cost in shipping.

3. *Operations in the European Theater:*

Operations in the European Theater will be conducted with the object of defeating Germany in 1943 with the maximum forces that can be brought to bear upon her by the United Nations.

4. The main lines of offensive action will be:

In the Mediterranean:

(a) The occupation of Sicily with the object of

(1) Making the Mediterranean line of communications more secure.

(2) Diverting German pressure from the Russian front.

(3) Intensifying the pressure on Italy.

(b) To create a situation in which Turkey can be enlisted as an active ally.

In the U.K.:

(c) The heaviest possible bomber offensive against the German war effort.

(d) Such limited offensive operations as may be practicable with the amphibious forces available.

(e) The assembly of the strongest possible force (subject to (a) and (b) above and paragraph 6 below) in constant readiness to reenter the Continent as soon as German resistance is weakened to the required extent.

5. In order to insure that these operations and preparations are not prejudiced by the necessity to divert forces to retrieve an adverse situation elsewhere, adequate forces shall be allocated to the Pacific and Far Eastern Theaters.

6. *Operations in the Pacific and Far East:*

(a) Operations in these theaters shall continue with the forces allocated, with the object of maintaining pressure on Japan, retaining the initiative and attaining a position of readiness for the full scale offensive against Japan by the United Nations as soon as Germany is defeated.

(b) These operations must be kept within such limits as will not, in the opinion of the Combined Chiefs of Staff, jeopardize the capacity of the United Nations to take advantage of any favorable opportunity that may present itself for the decisive defeat of Germany in 1943.

(c) Subject to the above reservation, plans and preparations shall be made for:

(1) The recapture of Burma (ANAKIM) beginning in 1943.
(2) Operations, after the capture of Rabaul, against the Marshalls and Carolines if time and resources allow without prejudice to ANAKIM.

3.9 Stalin Angrily Responds to the Continued Delays in Establishing a Second Front, June 24, 1943[9]

The postponement of cross-Channel operations yet again deeply angered Soviet leader Josef Stalin. In this June 1943 telegram to Churchill, he responded with a list of Anglo-American broken promises regarding the establishment of a second front in Western Europe—and a veiled threat regarding the future of the Grand Alliance.

From your [Winston Churchill's] messages of last year and this I gained the conviction that you and the President were fully aware of the difficulties of organising such an operation and were preparing the invasion accordingly, with due regard to the difficulties and the necessary exertion of forces and means. Even last year you told me that a large-scale invasion of Europe by Anglo-American troops would be effected in 1943. In the Aide-Mémoire handed to V. M. Molotov on June 10, 1942, you wrote:

> Finally, and most important of all, we are concentrating our maximum effort on the organisation and preparation of a large-scale invasion of the Continent of Europe by British and American forces in 1943. We are setting no limit to the scope and objectives of this campaign, which will be carried out in the first instance by over a million men, British and American, with air forces of appropriate strength.

Early this year you twice informed me, on your own behalf and on behalf of the President, of decisions concerning an Anglo-American invasion of Western Europe intended to "divert strong German land and air forces from the Russian front." You had set yourself the task of bringing

---

9. From Ministry of Foreign Affairs of the U.S.S.R., *Correspondence between the Chairman of the Council of Ministers of the U.S.S.R. and the Presidents of the U.S.A. and the Prime Ministers of Great Britain during the Great Patriotic War of 1941–1945*, vol. 2 (Moscow: Foreign Languages Publishing House, 1957), 73–76.

Germany to her knees as early as 1943, and named September as the latest date for the invasion.

In your message of January 26 you wrote:

> We have been in conference with our military advisers and have decided on the operations which are to be undertaken by the American and British forces in the first nine months of 1943. We wish to inform you of our intentions at once. We believe that these operations together with your powerful offensive, may well bring Germany to her knees in 1943.

In your next message, which I received on February 12, you wrote, specifying the date of the invasion of Western Europe, decided on by you and the President:

> We are also pushing preparations to the limit of our resources for a cross-Channel operation in August, in which British and United States units would participate. Here again, shipping and assault-landing craft will be the limiting factors. If the operation is delayed by the weather or other reasons, it will be prepared with stronger forces in September.

Last February, when you wrote to me about those plans and the date of invading Western Europe, the difficulties of that operation were greater than they are now. Since then the Germans have suffered more than one defeat: they were pushed back by our troops in the South, where they suffered appreciable loss; they were beaten in North Africa and expelled by the Anglo-American troops; in submarine warfare, too, the Germans found themselves in a bigger predicament than ever, while Anglo-American superiority increased substantially; it is also known that the Americans and British have won air superiority in Europe and that their navies and mercantile marines have grown in power.

It follows that the conditions for opening a second front in Western Europe during 1943, far from deteriorating, have, indeed, greatly improved.

That being so, the Soviet Government could not have imagined that the British and U.S. Governments would revise the decision to invade Western Europe, which they had adopted early this year. In fact, the Soviet Government was fully entitled to expect that the Anglo-American decision would be carried out, that appropriate preparations were under way and that the second front in Western Europe would at last be opened in 1943.

That is why, when you now write that "it would be no help to Russia if we threw away a hundred thousand men in a disastrous cross-Channel attack," all I can do is remind you of the following:

First, your own Aide-Mémoire of June 1942 in which you declared that preparations were under way for an invasion, not by a hundred thousand, but by an Anglo-American force exceeding one million men at the very start of the operation.

Second, your February message, which mentioned extensive measures preparatory to the invasion of Western Europe in August or September 1943, which, apparently envisaged an operation, not by a hundred thousand men, but by an adequate force.

So when you now declare: "I cannot see how a great British defeat and slaughter would aid the Soviet armies," is it not clear that a statement of this kind in relation to the Soviet Union is utterly groundless and directly contradicts your previous and responsible decisions, listed above, about extensive and vigorous measures by the British and Americans to organise the invasion this year, measures on which the complete success of the operation should hinge.

I shall not enlarge on the fact that this responsible decision, revoking your previous decisions on the invasion of Western Europe, was reached by you and the President without Soviet participation and without inviting its representatives to the Washington conference, although you cannot but be aware that the Soviet Union's role in the war against Germany and its interest in the problems of the second front are great enough.

There is no need to say that the Soviet Government cannot become reconciled to this disregard of vital Soviet interests in the war against the common enemy.

You say that you "quite understand" my disappointment. I must tell you that the point here is not just the disappointment of the Soviet Government, but the preservation of its confidence in its Allies, a confidence which is being subjected to severe stress. One should not forget that it is a question of saving millions of lives in the occupied areas of Western Europe and Russia and of reducing the enormous sacrifices of the Soviet armies, compared with which the sacrifices of the Anglo-American armies are insignificant.

3.10 President Roosevelt, Churchill, and Stalin Debate and Decide Future Allied Strategy at the Tehran Conference, November 29–30, 1943[10]

The ensuing 1943 crisis in Allied relations was resolved at the November "Big Three" summit conference in the Iranian capital of

---

10. From U.S. Department of State, *Foreign Relations of the United States: The Conferences at Cairo and Tehran, 1943* (Washington, DC: U.S. Government Printing Office, 1961), 536–39, 576–77.

Tehran. At that conference, Roosevelt and Stalin rejected Churchill's pleas for further delay in launching the cross-Channel operation, now renamed Overlord, in order to obtain additional prizes in the Mediterranean that had become available with the invasion and surrender of Italy that summer. In the following minutes from the November 29 meeting at the Tehran Conference, Churchill explains the gains to be obtained from such a delay while Stalin and Roosevelt make clear their preference and insistence on no further delay in launching Overlord—an insistence that resulted in the Allied strategic agreements reached on the following day. In addition to these agreements, Stalin also agreed to enter the war against Japan once Germany had been defeated.

November 29 Meeting

[Prime Minister Churchill] went on to say that personally all he wanted was landing craft for two divisions in the Mediterranean and that with such a force many operations would be feasible, for example, it could be used to facilitate the operations in Italy or to take the island of Rhodes if Turkey will enter the war, and could be used for these purposes for at least six months and then employed in support of OVERLORD. He pointed out that this force of landing craft could not be supplied for the forces in the Mediterranean without either delaying OVERLORD six to eight weeks or without withdrawing forces from the Indian theater. This is the dilemma. . . . The Prime Minister concluded that if Turkey declared war on Germany it would be a terrible blow to German morale, would neutralize Bulgaria and would directly affect Rumania which even now was seeking someone to surrender unconditionally to. Hungary likewise would be immediately affected. He said that now is the time to reap the crop if we will pay the small price of the reaping. He summed up the task before the conference as: (1) to survey the whole field of the Mediterranean, and (2), how to relieve Russia, and (3), how to help OVERLORD.

Marshal Stalin said that Mr. Churchill need have no worry about the Soviet attitude toward Bulgaria; that if Turkey entered the war the Soviet Union would go to war with Bulgaria, but even so he did not think Turkey would come in. He continued that there was no difference of opinion as to the importance of helping the Partisans, but that he must say that from the Russian point of view the question of Turkey, the Partisans and even the occupation of Rome were not really important operations. He said that OVERLORD was the most important and nothing should be done to distract attention from that operation. He felt that a directive should be given to the military staffs, and proposed the following one:

(1). In order that Russian help might be given from the east to the execution of OVERLORD, a date should be set and the operation should not be postponed. (2). If possible the attack in southern France should precede OVERLORD by two months, but if that is impossible, then simultaneously or even a little after OVERLORD. An operation in southern France would be a supporting operation as contrasted with diversionary operations in Rome or in the Balkans, and would assure the success of OVERLORD. (3). The appointment of a Commander-in-Chief for OVERLORD as soon as possible. Until that is done the OVERLORD operation cannot be considered as really in progress. Marshal Stalin added that the appointment of the Commander-in-Chief was the business of the President and Mr. Churchill but that it would be advantageous to have the appointment made here.

The President then said he had been most interested in hearing the various angles discussed from OVERLORD to Turkey. He attached great importance to the question of logistics and timing. He said it is clear that we are all agreed as to the importance of OVERLORD and the only question was one of when. He said the question was whether to carry out OVER-LORD at the appointed time or possibly postpone it for the sake of other operations in the Mediterranean. He felt that the danger of an expedition in the eastern Mediterranean might be that if not immediately successful it might draw away effectives which would delay OVERLORD. He said that in regard to the Balkans, the Partisans and other questions are pinning down some 40 Axis Divisions and it was therefore his thought that supplies and commando raids be increased to that area to insure these Divisions remaining there. The President then said he was in favor of adhering to the original date for OVERLORD set at Quebec, namely, the first part of May.

Marshal Stalin said he would like to see OVERLORD undertaken during the month of May; that he did not care whether it was the 1st, 15th, or 20th, but that a definite date was important.

The Prime Minister said it did not appear that the points of view were as far apart as it seemed. The British Government was anxious to begin OVERLORD as soon as possible but did not desire to neglect the great possibilities in the Mediterranean merely for the sake of avoiding a delay of a month or two.

Marshal Stalin said that the operations in the Mediterranean have a value but they are really only diversions.

The Prime Minister said in the British view the large British forces in the Mediterranean should not stand idle but should be pressing the enemy with vigor. He added that to break off the campaign in Italy where the allied forces were holding a German army would be impossible.

Marshal Stalin said it looked as though Mr. Churchill thought that the Russians were suggesting that the British armies do nothing.

The Prime Minister said that if landing craft [are] taken from the Mediterranean theater there will be no action. He added that at Moscow the conditions under which the British Government considered OVERLORD could be launched had been fully explained, and these were that there should not be more than 12 mobile German divisions behind the coastal troops and that German reinforcements for sixty days should not exceed 15 Divisions. He added that to fulfill these conditions it was necessary in the intervening period to press the enemy from all directions. He said that the Divisions now facing the allies in Italy had come . . . [for the most part from France], and to break off the action in Italy would only mean that they would return to France to oppose OVERLORD. Turning again to the question of Turkey, The Prime Minister said that all were agreed on the question of Turkey's entrance into the war. If she refused, then that was the end of it. If she does enter, the military needs will be slight, and it will give us the use of Turkish bases in Anatolia, and the taking of the island of Rhodes which he felt could be done with one assault Division. Once Rhodes was taken the other Aegean islands could be starved out and the way opened to the Dardanelles. Mr. Churchill pointed out that the operation against Rhodes was a limited operation and would not absorb more effectives, and that in any case the troops for this purpose would come from those now used for the defense of Egypt. Once Rhodes was taken these forces from Egypt could proceed forward against the enemy. All he wanted was a small quantity of landing craft. . . .

. . . Marshal Stalin then said he wished to ask Mr. Churchill an indiscreet question, namely, do the British really believe in OVERLORD or are they only saying so to reassure the Russians.

The Prime Minister replied that if the conditions set forth at Moscow were present it was the duty of the British Government to hurl every scrap of strength across the channel. He then suggested that the British and American staffs meet tomorrow morning in an endeavor to work out a joint point of view to be submitted to the conference. It was further agreed that the President, Marshal Stalin, and the Prime Minister would lunch together at 1:30. . . .

November 30 Meeting

General Brooke said that sitting in combined session the United States and British Staffs had reached the following agreement, which had been submitted for the approval of the President and the Prime Minister. It was agreed:

(1). That OVERLORD will be launched during the month of May, 1944.

(2). That there will be a supporting operation in southern France on as large a scale as possible, depending on the number of landing craft available for this operation. . . .

Marshal Stalin said he fully understood the importance of the decision reached and the difficulties which would be encountered in the execution of OVERLORD. He added that the danger in the beginning of the operation was that the Germans might attempt to transfer troops from the eastern front to oppose OVERLORD. In order to deny to the Germans the possibility of maneuvering he pledged that the Red Army would launch simultaneously with OVERLORD large scale offensives in a number of places for the purpose of pinning down German forces and preventing the transfer of German troops to the west. He said that he had already made the foregoing statement to the President, and Mr. Churchill but he thought it necessary to repeat it to the conference.

CHAPTER 4

FIGHTING AND DEFEATING NAZI GERMANY

The United States and its allies fought Germany on the high seas and in the air as well as on land, with numerous debates taking place within and among the separate military services as well as within the Grand Alliance as a whole (see Chapter 3) over what constituted the best strategies and the most appropriate priorities. In general, and far from surprisingly, each service (army, navy, air) argued that its role was the most important and should therefore receive priority in the allocation of resources and personnel.

One important argument focused on the proper use of aircraft, a relatively new weapon. Although they had been used in World War I, only in the interwar period did the armed forces begin to explore their full potential and debate the best way to use them. That debate continued throughout the war. Advocates of what was labeled "strategic" bombing, in both the United States Army Air Forces (AAF) and the British Royal Air Force (RAF) argued that massed bombers attacking German cities could destroy the industrial capacity of Germany to wage war as well as the will of its people to continue the conflict and thus guarantee victory without the use of major ground or naval forces. Critics within the army and the navy disagreed vehemently. Strategic bombing could not achieve these goals alone, they maintained; ground and naval power remained the keys to victory. They consequently pressed for a focus on what was known as the "tactical" use of airpower to support both ground forces fighting the German army in Europe and naval forces fighting the crucial Battle of the Atlantic against German submarines. Without victory in this campaign on the high seas, naval planners emphasized, the critical Atlantic supply lines to Britain and the Soviet Union would be cut and the war lost. Army planners similarly argued that victory ultimately depended on the defeat of the German army on the ground.

Inter-Allied as well as inter-service and intra-service disagreements over appropriate theater strategy and priorities also took place. The RAF, for example, favored nighttime area bombing of German cities designed to destroy civilian morale, while the AAF believed in daylight "precision" bombing designed to destroy critical German industries. Once Operation Overlord was launched in 1944, British and U.S. ground commanders argued incessantly over whose forces should receive priority in mission as well as supplies, and whether offensives against the German army should be launched along a "broad front" running from the English Channel to the Swiss border as Supreme Allied commander General Dwight D. Eisenhower desired or along the much narrower front proposed by some of his army commanders, most notably British General Bernard Montgomery and U.S. Generals Omar Bradley, George Patton, and Jacob Devers. These army commanders also argued with each other, with their arguments exacerbated by sharp personality conflicts, over which of them and with what forces should be responsible for this narrower thrust into Germany.

Behind these disputes rested the fate of all the soldiers, sailors, and airmen who participated in the war against Germany. Their personal experiences in ground, air, and naval campaigns are as much a part of this war as the disagreements within the U.S. and Allied high commands.

Many of the strategic disagreements discussed in this chapter continued after the war and down to the present. Scholars continue to disagree, for example, about the effectiveness as well as the morality of the strategic bombing campaign. Critics note that by itself, the campaign clearly did not defeat Nazi Germany as its proponents had claimed it could, and that it failed to destroy either German civilian morale or German war production; indeed, that production actually went up in 1943 and 1944 despite the campaign. They also point out that the AAF daylight campaign was far from the "precision bombing" claimed and in practice often similar to the indiscriminate nighttime area bombing of the RAF, and they note the enormous costs of the campaign in terms of human life as well as equipment; in this regard, U.S. bomber crews had one of the highest casualty rates of any service during the war. Defenders of the campaign claim that German war production would have gone up much more than it did without the campaign; that it forced the Germans to focus on the production of anti-aircraft weapons instead of those that could have been used on the Eastern Front; and that, with the advent of long-range fighter aircraft in 1944 to accompany the bombers, the campaign succeeded in destroying the German Luftwaffe fighter force and thereby ensured Allied control of the air during and after the cross-Channel invasion—without which success would not have been possible.

Historians also continue to disagree as to which ground campaign would have been the most effective—and under whose leadership. While Montgomery had been given command of all ground forces during the opening phases of the campaign, in early September Eisenhower assumed that command and divided his powerful forces into three army groups: a northern one composed primarily of British and Canadian forces under Montgomery's command, a central one composed primarily of U.S. forces under U.S. General Omar N. Bradley, and a southern one composed of U.S. and French forces under U.S. General Jacob Devers coming up from southern France after the successful mid-August landing there. Eisenhower's critics claim that the Germans could have been totally defeated and forced to surrender in 1944 instead of a year later had he agreed to give priority in supplies and offensive operations to one of these three army groups and commanders instead of pursuing his slower broad-front approach. His defenders counter that Montgomery failed to cross the Rhine in the Netherlands when given that priority in September (Operation Market Garden), that such a strategy risked German isolation and defeat of a single force whereas that would not be possible if all Allied forces advanced simultaneously, and that as an *Allied* commander he could not strongly favor the forces and commander of one nation over another without risking a rupture in the alliance.

The documents reproduced in this chapter deal with these strategic disagreements as well as the experiences of those who fought and raise a series of questions for you to consider. How effective in hindsight was the strategic bombing campaign? Was it worth its enormous human and material costs as well as the moral opprobrium attached to the killing of hundreds of thousands of civilians? Should it have received an even higher priority, or a lower one so that more critical air support could have been given to both the Allied effort against German submarines in the Atlantic and the German army in Europe? Why did Eisenhower favor a broad-front strategy while his ground commanders argued for a narrower approach? In retrospect, which approach was better? What were the most important factors in the eventual and total Allied victory over Germany? And what was the impact of the war in Europe on those Americans who fought in it?

* * * *

4.1 Army Ground versus Air Plans for the War against Germany: The "Victory Program" (with AWPD-1) of September 1941[1]

Although muted, the different strategic approaches of the various American services were nevertheless apparent in the prewar plans of

---

1. From "Over-all Production Requirements Required to Defeat United States Potential Enemies," RG 225, National Archives; repr. in *American War Plans*, vol. 5, ed. Steven T. Ross (New York: Garland, 1992), 190–91, 199–201, 210–17.

the U.S. Army ground and air forces contained within the so-called Victory Program of September 1941. Note in particular the different emphasis given to air, naval, and ground operations within the two excerpts reproduced here. In retrospect, which assessment was more accurate?

Ultimate Requirements Study Estimate of Army Ground Forces

1. The specific operations necessary to accomplish the defeat of the Axis Powers cannot be predicted at this time. Irrespective of the nature and scope of these operations, we must prepare to fight Germany by actually coming to grips with and defeating her ground forces and definitely breaking her will to combat. Such requirement establishes the necessity for powerful ground elements, flexibly organized into task forces which are equipped and trained to do their respective jobs. The Germans and their associates with between 11 and 12 million men under arms, now have approximately 300 divisions fully equipped and splendidly trained. It is estimated that they can have by 1943, a total of 400 divisions available in the European Theater.

2. The important influence of the air arm in modern combat has been irrefutably established. The degree of success attained by sea and ground forces will be determined by the effective and timely employment of air supporting units and the successful conduct of strategical missions. No major military operation in any theater will succeed without air superiority, or at least air superiority disputed. The necessity for a strong sea force, consisting principally of fast cruisers, destroyers, aircraft carriers, torpedo boats and submarines, continues in spite of the increased fighting potential of the air arm. Employment of enemy air units has not yet deprived naval vessels of their vital role on the high seas, but has greatly accelerated methods and changed the technique in their employment. It appears that the success of naval operations, assuming air support, will still be determined by sound strategic concepts and adroit leadership. A sea blockade will not accomplish an economic strangulation or military defeat of Germany. Nor will air operations alone bring victory. Air and sea forces will make important contributions but effective and adequate ground forces must be available to close with and destroy the enemy within his citadel. . . .

4. . . . Accepting the premise, that we must come to grips with the enemy ground forces, our principal theater of war is Central Europe. . . .

5. . . . Task Forces consisting principally of armored and motorized divisions, must be created for possible operations in North Africa, the Middle

East, France and the Low Countries. . . . The realization of our present national policies may require operations in distant theaters by military forces of unprecedented strength. It would be folly to create strong fighting forces without providing the transportation to move and maintain them in the contemplated theaters of operations. The maximum possible shipbuilding capacity of our country, coordinated of course with other essential demands upon industry and raw materials, must be exploited and continued in operation for the next several years.

6. The foregoing considerations clearly indicate the importance of creating a productive capacity in this country, that will provide the most modern equipment designed to give mobility and destructive power to our striking forces. The forces that we now estimate as necessary to realize our national objectives and for which production capacity must be provided, may not be adequate or appropriate. No one can predict the situation that will confront the United States in July, 1943. We may require much larger forces than those indicated below, and correspondingly greatly increased quantities of equipment. Emphasis has been placed on destructive power and mobility, with a view to offensive maneuvers in our principal theater of operations (Europe). The forces deemed necessary to accomplish the role of ground units in the supreme effort to defeat our potential enemies, total 5 Field Armies consisting of approximately 215 divisions (infantry, armored, motorized, airborne, mountain and cavalry) with appropriate supporting service elements.

Air Intelligence—Estimate of the Situation [AWPD-1]

3. *b.* The German offensive against Russia and the other German war operations have placed a considerable strain upon the economic structure of the Reich, and the Russian Campaign engaged a major portion of the German army and most of the German Air Force in Eastern Europe.

c. The declaration of war by Germany against Russia improved the conditions for enforcing the sea blockade and the means of applying pressure through economic warfare. Even in the event of Russian collapse, the German economic structure will continue to operate under heavy strain, and there will be a period of at least a year before Russian economy could be resuscitated and incorporated into the German system.

d. The extent of the economic strain on Germany is indicated by the following: at present there are 6½ million men under arms in the German army, 100,000 in the German Navy, and 1½ million in the German Air Force. Behind this armed front, there are 8½ million men engaged in armaments work alone, about half of whom are working in steel industries. Nearly 17 million men are directly engaged in this war, to the exclusion of all normal civil pursuits and production. Hence, there is a very heavy drain on the social and economic structure of the state. Destruction of that structure will virtually break down the capacity of the German nation to wage war. The basic conception on which this plan is based lies in the application of air power for the breakdown of the industrial and economic structure of Germany. This conception involves the selection of a system of objectives vital to continued German war effort, and to the means of livelihood of the German people, and tenaciously *concentrating all bombing* toward destruction of those objectives. The most effective manner of conducting such a decisive offensive is by destruction of precise objectives, at least initially. As German morale begins to crack, area bombing of civil concentrations may be effective.

e. It is improbable that a land invasion can be carried out against Germany proper within the next three years. If the air offensive is successful, a land offensive may not be necessary.

4.2 The Naval and Air Campaigns against German U-Boats and Cities Receive High Priority at the Casablanca Conference, January, 1943[2]

While the 1942 Anglo-American invasion of French North Africa (see Chapter 3) succeeded, German submarines throughout that year wreaked havoc on Anglo-American shipping in the Atlantic, sinking more tonnage than the Allies built and threatening their ability to continue, let alone win, the war. Consequently, the campaign against the German U-boats received a great deal of attention and top priority when Churchill, Roosevelt, and their military chiefs met in January at the recently captured city of Casablanca. As the excerpts from the Combined Chiefs of Staff minutes and memoranda reproduced here illustrate, this campaign included the use of heavy bombers that would otherwise have been used in the major campaign to bomb German cities and industry—a campaign that also received a very high priority at Casablanca. Note in this regard how the Combined Chiefs resolved this conflict, as well as

---

2. From U.S. Department of State, *Foreign Relations of the United States: The Conferences at Washington, 1941–1942, and Casablanca, 1943* (Washington, DC: U.S. Government Printing Office, 1968), 545, 565, 774, 781–82.

the Anglo-American dispute over British nighttime area bombing to destroy German morale versus U.S. daytime "precision" bombing to destroy the German economy.

Combined Chiefs of Staff Minutes, January 14, 1943

[General Marshall] repeated that our first concern must be the defeat of Germany's submarine warfare.

[British Air Chief] Sir Charles Portal then said that the British Chiefs of Staff also felt that the defeat of the submarine menace must be given first priority in the use of air power, particularly in the protection of our line of communications. . . .

Sir Charles Portal said that the air had proved the most effective weapon against the U-boat. The estimated German output of U-boats was twenty a month. He gave the following figures for attacks on U-boats during the last two months:

		November	*December*
U-Boats sunk	by aircraft	8	2
U-Boats damaged		24	9
U-Boats sunk	by other means	8	6
U-Boats damaged		7	6

Air patrols over the U-boat routes to the hunting grounds were very costly in aircraft since it was calculated that there was only one sighting for 250 hours flying time. Nevertheless, even if a large number of U-boats were not actually destroyed by this means, aircraft patrols had a good effect in compelling U-boats to remain submerged and thereby reducing their time on the hunting grounds. A further method of attack on U-boats was the laying of mines from the air at the exits of the U-boat bases and construction yards.

General Arnold inquired whether it was not possible to use flying boats for anti-submarine work, both over the hunting grounds and on the routes to them. This would avoid the use of valuable long-range bombers.

Sir Charles Portal said that the long-range bomber was essential for work over the convoys, since flying boats, owing to their slow speed, took too long to reach them after a call for assistance. Moreover, the load of the flying boat in bombs and depth charges was less than that of the Liberator. . . . A considerable number of Catalinas were being used in spite of these disadvantages. It was estimated that the minimum requirements for the whole of the Atlantic and British Home Waters was between 120 and 135 long-range bombers. . . .

Memorandum by the Combined Chiefs of Staff, January 19, 1943

Conduct of the War in 1943

The Combined Chiefs of Staff have agreed to submit the following recommendations for the conduct of the war in 1943.

1. *Security:*
The defeat of the U-boat must remain a first charge on the resources of the United Nations.

2. *Assistance to Russia:*
The Soviet forces must be sustained by the greatest volume of supplies that can be transported to Russia without prohibitive cost in shipping.

3. *Operations in the European Theater:*
Operations in the European Theater will be conducted with the object of defeating Germany in 1943 with the maximum forces that can be brought to bear upon her by the United Nations.

4. The main lines of offensive action will be:
In the Mediterranean:

(*a*) The occupation of Sicily with the object of:

(1) Making the Mediterranean line of communications more secure.

(2) Diverting German pressure from the Russian front.

(3) Intensifying the pressure on Italy.

(*b*) To create a situation in which Turkey can be enlisted as an active ally.

In the U.K.:

(*c*) The heaviest possible bomber offensive against the German war effort.

(*d*) Such limited offensive operations as may be practicable with the amphibious forces available. . . .

Memorandum by the Combined Chiefs of Staff, January 21, 1943

The Bomber Offensive from the United Kingdom

Directive to the appropriate British and U.S. Air Force Commanders, to govern the operation of the British and U.S. Bomber Commands in the

United Kingdom (Approved by the Combined Chiefs of Staff at their 65th Meeting on January 21, 1943)

1. Your primary object will be the progressive destruction and dislocation of the German military, industrial and economic system, and the undermining of the morale of the German people to a point where their capacity for armed resistance is fatally weakened.

2. Within that general concept, your primary objectives, subject to the exigencies of weather and of tactical feasibility, will for the present be in the following order of priority:

(*a*) German submarine construction yards.

(*b*) The German aircraft industry.

(*c*) Transportation.

(*d*) Oil plants.

(*e*) Other targets in enemy war industry.

The above order of priority may be varied from time to time according to developments in the strategical situation. Moreover, other objectives of great importance either from the political or military point of view must be attacked. Examples of these are:

(1) Submarine operating bases on the Biscay coast. If these can be put out of action, a great step forward will have been taken in the U-boat war which the C.C.S. [Combined Chiefs of Staff] have agreed to be a first charge on our resources. . . .

(2) Berlin, which should be attacked when conditions are suitable for the attainment of specially valuable results unfavorable to the morale of the enemy or favorable to that of Russia. . . .

5. You should take every opportunity to attack Germany by day, to destroy objectives that are unsuitable for night attack, to sustain continuous pressure on German morale, to impose heavy losses on the German day fighter force, and to contain German fighter strength away from the Russian and Mediterranean theaters of war.

4.3 A Mother Questions and General Henry H. "Hap" Arnold's Staff Defends the Bombing of German Cities[3]

Both during and after the war numerous questions were raised regarding the effectiveness and the morality of the bombing campaign, a

---

3. From "Suggested Reply," in "Humanitarian Aspects of Airpower" binder, Frederick L. Anderson Collection, Hoover Institution, Stanford University, Stanford, CA; repr. in Conrad C. Crane, *Bombs, Cities and Civilians: American Airpower Strategy in World War II* (Lawrence: University Press of Kansas, 1993), 28, 163–64.

campaign that resulted in the deaths of hundreds of thousands of German civilians. Reproduced here is a letter expressing concerns about the morality of this campaign from the mother of a bomber pilot who was also a friend of AAF chief General Henry H. "Hap" Arnold, followed by a defense and explanation of that controversial campaign written in response by one or more members of Arnold's AAF staff. Did the actual campaign reflect and validate this defense and explanation?

May 3, 1943

Dear Hap:

Last month my son Ted won his wings at Randolph Field. He is now going through a bombardment school, and in a short time expects to go to the front.

Will you tell me—has he become what our enemies call him, "A Hooligan of the Air?" Is he expected to scatter death on men, women, children—to wreck churches and shrines—to be a slaughterer, not a fighting man? . . .

Very sincerely,
/s/ Katherine A. Hooper
(Mrs. James E. Hooper)

Suggested Reply to Letters Questioning Humanitarian Aspects of Air Force

The most fundamental difference between beast and man is in the fact that the beast is a realist, taking life at its face value, while man attempts by his emotions to camouflage, and thereby to make more bearable, unpleasant prospects which he faces.

War, no matter how glorious the cause, is horrible by every civilized standard. Clothing it in shining armor does not hide the blood and suffering except from him who would be blind; neither does changing the vehicle of destruction alter the fact that death and destruction form the inevitable body and face of war.

By drawing aside the curtain, we see air warfare as being different only in the range of its potential destruction. The air gives uncurbed bestial instincts a wider field of expression, leaving only humanity and common sense to dictate limitations. Law cannot limit what physics makes possible. We can depend for moderation only upon reason and humane instincts when we exercise such a power.

We believe that we are using those curbs to the proper extent in our application of Air Power, but I can well understand your confusion in the light of propaganda and misguided reports of air operations. The fact that no adequate explanation has ever been offered has likewise confused others in a much better position to understand.

All of us have seen the result of air power as used by the beast. To one such as he, any horror is justified so long as his end is accomplished but he fails to realize that even his purpose could be better accomplished if he used methods which are more efficient and which happen, at the same time, to be most humane.

This can best be illustrated by our own concept of the proper role of air power in war. It works on the principle of the old adage to the effect that for the lack of a nail the house fell down. We take away the nail.

It has always been recognized that armies can be defeated through the killing of men; but are not modern armies as futile without weapons and equipment? The armored force is nothing without a tank, and we can take the tank by killing its occupants and, at the same time, suffering casualties on our part. But we can also take the tank away, in effect, "before it is born," thereby saving the casualties on both sides. We can hit the factory where it is built, the steel plant where the armor is made, or the refinery from which it gets its fuel. We do not mean the cities containing the factories, but by exercising the precision which is the keynote of America, we mean that we carefully select and, to the best of our ability, hit the precise spot which is most vital to the enemy. We hold no brief for terror bombing. True that will cause casualties on both sides, and there will still be ground fighting, but the final score in blood will be much less.

Those are the factors of reason and humanity which we allow to curb the awful weapon at our disposal. Those are the factors which the brute mind of the beast cannot conceive. With the understanding cooperation of you and thousands of others like you, we will prove to the beast that humanity pays and that Air Power is the most powerful urge for peace.

4.4 The Original Overlord Plan Proposes Landing on the Normandy Beaches and Explains the Problems to Be Overcome, July 27, 1943[4]

Even though the Allies invaded Sicily and Italy rather than northern France in 1943, the Combined Chiefs at the January Casablanca Conference also directed that a planning staff for cross-Channel operations

---

4. From U.S. Department of State, *Foreign Relations of the United States: The Conferences at Washington, 1941–1942, and Casablanca, 1943* (Washington, DC: U.S. Government Printing Office, 1970), 488–96.

be established and that it develop appropriate plans. By the summer that staff had developed the following plan for such an operation, now code-named Overlord. Note the target date, the reasons for the selection of the Normandy area of the French coast, and the major problems that needed to be overcome. The Combined Chiefs of Staff approved this plan at the August 1943 summit conference in Quebec. Its commanders would modify the plan in early 1944 by considerably expanding the size of the beachhead and the forces to be deployed to attain and hold it. Those forces, under the overall command of General Eisenhower, achieved success on June 6, 1944.

The object of Operation "Overlord" is to mount and carry out an operation with forces and equipment established in the United Kingdom, and with target date the 1st of May, 1944, to secure a lodgement on the Continent from which further offensive operations can be developed. The lodgement area must contain sufficient port facilities to maintain a force of some twenty-six to thirty divisions, and enable that force to be augmented by follow-up shipments from the United States or elsewhere of additional divisions and supporting units of the rate of three to five divisions per month.

Selection of a Lodgement Area

. . . 4. [T]aking beach capacity and air and naval considerations together, it appears that either the Pas de Calais area or the Caen-Cotentin [Normandy] area is the most suitable for the initial main landing.

5. As the area for the initial landing, the Pas de Calais has many obvious advantages such that good air support and quick turn round for our shipping can be achieved. On the other hand, it is a focal point of the enemy fighters disposed for defence, and maximum enemy air activity can be brought to bear over this area with the minimum movement of his air forces. Moreover, the Pas de Calais is the most strongly defended area on the whole French coast. The defences would require very heavy and sustained bombardment from sea and air: penetration would be slow, and the result of the bombardment of beach exits would severely limit the rate of build-up. Further, this area does not offer good opportunities for expansion. It would be necessary to develop the bridgehead to include either the Belgian ports as far as Antwerp or the Channel ports Westwards to include Havre and Rouen. But both any advance to Antwerp across the numerous water obstacles, and a long flank march of some 120 miles to the Seine ports must be considered

unsound operations of war unless the German forces are in a state not far short of final collapse. . . .

8. . . . The Caen sector is weakly held; the defences are relatively light and the beaches are of high capacity and sheltered from the prevailing winds. Inland the terrain is suitable for airfield development and for the consolidation of the initial bridgehead; and much of it is unfavorable for counterattacks by Panzer divisions. Maximum enemy air opposition can only be brought to bear at the expense of the enemy air defence screen covering the approaches to Germany; and the limited number of enemy airfields within range of the Caen area facilitates local neutralisation of the German fighter force. The sector suffers from the disadvantage that considerable effort will be required to provide adequate air support to our assault forces and some time must elapse before the capture of a major port.

After a landing in the Caen sector it would be necessary to seize either the Seine group of ports or the Brittany group of ports. To seize the Seine ports would entail forcing a crossing of the Seine, which is likely to require greater forces than we can build up through the Caen beaches and the port of Cherbourg. It should, however, be possible to seize the Brittany ports between Cherbourg and Nantes and on them build up sufficient forces for our final advance Eastwards.

Provided that the necessary air situation can first be achieved, the chances of a successful attack and of rapid subsequent development are so much greater in this sector than in any other that it is considered that the advantages far outweigh the disadvantages.

The Lodgement Area Selected

9. In the light of these factors, it is considered that our initial landing on the Continent should be effected in Caen area, with a view to the eventual seizure of a lodgement area comprising the Cherbourg-Brittany group of ports (from Cherbourg to Nantes).

Opening Phase up to the Capture of Cherbourg

. . . 11. The main limiting factors affecting such an operation are the possibility of attaining the necessary air situation; the number of offensive divisions which the enemy can make available for counter attack in the Caen area; the availability of landing ships and craft and of transport aircraft; and the capacity of the beaches and ports in the sector. . . .

Major Conditions Affecting Success of the Operation

32. It will be seen that the plan for the initial landing is based on two main principles—concentration of forces and tactical surprise. Concentration of the assault forces is considered essential if we are to ensure adequate air support and if our limited assault forces are to avoid defeat in detail. An attempt has been made to obtain tactical surprise by landing in a lightly defended area—presumably lightly defended as, due to its distance from a major port, the Germans consider a landing there unlikely to be successful. This action, of course, presupposes that we can offset the absence of a port in the initial stages by the provision of improvised sheltered waters. It is believed that this can be accomplished.

33. The operation calls for a much higher standard of performance on the part of the naval assault forces than any previous operation. This will depend upon their being formed in sufficient time to permit of adequate training.

34. Above all, it is essential that there should be an over-all reduction in the German fighter force between now and the time of the surface assault. From now onwards every practical method of achieving this end must be employed. This condition, above all others, will dictate the date by which the amphibious assault can be launched.

35. The next condition is that the number of German offensive divisions in reserve must not exceed a certain figure on the target date if the operation is to have reasonable chance of success. The German reserves in France and the Low Countries as a whole, excluding divisions holding the coast, G. A. F. [German Air Force] division and training divisions, should not exceed on the day of the assault twelve full-strength first-quality divisions. In addition, the Germans should not be able to transfer more than fifteen first-quality divisions from Russia during the first two months. Moreover, on the target date the divisions in reserve should be so located that the number of first-quality divisions which the Germans could deploy in the Caen area to support the divisions holding the coast should not exceed three divisions on D day, five divisions by D plus 2, or nine divisions by D plus 8.

During the preliminary period, therefore, every effort must be made to dissipate and divert German formations, lower their fighting efficiency and disrupt communications.

36. Finally, there is the question of maintenance. Maintenance will have to be carried out over beaches for a period of some three months for a number of formations, varying from a maximum of eighteen divisions in the first month to twelve divisions in the second month, rapidly diminishing to nil in the third month. Unless adequate measures are

taken to provide sheltered waters by artificial means, the operation will be at the mercy of the weather. Moreover, special facilities and equipment will be required to prevent undue damage to craft during this extended period. Immediate action for the provision of the necessary requirements is essential.

37. Given these conditions—a reduced G. A. F., a limitation in the number or effectiveness of German offensive formations in France, and adequate arrangements to provide improvised sheltered waters— it is considered that Operation "Overlord" has a reasonable prospect of success. To ensure these conditions being attained by the 1st May, 1944, action must start *now* and every possible effort made by all means in our power to soften German resistance and to speed up our own preparations.

4.5 Generals Eisenhower and Montgomery Debate Broad versus Narrow Front Strategies, September 1944[5]

Allied forces landing in Normandy on June 6 achieved startling success in the summer of 1944 and by the end of August had liberated most of France and Belgium. By that time sufficient forces had landed for Eisenhower to form the Anglo-Canadian 21st Army Group under the command of British General Bernard Montgomery and the U.S. 12th Army Group under the command of U.S. General Omar Bradley, soon supplemented by the U.S.-French 6th Army Group under U.S. General Jacob Devers that had successfully invaded southern France a few weeks earlier.

Eisenhower and Montgomery had very different ideas as to the correct military strategy to follow in the aftermath of their summer victories, with Eisenhower favoring a broad-front approach that would have all Allied forces advancing on Germany simultaneously while Montgomery favored a narrower and more concentrated approach whereby his 21st Army Group, supplemented by some of Bradley's U.S. forces on his right flank, would receive the bulk of available supplies and drive toward the Ruhr and Berlin. In mid-September each general explained and defended his approach.

5. From Dwight D. Eisenhower Papers, Eisenhower Presidential Library, Abilene, KS; repr. in *The Papers of Dwight David Eisenhower: The War Years*, vol. 4, ed. Alfred D. Chandler Jr. (Baltimore: Johns Hopkins Press, 1970), 2148–49, 2164–65; and in *The Memoirs of Field-Marshal Montgomery* (Cleveland: World Publishing, 1958), 248–53.

September 15, 1944

Dear Montgomery:

... I have been considering our next move.

As I see it, the Germans will have stood in defense of the Ruhr and Frankfurt and will have had a sharp defeat inflicted on them. Their dwindling forces, reinforced perhaps by material hastily scratched together or dragged from other theaters, will probably try to check our advance on the remaining important objectives in Germany. By attacking such objectives we shall create opportunities of dealing effectively with the last remnants of the German forces in the West. Moreover, we shall be occupying further key centers and increasing our stranglehold on the German peoples.

Clearly, Berlin is the main prize, and the prize in defense of which the enemy is likely to concentrate the bulk of his forces. There is no doubt whatsoever, in my mind, that we should concentrate all our energies and resources on a rapid thrust to Berlin.

Our strategy, however, will have to be coordinated with that of the Russians, so we must also consider alternative objectives.

There is the area of the northern ports, Kiel-Lubeck-Hamburg-Bremen. Its occupation would not only give us control of the German Navy and North Sea bases, of the Kiel Canal and of a large industrial area, but would enable us to form a barrier against the withdrawal of German forces from Norway and Denmark. Further, this area, or a part of it, might have to be occupied as flank protection to our thrust on Berlin.

There are the areas Hanover-Brunswick and Leipzig-Dresden. They are important industrial and administrative areas and centers of communications, on the direct routes from the Ruhr and Frankfurt to Berlin, so the Germans will probably hold them as intermediate positions covering Berlin.

There are the Nurnberg-Regensburg and the Augsburg-Munich areas. Apart from their economical and administrative importance, there is the transcending political importance of Munich. Moreover, there may be an impelling demand to occupy these areas and cut off enemy forces withdrawing from Italy and the Balkans.

Clearly, therefore, our objectives cannot be precisely determined until nearer the time, so we must be prepared for one or more of the following:

a. To direct forces of both Army Groups on Berlin astride the axes Ruhr-Hanover-Berlin *or* Frankfurt-Leipzig-Berlin, *or* both.
b. Should the Russians beat us to Berlin, the Northern Group of Armies would seize the Hanover area and the Hamburg group of ports. The Central Group of Armies would seize part, or the whole, of Leipzig-Dresden, depending upon the progress of the Russian advance.

c. In any event, the Southern Group of Armies would seize Augsburg-Munich. The area Nurnberg-Regensburg would be seized by Central or Southern Group of Armies, depending on the situation at the time.

Simply stated, it is my desire to move on Berlin by the most direct and expeditious route, with combined U.S.-British forces supported by other available forces moving through key centers and occupying strategic areas on the flanks, all in one coordinated, concerted operation.

It is not possible at this stage to indicate the timing of these thrusts or their strengths, but I shall be glad to have your views on the general questions raised in this letter.

Sincerely,
[Dwight D. Eisenhower]

18th September

My dear Ike,

I have received your letter dated 15-9-44, and I give below my general views on the questions you raise—as asked for by you.

1. I suggest that the whole matter as to what is possible, and what is NOT possible, is very closely linked up with the administrative situation. The vital factor is time; what we have to do, we must do quickly.

2. In view of para. 1, it is my opinion that a concerted operation in which all the available land armies move forward into Germany is not possible; the maintenance resources, and the general administrative situation, will not allow of this being done QUICKLY.

3. But forces adequate in the strength for the job in hand could be supplied and maintained, provided the general axis of advance was suitable, and provided these forces had complete priority in all respects as regards maintenance.

4. It is my own personal opinion that we shall not achieve what we want by going for objectives such as Nurnberg, Augsburg, Munich, etc., and by establishing our forces in central Germany.

5. I consider that the best objective is the Ruhr, and thence on to Berlin by the northern route. . . .

6. If you agree with para. 5, then I consider that 21 Army Group, plus First U.S. Army of nine divisions, would be adequate. Such a force must have *everything it needed in the maintenance line*; other Armies would do the best they could with what was left over.

7. If you consider that para. 5 is not right, and that the proper axis of advance is by Frankfurt and central Germany, then I suggest that 12 Army Group of three Armies would be used and would have all the maintenance. 21 Army Group would do the best it could with what was left over; or

possibly the Second British Army would be wanted in a secondary role on the left flank of the movement.

8. In brief, I consider that as time is so very important we have got to decide what is necessary to go to Berlin and finish the war; the remainder must play a secondary role. It is my opinion that three Armies are enough, if you select the northern route, and I consider that, from a maintenance point of view, it could be done. I have not studied the southern route.

9. I consider that our plan, and objectives, should be decided NOW, and everything arranged accordingly. I would not myself agree that we can wait until nearer the time, as suggested in your letter.

10. Finally to sum up.

I recommend the northern route of advance via the Ruhr, vide para. 5. Para. 6 would then apply. . . .

Yours ever
(Sgd) B. L. Montgomery

20th September

Dear Monty,

Generally speaking I find myself so completely in agreement with your letter of 18 September (M-526) that I cannot believe there is any great difference in our concepts.

Never at any time have I implied that I was considering an advance into Germany with all armies moving abreast.

Specifically I agree with you in the following: My choice of routes for making the all-out offensive into Germany is from the Ruhr to Berlin. A prerequisite from the maintenance viewpoint is the early capture of the approaches to Antwerp so that that flank may be adequately supplied.

Incidentally I do not yet have your calculations in the tonnage that will be necessary to support the 21 Army Group on this move. There is one point, however, on which we do not agree, if I interpret your ideas correctly. As I read your letter you imply that all the divisions that we have, except those of the 21st Army Group and approximately nine of the 12th Army Group, can stop in place *where they are* and that we can strip all these additional divisions from their transport and everything else to support one single knife-like drive towards Berlin. This may not be exactly what you mean but it is certainly not possible.

What I do believe is that we must marshal our strength up along the Western borders of Germany, to the Rhine if possible, insure adequate maintenance by getting Antwerp working at full blast at the earliest possible moment and then carry out the drive you suggest. All of Bradley's Army Group, except his left Army, which makes his main effort, will move forward sufficiently so as always to be in supporting position for the main drive and to prevent concentration of German forces against its front and flanks. . . .

As you know I have been giving preference to my left all the way through this campaign including attaching the First Airborne Force to you and adopting every possible expedient to assure your maintenance. All other forces have been fighting with a halter around their necks in the way of supplies. You may not know that for four days straight Patton has been receiving serious counterattacks and during the last seven days, without attempting any real advance himself, has captured about 9,000 prisoners and knocked out 270 tanks. . . .

Sincerely,
(Sgd) Dwight D. Eisenhower

21st September

Dear Ike, thank you very much for your letter of 20 Sep sent via Gale. I cannot agree that our concepts are the same and I am sure you would wish me to be quite frank and open in the matter. I have always said stop the right and go on with left, but the right has been allowed to go on so far that it has outstripped its maintenance and we have lost flexibility. In your letter you still want to go on further with your right and you state in your para. 6 that all of Bradley's Army Group will move forward sufficiently etc. I would say that the right flank of 12 Army Group should be given a very direct order to halt and if this order is not obeyed we shall get into greater difficulties. The net result of the matter in my opinion is that if you want to get the Ruhr you will have to put every single thing into the left hook and stop everything else. It is my opinion that if this is not done then you will not get the Ruhr. Your very great friend Monty.

4.6 Generals Bradley and Patton Express Their Anger at Montgomery, April 1943 and December 1944[6]

The 1944 strategic dispute between Eisenhower and Montgomery was far from the first or the only disagreement between them and between Montgomery and other U.S. commanders such as Generals Bradley and Patton, who not only disagreed with the British general's strategic ideas but also found his attitude and arrogance insufferable.

6. From Omar N. Bradley and Clay Blair, *A General's Life* (New York: Simon & Schuster, 1983), 165–66, 369–72, 375–76.

Reproduced here are excerpts from Bradley's 1983 memoirs, in which he describes their conflicts during both the 1943 planning for the invasion of Sicily and the late 1944 planning for the invasion of Germany.

During the December Battle of the Bulge, German forces had attacked General Courtney Hodges's U.S. 1st Army, driving a deep wedge into Bradley's 12th Army Group. As a result, Eisenhower gave Montgomery temporary command over the 1st Army as well as General William Simpson's U.S. 9th Army to its north, leaving Bradley in command of only General Patton's 3rd U.S. Army. Once the German advance had been halted, conflict erupted once again at SHAEF (Supreme Headquarters, Allied Expeditionary Forces) over how to proceed, with Montgomery pressing for retention of the two U.S. armies and a single thrust into Germany by his now reinforced 21st Army Group and Bradley as well as Patton for their return to 12th Army Group and a very different plan for the invasion and conquest of Germany. By year's end the personality and strategic conflicts had reached a boiling point.

. . . In the following week there were new, urgent and acrimonious Allied meetings all across North Africa, culminating in an emergency meeting of the board in Algiers May 2 to hear a new plan conceived by Monty. Montgomery, Cunningham and Tedder made it, but Alexander and Patton were grounded by bad weather. Monty buttonholed Bedell Smith in the men's room and "sold" his plan with little difficulty. Basically, Monty proposed that Patton's landing at Palermo be canceled and his Seventh Army shifted across the island to land adjacent to Monty's Eighth Army on the south coast near Gela. In sum: a massive concentration of Allied strength in a single area, rather than the dispersed pincer concept.

When the full board finally got together in Algiers in subsequent days, Ike and Alexander fully endorsed Monty's radical changes. Tedder and Cunningham voiced many grave reservations. Basically, they did not want to forgo the pincer concept and thought Monty's plan too conservative. However, in the end, they yielded, Cunningham very reluctantly. Throughout the discussions, Patton, though he disapproved of Monty's plan, was untypically reserved and closed-mouthed. He assumed the pose of a loyal soldier who would follow whatever orders were given him.

In these various meetings, which for the first time brought Monty into close association with the Americans, he came across as pompous, abrasive, demanding and almost insufferably vain. Ike summed up his opinion of Monty in a letter to Marshall:

> Montgomery is of different caliber from some of the outstanding British leaders you have met. He is unquestionably able, but very conceited. For your most secret and confidential information, I will give you my opinion

which is that he is so proud of his successes to date that he will never willingly make a single move until he is absolutely certain of success—in other
words, until he has concentrated enough resources so that anybody could
practically guarantee the outcome. . . . Unquestionably he is an able tactician
and organizer and, provided only that Alexander will never let him forget
for one second who is the boss, he should deliver in good style. . . .

What none of the board members quite realized at the time was that
Montgomery had set a stage on which he meant to be the principal actor.
Sicily would merely become a larger-scale version of Monty's Mareth line
breakout, with Patton's Seventh Army playing a supporting role, just as our
II Corps had played a supporting role to the Eighth Army in Tunisia. In
part, Alexander had ceded this leading role to Monty because of his linger-
ing distrust of the American GI. . . .

* * * *

On Christmas Day Monty telephoned, suggesting an immediate conference to coordinate our maneuvers. I welcomed the invitation, hoping it
might give me an opportunity to build a fire under him. I flew to his headquarters near St. Trond, Belgium. There was no aide at the airport to meet
us—not even a car and driver. This I took to be a calculated insult. I was so
put out I told my aide Chet Hansen we should go home. But Hansen found
one of Hodges' staffers, who offered his car. After a fumbling search through
unfamiliar ground, we located Monty's headquarters. Neither Monty nor
anyone else offered us anything to eat or drink. I determined to make my
visit as short as possible and, in fact, it lasted a mere thirty minutes.

Monty was more arrogant and egotistical than I had ever seen him. He
began by lecturing and scolding me like a schoolboy. . . .

Never in my life had I been so enraged and so utterly exasperated. It
required every fiber of my strength to restrain myself from an insulting
outburst. Somehow I remained silent, seething inside, nodding as Monty
imperiously rattled on. I admitted to nothing. In fact, I silently disagreed
with every word he uttered. However, to avoid a potentially crippling
breakdown in the Allied command, I kept my counsel.

Even more dismaying was Monty's view of future courses of action. Far
from being beaten, the Germans had sufficient strength for another blow,
he believed. Hodges' First Army was too weak to do anything but hold.
Hodges desperately needed replacements. It would be *three months* before
Hodges would be ready for a major offensive. Patton's offensive was futile;
it was too weak and would accomplish nothing. Patton should break off

the attack and withdraw to defensive positions along a line the Saar River–Vosges Mountains or even the Moselle River and supply Hodges with more divisions. In sum, Monty's view was that all Allied armies should go completely to the defensive, regroup and gear up for a single-thrust offensive led by him, some time in the distant future.

Although Monty's penchant for tedious planning, the massive build-up and the "set piece" battle were only too well known, it seemed to me that he talked like a man who had lost touch with reality. Every scrap of intelligence we had available, including a mountain of Ultra, indicated beyond doubt that owing to our rapid and effective countermeasures and the courage of the individual American soldier, Hitler's last great ill-advised gamble had failed. His panzers had run out of gas and ammo. He had suffered enormous casualties. His air power had not been effective in the slightest; with the coming of favorable weather, we were now in a position to savagely apply our own overwhelming air power. *Now* was the time to hit back. Not three months from now.

I flew back to my headquarters in a dark mood. Later that evening I had a long talk with Patton, relaying the substance of Monty's views. Patton was apoplectic. He wrote in his diary: "I feel this is disgusting. . . . If ordered to fall back, I think I will ask to be relieved."

The next morning I got Bedell Smith on the telephone. This time I was no shrinking violet. I let him have it with both barrels. I told him Monty insisted on going over to the defensive and was throwing away an opportunity to inflict a devastating defeat on the enemy. I asked in no uncertain terms that the First and Ninth armies be returned to my operation command so that I could get some action in the north. I would move my headquarters to Namur to assure coordination of all U.S. forces. I stressed that we *had to act now.* . . .

My pressure on SHAEF compelled an immediate reconsideration of future planning. Tedder noted that I was "very disturbed" at Monty's "purely defensive view." My own views could no longer be ignored or dismissed. Accordingly, Ike called for a meeting in Brussels for the next day, December 27, with Monty and me. . . .

The Brussels meeting had to be postponed by one day, to December 28, because the train Ike was scheduled to take had been bombed by the Luftwaffe. Owing to that development, Ike suggested that I meet him at SHAEF on the 27th. I welcomed the opportunity to see Ike before he saw Monty. It would give me further opportunity to stress the urgent need for a quick and decisive action. Patton wrote in his diary: "Bradley left at 1000 to see Ike. . . . If Ike will put Bradley back in command of the First and Ninth Armies, we can bag the whole German Army. I wish Ike were more of a gambler, but he is certainly a lion compared to Montgomery, and

Bradley is better than Ike as far as nerve is concerned. . . . Monty is a tired little fart. War requires the taking of risks and he won't take them." . . .

My presentation included both short-term and long-term strategy proposals. For the short term I urged an immediate pincer attack against the waist of the German salient. . . . I would move my Twelfth Army Group headquarters to Namur or Dinant in order to coordinate operations of both Patton and Hodges. I urged that this attack begin *at once.*

For the long term, I proposed a substantial change in Allied strategy, designed to quickly exploit Hitler's blunder of the Bulge. Instead of putting our main effort to reach the Rhine in the north under Monty as originally planned, I proposed that we now put our main effort through the center under me. The armies of Hodges and Patton would advance eastward abreast, on a north-south line commencing just south of the Roer dam area and extending farther south into the Ardennes. This great mass would follow in hot pursuit of the retreating Germans through the Eifel to the Bonn area, cross the Rhine and proceed toward the good open tank country lying between Frankfurt and Kassel. At the same time Monty, with his British and Canadian armies, would cross the Rhine and go north of the Ruhr, protecting our left flank. Devers would remain on the defensive in the Saar area. . . .

Ike was more forceful and commanding that I had ever seen him. "Calamity acted on Eisenhower like a restorative," Alan Brooke wrote, "and brought out all the greatness in his character." This was true and the change was remarkable. I soon saw that Ike was not going to rubber-stamp my plans as he had so often done in the past. From now on, Ike would run the war; he would make the major decisions.

He would not make any formal decisions until he met with Monty. However, he did agree with me completely on the short-term strategy: cutting the German salient in the waist at Houffalize. Monty, I then learned, was also now apparently swinging to my point of view. Earlier in the day he had telephoned Ike to say that he was now ready to consider a definite counterattack, leading Ike to comment, "Praise God from Whom all blessings flow." He likewise agreed that I should shift my headquarters to the Namur area. But he refused to return control of Hodges to me until his forces and Patton's had screwed the cap on the tub at Houffalize. That was a sharp personal disappointment.

As to my long-term proposal for a "hurry up" offensive through the center, Ike was less enthusiastic. He now held the view that nobody was going to jump on the Rhine on the run, as we had jumped the Seine. He would risk no more Bulges; he wanted a strong, easily defended line from which he would plunge into the heart of Germany. The most easily defended line was the Rhine River. Ike believed we must wipe out German forces west of the Rhine along its entire length, then all draw up to the Rhine abreast before the final big push. For that big push, he still favored putting the bulk of our weight in the north under Monty, with Simpson's Ninth Army reinforcing him.

At the same time, however, he saw the advantages of my "hurry up" offensive. If successful, it could at least get the Allied center to the Rhine. It would keep pressure on the Germans until Monty regrouped from his Bulge redeployment. Ike approved it, informally, with sharp limitations. If my attack failed to achieve early promise of "decisive success" he would halt it. He did not want it to develop into another ghastly war of attrition. Moreover, the plan was subject to review at any time, and if Ike so decided, I was to go on the defensive without questions or objection.

There was one final sticky point. Under my plan, Simpson's Ninth Army would assist in the "hurry up" offensive by taking over the First Army front in the Roer dam area. Although I had long reconciled myself to the fact that Monty would keep the Ninth Army, I thought it would be advantageous for U.S. morale if the Ninth Army returned to my command temporarily for the "hurry up" offensive. If Hodges bogged down in the Eifel, I could use Simpson to put pressure on the Düren area. But Ike was adamant on this point. Now that Monty had the Ninth Army, it would remain under his command. He said that he had "fought the propaganda to put Marshal Montgomery in command [of all ground forces] so long it was wearing him out." By leaving the Ninth Army under Monty, "he might be able to shut up the element that was trying to put everything under Marshal Montgomery." I was extremely disappointed in this decision, angered that political decisions were adversely affecting tactical operations.

The next day, December 28, Ike went by train to confer with Monty. Poor weather conditions compelled them to meet in Hasselt, Belgium. Since I had already made my views quite clear, there was no need for me to attend this meeting. When they sat down to talk, Ike was keenly disappointed to learn that Monty's apparent willingness to go immediately to the offensive against the German salient was not quite true. Based on Ultra reports, Monty was now convinced that the Germans would stage one last great attack in the north against Hodges. He thought the best strategy was to absorb this attack, *then* counterattack. . . .

Heretofore Ike had been reluctant to impose his operational ideas and plans on Monty, leaving him a free hand. But this time he was not. He compelled Monty to commit to a quick, definite plan. If the German offensive did not materialize within three days, by January 1, Monty was to "start driving." That is, launch Collins' VII Corps in a counter offensive, with Ridgway's XVIII Airborne Corps supporting his left flank. If the German attack did come, Monty was to absorb it and then "drive in on him on the rebound." Under no circumstances was there to be a typical long Montgomery-type buildup followed by a set-piece battle.

Beyond that, Ike and Monty discussed long-term strategy. Ike described my plan for the "hurry up" offensive and stated his own desire to have everybody draw up to the Rhine before launching the final big push. This news apparently came as a shock to Monty, leading him to lecture and scold Ike as he had me. Brooke noted in his diary: "Monty had another interview with Ike. I do not like the account of it. It looks to me as if Monty, with his usual lack of tact, has been rubbing into Ike the results of not having listened to Monty's advice." Monty took sharp exception both to my "hurry up" offensive and Ike's broad-front approach to the Rhine River. My offensive would be a waste of precious resources. He insisted that it be canceled, that all fronts other than his go on the defensive so that he could lead a single massive assault into Germany's heartland. For best results, I should come completely under his command. Monty later wrote Alan Brooke to say that Ike had agreed with his strategic concepts, but this was either another gross misunderstanding or a deliberate distortion on Monty's part.

On returning to SHAEF, Ike, having now conferred with both Monty and me, drew up an "outline plan" for short- and long-term operations. The plan approved two of my major proposals: a short-term offensive to close pincers on the waist of the German salient and my long-term "hurry up" offensive with the aforementioned restrictions. To prod Monty and make it clear that he expected an all-out effort from the north on the short-term strategy, Ike specified to Monty that we would utilize "everything consistent with minimum security requirements." Following that operation, I would resume command of the First Army (but not the Ninth) for my offensive, which would go northeast toward Bonn and "eventually to the Rhine." When all enemy forces west of the Rhine had been destroyed, we would prepare to cross the Rhine with the *main effort north of the Ruhr.* (Ike's italics.)

Monty clearly lost this round. I had not had my way completely, but at least Monty had been ordered to go all-out on the short-term effort to cut the German salient at the waist; and, against Monty's counsel, Ike had approved my limited offensive.

Before Ike could cable this plan to us, Monty composed and sent to Ike a formal letter summarizing his views on long-term operations. This letter was an arrogant and unequivocal *demand* that my "hurry up" offensive be canceled, that I and all my armies be placed under Monty's operational control (making Monty, in effect, land commander) for a single massive Allied thrust north of the Ruhr, and that Ike's plan to draw all armies up to the Rhine be scrapped.

"I think we want to be careful," Monty wrote, "because we have had one very definite failure. . . . I therefore consider that it will be necessary for you to be very firm on the subject, and any loosely worded statement will be quite useless." He went on to say that since Ike "cannot possibly" be land commander himself, "you would have to nominate someone else." That person, Monty said, should be "C in C 21 Army Group"—Monty. He would have "full operational direction, control and coordinate of" all operations in the north. "I put this matter to you again because I am so anxious not to have another failure," he continued. He was "absolutely convinced" that *all* offensive power had to be thrown behind his northern operation and that "a sound set-up for command" had to be established. "I am certain," he concluded, "that if we do not comply with these two basic conditions, then we will fail again." . . .

Monty's letter, the pro-Monty and anti-Ike press campaign in Britain, and the news that Monty would not launch Collins and Ridgway until January 3 (five days behind Patton's attack), sent Ike and Bedell Smith into a towering rage and precipitated a command High Noon. Ike, now reassured of his position by Marshall, began drafting a letter to the Combined Chiefs of Staff in which he, in effect, asked them to choose between him and Monty. Inasmuch as the United States now had the preponderance of military power on the Continent, there would be no question about the outcome: Monty would be sacked.

That same day, December 30, Monty's chief of staff, Freddie de Guingand, after talking to Bigland and Bedell Smith, realized that an "extremely dangerous situation had developed." Determined to seek peace, he flew through a snowstorm to Paris, raced to SHAEF by car, and hurried on to Bedell Smith's office. Smith told de Guingand that "the matter had practically reached a stage where nothing more could be done about it." Nonetheless, Smith escorted him to see Ike.

Ike was in conference with Tedder, editing the me-or-Monty cable to the Combined Chiefs. De Guingand recalled: "The Supreme Commander looked really tired and worried. He very quietly started to explain how serious matters were. He told me that Bradley's position had become intolerable, and that there was every chance that he would lose the confidence of his troops. This would be most unfortunate and might mean his losing one of his ablest commanders. He asked me whether my Chief fully realized the effects of the line taken up by the British Press, and how Monty himself had helped to create this crisis by his campaign for a Land Force Commander and by the indiscreet remarks he had passed. Eisenhower went on to say that he was tired of the whole business, and had come to the conclusion that it was now a matter for the Combined Chiefs to make a decision. It was quite obvious that with Montgomery still pressing for a Land Force Commander it was impossible for the two of them to carry on working in harness together." Ike then gave de Guingand the cable to read. De Guingand saw that Ike had gone so far as to propose Alexander as Monty's replacement.

De Guingand was "stunned." He implored Ike to delay the cable twenty-four hours to give him an opportunity to "solve the impasse." He was "absolutely convinced" Monty had no idea "things had become so serious." Neither Ike nor Tedder was inclined to delay, stressing the "damage which had already been done." But Bedell Smith, to de Guingand's "intense relief," advised giving de Guingand a chance, and after "quite a time," Ike and Tedder relented.

The next day, December 31, de Guingand, racing against time, and suffering "a very bad attack of nerves," flew back through heavy weather to Monty's headquarters. He briefed his boss on his impending professional catastrophe, pointedly showing him a copy of Marshall's cable to Ike, and mentioning that Alexander had been proposed as Monty's replacement. Monty appeared to be "genuinely and completely taken by surprise" and found it "difficult to grasp" what de Guingand was saying, and "extremely hard to believe it possible" that he might be relieved of command. When Monty did at last grasp the gravity of the crisis, de Guingand recalled, "He looked completely non-plussed—I don't think I had ever seen him so deflated. It was as if a cloak of loneliness had descended upon him."

"What shall I do, Freddie?" Monty asked helplessly.

De Guingand had already anticipated that question and drafted a letter of apology and retreat to Ike. Monty read the signal, marked it "most immediate," "top secret," and "personal for Eisenhower, for his eyes only," and sent it off. The letter:

> Dear Ike, Have seen Freddie and understand you are greatly worried by many considerations in these very difficult days. I have given you my frank views because I have felt you like this. I am sure there are many factors which have a bearing quite beyond anything I realize. Whatever your decision may be you can rely on me one hundred per cent to make it work, and I know Brad will do the same. Very distressed that my letter may have upset you and I would ask you to tear it up. Your very devoted servant, Monty.

The letter did the trick. With it, de Guingand pulled Monty's chestnuts out of the fire. Ike apparently destroyed his own letter to the Combined Chiefs; no trace of it was ever found. De Guingand met with a committee of British war correspondents, frankly described what had happened and pleaded with them to ask their editors to cool the pro-Monty, anti-American propaganda and the campaign to make Monty lead commander. There followed an abrupt silence on the matter in most responsible Fleet Street organs.

On December 31, Ike forwarded his "outline plan" to Monty and me. In a covering letter to Monty, he wrote, tactfully but firmly:

> You know how greatly I've appreciated and depended upon your frank and friendly counsel, but in your latest letter you disturb me by predictions of "failure" unless your exact opinions in the matter of giving you command over Bradley are met in detail. I assure you that in this matter I can go no further. . . . For my part I would deplore the development of such an unbridgeable gulf of convictions between us that we would have to present our differences to the Combined Chiefs of Staff. The confusion and debate that would follow would certainly damage the good will and devotion to a common cause that have made this Allied Force unique in history.

I have the greatest admiration for the firm manner in which Ike handled this episode, the most taxing command crisis of the war. But the attack was not yet over. In the distance, Alan Brooke and Churchill were preparing for another assault on the U.S. command.

4.7 General Marshall Explains the Key Military Events in German Defeat as Perceived by Captured Members of the German High Command, September 1945[7]

In his 1945 public biennial report, Army Chief of Staff General George C. Marshall listed and explained seven key military events that led to German defeat as perceived by captured members of the German High Command. Note how many of these did and how many did not involve U.S. forces as opposed to solely British or solely Soviet forces.

The steps in the German defeat, as described by captured members of the High Command, were:

1. *Failure to invade England.* Hitler's first military setback occurred when, after the collapse of France, England did not capitulate. According to Colonel General Jodl, Chief of the Operations Staff of the German High Command, the campaign in France had been undertaken because it was estimated that with the fall of France, England would not continue to fight. The unexpectedly swift victory over France and Great Britain's

---

7. From *Biennial Reports of the Chief of Staff of the United States Army to the Secretary of War, 1 July 1939 to 30 June 1945* (Washington, DC: U.S. Army Center of Military History, 1996), 108–9.

continuation of the war found the General Staff unprepared for an invasion of England. . . .

2. *The Campaign of 1941 in the Soviet Union.* In the autumn of 1941 after the battle of Vysma, the Germans stood exhausted but apparently victorious before Moscow. According to Jodl, the General Staff of the armed forces considered that one last energetic push would be sufficient to finish the Soviets. The German High Command had neither envisioned nor planned for a winter campaign. A sudden storm, and extremely unseasonable cold in the Christmas week of 1941 precipitated the strategic defeat of the German armed forces. Impatient of all restraint, Hitler publicly announced that he had more faith in his own intuition than in the judgment of his military advisers. He relieved the Commander in Chief of the Army, General Von Brauschitsch. It was the turning point of the war.

3. *Stalingrad.* Even after the reverse before Moscow in 1941, Germany might have avoided defeat had it not been for the campaign in 1942 which culminated in the disaster at Stalingrad. Disregarding the military lessons of history, Hitler, instead of attacking the Soviet armies massed in the north, personally planned and directed a campaign of which the immediate objectives were to deprive the Soviet Union of her vital industries and raw materials by cutting the Volga at Stalingrad and seizing the Caucasian oil fields. Beyond these concrete objectives was evidently the Napoleonic dream of a conquest of the Middle East and India by a gigantic double envelopment with one pincer descending from the Caucasus through Tiflis and the other from North Africa across Egypt, Palestine, and the Arabian desert. The campaign collapsed before Stalingrad with the magnificent Russian defense of that city and in the northern foothills of the Caucasus. . . .

4. *Invasion of North Africa.* Allied landings in North Africa came as a surprise to the German High Command. . . . Allied security and deception measures for the landing operations were found to have been highly effective. . . .

5. *The Invasion of France.* All German headquarters expected the Allied invasion of France. According to Colonel General Jodl, both the general direction and the strength of the initial assault in Normandy were correctly estimated; but Field Marshal Keitel states that the Germans were not sure exactly where the Allies would strike and considered Brittany as more probable because of the three major U-boat bases located in that region. Both agree that the belief of the German High Command that a second assault would be launched, probably by an army under General Patton, held large German forces in the Pas-de-Calais area. Both Keitel and Jodl believed that the invasion could be repulsed or at worst contained, and both named the Allied air arm as the decisive factor in the German failure. . . .

6. *The Ardennes Counterattack.* The German offensive in December 1944 was Hitler's personal conception. According to Jodl, the objective of the attack was Antwerp. It was hoped that overcast weather would neutralize Allied air superiority, and that an exceptionally rapid initial break-through could be achieved. Other German officers believe that this operation was reckless in the extreme, in that it irreparably damaged the comparatively fresh armored divisions of the Sixth Panzer Army, the principal element of Germany's strategic reserve, at a moment when every available reserve was needed to repulse the expected Soviet attack in the east.

7. *The Crossing of the Rhine.* Even after the failure of the German counteroffensive in the Ardennes, the Germans believed that the Rhine line could be held. The loss of the Remagen bridge, however, exploded this hope. The entire Rhine defensive line had to be weakened in the attempt to contain the bridgehead, and the disorderly German retreat in the Saar and Palatinate rendered easy the subsequent drive eastward of the Allied armies toward Hamburg, Leipzig, and Munich.

4.8 Tuskegee Airman Lieutenant Alexander Jefferson Recalls His Combat Missions and Internment, 1944[8]

The American servicemen who fought in World War II came from diverse backgrounds, and many of them faced racial discrimination in the armed forces as well as at home. African Americans, for example, were racially segregated within each service as well as within civilian society, and they were frequently assigned only to menial, noncombat tasks during the war. One of the most notable exceptions to this pattern were the Tuskegee Airmen, Black fighter pilots who amassed a superb record. This document comes from the memoirs of one of those pilots, Lieutenant Alexander Jefferson, who was shot down by the Germans in 1944 and became a prisoner of war (POW). Jefferson later rose to the rank of lieutenant colonel and in civilian life became a public school science teacher and assistant principal in Detroit.

I have no detailed record of the missions I flew, but I know I flew eighteen without ever missing a scheduled mission until I was shot down on August 12, 1944. We normally flew long-range missions, escorting B-24s and

---

8. From Alexander Jefferson, "Memoirs of a Luft Gan[g]ster"; repr. in Alexander Jefferson, *Red Tail Captured, Red Tail Free: The Memoirs of a Tuskegee Airman and POW* (New York: Fordham University Press, 2005), 40–47, 52–58, 76, 106–7.

B-17s to their targets over Greece, Bulgaria, Hungary, Poland, Germany, and France, but we also flew strafing missions. I flew mostly as a wingman and did not have my own plane until just before my final missions. When new planes arrived or new engines were installed, the older pilots always had first choice. As a replacement pilot, I had to fly what was left. When I finally did get my own plane, I named her *Margo*, for the young lady I met while on leave in Washington, D.C.

Our missions followed a prescribed routine. We'd awake by any means we could, trying not to disturb our tent mates in case they were not scheduled to fly and wanted to sleep. We'd wash, shave, brush our teeth, and then head for the mess tent, where we'd eat some very strange-tasting food that I suspect was flavored by the hundred-octane gas that fueled the stoves. After this unsavory breakfast, we'd return to our tents, put on our flying suits, boots, gloves, chutes, goggles, and watches, grab our cigarettes, and head to the group briefing tent. The briefing officer was usually Colonel Davis, the group commander, or his operations officer, Major Ed Gleed. A huge map of the entire European theater covered the wall. If a red string extended from Ramitelli and a green string from another airfield in Italy came together around the coast of Yugoslavia, we knew it would be an escort mission.

Someone would shout, "Attention," and the briefing officer would enter. We would pop to and stand at attention. The briefing officer would respond, "At ease!" and everyone would sit down.

If the briefing officer said "Gentlemen, today we go to Ploiesti," he would be greeted with a resounding "Oh s-----!" If there was only one red string ending in an area occupied by the enemy, it was a strafing mission, which usually also brought expletives from the fighter pilots because this meant being exposed to ground fire from enemy troops. If it was an escort mission, we would also be told whether we would be protecting B-17s or B-24s. We much preferred B-24s because the B-17s were slower, and we had to stay with them longer, which meant we used too much of our precious fuel.

The briefing officer would tell us the type of mission, the mission target, intelligence reports on anticipated ground fire and aerial attacks at the target, and possible partisan support, including what they might be wearing and their identifying armbands or headbands.

For a mission to Ploiesti, Romania, the line would angle northeast with a dip marking the place and time where we would pick up the bombers and another dip showing the time and place we would release them and to whom. We would then mark course, altitude, position, and bomber and fighter IDs on pads strapped to our knees.

We would synchronize our watches and received our engine startup and takeoff time, as well as our start-on course time, our estimated rendezvous time and place, and the estimated total mission time. An intelligence officer would then come in and give the latest flak report, informing us which areas to avoid because of heavy concentrations. These reports were invariably wrong, as we almost always encountered the most devastating flak over areas that intelligence had assured us were perfectly safe. In fact, for many World War II airmen, the term "military intelligence" still evokes laughter. . . .

We would pile out of the briefing shack, get in jeeps and trucks, and ride to our planes. In the meantime, our mechanics had been up most of the night preflighting our aircraft. We would walk around our planes and talk with the crew chiefs about any concerns. We'd then strap ourselves in, start the engines, check the dials, and clamp our feet on the brakes to prevent any premature movement of the 10,000-pound plane. For these missions, we had 92 gallons of gas inside each wing, 100 gallons hanging under each wing, and another 85 gallons in a tank behind the pilot. We also had two 50-caliber guns in each wing with 300 rounds for each gun.

We had only one runway from which all four squadrons would take off. Two squadrons would take off from each end. After the magneto engine check, the planes would sit idling until takeoff time. The lead plane would taxi onto the runway, waiting for the tower to fire off a green flare exactly at takeoff time. The Group Leader would then start rolling down the runway. Number two would follow close behind. Number three would move into place so he could follow. Fighting the turbulence of the preceding planes now became a challenge. This continued until sixteen planes and the two spares had taken off. It was then that the lead plane of the second squadron would start his takeoff from the other end of the same runway.

While awaiting takeoff, with that big eleven-foot prop spinning and those 1,500 horses pulling the plane, your pulse begins to race, especially when you look down the line and see the other fifteen planes in your squadron slowly easing forward to begin taxiing down the ramp. Canopies are open, and the noise is deafening but exhilarating. You just hope the bastard behind you doesn't let up on his brakes and chew your tail off, or that the so-and-so on your left has his gun switch off or his finger off the trigger so he doesn't blow you to smithereens. You sit at the end of the runway and wait, your plane throbbing and threatening to bolt. Your legs are tied in knots from clamping your feet on the brakes. Fumes and dust penetrate your oxygen mask. There you sit, locked in, unable to move, worrying about somebody's prop chewing on your left and your prop threatening the guy on your right. Finally, you look to your left and watch the 99th beginning to take off from the other end of the strip directly toward you. The first few guys pass over about fifty feet out in front of you. As number five and six begin to hit the turbulence of the previous guys, they wobble back and forth. You look up, and a P-51 sails over your head with about ten to fifteen feet to spare!

After the eighteen get off, sixteen plus two spares, it finally becomes our turn. Bubble Blue Leader wheels out and we turn and taxi out to take off behind him. Throttle forward, engine pulling sixty inches of mercury, mixture rich, using left main tank, mags checked, dials in the green, prop pitch low, throttle pushed forward, forced back in seat by the tremendous acceleration, watching airspeed, easing off a bit, watching the torque, queuing in on the element leader, cutting him off, while he's cutting off the flight leader who is cutting of the squadron leader, who is cutting off the group leader: a giant luftberry in the sky, made up of seventy-two circling planes. The group circles the field twice before everyone is ready to get into tight formation: Four squadrons, seventy-two planes, off to pick up B-17s or B-24s.

One of my most vivid memories of combat is sitting above those B-17s. It was always mind-boggling to look back as far as the eye could reach and see that ten to fifteen-mile string of bombers that might include as many as a thousand planes. Up above, you'd see the contrails of our P-51s zigzagging back and forth over the straight contrails of the bombers. Typically, if the B-17s were flying at 24,000 feet, the 99th squadron would be at 25,000 feet, the 100th at 26,000 feet, the 101st at 27,000 feet, and the 302nd at 28,000 feet. Because the bombers were so much slower, each fighter squadron would zigzag back and forth at 220 mph over the B-17s, which were flying at 160 mph. Occasionally a squadron might be forced up to 32,000 feet, but in such thin air, one had to avoid sharp maneuvers, or the mushy controls might cause the plane to spin out.

So many things happen simultaneously: planes switching tanks, radios squawking, "Bogies (meaning unknown planes) at three o'clock," and then a loose, ragged formation automatically tightening when someone hollers, "Get the hell out of my ass!" Eyes get sharper, breathing becomes more rapid, heads weave right and left. Bubble Blue Leader comes in curt and sharp, "Bubble Blue, drop tanks on mark." Immediately you switch your fuel from wing tanks to internal. Most of us had already done so when we first heard someone holler, "Bogie." The sight of sixteen P-51s dropping tanks was spectacular: thirty-two silvery, bullet-shaped objects dropping like huge drops of rain, and often seeing the German planes turning away and refusing to come in.

Many escort missions were monotonous, five or six-hour rides, but they could also be exhilarating. I remember on my fourth or fifth mission our squadron got eight or nine kills. I didn't see a single one, because I was too busy flying my element's wing, protecting his rear end. Above all, there was a great feeling of relief when all our planes returned safely to base.

My most unforgettable mission was flying cover over the Ploiesti oil fields. After we picked up our bombers at the border of Hungary and Romania, we encountered only sporadic anti-aircraft fire on the way to the target. Then, some fifteen or twenty miles ahead, I saw a huge black cloud, shaped like a hockey puck, from 20,000 feet to about 26,000 feet. I could see a series of fires and lots of smoke rising from the ground underneath it, which appeared to be an oil refinery complex. The B-17s flew out on a sixty-degree angle and then aimed directly for that black cloud. We pulled off to the left and orbited while they disappeared into the black cloud. Then, we saw four or five B-17s falling out of the bottom of the cloud, spinning down lazily, trailing smoke and flames. Unconsciously, I yelled, "Bail out, damn it! Get out of there!" Out of one of the planes I counted one, two, three chutes opening up. Then there was a big whoosh. The B-17 had exploded in a huge red ball of flames. Realism set in: three chutes had opened; that meant seven men had died, right there in front of my eyes. Seven men no longer existed. I threw up into my oxygen mask— at 31,000 feet. That experience—including my crew chief's refusing to clean my oxygen mask after I returned to base—burned itself into my mind. . . .

On August 12, 1944, I was a pilot with the 301st Fighter Squadron, 332nd Fighter Group, 15th Air Force. I was flying my nineteenth mission, which was to strafe and knock out radar stations at Toulon Harbor on the southern coast of France to prevent the Germans from detecting the Allied invasion ships, which three days later, as part of Operation Dragoon, would land between Marseilles and Nice.

It was a beautiful clear day, with unlimited visibility, when our sixteen P-51s flew in over the coast in four flights of four each. The first three sets of four went in, hit the target at low level, and flew out to sea. We were the last flight. As we dived in from 15,000 feet at about 400 knots, I was Tail-End Charlie, which meant I was the last plane to go in. When our squadron leader called for us to drop our hundred-gallon tanks, somehow my tanks got hung up and I was slow dropping them. In order to catch up, I had to push everything to the wall, with my airspeed almost redlined. I was pulling about sixty inches of manifold pressure, the plane was shaking and rocking, but I did get back into position just before our flight began to fire on the target.

Halfway down, I could see blinking red lights over the target; in fact, the entire side of the cliff in front of the radar towers was covered with anti-aircraft fire. About a thousand yards from the target, out of the corner of my eye, I saw Bob Daniels's number two plane take two direct hits. He began trailing black smoke and headed out to sea. I found out later he had elected to set down on the water, which was not advised, because the air scoop could pull the plane under water before the pilot could extricate himself. Nevertheless, Daniels got out and floated on the water until the Germans picked him up.

By this time, we were down to three hundred feet, flying at more than 400 mph. Looking ahead, I could see the first flight of four getting hits on the towers and veering out to sea. Right behind them came the second and third flights, which also got their hits and banked out to sea. Then we came into position. With the target in range, my ship was bucking and shaking. Anti-aircraft fire was coming up on all sides. My oil pressure and coolant temp needles were in the red, with everything else at the top of the green, about to go red.

As I passed over the target at about fifty feet, I felt a loud thump shake the plane. I glanced at the instrument panel, and now everything was in the red. I felt a tremendous rush of air. I looked up and there was a hole in the top of my canopy just in front of my head. I thought, "What the hell?" Fire and smoke were filling the cockpit. I looked down and saw that flames were coming up through a hole in the floor between my feet and scorching my gloves and boots. I pulled up into a loop to get some altitude, jerked the red knob on the instrument panel, and popped the canopy. At the same time, I racked in the forward trim tab on the elevator with my left hand. At the top of the loop, I punched the safety belt release and let go of the stick. The forward trim tab was supposed to pitch the nose down, but because the plane was upside down, the nose went up abruptly and I was thrown out. I figure I got out at about eight hundred feet.

I can still see the tail, including the rivets, as it went whizzing by. I pulled the D-ring. I looked at it in my hand and thought, "Some SOB sold the silk." The rumor back at the base was that someone had been stealing the silk out of the parachutes and selling it to the Italians. So when my chute did not immediately open, I thought that had happened to me. But just then the chute popped, and all I could see was green. I fell through some trees and hit squarely on my feet and rolled over. I sustained cuts and bruises on my arms and legs. Fortunately, I was wearing paratrooper jump boots because they gave extra support to my ankles.

At the time, things are happening so fast you don't have time to get scared. It's only a couple of days later, when you have time to think about what happened, that it all hits you. Intelligence had told us French resistance fighters were in the area, so we were supposed to dig a hole, hide our parachute, and wait for the French to find us. Hell, I hit the ground, rolled over, and looked up into the muzzle of a Mauser and a German soldier saying, "Ja, Ja, Herr Lieutenant. Für Sie ist der Krieg vorbei." ("Ah, yes Lieutenant. For you the war is over.") I had landed right in the middle of the 20 mm gun crew that had shot me down.

The other guys in my flight had looked back and saw my plane go in, but they didn't see me get out. They thought I had bought the farm and reported me killed in action. My mother and dad subsequently received the dreaded KIA telegram. Not until several weeks later did the International Red Cross notify them that I was a prisoner of war.

The first things my captors took were my cigarettes, my Parker pen, and my wristwatch. They then transported me in a car several miles east of Toulon to a small villa overlooking the Mediterranean. A German officer was seated at a glass table on the veranda. I saluted because he had rank on his shoulders. In perfect English, he said, "Have a seat, lieutenant, and thanks for the Lucky Strikes!" He spoke very formally and asked me how things were in the States. I replied, as S-2 had instructed us, with name, rank and serial number. He ignored this and asked if I had ever been in Atlanta. I told him I hadn't, although of course, I had spent four years attending Clark College. He talked about the black clubs on Auburn Avenue and the good times he had enjoyed in the various bars and hotels. He then asked if I had ever been in Washington, D.C. I again told him no, even though I had attended Howard University.

He then proceeded to tell me about his days at the University of Michigan, naming streets, fraternity houses, and restaurants. It turned out he had graduated from the University of Michigan in 1936, with a Ph.D. in political science.

After returning to Germany, he was called into the army and eventually assigned to the anti-aircraft unit that shot me down. He was a jazz fan and talked about the Howard Theater and the Crystal Caverns nightclub in Washington, where all the black jazz artists appeared, and then he started talking about Detroit's Paradise Valley. His whole demeanor changed and he became much friendlier. He told me about boarding the Oakland streetcar next to the library behind the J. L. Hudson Department Store in downtown Detroit, and how it proceeded east on Adams, past the "Colored" YMCA and the Three Sixes Nightclub and then turned north on Hastings and then west on Forest Street, where Sonny Wilson's Bar was on the corner. He even named the bartenders and the girls across the street in the "hotel." For the next thirty minutes or so, I sat listening while he smoked my Lucky Strikes and excitedly told me about his Detroit experiences, especially about all the fun he had while drinking and carousing with the local girls. He finally said to me, "Some of the best times in my life were spent in the Valley. Let's hope this war ends soon so we can get back to the things that really matter." With that he offered me one of my cigarettes, shook my hand, then stood on the porch in a typical Nazi stance, watching silently and forlornly as they loaded me aboard a truck to be transported to a POW camp in Germany. I thought to myself, it really is a small world. At first, he had rubbed my feelings a little raw, hearing him speak about the "good" loving he received from our black girls back home. In the end, however, I was truly thankful for their efforts on behalf of the war. Truly thankful, indeed. . . .

Surprisingly, there were few fighter pilots in Stalag Luft III. Most American prisoners had flown bombers. Of course, as Tuskegee Airmen, we were held in high esteem. We were also a bit older and more mature. All of us were college graduates, although some of the white pilots were not.

Did I experience any overt racism or general resentment on the part of the white POWs? Understandably, I felt an undercurrent of hesitancy and a kind of guarded inquisitiveness. Some of these men had been prisoners for more than two years and had no idea that blacks were now pilots and officers in the Army Air Corps. This was very strange to them, but then one day a B-17 crewmember arrived in Stalag Luft III. When he spotted me, he ran over, grabbed and hugged me, and exclaimed, "You're a Red Tail! You goddam Red Tails are the best damned unit! If the Red Tails had been with us, we'd have made it back home! You guys saved our asses so many times!" After that encounter, the reputation of the 332nd Fighter Group spread quickly throughout the camp. . . .

We steamed into New York on June 7. The ship's horns were blasting and all of us were shouting at the top of our lungs. Spirits soared when the skyline of New York came into focus, and rose even higher when we spotted the Statue of Liberty and finally docked. What a feeling of indescribable jubilation! But then, going down the gangplank, a short, smug, white buck private shouted, "Whites to the right, niggers to the left."

It was very discouraging, upon returning to the United States, to find racism, segregation, and other social ills alive and well. I knew then I was back home.

4.9 Sergeant Bernard Bellush Recalls D-Day on Omaha Beach, November 14, 1944, and March 16, 2000[9]

Jewish Americans also faced discrimination and often de facto segregation at home, though not in the armed forces. One of them was Sergeant Bernard Bellush from New York City, who landed on bloody Omaha Beach in Normandy on D-Day and remained there for many months. The document here comes from his unpublished wartime history of his ammunition company and from his postwar recollections of

9. From Bernard Bellush, "The Making of an Ammunition Company" (616th Ord. Amm. Co.), November 14, 1944, National Archives, and author's March 16, 2000, afterword.

what took place on board the landing craft that took him to Omaha on June 6, 1944. After the war Bellush became a professor of history at the City College of New York.

During the evening of June 3rd, our LST [landing ship, tank] 376 pulled up anchor and headed out for the open channel waters, only to be called back to port at about 0700 the following morning. The channel was too stormy for an amphibious assault. This respite was short-lived for the evening of the 4th found us off again, this time to be halted only when 10 miles off the French coastline. We slept fairly well that night. During the morning of the 5th, after hearing the announcement over the loudspeaker that "France is now dead ahead," we cleaned our carbines, had our final briefing and made last minute preparations. As far as the eye could see were LSTs, and their rhinos [pontoon barges] in tow, LCTs [landing craft, tank], LCCs [landing craft, control] with their tremendous antennae, and American destroyers flitting between their protected breed. Navy men aboard our LST were continuously at battle stations, with lookouts identifying the endless squadrons of friendly planes flying overhead towards France. All was in readiness for any eventuality, yet tragedy, in the form of a torpedo, was to strike her a few days later. In the early afternoon the First team assembled forward on the top deck for mixed services. Sgt. Bernard Bellush of The Bronx, N.Y., read the convocation and offered the sermon, while Sgt. Sam Godino of Jersey City, N.J., led us in The Lord's Prayer. With this completed we returned to our "Cubby holes" to while away the time playing cards, reading or just talking. Darkness finally descended and we tried to snatch a few hours of sleep. About 0300 on June 6th the motors went dead—we were 10 miles from France. The Navy "Huskies" aboard rocket firing speedboats were lowered away to the rough waters and then slid off into the darkness. Within an hour, the 105 Howitzer-laden dukws [army amphibious truck] backed out of the tank deck into the water and then moved off. All was in readiness for our transfer to the rhino ferry which was to carry us to shore. Off in the distance could be seen flashes of exploding shells and rockets. Finally, when darkness gave way to light, we found ourselves surrounded by LSTs, troop transports and smaller type vessels. Overhead P-38s flew by in an unending line, ranging over the entire sky. We anxiously waited for the rhino-ferry to swing around and back up to the bow of the ship. Twice the rough waters squelched the plans of the Seabees, but the third attempt was successful. We shook hands all around as we said farewell to our navy friends, many who now lie interred with the 376 in Davey Jones' locker. May their stay there be peaceful. . . .

The water was choppy, and though we rocked slightly—and continued to do so for days after hitting the beach—men of the first team became sick. We were eleven miles out to sea when we started for shore and so did not come close to land until 1300 hours. There was little movement on shore. Shells could be seen bursting on all sides, with many vehicles aflame. An LCI [landing craft, infantry] ordered us back and we heaved a deep sigh of relief, especially after seeing the rhino dead ahead of us receive direct hits and burst into flames. Things looked bad. As we moved aimlessly, paralleling the beach, mention was heard of this invasion being a failure, and our returning to England for another year of training and preparation. This pessimist was quickly corrected by the expressed thoughts of another who maintained that we couldn't fail. We had unlimited, and overpowering, supplies of men and material. And we had complete mastery of the skies. No! Success was inevitable. They couldn't stop us. In the midst of these thoughts we were ordered onto the beach once more by a passing LCC which told us to "Get going." On went our packs and pistol belts, as we silently prayed for our safety, while verbally cursing the cumbersome loads on our shoulders. Later, we were to be grateful that we had kept most of our stuff, especially the blankets.

As we approached the shrapnel-strewn shore a second time, an LCI with a loudspeaker attached, told us to "get the hell away from the beach." And once more we felt deeply relieved. The boys on the beach were going through hell. . . .

And what of the third team of the company? They had left their transport on two LCVPs [landing craft, vehicle and personnel], led by Lt. Bertram I. Sherman, of Cleveland Heights, Ohio, and Lt. Richard D. Cameron, of Battle Creek, Michigan. After circling for over an hour with eight other LCVPs, they headed for shore, but only four of these vessels beached at about 1330 hours. The other six had found things too hot because of 88 shells, and machine gun fire which had ricocheted off the front ramps. Meanwhile some 80 per cent of the men became sick—and were they sick. With the lowering of the front ramps the men jumped into water up to their necks, and shuffled shorewards for the psychological protection of the beach. [There they found] the rock-laden sands already strewn with wounded and dead. The time table had been upset. We were lying side by side with the infantry men of the 26th Regt. of the First Division. We had been warned time and again, but had never believed, that we might someday be fighting alongside infantrymen. Shrapnel was hitting all about us, cutting through the trousers of our evil-smelling impregnated clothes (chemically treated against possible gas attacks), lifting helmets from heads and bodies from the ground. We crawled behind a wrecked LCI and LCT for protection, then edged farther up the beach behind stalled half-tracks. A few minutes after leaving the "protection" of those vehicles they were blown to smithereens by direct mortar hits. And before we could finally edge our way through the mine field to safe shelter at the base of the cliff, we left James S. Isbell, of Falkville, Alabama, a fervently religious lad, fatally wounded, and two shrapnel-hit men, James Devine, of Philadelphia, Pennsylvania, and Carl Umhelts, of Sunbury, Pennsylvania. We had had our first taste of actual combat, and we didn't like it. . . .

And so we all dug in for the night, hoping that falling ack-ack and enemy bombs—would not strike us. It was a cold, damp night of fitful snatches of sleep—a night to forget. Before dawn of D plus 1, we were told by messenger to prepare ourselves to advance to the front lines as replacements for the infantry. But the final orders never came through. Our footsloggers were suffering terrific casualties. . . .

On the morning of D plus 1 the third team sent two men in search of the separated group of twelve men. They eventually returned with them late in the afternoon. At the same time a group of men . . . were detailed . . . to remove German ammunition from a concrete emplacement on the beach. Despite possible booby traps attached to the German ammunition, American wounded lying within the emplacement, and mortar shells falling without, the dangerous task was completed by early afternoon. Outside the emplacement Father Schultz, our Catholic Chaplain from Washington, D.C., calmly gave last rites to our dying, as mortars and shrapnel continued to fall nearby.

Some other men were directed to unload the only munition-laden LCT to land safely on our beach. And they continued to do so despite mortar fire and exploding mines which shook you so that you soon felt that you had just been through a clothes wringer. They were shortly joined in this task by men from the separated group of the first team. Continued mortar firing, and increased temperature readings, made it uncomfortably hot as we struggled to empty the craft of its valuable cargo—the only reserve ammunition for our valiant fighting men up front. Have you ever lifted, and then carried, a 155mm shell across, and up a large pebble-strewn beach, with the sand giving way under every step, and then stacked them amongst our tarp-covered dead? It's a heartbreaking and wearying task. We finally left the work when ordered back to our outfit, which we rejoined late that afternoon. But before we left the beach we had been told by a Colonel from our Brigade that our ammunition company was the most important outfit on the beach that day. It is true that he exaggerated the situation, but we later learned that up to D plus 6, ours was the only ammunition dump on this beach supplying practically any ammunition to the boys up front.

By early evening of D plus 1, we were still unable to open either of the pre-determined ASP [Ammunition Supply Point] sites, because the areas had not been demined. Thus, we set up shop about an eighth of a mile from the beach and ammunition started trickling and then flowing in. We didn't have to go far to supply the artillery for our 105s were shooting from fields next to us. . . .

. . . We received and issued ammunition during the night of D plus 1, although the dump was often lit up as pre-war Times Square by the anti-aircraft fire which greeted Jerry flying overhead. Those of us who did have opportunity to rest fell asleep from sheer exhaustion and were not awaked by the AA [anti-aircraft] fire, falling ack-ack, nor even sniper or machine gun fire. We slept in the inevitable hedgerow of Normandy, which offered excellent natural protection. Most of us froze that night because the duffel bags containing our blankets had not yet arrived. . . .

. . . The S.O.P. [Standard Operating Procedure], set during maneuvers in Tennessee, S. Wales, and S. England, provided for a bivouac site some distance away from the ammunition. But this is war in all its reality, and cruelty. Thus, we camped in the hedgerows, surrounded on all sides by TNT, 155mm shells, charges, and ground force ammunition of all types. One lucky hit from Jerry's nightly visits and——: well, let's forget about it. Our work was cut out for us and we did it, and we're darn proud of our achievements. . . .

Respectfully submitted by,
Sgt. Bernard Bellush, 32629761
November 14, 1944

Fifty-six years after the completion of this manuscript, I was able to secure a copy of it from the National Archives and read it once more. . . .

During a quick reading of the manuscript, . . . I realized that there were a number of instances where the narrative could have been more fully developed. One of them was a very brief reference to a sermon I gave on LST 376 while we were crossing the English Channel, on our way to Omaha Beach. The other was too brief references to my feelings and actions as our rhino ferry approached the beach. So, let me try to expand on at least these two events.

On that bitterly cold and blustery day of June 5th, as the Allied armada was slowly making its way across the English Channel towards Omaha Beach, my shortish commanding officer suddenly approached me. He remarked that there was no Chaplain aboard our LST to conduct religious services and then said that he was appointing me Acting Chaplain, but only for that day. My assignment was to shortly conduct religious services for the men of our company. I called upon the help of a Catholic as well as a Protestant member of our Army unit, and asked one to read the Lord's Prayer and the other another relevant section from the Army Prayer book.

They did their chores after we gathered our unit together on the heaving deck of this lumbering ship.

In the short space of time accorded me, I decided to offer a sermon based upon the tragic but memorable experiences of the Jewish fighters of the Warsaw Ghetto. Apparently, from reading the weekly *New Republic* magazine, which reached me regularly overseas, I had learned about this comparatively recent revolt long before the general public was alerted to it. Surrounded by ships as far as the eye could see, and looking into the eyes of fearful men who knew not what to expect the next day on the beaches of Normandy, I sought to reassure them as best I could.

I reminded them that the Warsaw Ghetto Jews had revolted against the mighty German Nazi Army with a miniscule number of rifles and grenades. And despite the overwhelming German cannon, machine guns, howitzers and lumbering, huge tanks which mowed them down street by street, the Jews of Warsaw fought on courageously to the last man and woman. At the least, they were models for us to emulate. We, on the other hand, I reminded my companions, would land on Omaha Beach supported by the greatest array of armament, ships and planes ever assembled by any one group of nations in the history of man and womankind. Did I calm or strengthen any of these soldiers? I don't know to this day.

But I do know that it took over half a century before someone confirmed the fact that I had given a sermon on the Warsaw Ghetto uprising, aboard LST 376, the day before we landed on Omaha Beach. In my manuscript on the history of the 616th Ordinance Ammunition Company, I had apparently avoided devoting too much space to myself by detailing the contents of the sermon. Thus, there was no written or oral record of its contents, except from my own recollections. This situation was finally altered in the Fall of 1998.

After a luncheon in New York's Marriot Hotel, in late September of 1998, where I had just debated a conservative economist on the merits of our nation's tax system before some 500 retired unionists, I was approached by a shortish man in his late sixties. He asked me, "What does the 616th Ordinance Ammunition Company mean to you." I immediately replied that it was my army unit during World War II. He then excitedly threw his hands around me and blurted out: "I am Tony Bisogno and I was in the same outfit with you. And I remembered you giving the sermon on the Warsaw Ghetto Jews on LST 376 as we were crossing the English Channel."

Fifty-four years after D-Day, I lived to hear Tony Bisogno, from Long Island, confirm my memories and the Warsaw Ghetto sermon I had given on LST 376.

Why didn't I originally describe, in much greater detail, the reactions of the men of the 616th Ordinance Ammunition Company, as we left LST

376? I don't know. But I knew we were heading for Omaha Beach, directly in line with the Church spire at Colleville-sur-Mer. But, let me now, fifty-six years later, try to remedy that situation. . . .

. . . While heading towards the beach, we passed an endless array of battleships, cruisers and then destroyers, all of which were firing away at German defenses and embankments on and beyond the beach.

Finally, we spotted the beach and, to our utter amazement, gradually discerned immense, overhanging cliffs. The indoctrination lectures given us in England, just before we shoved off across the Channel, never adequately described these mountainous heights. They reminded those of us who came from the New York area of the towering Palisades which line the west side of the Hudson River, north of the George Washington Bridge. Unlike Utah Beach, which was level into the surrounding countryside, those GIs who landed on Omaha Beach in the early morning hours of D-Day were decimated by the bristling German armor on the beach and above it in the awesome Palisades.

A rhino ferry, which is almost a basketball court wide, has no side walls. Thus, we were afforded no psychological protection, especially when we observed German artillery shells hitting a rhino ferry to our right, and then another to our left, setting them ablaze. Fearing that we would be the next ones hit, and expecting then to have to jump into the water and swim to shore to save our lives, I started shedding clothes from my overweight knapsack. The most valuable items I threw overboard, which really made no sense or logic, because of their infinitesimal weight, were my size 14 socks—an extremely rare item in Uncle Sam's army. But who, at this critical moment, was sensible or logical. We were never more frightened in our entire lives. Fortunately, our rhino-ferry was not hit that day, and we survived to hit hellish Omaha Beach long after we were scheduled to do so. But we had survived.

Bernie Bellush
March 16, 2000

4.10 Newspaper Columnist Ernie Pyle Depicts the Realities of War for Americans at Home, 1943[10]

Ernie Pyle was one of the most popular and best known of all the U.S. journalists sent overseas to cover the war. Reproduced here is an

10. From Ernie Pyle, *Here Is Your War* (New York: Henry Holt, 1943), 295–99, 304.

excerpt from the last chapter of his 1943 *Here Is Your War*, in which he describes the attitudes of American soldiers at the end of the Tunisian campaign in the spring of 1943. Pyle was killed on April 18, 1945, while covering the U.S. invasion of Okinawa in the Pacific.

The Tunisian campaign was ended. Our air forces moved on farther into Tunisia, to the very edge of the chasm of sea that separated them only so little from Sicily and Sardinia and then from Europe itself. We and the British leaped upon the demolished ports we had captured, cleared out enough wreckage for a foothold for ships, and as the ports grew and grew in usefulness they swarmed with thousands of men, and ships, and trucks. Our combat troops moved back—out of range of enemy strafers—to be cheered and acclaimed momentarily by the cities in the rear, to take a few days of wild and hell-roaring rest, and then to go into an invasion practice that was in every respect, except the one of actually getting shot, as rigorous as a real invasion.

Surely before autumn we of Tunisia would be deep into something new. Most of us realized and admitted to ourselves that horrible days lay ahead. The holocaust that at times seemed so big to us in Tunisia would pale in our memories beside the things we would see and do before another year ran out. . . .

It is hard for you at home to realize what an immense, complicated, sprawling institution a theater of war actually is. As it appears to you in the newspapers, war is a clear-cut matter of landing so many men overseas, moving them from the port to the battlefield, advancing them against the enemy with guns firing, and they win or lose.

To look at war that way is like seeing a trailer of a movie, and saying you've seen the whole picture. I actually don't know what percentage of our troops in Africa were in the battle lines, but I believe it safe to say that only comparatively few ever saw the enemy, ever shot at him, or were shot at by him. All the rest of those hundreds of thousands of men were churning the highways for two thousand miles behind the lines with their endless supply trucks, they were unloading the ships, cooking the meals, pounding the typewriters, fixing the roads, making the maps, repairing the engines, decoding the messages, training the reserves, pondering the plans.

To get all that colossal writhing chaos shaped into something that intermeshed and moved forward with efficiency was a task closely akin to weaving a cloth out of a tubful of spaghetti. . . .

What I have seen in North Africa has altered my own feelings in one respect. There were days when I sat in my tent alone and gloomed with the desperate belief that it was actually possible for us to lose this war. I don't feel that way any more. Despite our strikes and bickering and confusion back home, America is producing and no one can deny that. Even here at the far end of just one line the trickle has grown into an impressive stream. We are producing at home and we are hardening overseas. Apparently it takes a country like America about two years to become wholly at war. We had to go through that transition period of letting loose of life as it was, and then live the new war life so long that it finally became the normal life to us. It was a form of growth, and we couldn't press it. Only time can produce that change. . . . [W]e have about changed our character and become a war nation. I can't yet see when we shall win, or over what route geographically, or by which of the many means of warfare. But no longer do I have any doubts at all that we shall win.

The men over here have changed too. . . .

For a year, everywhere I went, soldiers inevitably asked me two questions: "When do you think we'll get to go home?" and "When will the war be over?" The home-going desire was once so dominant that I believe our soldiers over here would have voted—if the question had been put—to go home immediately, even if it meant peace on terms of something less than unconditional surrender by the enemy.

That isn't true now. Sure, they all still want to go home. So do I. But there is something deeper than that, which didn't exist six months ago. I can't quite put it into words—it isn't any theatrical proclamation that the enemy must be destroyed in the name of freedom; it's just a vague but growing individual acceptance of the bitter fact that we must win the war or else, and that it can't be won by running excursion boats back and forth across the Atlantic carrying homesick vacationers.

A year is a long time to be away from home, especially if a person has never been away before, as was true of the bulk of our troops. At first homesickness can almost kill a man. But time takes care of that. It isn't normal to moon in the past forever. Home gradually grows less vivid; the separation from it less agonizing. There finally comes a day—not suddenly but gradually, as a sunset-touched cloud changes its color—when a man is living almost wholly wherever he is. His life has caught up with his body, and his days become full war days, instead of American days simply transplanted to Africa.

That's the stage our soldiers are in now. . . .

Our men, still thinking of home, are impatient with the strange peoples and customs of the countries they now inhabit. They say that if they ever get home they never want to see another foreign country. But I know how it will be. The day will come when they'll look back and brag about how they learned a little Arabic, and how swell the girls were in England, and how pretty the hills of Germany were. Every day their scope is broadening despite themselves, and once they all get back with their global yarns and their foreign-tinged views, I cannot conceive of our nation ever being isolationist again. The men don't feel very international right now, but the influences are at work and the time will come. . . .

On the day of final peace, the last stroke of what we call the "Big Picture" will be drawn. I haven't written anything about the "Big Picture," because I don't know anything about it. I only know what we see from our worm's-eye view, and our segment of the picture consists only of tired and dirty soldiers who are alive and don't want to die; of long darkened convoys in the middle of the night; of shocked silent men wandering back down the hill from battle; of chow lines and Atabrine tablets and foxholes and burning tanks and Arabs holding up eggs and the rustle of high-flown shells; of jeeps and petrol dumps and smelly bedding rolls and C rations and cactus patches and blown bridges and dead mules and hospital tents and shirt collars greasy-black from months of wearing; and of laughter too, and anger and wine and lovely flowers and constant cussing. All these it is composed of; and of graves and graves and graves.

That is our war, and we will carry it with us as we go on from one battleground to another until it is all over, leaving some of us behind on every beach, in every field. We are just beginning with the ones who lie back of us here in Tunisia. I don't know whether it was their good fortune or their misfortune to get out of it so early in the game. I guess it doesn't make any difference, once a man has gone. Medals and speeches and victories are nothing to them any more. They died and others lived and nobody knows why it is so. They died and thereby the rest of us can go on and on. When we leave here for the next shore, there is nothing we can do for the ones beneath the wooden crosses, except perhaps to pause and murmur, "Thanks, pal."

CHAPTER 5

THE WAR AGAINST JAPAN—AND THE JAPANESE

The war against Japan differed in many ways from the war against Germany. Inter-service disagreements about the relative importance of ground, naval, and air operations admittedly took place in both conflicts, but those regarding Asia and the Pacific were quite different from those regarding Europe. So were Allied political disagreements and the nature of the actual fighting.

Despite official maintenance of the Germany-first strategy enunciated before U.S. entry into the war and reaffirmed soon after Pearl Harbor (see Chapter 3), the United States sent major forces to the Pacific in 1942 in an effort to halt the numerous Japanese offensives that followed the attack on Pearl Harbor. Such an effort was demanded by the Chinese, Australian, and New Zealand governments, by the U.S. Navy, by Philippine Commander General Douglas MacArthur, and by an American public desirous of immediate revenge for the Pearl Harbor attack. Consequently, by the end of 1942, and even through much of 1943, more U.S. forces were deployed against Japan than against Germany. Those forces did not succeed in preventing Japanese conquest of the Philippines, Burma, the Dutch East Indies, Malaya, and all the other European colonies in Southeast Asia by the spring of 1942, but they did halt additional Japanese offensives in the May–June 1942 naval Battles of Coral Sea and Midway and the lengthy six-month campaign that began in August for control of the island of Guadalcanal in the South Pacific Solomon Islands chain. Yet the Japanese still possessed in 1943 one of the largest empires in history, and how to defeat them became a matter of intense inter-service and inter-Allied dispute.

Reversing the precision bombing strategy they championed in the war against Germany, U.S. military planners came to favor the eventual area bombing of Japanese cities. How to get within bombing range of those cities, however, and whether bombing alone would be sufficient to obtain Japanese surrender, led to major debates over the relative importance of different geographic areas and types of forces to be used.

The vast Pacific theater had in early 1942 been placed under the control of the U.S. Joint Chiefs of Staff and divided in two: Pacific Ocean Areas (POA) under Admiral Chester W. Nimitz, headquartered in Hawaii, and the Southwest Pacific (SWPA) under General Douglas MacArthur, now in Australia. From this base MacArthur called for offensives in New Guinea and New Britain to destroy the major Japanese base at Rabaul and then to advance northwest to the Philippines. Nimitz and naval Chief Admiral Ernest J. King, on the other hand, pressed instead for a naval drive westward across the Central Pacific, through the Gilbert, Marshall, Caroline, and Marianas island groups, to the island of Formosa off the coast of China. Either approach would require major amphibious assaults, and thus the use of ground and air as well as naval forces.

The bulk of the Japanese Army was already deployed in China against the forces of Chinese leader Chiang Kai-shek, a situation U.S. military planners hoped to maintain. So did President Roosevelt, who wanted China to play a major role in the war and become one of his "Four Policemen" in the postwar world (see Chapter 11). China consequently constituted a third important geographic area in the war against Japan. To maintain and support Chiang's forces, General Joseph Stilwell was appointed his Allied chief of staff as well as Lend-Lease administrator and commander of all U.S. forces in the China-Burma-India (CBI) theater. His major tasks were to train Chiang's armies and, in conjunction with British and some U.S. forces, to reconquer northern Burma so that a land route could be re-created for Chinese forces to receive badly needed supplies.

Numerous military and political disagreements plagued Stilwell's mission. General Claire Chennault, who commanded U.S. Army Air Forces in China, discounted the need for major ground operations and pressed instead for the establishment of air bases from which to bomb the Japanese. Stilwell disagreed, but Chiang supported Chennault's proposals—at least partially, as Stilwell discovered, because he did not wish to risk his armies in additional battles against the Japanese; instead he wanted to obtain for his forces U.S. supplies and training so that they could be effectively used, after the war against Japan ended, in the civil war against Mao Zedong's Communists that had begun before the Japanese invasion. Nor were the British anxious to conduct operations in Burma or for China to play a major role in the war—or in the postwar world. Indeed, Churchill did not believe China was or should be considered a great power, and he clashed sharply with Roosevelt over the future of colonialism in Asia.

These factors resulted in numerous military failures in the China-Burma-India theater. In contrast, Nimitz and MacArthur were both highly successful in the Pacific, where each had been allowed to pursue his own favored approach. By late 1944, their forces in this "dual offensive" had reached the Marianas within bombing range of the Japanese home islands and the Philippines, thereby cutting off Japan from the resources of Southeast Asia.

This dual advance in the Pacific was marked by warfare quite different from what was taking place in Europe. As in the war against Germany, control of the seas was critical, but it was U.S. rather than German submarines that took the offensive in the Pacific, where they successfully destroyed much of the Japanese merchant fleet. Furthermore, naval combat in this theater focused much more than in the Atlantic on battles between surface warships—most notably though far from exclusively on aircraft carriers that during the war replaced battleships as the key capital vessels of both nations. Indeed, the range and power of the aircraft on these carriers was so great that they could and did destroy surface warships not possessing adequate air defense; and they operated over such distances that in many naval air battles the opposing fleets did not even see each other.

Between 1942 and 1944, in such battles as Coral Sea, Midway, Philippine Sea, and Leyte Gulf, U.S. ships and aircraft virtually destroyed Japan's carrier fleet and naval air forces as well as its other surface ships. Along with many of these naval battles came amphibious landings and major land campaigns on numerous islands by both marine and army units. These battles were particularly brutal, with little if any quarter asked for or given by either side. In effect it became a race war in which each side, convinced of its own racial superiority, treated the other as inferior and not subject to the established rules of warfare. They were not alone: similar conclusions and behavior marked both the German war first against Poland and then against the Soviet Union and Japan's war against China, where millions of civilians would die. Since most of the islands in the Pacific on which major battles were fought did not contain large numbers of civilians, however, the bulk of the casualties and deaths there were military.

The American war against Japan extended to the thousands of Japanese who had emigrated to or been born in the United States. Despite a lack of evidence, these Issei and Nisei were perceived as remaining loyal to Japan and thus potential threats to national security as well as racially inferior. In the war hysteria that swept the nation after Pearl Harbor the federal government ordered their expulsion from the West Coast and internment in a series of camps established for that purpose. In 1988, the U.S. Congress apologized for this gross violation of civil liberties and offered some financial compensation to the victims.

Historical disagreements regarding the war against the Japanese have focused on four major issues: the dual advance in the Pacific; the failures in China; the role of racism in both the war itself and the decision to intern the Japanese in the United States; and the decision to use the atomic bomb against Japan. This last issue has generated the largest and most heated interpretive disputes and consequently is treated separately in Chapter 12. In regard to the dual offensive, the decision to divide the huge Pacific theater into two theaters with different commanders violated the Allied principle of unity of command and, according to some critics, dissipated the U.S. effort and led to some unnecessary battles and casualties. Those unnecessary battles and casualties have in turn led to debate over the decisions and behavior of MacArthur, Nimitz, and their subordinate commanders. The continued American failures in China once the war ended, culminating in the Communists' 1949 victory over Chiang's Nationalists, led to intense political as well as historical attacks on U.S. policies and policy makers during the early years of the Cold War. During the 1970s, however—a period marked by reduced Soviet-American and Sino-American tensions—numerous historians began to reexamine and reevaluate these policies and policy makers. The historical debates over racism against the Japanese revolve not around its existence but rather its role in the decision to relocate and intern not only the non-citizen Issei, but also the American-born Nissei.

Numerous questions remain regarding the nature of this war against Japan—and against the Japanese living in the United States. Was too much, too little, or just the right amount of attention given to the war in the Pacific and Asia compared to the war in Europe? Why did the Joint Chiefs of Staff violate their unity of command principle in the Pacific by allowing competing theaters to exist under Nimitz and MacArthur, and was the ensuing dual offensive effective or counterproductive? Why were the Pacific island battles so bloody, and why were so few prisoners taken? Why did U.S. military and diplomatic efforts in China fail, and with what consequences? And what impact did all of the above have on the 1945 decision to use the atomic bomb against Japan in 1945?

Within the United States, why were the civil liberties of Japanese living in the country violated? Why were they forcibly removed from their West Coast homes and interned during the war? In hindsight, to what extent and in what ways was this removal and internment related to the war against Japan as opposed to purely domestic factors?

* * * *

5.1 Public Opinion Favors a Japan-First Strategy, 1942–1943[1]

Officially the United States adhered throughout the war to a global strategy designed to defeat Germany before Japan. Throughout 1942 and 1943, however, numerous high-ranking military officials called for

---

1. From George Gallup, *The Gallup Poll: Public Opinion, 1935–1971*, vol. 1 (New York: Random House, 1972), 370.

a modification or a reversal of this strategy (see Chapter 3, Documents 1, 2, 3, and 6). So did a large percentage of the American people, as the public opinion polls reproduced here illustrate.

Japan First or Germany First, 1942

40. . . . . Granting that it's important for us to fight the Axis every place we can, which do you think is more important for the United States to do right now?

	Mar 28 '42	June 17, '42
Put most of our effort into fighting Japan	62%	37%
Put most of our effort into fighting Germany	21	46
Don't know	17	14
Both		1
No answer		2

Nation's Chief Enemy, 1943

Interviewing Date 2/5–10/43

Survey #289-K	Question #1

In this war, which do you think is our chief enemy—Japan or Germany?

Japan	53%
Germany	34
No opinion	13

5.2 The Military Plans for the Defeat of Japan, May 21, 1943[2]

As this Joint and Combined Chiefs of Staff document of May 1943 illustrates, planning for the defeat of Japan involved numerous operations in Asia as well as the Pacific. Which of these operations eventually obtained top priority, and why?

---

2. From U.S. Department of State, *Foreign Relations of the United States: The Conferences at Washington and Quebec, 1943* (Washington, DC: U.S. Government Printing Office, 1970), 349–50.

4. Burma-China Theater

The Combined Chiefs of Staff have agreed on:

a. The concentration of available resources as first priority within the Assam-Burma Theater on the building up and increasing of the air route to China to a capacity of 10,000 tons a month by early fall, and the development of air facilities in Assam with a view to—

(1) Intensifying air operations against the Japanese in Burma;

(2) Maintaining increased American air forces in China;

(3) Maintaining the flow of airborne supplies to China.

b. Vigorous and aggressive land and air operations from Assam into Burma via Ledo and Imphal, in step with an advance by Chinese forces from Yunnan, with the object of containing as many Japanese forces as possible, covering the air route to China, and as an essential step towards the opening of the Burma Road.

c. The capture of Akyab and of Ramree Island by amphibious operations.

d. The interruption of Japanese sea communications into Burma.

5. Operations in the Pacific—1943–44

The courses of action examined by the Combined Chiefs of Staff and the conclusions reached by them are as follows:

a. Far Eastern Theater.

(1) *Operations in Burma to Augment Supplies to China.*

Vital to implementing the strategic plan for the defeat of Japan and to keeping China in the war.

(2) *Air Operations in and from China.*

Close coordination with other elements of plan are essential.

b. Pacific Theater.

(1) *Operations in the Solomons and Bismarck Archipelago.*

Provides for retaining the initiative, maintaining pressure on Japan, and the defense of Australia.

(2) *Operations in New Guinea.*

The capture of New Guinea will facilitate the opening of a line of communications to the Celebes Sea and contribute to the defense of Australia.

(3) *Operations in Eastern Netherlands East Indies.*

Due to limitations of forces, operations other than air warfare should be restricted to the seizure of those islands necessary to the capture of New Guinea.

(4) *Operations in the Marshall Islands.*

Shortens lines of communications to Southwest Pacific and Celebes Sea.

(5) *Operations in the Caroline Islands.*

Necessary to gain control of central Pacific, thereby facilitating establishment of line of communications to Celebes Sea. Will enable United Nations forces to directly threaten the Japanese Archipelago.

(6) Intensification of Operations Against Enemy Lines of Communication.

All the foregoing operations are essential to the attainment of positions which enable the intensification and expansion of attacks on the enemy lines of communication in the Pacific.

Conclusions

a. Offensive operations in the Pacific and Far East in 1943–1944 should have the following objectives:

(1) Conduct of air operations in and from China.

(2) Operations in Burma to augment supplies in China.

(3) Ejection of the Japanese from the Aleutians.

(4) Seizure of the Marshall and Caroline Islands.

(5) Seizure of the Solomons, the Bismarck Archipelago, and Japanese held New Guinea.

(6) Intensification of operations against enemy lines of communication.

b. Operations to gain these objectives will be restricted by the availability of trained amphibious divisions and amphibious craft.

5.3 Army Nurse Lieutenant Juanita Redmond Describes a Japanese Air Attack on Bataan in the Philippines, April 1942[3]

This document and the three that follow it are personal accounts of the different types of warfare that took place in Asia and the Pacific. The one reproduced here comes from the memoir of U.S. Army nurse Juanita Redmond on the Bataan Peninsula in the Philippines, where U.S. and Filipino forces on the island of Luzon withdrew in 1942 and made their unsuccessful defense against the Japanese invasion. Their surrender was followed by the notorious Bataan death march, in which numerous survivors of the actual campaign died. How did the

3. From Juanita Redmond, *I Served on Bataan* (Philadelphia: J. B. Lippincott, 1943), 106–11, 117–18.

air attack on the hospital where she was working change Redmond's opinion of the Japanese and the nature of the war?

At ten o'clock on Easter Monday the first wave of bombers struck us.

Someone yelled, "Planes overhead!" But those had become such familiar words that most of us paid them little attention. I went on pouring medications, and then the drone of the planes was lost in the shrill crescendo and roar of a crashing bomb.

It landed at the hospital entrance and blew up an ammunition truck that was passing. The concussion threw me to the floor. There was a spattering of shrapnel and pebbles and earth on the tin roof. Then silence for a few minutes.

I heard the corpsmen rushing out with litters, and I pulled myself to my feet. Precious medicines were dripping to the ground from the shattered dressing carts, and I tried to salvage as much as possible.

The first casualties came in. The boys in the ammunition truck had been killed, but the two guards at the hospital gate had jumped into their fox holes. By the time they were extricated from the debris that filled up the holes they were both shell-shock cases.

There were plenty of others.

Outside the shed a guard yelled, "They're coming back!"

They were after us, all right.

In the Orthopedic ward nurses and corpsmen began to cut the traction ropes so that the patients could roll out of bed if necessary, broken bones and all. In my ward several of the men became hysterical; I would have joined them if I could. It was all I could do to go on being calm and acting as if everything were all right and I had everything under control.

"They're very near us!" came the warning from outside.

Father Cummins had come in, and standing in the middle of the shed where all the boys could see him, he asked us to repeat the Lord's Prayer with him.

Then the second wave of bombs fell.

That one hit the mess and the Doctors' and Nurses' Quarters. When the ripping and tearing sound of crashing wood and the roar of minor explosions diminished, I could hear shrieks of pain outside, the helpless sobbing of the men in the wards, and Father Cummins' quiet voice praying.

Through the open sides of the sheds came flying debris, clouds of dust, wrenched boards with protruding nails, limbs of trees.

It wasn't over.

Even in the first few moments of quiet, we heard the planes coming back.

We couldn't do anything but wait. That was the awful part; we couldn't do anything.

This time they scored a direct hit on the wards. A thousand-pound bomb pulverized the bamboo sheds, smashed the tin roofs into flying pieces; the iron beds doubled and broke jaggedly like paper matches. Sergeant May had pulled me under a desk, but the desk was blown into the air, he and I with it. I heard myself gasping. My eyes were being gouged out of their sockets, my whole body was swollen and torn apart by the violent pressure. This is the end, I thought.

Then I fell back to the floor, the desk landing on top of me and bouncing around drunkenly. Sergeant May knocked it away from me, and gasping for breath, bruised and aching, sick from swallowing the smoke of the explosive, I dragged myself to my feet. I heard Freeman, our boy with no legs, calling out:

"Where's Miss Redmond? Is Miss Redmond alive?"

He was being carried out; fortunately, he had rolled out of bed and, though he had been covered with debris, except for a few scratches he was unhurt.

Father Cummins said calmly: "Somebody take over, I'm wounded." He had shrapnel in his shoulder.

Only one small section of my ward remained standing. Part of the roof had been blown into the jungle. There were mangled bodies under the ruins; a blood-stained hand stuck up through a pile of scrap; arms and legs had been ripped off and flung among the rubbish. Some of the mangled torsos were almost impossible to identify. One of the few corpsmen who had survived unhurt climbed a tree to bring down a body blown into the top branches. Blankets, mattresses, pajama tops hung in the shattered trees.

We worked wildly to get to the men who might be buried, still alive, under the mass of wreckage, tearing apart the smashed beds to reach the wounded and the dead. These men were our patients, our responsibility; I think we were all tortured by an instinctive, irrational feeling that we had failed them.

The bombing had stopped, but the air was rent by the awful screams of the new-wounded and the dying, trees were still crashing in the jungle and when one nearby fell on the remaining segment of tin roof it sounded like shellfire. We were shaking and sick at our stomachs, but none of us who was able to go on dared to stop even for a moment. . . .

That night we stayed in our fox holes. I didn't sleep. We hadn't eaten since breakfast, but I wasn't hungry. We were like hunted animals, waiting for the kill, almost hoping it would happen quickly so that the torment of waiting would end. But stronger than that was anger; anger and hate and a hot desire to fight back, to avenge our dead.

What kind of human beings would deliberately bomb a hospital, defense-less, openly marked for what it was, filled with the wounded and the sick?

I don't know. The only answer I had found when I crawled out of my hole in the morning, my head aching, a crick in my back, my legs cramped, was not an answer but a conviction. This isn't a war in which anybody—*anybody*—is let off. Each single individual of us is in it and each must give everything he has to give. An enemy that will bomb hospitals and unde-fended cities—sick and injured men, or women and children and helpless old people—isn't an enemy you can ever come to terms with; not in the usual meaning of the phrase. The war must end without compromise.

It wasn't particularly original thinking, I know, but somehow it com-forted me to have it clear and simple in my own mind. I could put the long thoughts of the people I would never see again into the background and go on about my work.

5.4 Navy Pilot George Gay Survives the Battle of Midway, June 1942[4]

Unlike most battles and campaigns in World War II, the Battle of Mid-way was both brief and decisive. Japanese naval commander Isoroku Yamamoto sought to surprise the Americans as he had at Pearl Har-bor and destroy the U.S. aircraft carriers that had not been there on December 7, 1941. This time, however, it was Yamamoto who was surprised as U.S. intelligence discovered his plan and with naval air-craft sank four of his large aircraft carriers, three of them in a fifteen-minute time span on June 4, 1942. This permanently tipped the naval air balance in the Pacific. Navy pilot George Gay, a participant in the battle and the author of the following document, was the sole survivor of a U.S. torpedo squadron that failed to break through Japanese air defenses but paved the way for the ensuing success of U.S. Navy dive bombers. Here he describes naval air combat that he experienced and the ensuing dive bomber success that he watched from the water.

We were now in a position, those of us still left, to turn west again to intercept the ship we had chosen to attack, but the Zeros were still intent on not letting us through, and our planes kept falling all around me. We were on the ship's starboard side, or to the right and ahead of our target,

4. From George Gay, *Sole Survivor: A Personal Story about the Battle of Midway*, rev. ed. (Naples, FL: Midway Publishers, 1986), 121–26.

and as we closed range, the big carrier began to turn towards us. I knew immediately from what the skipper had said so often in his lectures that if she got into a good turn she could not straighten out right away, and I was glad that she had committed herself. At that moment there were only two planes left of our squadron besides our own. One was almost directly ahead of me, and I could hardly see him over the nose of my plane. The other was also ahead of me, but off just a bit to my left. I skidded to the left and avoided more 20 MM slugs just in time to pull my nose up and fire another Zero as he got in front of me. I only had one .30 caliber gun, and although I knew I hit this Zero also, it did little damage. I had a number of such chances, but I didn't get anywhere near the satisfaction that I wanted out of spitting at those Zeros with that one pea-shooter. When I turned back to the right, the plane that had been directly ahead of me was gone, and the other was out of control. . . .

My target, which I think was the *Kaga*, was now in a hard turn to starboard and I was going toward her forward port quarter. I figured that by the time a torpedo could travel the distance it should be in the water, the ship should be broadside. I aimed about one quarter of the ship's length ahead of her bow, and reached out with my left hand to pull back the throttle. It had been calculated that we should be at about 80 knots when we dropped these things, so I had to slow down.

I had just got hold of the throttle, when something hit the back of my hand and it hurt like hell. My hand didn't seem to be working right, so I had to pull the throttle back mostly with my thumb. You can well imagine that I was not being exactly neat about all this, I was simply trying to do what I had come out to do. When I figured that I had things about as good as I was going to get them, I punched the torpedo release button.

Nothing happened. "Damn those tracers," I thought. "They've goofed up my electrical release and I'm getting inside my range." I had been told that the ideal drop was 1,000 yards range, 80 knots speed, and 80 feet or so of altitude. But by the time I got the control stick between my knees and put my left hand on top of it to fly the plane, and reached across to pull the cable release with my good right hand, I was into about 850 yards. The cable, or mechanical release, came out of the instrument panel on the left side, designed to be pulled with the left hand. But those damn Zeros had messed up my program. My left hand did not work. Anyhow, it was awkward, and I almost lost control of the plane trying to pull out that cable by the roots. I can't honestly say I got rid of that torpedo. It felt like it. I had never done it before so I couldn't be sure, and with the plane pitching like a bronco, I had to be content with trying my best.

"Okay, so I've gotten rid of the G.D. torpedo. Now what do I do?" Slamming that throttle forward was no problem. Now it was "balls to the wall" as we would say. We had talked about this and decided that this was no place to turn around. If you threw your belly up to all those guns on that ship, you would increase your size by about 300 per cent. The only thing to do was fly right at them and present the smallest target possible.

God, but that ship looked big! I remember thinking, "Why in the hell doesn't the *Hornet* look that big when I'm trying to land on her?" There was a Jap on a Pom-Pom gun shooting at me, and I just bore-sighted right back at him and flew him eye to eye. He must have thought I was fool enough to be one of his kamikaze types, because he jumped off his gun and I flew right over him.

I looked up on the bridge, and I could see a guy there waving his arms. I could even see a pair of binoculars in one hand and a Samurai sword in the other. He was pointing at me like they couldn't see me. I think he was the captain.

Here again, you just keep thinking. I remember that I did not want to fly out over the starboard side and let all those gunners have a chance at me, so I headed out over the stern.

Maybe that guy back there on that Pom-Pom hadn't been so wrong after all. I looked down on the flight deck and there were not only planes and men there, but bombs, torpedoes, gas hoses, and all kinds of gear.

I thought, "I could crash into all this and make one great big mess, maybe even get myself a whole carrier, but I'm feeling passably good, and my plane is still flying, so the hell with that—I'll keep going. Maybe I'll get another crack at them and do more damage in the long run.". . .

Flying as low as I could, I went between a couple of cruisers, and out past the destroyers. If you have ever seen movies of this sort of thing, you may wonder how anything could get through all that gunfire. I am alive to tell you that it *can* be done. I think my plane was hit a few times, but here again, I really wasn't going to the trouble to keep track of these small details.

The Zeros had broken off me when I got into ack-ack, but they had no trouble going around to meet me on the other side. A 20 MM cannon slug hit my left rudder pedal just outside my little toe, blew the pedal apart and knocked a hole in the firewall. This set the engine on fire, and it was burning my left leg through that hole.

When the rudder pedal went, the control wire to the ailerons and the rudder went with it. Don't ask me how or why, but the thing that was left for me was the only thing I had to have. I had the elevators so I could pull the nose up. Reaching over with my right hand, I cut the switch. That was also on the left side. Anyhow, I was able to hold the nose up and slow down to almost a decent ditching speed.

Most airplanes will level out if you turn them loose, especially if they are properly trimmed. Mine was almost making it, but I was crosswind, so the right wing hit first. This slammed me into the water in a cartwheel fashion and banged the hood shut over me before it twisted the frame and jammed the hood tight.

As I unbuckled, water was rising to my waist. The nose of the plane was down, so I turned around and sat on the instrument panel while trying to get that hood open. It wouldn't budge. When that water got up to my armpits and started lapping at my chin, I got scared—and I mean really scared. I knew the plane would dive as soon as it lost buoyancy and I didn't want to drown in there. I panicked, stood up and busted my way out.

The Zeros were diving and shooting at me, but my first thought now was of Bob Huntington. I was almost positive he was dead. I think he took at least one of those cannon slugs right in the chest, but I thought that the water might revive him and I had to try and help him. I got back to him just as the plane took that dive, and I went down with it trying to unbuckle his straps and get him out.

The beautiful water exploded into a deep red, and I lost sight of everything. What I had seen confirmed my opinion of his condition and I had to let Bob go. The tail took a gentle swipe at me as if to say goodbye and I came up choking. . . . Zeros were still strafing me and I ducked under a couple of times as those twacking slugs came close. As I came up for air once, I bumped my head on my life raft out of the plane. . . .

I noticed that the Zeros had stopped strafing me and I wondered why. Looking around, I saw the whole Jap Navy steaming right down on me. They were landing planes again, and though I thought they were going to run right over me, I was fascinated by their landing procedure. Their planes did not come by the ship downwind as we did, then turn for a base leg and come off the final turn at the cut. They were coming straight in from astern and I thought, "How awkward. How do they get the proper interval? That doesn't give them much of a chance to judge relative speed."

Then I saw why the Zeros had left me. Our dive bombers were coming down. There is no way I can describe what a beautiful sight that was! I could see that the Zeros that had come down after us were not up there bothering them and I knew that some of those fellows were not only pushing over in their first dive, but it was also their first time they had ever flown that type of a plane. They were magnificent and I did not see a single splash indicating a miss! They laid those bombs right where they belonged and caused the most devastating damage possible. Some pilots would see their target explode, and pull off to pick another one and then come on down. It was almost unbelievable, but I was seeing it. Almost simultaneously, three Jap carriers were wiped out. I knew what that meant. By golly, we did it! We caught them just as we had hoped to while they were retrieving aircraft that were low on fuel and out of bombs and ammunition.

5.5 Marine Private E. B. Sledge Remembers the Hellish Battle of Okinawa, 1945[5]

The first six months of 1945 witnessed the two bloodiest battles of the Pacific War, as massive U.S. ground, naval, and air forces invaded two heavily defended islands within bombing distance of Japan: Iwo Jima in February and Okinawa in April. In both campaigns the Americans faced fierce and suicidal Japanese resistance. On Iwo Jima, total U.S. casualties (dead, wounded, and missing) for the first time exceeded those of the Japanese, who fought nearly to the last man. The Okinawa campaign was even worse, lasting nearly three months and resulting in the highest casualty totals for both sides in the entire Pacific War: 50,000 for the Americans and 100,000 for the Japanese. What role do you think these high casualties played in American decision making regarding first the conventional and then the atomic bombing of Japan?

Marine Corps volunteer Eugene B. Sledge fought on Okinawa after surviving the bloody battle for the island of Peleliu in late 1944. The following excerpt from his highly regarded 1981 memoir describes the horrors he experienced on Okinawa. Sledge eventually became a college biology professor in his native Alabama.

After digging in the gun, registering in on the aiming stakes, and preparing ammo for future use, I had my first opportunity to look around our position. It was the most ghastly corner of hell I had ever witnessed. As far as I could see, an area that previously had been a low grassy valley with a picturesque stream meandering through it was a muddy, repulsive, open sore on the land. The place was choked with the putrefaction of death, decay, and destruction. In a shallow defilade to our right, between my gun pit and the railroad, lay about twenty dead Marines, each on a stretcher and covered to his ankles with a poncho—a commonplace, albeit tragic, scene to every veteran. Those bodies had been placed there to await transport to the rear for burial. At least those dead were covered from the torrents of rain that had made them miserable in life and from the swarms of flies that sought to hasten their decay. But as I looked about, I saw that other Marine dead couldn't be tended properly. The whole area was pocked with shell craters and churned up by explosions. Every crater was half full of water, and many of them held a Marine corpse. The bodies lay pathetically just as they had been killed, half submerged in muck and water, rusting weapons still in hand. Swarms of big flies hovered about them.

5. From E. B. Sledge, *With the Old Breed at Peleliu and Okinawa* (Novato, CA: Presidio Press, 1981), 252–53, 267, 276–78.

"Why ain't them poor guys been covered with ponchos?" mumbled my foxhole buddy as he glanced grimly about with a distraught expression on his grizzled face. His answer came the moment he spoke. Japanese 75mm shells came whining and whistling into the area. We cowered in our hole as they crashed and thundered around us. The enemy gunners on the commanding Shuri Heights were registering their artillery and mortars on our positions. We realized quickly that anytime any of us moved out of our holes, the shelling began immediately. We had a terrible time getting our wounded evacuated through the shell fire and mud without the casualty- and stretcher-bearers getting hit. Thus it was perfectly clear why the Marine dead were left where they had fallen.

Everywhere lay Japanese corpses killed in the heavy fighting. Infantry equipment of every type, U.S. and Japanese, was scattered about. Helmets, rifles, BARs [Browning automatic rifles], packs, cartridge belts, canteens, shoes, ammo boxes, shell cases, machine-gun ammo belts, all were strewn around us up to and all over Half Moon.

The mud was knee deep in some places, probably deeper in others if one dared venture there. For several feet around every corpse, maggots crawled about in the muck and then were washed away by the runoff of the rain. There wasn't a tree or bush left. All was open country. Shells had torn up the turf so completely that ground cover was nonexistent. The rain poured down on us as evening approached. The scene was nothing but mud; shell fire; flooded craters with their silent, pathetic, rotting occupants; knocked-out tanks and amtracs; and discarded equipment—utter desolation.

The stench of death was overpowering. The only way I could bear the monstrous horror of it all was to look upward away from the earthly reality surrounding us, watch the leaden gray clouds go skidding over, and repeat over and over to myself that the situation was unreal—just a nightmare—that I would soon awake and find myself somewhere else. But the ever-present smell of death saturated my nostrils. It was there with every breath I took.

I existed from moment to moment, sometimes thinking death would have been preferable. We were in the depths of the abyss, the ultimate horror of war. During the fighting around the Umurbrogol Pocket on Peleliu, I had been depressed by the wastage of human lives. But in the mud and driving rain before Shuri, we were surrounded by maggots and decay. Men struggled and fought and bled in an environment so degrading I believed we had been flung into hell's own cesspool. . . .

Our buddies who had gone back had been greeted enthusiastically—as those of us who survived were received later on. But the folks back home didn't, and in retrospect couldn't have been expected to, understand what we had experienced, what in our minds seemed to set us apart forever from anyone who hadn't been in combat. We didn't want to indulge in self-pity. We just wished that people back home could understand how lucky they were and stop complaining about trivial inconveniences. . . .

At dusk on one of those last few days of May, we moved onto a muddy, slippery ridge and were told to dig in along the crest. One of the three 60mm mortar squads was to set up its gun down behind the ridge, but my squad and the remaining squad were ordered to dig in along the ridge crest and to function as riflemen during the night. The weather turned bad again, and it started to rain.

Mac, our mortar section leader, was nowhere to be seen. But Duke, who had been our section leader on Peleliu and who was by then leading the battalion's 81mm mortar platoon, came up to take charge. He ordered an NCO to have us dig two-man foxholes five yards apart along the crest of the ridge. My buddy went off down the ridge to draw ammo and chow while I prepared to dig.

The ridge was about a hundred feet high, quite steep, and we were on a narrow crest. Several discarded Japanese packs, helmets, and other gear lay scattered along the crest. From the looks of the muddy soil, the place had been shelled heavily for a long time. The ridge was a putrid place. Our artillery must have killed Japanese there earlier, because the air was foul with the odor of rotting flesh. It was just like being back at Half Moon Hill. Off toward our front, to the south, I had only a dim view through the gathering gloom and curtain of rain of the muddy valley below.

The men digging in on both sides of me cursed the stench and the mud. I began moving the heavy, sticky clay mud with my entrenching shovel to shape out the extent of the foxhole before digging deeper. Each shovelful had to be knocked off the spade, because it stuck like glue. I was thoroughly exhausted and thought my strength wouldn't last from one sticky shovelful to the next.

Kneeling on the mud, I had dug a hole no more than six or eight inches deep when the odor of rotting flesh got worse. There was nothing to do but continue to dig, so I closed my mouth and inhaled with short shallow breaths. Another spadeful of soil out of the hole released a mass of wriggling maggots that came welling up as though those beneath were pushing them out. I cursed, and told the NCO as he came by what a mess I was digging into.

"You heard him, he said put the holes five yards apart."

In disgust, I drove the spade into the soil, scooped out the insects, and threw them down the front of the ridge. The next stroke of the spade unearthed buttons and scraps of cloth from a Japanese army jacket buried in the mud—and another mass of maggots. I kept on doggedly. With the next thrust, metal hit the breastbone of a rotting Japanese corpse. I gazed down in horror and disbelief as the metal scraped a clean track through the mud along the dirty whitish bone and cartilage with ribs attached. The shovel skidded into the rotting abdomen with a squishing sound. The odor nearly overwhelmed me as I rocked back on my heels.

I began choking and gagging as I yelled in desperation, "I can't dig in here! There's a dead Nip here?"

The NCO came over, looked down at my problem and at me, and growled, "You heard him; he said put the holes five yards apart."

"How the hell can I dig a foxhole through a dead Nip?" I protested.

Just then Duke came along the ridge and said, "What's the matter, Sledgehammer?"

I pointed to the partially exhumed corpse. Duke immediately told the NCO to have me dig in a little to the side away from the rotting remains. I thanked Duke and glared at the NCO. How I managed not to vomit during the vile experience I don't know. Perhaps my senses and nerves had been so dulled by constant foulness for so long that nothing could evoke any other response but to cry out and move back.

5.6 Japanese Civilians Tomizawa and Kobayashi Hiroyasu Live through the Firebombing of Tokyo, 1945[6]

Once U.S. forces had conquered Pacific islands within bombing distance of the Japanese home islands, the AAF launched a major area bombing campaign against Japanese cities. The results were devastating given the wooden structure of many Japanese buildings and the lack of adequate air defense as well as the greater size and range of the new American B-29 "Superfortress" bombers. According to the U.S. Strategic Bombing Survey, the massive firebombing attack on Tokyo on March 9–10 resulted in 88,000 deaths; historians have since questioned these official figures, arguing that the death toll was much higher—thus making the Tokyo bombing even deadlier than the atomic attacks on Hiroshima or Nagasaki. In the oral history reproduced here, two Japanese civilians who survived the attack on Tokyo describe some of the ensuing horrors.

Kobayashi: March 9, 1945. I was there. Air-raid warnings came every day, so we weren't particularly shaken when we saw red spots far away, but soon the airplanes were flying above us. Places near us were turning red. Over there, it's red. Here, it's red! Some were still at the switchboards.

---

6. From Haruko Taya Cook and Theodore F. Cook, *Japan at War: An Oral History* (New York: New Press, 1992), 351–53.

The others were trying to extinguish the flames after the building caught fire. Outside, huge telephone poles, set against the building and meant to protect the windows and withstand any bomb blast, became like kindling under the incendiary bombs. When the poles started burning, there were still some working the phone lines.

Tomizawa: Our place had communication lines to the antiaircraft batteries and the fire-fighting units for the whole Shitamachi area. There weren't any wireless communications in use then, so crucial government lines passed through our switchboard. Until the last second, many operators were still working, plugging lines into the jacks.

Kobayashi: Parts of the building were still made of wood. The window frames, for instance, and the rest areas. Wood, covered with stucco. Up on the roof, there was a water tank. Through pipes, it was supposed to lay down a curtain of water over the whole building. But the water in the tank, when it was released, was soon exhausted. We opened up fire plugs, and though water poured out fast at first, everyone was using them, too, so it soon trickled to a stop. We had a small pond, maybe two meters long. It had goldfish we kept for fun. We drained that water, throwing it onto the windows to cool them down. The glass shattered, "*Ping!*" because of the heat. I remember those kids carrying buckets. Helter-skelter. Even the water in the teakettle was used up.

Outside, the world was ablaze. We had no more water. It was all gone. That was it. The operators and the night supervisor, Matsumoto Shūji, were there. Mr. Matsumoto was found dead in the shelter. Burned to death. He was a marathon runner, but he was responsible for them. According to a survivor, Miss Tanaka, they finally did try to leave the building. "Get out, get out!" they were told, but the flames were too strong. They couldn't flee.

Tomizawa: Only four of them survived. Fortunate to escape that dangerous situation. The remaining thirty-one all perished.

Kobayashi: When we left, we men thought we were the last ones. We couldn't really get the gate open, so we climbed over the side wall. The bridge over the Arakawa was jammed. People coming this way from the far side, and trying to go there from this side. They packed together in the middle and couldn't move. People are greedy. Even at times like that, people are carrying things. Our phone cable was next to the bridge, partially submerged in the water. We took a chance. There was no other way. We hung on to it and moved across hand over hand, our bodies in the water. All the way across the river to escape the burning air. It was like a circus act.

If there'd still been water, water coming from the hydrants, we probably wouldn't have made it. But there was no water. No way to fight the fire. Besides, our line of command was separate from that of the girls. We were later questioned. "Why did only the men flee?" They wanted to know why we didn't take more girls with us. But when they investigated, they found that even the coin boxes on the public phones had melted completely. Then they understood.

Not even a single line was still operational. When I returned the next day, where the thick cables went in, they had melted down. There were no window frames. All the metallic things had melted in the heat and were bowing down, all bent over. The switchboards, anything made of wood, all burned. Gone.

Tomizawa: The interior cables were still hanging in the empty concrete box. A chill went through me.

Kobayashi: Some people could be identified. By their stomach wraps. Where it had been tight against their skin a name could be found written on it. It wasn't burned. To tell you the truth, I couldn't tell if they were men or women. They weren't even full skeletons. Piled on top of each other. The bottom of the pile, all stuck together. A few bits of clothing could be found on them. The underpants of Mr. Matsumoto were left. Touching the wall of the shelter. When Matsumoto-san's wife came, nobody could bear to tell her that her husband was not there anymore. "You have to tell her," everyone told me. "You were on night duty together." There's nothing more painful than that. His wife confirmed that they were her husband's underwear.

Even after all the bones were buried, when it rained, a blue flame burned. From the phosphorus. Soldiers stationed there used to say, "Maybe they'll come out tonight," thinking of the ghosts and the blue flames.

I wonder what war is. I wonder why we did it. I'm not talking about victory or loss. I merely feel heartbroken for those who died. It's not an issue of whether I hate the enemy or not. However much you're glorified, if you're dead, that's it. Young kids worked so hard. Without complaint. It makes me seethe. Burning flames, huge planes flying over, dropping bombs. My feeling of hatred—"You bastards! Bastards!" you shout. But there was no sense that you're capable of doing anything about it. If you win, you're the victors. You can justify anything. It's all right if the ones who have rifles are killed. That's OK. But these kids didn't have weapons, they had only their breasts. Those are the ones whose end was tragic.

I wonder, does war bring happiness to anyone? The ones who perished here on duty were merely promoted two ranks. They got a medal from the Emperor. A long time afterwards. Their parents didn't even get their pensions. Only the men with stars are enshrined in Yasukuni. But where are those who perished here? Girls of fifteen and sixteen. Who did their best. [*His voice breaks.*] People even ask, "Why didn't they escape earlier? They should have fled earlier."

Tomizawa: They are the ones who should be enshrined.
Kobayashi: No! Not that! Their parents want them back!

5.7 General Joseph Stilwell Bitterly Explains His Problems in China, 1944[7]

The following excerpts from General Joseph W. Stilwell's diaries and letters to his wife, which were never intended to be seen by anyone else, illustrate the numerous political as well as the military problems and frustrations he faced in the China theater, with particular reference to the 1944 crisis that led to his recall.

September 17, The Manure Pile: Letter to Mrs. Stilwell

We are in the midst of a battle with the Peanut [Chiang Kai-shek], and it is wearing us out. Crises are rising in quick succession here and there; there is disaster in Hunan and Kwangsi: Dorn [in command on the Salween] is screaming for help: and hell to pay generally. Hell has been to pay before so I guess we can take it again. You may be interested to know that everything is turning out exactly as I told them it would in May 1943, when I was the Voice of One Howling in the Wilderness and when I was voted the Horse's-Neck-Most-Likely-to-Succeed-in-that-Role. I don't know if the Knowitalls have learned their lesson or not, but even if they have it has been an expensive experiment for me. A year and a half lost. In the so-called campaign for Changsha, Hengyang and Kweilin, the Peanut insisted on conducting operations by remote control and by intuition as usual, with catastrophic results. The enormity of this stupidity is shown by the fact that he thinks it was a pretty good show, considering. Considering what? I don't know. They throw away 300,000 men in Hunan [East China] without batting an eye and I break my back trying to get 10,000 to replace battle casualties [in the Burma campaign]. Co-operation in capital letters. Why can't sudden death for once strike in the proper place. It would really be funny if it weren't so tragic. The picture of this little rattlesnake being backed up by a great democracy, and showing his backside in everything he says and does, would convulse you if you could get rid of your gall bladder. But to have to sit there and be dignified, instead of bursting into guffaws, is too much to ask for the pay I get. What will the American people say when they finally learn the truth?

---

7. From Theodore H. White, ed., *The Stilwell Papers* (New York: William Sloan Associates, 1948; repr. Shocken Books, 1972), 331–33, 339–41.

I see that the Limeys [British] are going to rush to our rescue in the Pacific. Like hell. They are going to continue this fight with their mouths. Four or five old battleships will appear and about ten RAF planes will go to Australia but in twenty years the schoolbooks will be talking about "shoulder to shoulder" and "the Empire struck with all its might against the common enemy" and all that crap. The idea, of course, is to horn in at Hongkong again, and our Booby is sucked in. . . .

September 19

Mark this day in red on the calendar of life. At long, at very long last, F.D.R. has finally spoken plain words, and plenty of them, with a firecracker in every sentence. "Get busy or else." A hot firecracker. I handed this bundle of paprika to the Peanut and then sank back with a sigh. The harpoon hit the little bugger right in the solar plexus, and went right through him. It was a clean hit, but beyond turning green and losing the power of speech, he did not bat an eye. He just said to me, "I understand." And sat in silence, jiggling one foot. We are now a long way from the "tribal chieftain" bawling out. *Two long years lost*, but at least F.D.R.'s eyes have been opened and he has thrown a good hefty punch.

I came home. Pretty sight crossing the river: lights all on in Chungking.

September 21, Letter to Mrs. Stilwell

A lot of mail but nothing but junk. I throw it at Carl. The only mail I want to see has the Carmel postmark. It has taken two and a half years for the Big Boys to see the light, but it dawned finally and I played the avenging angel.

> I've waited long for vengeance—
> At last I've had my chance.
> I've looked the Peanut in the eye
> And kicked him in the pants.
>
> The old harpoon was ready
> With aim and timing true,
> I sank it to the handle,
> And stung him through and through.
>
> The little bastard shivered,
> And lost the power of speech.
> His face turned green and quivered
> As he struggled not to screech.

For all my weary battles,
For all my hours of woe,
At last I've had my innings
And laid the Peanut low.

I know I've still to suffer,
And run a weary race,
But oh! the blessed pleasure
I've wrecked the Peanut's face.

***

[October 1], Letter to Mrs. Stilwell

It looks very much as though they had gotten me at last. The Peanut has gone off his rocker and Roosevelt has apparently let me down completely. If old softy gives in on this, as he apparently has, the Peanut will be out of control from now on. A proper fizzle. My conscience is clear. I have carried out my orders. I have no regrets. Except to see the U.S.A. sold down the river. So be ready, in case the news isn't out sooner, to have me thrown out on the garbage pile. At least, I'll probably get home and tell you all about it. God help the next man.

It hasn't happened yet, but it is a thousand to one that it will soon.

5.8 President Franklin D. Roosevelt Orders Japanese Relocation, 1942[8]

Before Pearl Harbor approximately 90 percent of the 125,000 Americans of Japanese ancestry in the United States lived in California, Oregon, and Washington. Two-thirds of them were Nisei, native-born American citizens, while the other third were Issei, born in Japan and thus ineligible for citizenship under the 1882 and 1924 immigration laws. Wartime hysteria and fear of a possible Japanese invasion as well as racism led to calls for the removal of all people of Japanese descent from these states. In February of 1942, President Roosevelt issued Executive Order 9066, which authorized the army to "prescribe military areas" from which "any or all persons" could be excluded

---

8. From Exec. Order No. 9066 (February 19, 1942), *Federal Register* 7, no. 38 (February 25, 1942): 1407.

for security reasons. The army interpreted this order to encompass the entire West Coast and all persons of Japanese ancestry. This resulted in removal from their homes to internment camps set up in the interior of the country, after they had been forced to register with the local police and turn over all items in their possession that might foster sabotage—including weapons, chemicals, shortwave radios, and cameras. In 1944, the Supreme Court in the case of *Korematsu v. the United States* agreed in a 5–3 decision that this relocation and denial of civil liberties was a wartime necessity, but in 1988 Congress recognized the injustice that had been done and awarded $20,000 and a public apology to each of the 60,000 survivors of the 120,000 who had been interned.

Reproduced here are Roosevelt's executive order and a map of the centers and camps to which these Japanese Americans were sent.

Authorizing the Secretary of War to Prescribe Military Areas, Executive Order No. 9066

Whereas the successful prosecution of the war requires every possible protection against espionage and against sabotage to national-defense material, national-defense premises, and national-defense utilities as defined in section 4, Act of April 20, 1918, 40 Stat. 533, as amended by the Act of November 30, 1940, 54 Stat. 1220, and the Act of August 21, 1941, 55 Stat. 655 (U. S. C., Title 50, Sec. 104):

Now, therefore, by virtue of the authority vested in me as President of the United States, and Commander in Chief of the Army and Navy, I hereby authorize and direct the Secretary of War, and the Military Commanders whom he may from time to time designate, whenever he or any designated Commander deems such actions necessary or desirable, to prescribe military areas in such places and of such extent as he or the appropriate Military Commanders may determine, from which any or all persons may be excluded, and with such respect to which, the right of any person to enter, remain in, or leave shall be subject to whatever restrictions the Secretary of War or the appropriate Military Commander may impose in his discretion. The Secretary of War is hereby authorized to provide for residents of any such area who are excluded therefrom, such transportation, food, shelter, and other accommodations as may be necessary, in the judgment of the Secretary of War or the said Military Commander, and until other arrangements are made, to accomplish the purpose of this order. The designation of military areas in any region or locality shall supersede designations of prohibited and restricted areas by the Attorney General under the Proclamations of December 7 and 8, 1941, and shall supersede the responsibility and authority of the Attorney General under the said Proclamations in respect of such prohibited and restricted areas.

I hereby further authorize and direct the Secretary of War and the said Military Commanders to take such other steps as he or the appropriate Military Commander may deem advisable to enforce compliance with the restrictions applicable to each Military area hereinabove authorized to be designated, including the use of Federal troops and other Federal Agencies, with authority to accept assistance of state and local agencies.

I hereby further authorize and direct all Executive Departments, independent establishments and other Federal Agencies, to assist the Secretary of War or the said Military Commanders in carrying out this Executive Order, including the furnishing of medical aid, hospitalization, food, clothing, transportation, use of land, shelter, and other supplies, equipment, utilities, facilities and services.

This order shall not be construed as modifying or limiting in any way the authority heretofore granted under Executive Order No. 8972, dated December 12, 1941, nor shall it be construed as limiting or modifying the duty and responsibility of the Federal Bureau of Investigation, with respect to the investigation of alleged acts of sabotage or the duty and responsibility of the Attorney General and the Department of Justice under the Proclamations of December 7 and 8, 1941, prescribing regulations for the conduct and control of alien enemies, except as such duty and responsibility is superseded by the designation of military areas hereunder.

Franklin D. Roosevelt
February 19, 1942

Relocation Centers and Internment Camps

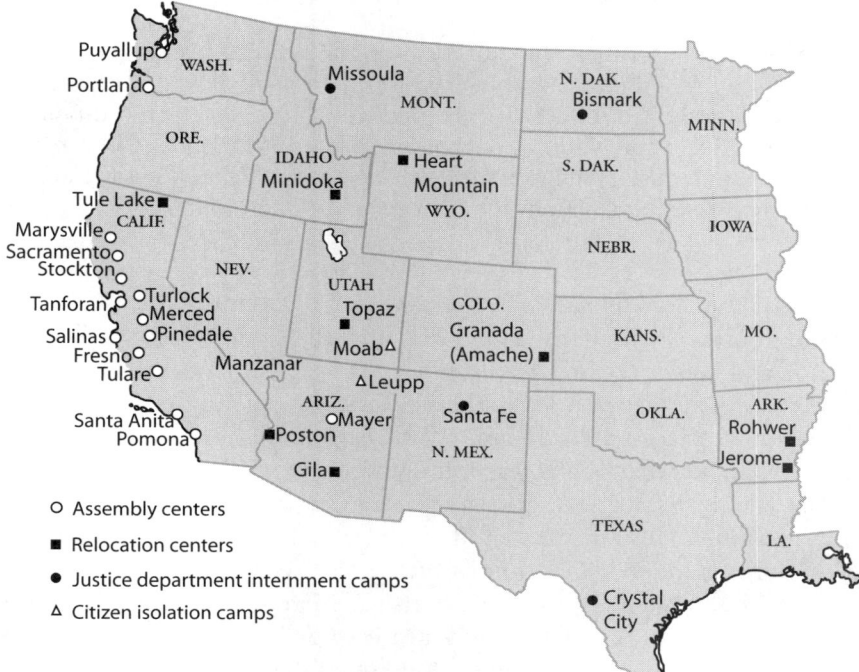

From Michi Weglyn, *Year of Infamy: The Untold Story of America's Concentration Camps* (New York: Morrow, 1976). *Who Built America?* by Nelson Lichtenstein, Susan Strasser, and Roy Rosenzweig. Copyright © 2000 by American Social History Productions, Inc. Used with the permission of Worth Publishers.

5.9 Japanese American Mikiso Hane
Remembers His Wartime Internment[9]

As a young Nisei man, Mikiso Hane and the rest of his family were forced to leave their California farm for internment at a camp in Arizona. After the war ended he attended Yale University, received both undergraduate and graduate degrees from that institution, and became a professor of history at Knox College. The excerpt that follows is taken from his 1990 recollections for the *Journal of American History*.

I suppose the place to start is "Where was I on December 7, 1941?" I was helping on the family farm. I had just learned to maneuver the Farmall tractor and was spreading fertilizer on the field all day that Sunday. It wasn't until after five that I went home. That was when I first heard about the Japanese attack on Pearl Harbor. My reaction was one of shock . . . and then fear about what public reaction toward us would be like.

For Japanese-American citizens growing up in California, racial bias and discrimination were facts of life that we had been conditioned to live with since childhood. Discrimination against Asian immigrants started with measures taken against the Chinese immigrants, culminating in the Chinese Exclusion Act of 1882 and the Geary Act of 1892. The next wave of Asian immigrants who became the target of the exclusionists was made up of Japanese. The door to Japanese immigrants was closed by the Immigration Act of 1924.

After 1924 anti-Japanese sentiments abated somewhat, but in the 1930s when Japan began to commit acts of aggression against China, the antagonism felt toward Japan resurfaced and was once again directed against people of Japanese descent on the West Coast. So our situation was fraught with a double-edged threat: the traditional anti-immigrant, racist sentiment and the anger at Japanese imperialism.

I was especially sensitive about this in 1941 because I had just returned from Japan in 1940. I was one of four sons and my parents, hoping to strike it rich in America and to retire in Japan, wanted one of us there. So in 1932 when I was ten I was sent back to a village near the outskirts of Hiroshima to live with my uncle's family and attend school. When relationships between the United States and Japan began to worsen and there was talk of the possibility of war breaking out between Japan and the United States, I asked my parents if I could return to the States. To my surprise they

9. From Mikiso Hane, "Wartime Internment," *Journal of American History* 77, no. 2 (September 1990): 569–75.

agreed to let me come back. The eight years in Japan made me feel that the American perception that all Japanese were different and not acceptable as Americans would apply more directly to me than to other Nisei (second-generation Japanese). I would be classified as a Kibei—a returnee to America, less of an American than Nisei, who were also not regarded as "real" Americans by the white populations.

Because I had returned to the U.S. after eight years I was still in high school as an overaged nineteen-year-old student in 1941. I think all Nisei went to school on December 8 with an acute sense of anxiety and trepidation. The most uncomfortable experience that day was congregating in the assembly hall to listen to President Franklin D. Roosevelt deliver his "day of infamy" speech.

Our schoolmates and teachers did not show any overt hostility toward us, so we continued going to school without suffering any untoward incidents. . . .

But the atmosphere in the society at large was a different matter. Almost immediately there was a hue and cry about spies in the Japanese community. All "Japs" were seen as sneaky, treacherous, disloyal, untrustworthy elements. A curfew was established to keep us from traveling beyond a certain limit, and during the hours from 8 p.m. to 6 a.m., we were confined to our homes. Japanese community leaders were immediately arrested by the Federal Bureau of Investigation (FBI). (On the first day, 736 Japanese immigrant leaders were detained; 2,191 people had been picked up by the FBI by February.) It was said that anyone who possessed books, magazines, or letters in the Japanese language could be apprehended. I had such materials, so I immediately disposed of all my books, magazines, photographs, letters, and diaries. I either burned them or dumped them in the outhouse.

Soon rumors began to spread about lynch mobs and about people being attacked in other communities. We had no way of verifying these rumors, but the hysteria being whipped up by the press led us to believe that some of the stories must be true. In fact two Nisei sisters in the neighboring town were abducted and raped. All things considered, the actual number of acts of violence was not as horrendous as we had feared it would be: seven killings and thirty-six other acts of violence. When the evacuation and internment order came, there was talk that all of us were going to be herded into camps and machine-gunned to death. . . . Gen. John L. De Witt, who was in charge of evacuating us, asserted that there was no distinction between Japanese in Japan and Japanese Americans in the United States. "A Jap's a Jap," he asserted. In testifying before a congressional committee in early 1943, he said, "We will have to worry about the Japs until they are wiped off the face of the map." In other words, what he had in mind was akin to Adolph Hitler's "final solution." In this respect we were fortunate that the administration of the camps was turned over to a civilian agency and not kept under the control of the army. . . .

. . . President Roosevelt signed Executive Order No. 9066 on February 19, 1942, authorizing the evacuation and internment of all West Coast Japanese including Japanese-American citizens. . . .

Ultimately, 119,803 of us ended up behind barbed wire fences. Sixty-five percent of those were American citizens. . . .

Well, in May 1942 those of us living in Hollister were rounded up and bused to Salinas to a temporary camp set up in the old rodeo grounds. Then in August we were put on the train with armed guards and sent to the interment camp in Poston, Arizona, a barren desert where the temperature in the summer hit about 120 degrees. Eventually twenty thousand of us were interned in Poston.

We arrived late at night but it was still oppressively hot. We trudged through the ankle-deep sand, headed to the empty barracks with our mattresses (straw-filled cloth sacks), and tried to sleep, wondering what was in store for us. For the next several months we struggled with the heat, the sandstorms, the scorpions, the rattlesnakes, the confusion, the overcrowded barracks, and the lack of privacy. But eventually a semblance of order and normality set in. We were all asked to serve in some capacity to make the camp a livable place. I took a job as a kitchen helper in the community mess hall. Water was drawn into the camp; grass and trees were planted; vegetables were grown.

In retrospect it is clear that the decision to evacuate and intern all people of Japanese blood from the West Coast was based not on military but on racial and political grounds. . . . Of course this was not clear to us then, and we succumbed to the mass hysteria that was overwhelming us and meekly accepted our plight. Virtually no one, except three persons, had the courage to challenge the authorities.

Why didn't the Nisei leadership lodge even a pro forma protest rather than urging us to cooperate fully with the authorities? . . . To explain the lack of strong leadership, we could note that most Nisei were very young, had very little political experience, and were conditioned by their parents to be submissive and obedient to authority.

If our inability to resist the evacuation and internment is understandable, how can we justify our meek behavior in camp when we were asked to prove our loyalty after we had been judged as potentially dangerous enemy aliens and had been interned? On this occasion we might have shown some gumption and defied the authorities by refusing to say yes to the loyalty questions. (They were questions 27: "Are you willing to serve in the armed forces of the United States on combat duty, wherever ordered?"

and 28: "Will you swear unqualified allegiance to the United States of America and faithfully defend the United States from any or all attack by foreign or domestic forces, and forswear any form of allegiance or obedience to the Japanese emperor, to any other foreign government, power or organization?")

Not only did the Japanese-American leadership urge us to answer yes to these questions, but we were also encouraged to volunteer for the Japanese-American combat team. . . . I recall reading in an article in a Hearst paper that we were digging cellars under our barracks to hoard food for the Japanese force whose invasion we were anticipating. In fact, we were digging cellars under the barracks to try to stay cool. We would sit around in the hole and play cards to while our time away. That is where I learned to play pinochle.

Well, most of us, 65,000 out of 75,000 citizens, complied and said yes to questions 27 and 28. There were some, however, who had the courage to say no. But instead of praising them for their courage, the Japanese-American loyalists condemned them. Those who answered no to the loyalty questions were segregated and sent to the camp in Tule Lake, California, which came to resemble a high-pressure concentration camp.

After answering yes to questions 27 and 28, I even volunteered for combat—not out of patriotism or courage or desire to join the army, but essentially because of faintheartedness. After I said yes to questions 27 and 28, the sergeant who had processed my answer then asked me if I was willing to volunteer for the Japanese-American combat unit. I was nonplussed by this question because I had just said I was loyal to the United States and was willing to serve in the army. If I said no to his question then logically he could conclude that I was lying when I said yes to questions 27 and 28. I was already afraid that I was more vulnerable than other Nisei because I was a Kibei. If I did not volunteer, it was possible, I thought, that I would be included among those who answered no to questions 27 and 28 and be sent off to a camp set up for disloyal Nisei and eventually be sent back to Japan. At any rate the situation seemed ominous. So I said yes and signed on the dotted line.

Eventually I was turned down by the army who classified me as 4-C, an enemy alien. So my concern that I would automatically be judged disloyal because I had just returned from Japan may not have been far off the mark.

By mid-1943 the War Relocation Authority began to allow internees to leave the camps if they received FBI clearances and could find employment away from the West Coast. Soon after I received a letter from Adj. Gen. J. A. Ulio declining my services as a soldier, I got an opportunity to leave the camp to become a tutor in Japanese in the army specialized training program at Yale University. The camp authorities gave me a temporary pass, so I left camp for New Haven in October 1943.

I cannot say that I had suffered much living in camp. So far as life in camp was concerned, for me it was merely a matter of inconvenience, time lost, and discomfort, and of course the humiliation and indignity that we experienced. But my reaction to life in camp would not be typical because I had lived in somewhat straitened circumstances as a peasant boy in Japan.

Those who underwent greater hardships were people who had more to lose that I did, especially professional people. I was paid sixteen dollars a month as kitchen help in the community kitchen. Doctors, who labored day and night with only primitive facilities at their disposal to take care of many of us who got sick, were paid nineteen dollars a month. When I entered the barracks hospital, after collapsing from spontaneous pneumothorax, the young doctor who took care of patients in the crowded ward worked tirelessly day and night. The doctors and the nurses are the unsung heroes of Poston and all the other internment camps. . . .

. . . When my oldest brother returned to Hollister to see if it would be possible to resume farming there, he saw nothing but signs that said, "No Japs allowed." He had to find a place to eat, so he finally entered a small diner, hoping that, it being a simple place, he would be allowed to have a hot dog. The owner pulled out a shotgun and threatened to shoot him if he didn't get the hell out of there. That was the end of his attempt to return to Hollister.

As for the impact that the internment and evacuation had on my life, it turned out to have positive results. It got me out to the East Coast, gave me an opportunity to work in an army language program in a university setting, and eventually provided me with the chance to go on to college and graduate school and enter the teaching profession. I shudder to think what my life would have been like if I had not been allowed to return to the States in 1940. Recently I was asked to review a book about the experiences of Japanese widows who lost their husbands in the atomic holocaust. Their vivid accounts made me reflect upon what might have happened to me if I had stayed in Hiroshima working in the post office where I had started to work just before I returned to the States. I too could well have been food for the maggots and worms because the boardinghouse where I lived was in the epicenter of the blast. If I, like other Japanese Americans, was destined to pay for the military actions of Japan because of our race, I am grateful that I paid for them in Poston rather than in Hiroshima.

CHAPTER 6

FOR THE DURATION: LIFE AND SOCIETY ON THE AMERICAN HOME FRONT

World War II transformed life and society on the American home front. The booming economy opened up new job opportunities to millions of Americans. Unemployment declined, wages rose, and business—especially big business—flourished. Thanks to a wartime labor shortage women and racial minorities—including African Americans, Mexicans, and Mexican Americans—found new opportunities in the country's booming economy.

The war also transformed the nation's landscape. The wartime boom attracted hundreds of thousands of new workers to urban and industrial centers. Wartime production reignited the Great Migration of African Americans from the rural South to the industrial North, Midwest, and after the 1940s, Far West. More than a half a million black Southerners left that region during the war in search of good jobs, as well as the kind of social and political freedom denied to them in the Jim Crow South. Unfortunately, these migrants did not find the "promised land" outside of the South. As noted in Chapter 2, black Americans faced persistent housing and labor market discrimination. Black workers were often the last hired and the first fired, and generally earned far less than their white counterparts. Landlords often refused to rent to black tenants, or relegated them to substandard and crowded housing.

The movement of African American workers to the industrial North often produced sharp and violent responses from white Americans anxious about racial change. In 1943, racial violence swept Detroit, a response in part to major changes in the city's demographics. Detroit's black population more than doubled between 1930 and 1950, triggering a sharp backlash among some white residents. The 1943 riot was triggered by a black swimmer's transgression of an invisible line at a local beach. The ensuing violence lasted for three days, destroyed $2 million in property, and cost 34 people their lives. Another 675 people were seriously injured, and 1,863 were arrested before federal troops finally managed to restore order.

Racial tensions flared in other cities as well. In 1942, the United States negotiated an agreement with Mexico to allow Mexican agricultural laborers to come to the United States. Some 200,000 Mexicans entered

the United States as farmworkers under the terms of this *bracero* agreement; a similar number entered as undocumented workers. Many of these
immigrants ended up in Los Angeles where they were greeted by a steady
stream of hostile press and intermittent violence. Tensions came to a head
in 1943 when groups of white servicemen joined by thousands of white
Angelenos, rampaged through the city, assaulting Hispanics, Filipinos,
and black Americans. This weeklong spate of violence became known as
the Zoot Suit Riots, for the colorful attire favored by some of the city's
young Mexican population.

The war also disrupted more intimate relations. The draft took many
young men away from their families. The wartime labor shortage created
new opportunities for women to work for wages outside the home. Young
men and women alike seized new employment opportunities even when
those jobs took them far away from their families and their hometowns.
Many experts worried that wartime disruptions to traditional domestic
arrangements would lead to fundamental and lasting changes in gender
roles at home and in the public sphere. This never happened. Indeed, the
wartime experience seems to have reinforced, rather than weakened, the
appeal of domesticity. Marriage and birthrates, which had plummeted
during the Great Depression, began to rise in 1940. American men and
women were getting married younger and having more children. According to one study, 1 million more children were born in the United States
between 1940 and 1943 than would have been absent the war emergency.
Between 1940 and 1945, the birthrate rose from 19.4 per 1,000 people to
24.5 per 1,000 people. The postwar baby boom simply reflected and mag-
nified wartime trends in marriage and childbearing.

Official policy and popular culture reinforced traditional gender roles
throughout the war. Government policy urged women to "make history working for victory," at the same time as it made clear that women's
work outside the home would be acceptable only "for the duration" of
the war. Indeed, the return to the domestic norm was one of the key reasons given for fighting. Popular culture echoed these sentiments. Mass
circulation magazines urged "war brides" to maintain their femininity and
sexual purity while their soldiers fought for the American way in Europe
or the Pacific. Wartime campaigns to stem the tide of venereal diseases
reflected widespread anxieties about unchecked female sexuality. Public
health campaigns to educate men about these sexually transmitted diseases almost always blamed women—whether they be prostitutes or so-
called victory girls—for their transmission. On the other hand, female
sexuality could also be yoked to the war. Pinups like Betty Grable—whose
"girl next door" image was only enhanced when she became a wife and
mother—harnessed male sexual fantasies to American war aims. Pinups

circulated widely during the war, and wives and girlfriends were encouraged to imitate the more famous pinups in photographs for their husbands and sweethearts.

For nonwhite women the war presented both danger and opportunities. Before the war, black women were all but locked out of well-paid, industrial work; most worked in domestic service. The war opened up new opportunities for these women. Indeed, the percentage of black women in domestic service dropped from 59.9 percent to 44.6 percent between 1940 and 1944. But black women faced terrible discrimination on the job, both from men and from white women, and had to adopt a variety of strategies to cope with persistent harassment and unequal treatment from unions, employers, and other workers.

The wartime boom itself produced vexing political and economic problems. Across the board, Americans were earning more and living better than ever before. But the boom raised the frightening specter of inflation. Policy makers remembered all too well the price spiral that accompanied the First World War, and the deflation that followed and, some believed, had led directly to the Great Depression. Concerned to check inflation, but also committed to a free market philosophy and constrained by politics, the Roosevelt administration pursued a limited anti-inflation policy that produced mixed results. As soon as the United States entered the war, the government rationed certain goods critical to the war effort: rubber, gasoline, and sugar (which was used in torpedoes, some dynamites, and smokeless powder). The government supplemented this system with relatively weak price controls and a tax policy (see Chapter 2) designed at least in part to drain excess buying power from the economy. In April of 1942, President Roosevelt exhorted the American people to pay the "price for civilization" in "hard work and sorrow and blood." Despite widespread talk about "sacrifice" however, and constant grumbling about rationing, the economist J. K. Galbraith later acidly concluded: "Never in the long history of human combat have so many talked so much about sacrifice with so little deprivation as in the United States in World War II."

The documents in this chapter encourage students to think about how wartime changes affected American life and how these changes varied according to race, gender, and class. Was World War II really a watershed for American women with regard to both family and paid labor outside the home? How did the war influence the lives of people of color? What long-term effects did the war—and its manifold disruptions—have on American society? On the American family? On American culture?

* * * *

6.1 War Jobs Trigger the Second Great Migration[1]

Close to 1.5 million African Americans left the South for the industrial North, Midwest, and Far West in the World War II period. Lured by the possibility of good work in war industries, the vast majority of migrants moved to urban areas. Those who hoped to discover the "promised land" in these industrial cities were often disappointed. Black migrants were often relegated to the most poorly paid and dangerous jobs, locked out of labor unions, and segregated within racialized ghettos. The second Great Migration, which continued until 1980, eventually transformed the geography of race in the United States, altered the demographics of American cities, and ultimately transformed both the Republican and Democratic Parties. The implications of this migration were apparent almost immediately. In 1947, the Millbank Fund commissioned a study by Ira D. A. Reid, an African American sociologist, author, and activist, into the causes and consequences of wartime migration.

The recent war, like World War I, has permanently influenced the distribution of the Negro population. . . . The southern Negro population is largely a rural one (63.5 per cent) while the Negro populations of the West and North are predominantly urban—89.4 per cent in the North and 83.1 per cent in the West.

Changes in the structure and location of economic activities during the period of defense and war mobilization brought about an extensive redistribution of the nation's population. Negroes participated with other groups in that migration, but with some striking differences:

. . . The beginning and the peak of large-scale Negro migration lagged behind similar phases in the general population shift. . . . Once the Negro migration got under way, the number involved was disproportionately large and the rate of migration more intense. . . . The proportion of Negroes remaining in the centers of in-migration appeared to be significantly higher than the average for all in-migrants. . . .

. . . In a later analysis the Bureau of the Census pointed out that the major Negro migration since the beginning of World War II started in the South and terminated in war-boom cities, regardless of location. The peculiar aspect of wartime migration was that between 1940 and 1944 Negro population movements usually started in the South and ended at such industrial points as Detroit, Norfolk, San Francisco, and Los Angeles,

---

1. Ira D. Reid, *Postwar Problems in Migration* (New York: Milbank Memorial Fund, 1947), available at http://www.inmotionaame.org/texts/index.cfm?migration=9&topic=99&type =text.

where Negroes could find employment in war activities. In ten Congested Production Areas the increase in Negro population from 1940 to 1944 of 49 per cent was substantially above the 19 per cent rise in the total population. . . .

. . . The Negro migration also differed from the general movement in the timing of its various phases. Whereas the peak of total migration was reached in late 1943, it was not until early 1945 that the corresponding phase of the population shift among Negroes was reached. The main stream of Negro migration did not start moving until after mid-1942. . . . The most important factor to influence the proportionately high Negro interstate and inter-regional migration was the racial patterning of defense training and war employment. . . . Restrictions on their employment after they had been trained forced many Negroes to leave their communities in the South in order to get the jobs for which they were qualified. . . .

. . . Discriminatory administration by state and local education officials of training programs financed from Federal funds seriously handicapped Negro workers. In the states of out-migration where three-fourths of the Negro labor was to be found, training facilities were either inadequate or nonexistent. In January, 1942, Negroes constituted only 4 per cent of the total trainees for war industries in the eighteen southern and border states where they constituted 22 per cent of the total population. The only permissive outlets for full training were in the large cities of the East and mid-West; the only permissive outlets for war employment were on the Pacific Coast. The Federal government acting under its creed of training and employment "without regard as to race, creed, or color" frequently sent workers from Georgia and Alabama to Kansas, Missouri, California, and Washington when the demands were at their peaks.

Now that the war is done, there is every indication that most of the Negro in-migrants will remain in or near these congested centers and that much of the interstate migration from the South will not be reversed. . . .

. . . As a result of this wartime migration, the development of social machinery wherewith to effect democratic adjustments in human relations has become a critical problem. The movements of populations have nationalized the problems of minorities and have promoted newer types of race attitudes and feelings. The racial tensions that accompany postwar or post-migration adjustments have begun to be felt keenly in centers that appear ill-equipped to absorb large permanent populations. . . .

. . . [A]ny further abridgment of political rights for Negroes in southern states, as is threatened in Alabama and Georgia, and as has already taken place in Arkansas and South Carolina, will assure a steady stream of settlers in urban areas of the North and West where the racial accommodation pattern is less partial and more easily manipulated.

6.2 The NAACP Explains What Caused the Detroit Race Riots, 1943[2]

No American city better represented the "arsenal of democracy" celebrated by Franklin Roosevelt than Detroit, Michigan. Thanks to the
automobile industry, Detroit grew by leaps and bounds after 1910. The
city's population more than doubled between 1910 and 1920, and
then doubled again between 1920 and 1950. Much of this growth was
fueled by African American migration to the city, particularly during
World War II. Between 1940 and 1950, the number of African Americans in Detroit rose from 149,110 to 300,506—and increase of just
over 100 percent. As in other cities, demographic change sometimes
provoked racist resistance and even violence on the part of white residents. In June 1943, Detroit exploded in a race riot that lasted for three
days. Thirty-four people were killed; twenty-five were African American; of these sixteen were killed by the police. In this document the
NAACP traces the roots of the violence to housing and job discrimination, the weakness of the Fair Employment Practice Committee, and
police brutality.

Preface

On June 20 a race riot erupted in Detroit—arsenal of democracy—which
took the lives of thirty-four Detroiters. Because this tragedy can happen
in other American cities, the National Association for the Advancement
of Colored People publishes herewith a two-part, detailed analysis of the
riot and its causes.

Long before the riot came, the NAACP worked indefatigably to arouse
public opinion regarding the impending danger and to get public officials
to act against police brutality, mob attacks upon the homes and persons
of Negro citizens, job discrimination, and other inequities based upon
color. More than a year before the riot the Office of War Information had
warned that "all hell will break loose in Detroit," unless positive action
were taken by public officials. *Life Magazine* in August, 1942, published a
nine-page illustrated warning under the caption, "Detroit Is Dynamite."
But boom town profits, political exigencies, other factors had stopped cor-
rective action.

---

2. From Walter White and Thurgood Marshall, *What Caused the Detroit Race Riot, An
Analysis* (New York: National Association for the Advancement of Colored People, 1943),
available at https://archive.org/stream/whatcauseddetroi00whit/whatcauseddetroi00whit_
djvu.txt.

It is hoped that the facts as set forth in the succeeding pages will help to arouse both public officials and private citizens to the necessity of action not alone as a war measure but to prevent other Detroits in the post-war years. These are inevitable unless courage and intelligence are exhibited by both white and Negro Americans.

What Caused the Detroit Riots?

Section I
By Walter White

In 1916 there were 8,000 Negroes in Detroit's population of 536,650. In 1925 the number of Negroes in Detroit had been multiplied by ten to a total of 85,000. In 1940, the total had jumped to 149,119. In June, 1943, between 190,000 and 200,000 lived in the Motor City.

According to the War Manpower Commission, approximately 500,000 in-migrants moved to Detroit between June, 1940, and June, 1943. Because of discrimination against employment of Negroes in industry, the overwhelming majority—between 40,000 and 50,000—of the approximately 50,000 Negroes who went to Detroit in this three-year period moved there during the fifteen months prior to the race riot of June, 1943. According to Governor Harry S. Kelly, of Michigan, a total of 345,000 persons moved into Detroit during that same fifteen-month period. There was comparatively little out-migration as industry called for more and more workers in one of the tightest labor markets in the United States. The War Manpower Commission failed almost completely to enforce its edict that no in-migration be permitted into any industrial area until all available local labor was utilized. Thus a huge reservoir of Negro labor existed in Detroit, crowded into highly congested slum areas. But they did have housing of a sort and this labor was already in Detroit. The coming of white workers recruited chiefly in the South not only gravely complicated the housing, transportation, educational and recreation facilities of Detroit, but they brought with them the traditional prejudices of Mississippi, Arkansas, Louisiana, and other Deep South states against the Negro. . . .

. . . This was particularly noticeable when Negroes were forced by sheer necessity to purchase or rent houses outside the so-called Negro area. For years preceding the riot, there had been mob attacks dating back as far as the famous Sweet case in 1925 upon the homes of Negroes. In some instances there had been police connivance in these attacks. In practically no cases had there been arrests of whites who had stoned or bombed the homes of Negroes. During July, 1941, there had been an epidemic of riots allegedly by Polish youths which had terrorized colored residents in Detroit, Hamtramack and other sections in and about Detroit. Homes of Negroes on Horton, Chippewa, West Grand Boulevard and other streets close to but outside of the so-called Negro areas were attacked by mobs with no police interference.

Detroit's 200,000 Negroes are today largely packed into two segregated areas. . . . In addition to these two wholly Negro areas, there are scattered locations throughout Detroit of mixed occupancy in which, significantly, there was during the riot less friction that in any other area.

The desperate scarcity of housing for whites, however, limited Negroes in finding places to live outside of the Negro areas. The Detroit newspapers have contained for months many advertisements offering rewards for housing of any nature or quality for whites. Meantime, but little public housing was created to meet the tragic need for housing of both whites and Negroes in Detroit. Even this was characterized by shameful vacillation and weakness in Washington which only added fuel to the flames of racial tension in Detroit. The notorious riots revolving about the question of who should occupy the Sojourner Truth housing project in February, 1942, are an example of this. These riots resulted when fascist elements, emboldened by the vacillation of the National Housing Administration which reversed itself several times on Negro occupancy, joined with pressure of real estate interests to bring to a head the mob violence which led to the smashing of the furniture and beating of Negro tenants attempting to move into the project. . . .

Jobs

Early in June, 1943, 25,000 employees of the Packard Plant, which was making Rolls-Royce engines for American bombers and marine engines for the famous PT boats, ceased work in protest against the upgrading of three Negroes. Subsequent investigation indicated that only a relatively small percentage of the Packard workers actually wanted to go on strike. The UAW-CIO bitterly fought the strike. But a handful of agitators charged by R. J. Thomas, president of the UAW-CIO, with being members of the Ku Klux Klan, had whipped up sentiment particularly among the Southern whites employed by Packard against the promotion of Negro workers. During the short-lived strike, a thick Southern voice outside the plant harangued a crowd shouting, "I'd rather see Hitler and Hirohito win than work beside a nigger on the assembly line.". . . The racial hatred created, released, and crystallized by the Packard strike played a considerable role in the race riot which was soon to follow. It also was the culmination of a long and bitter fight to prevent the employment of Negroes in wartime industry. . . .

. . . Ingrained or stimulated prejudice against the Negro has been used as much against organized labor as it has been against the Negro. Employers and employer associations have been apathetic to the storm which was brewing. Apparently they were interested only in the size and continuation of profits. It has been frequently charged and not disproved that some of the employers have financed or contributed heavily to some of the organizations which have organized and capitalized upon race prejudice as a means of checking the organization of workers in Detroit plants.

Detroit Labor Unions and the Negro

. . . The Detroit riot brought into sharp focus one of the most extraordinary labor situations in the United States. Prior to the Ford strike of 1941 many Negroes in Detroit considered Ford their "great white father" because the Ford plant almost alone of Detroit industries employed Negroes. When the UAW-CIO and the UAW-AFL sought to organize Ford workers, their approach at the beginning was a surreptitious one. The unions felt that the very high percentage of Southern whites in Detroit would refuse to join the Union if Negroes were too obviously participating. But when the strike broke, far-sighted Negro leaders in Detroit took an unequivocal position on behalf of the organization of workers. A serious racial clash was averted by the intercession of thoughtful whites and Negroes. Following the winning of the NLRB election by the union, it began to take a broader and more unequivocal position that all workers and union members should share in the benefits of union agreements irrespective of race, creed, or color.

During the recent riot, R. J. Thomas, president of the UAW-CIO proposed an eight-point program which was widely published, and which helped to emphasize the basic causes of the riot. These points included: (1) creation of a special grand jury to investigate the cause of the riots and to return justifiable indictments, with a competent Negro attorney appointed as an assistant Prosecutor of work with the grand jury; (2) immediate construction and opening of adequate park and recreation facilities. Thomas called it "disgraceful that the City's normal, inadequate park space was permitted to be overtaxed further by the influx of hundreds of thousands of new war workers"; (3) immediate and practical plans for rehousing Negro slum dwellers in decent, Government-financed housing developments; (4) insistence that plant managements as well as workers recognize the right of Negroes to jobs in line with their skill and seniority; (5) a full investigation by the special grand jury of the conduct of the Police Department during the riots; (6) special care by the courts in dealing with many persons arrested. Those found guilty should be severely punished, and there must be no discrimination between white and Negro rioters; (7) the loss of homes and small businesses, as well as personal injuries, is the responsibility of the community, and the city should create a fund to make good these losses; (8) creation by the Mayor of a special biracial committee of ten persons to make further recommendations looking toward elimination of racial differences and frictions, this committee to have a special job in connection with high schools "where racial hatred has been permitted to grow and thrive in recent years."

Vacillation on Fair Employment Practice Committee

A contributory factor to the breakdown of discrimination in employment in Detroit was the issuance on June 25, 1941, by President Roosevelt of Executive Order 8802 under which was established the President's Committee on Fair Employment Practice. Although limited in personnel, budget, and authority, the FEPC as the affirmative expression of a moral principle had strengthened the efforts to eliminate discrimination in Detroit was plants. . . .

But in the summer of 1942, the FEPC was robbed of its independent status and placed under the control of the War Manpower Commission. The conviction in Detroit and other places began to grow that the FEPC was being quietly shelved and that the government no longer was insistent that discrimination in employment be abolished. . . . As the FEPC lapsed into total inactivity fear of Federal action died among those who were guilty of discrimination. Anti-Negro organizations and individuals renewed and increased their agitation against the employment and upgrading of Negroes. Despair deepened in the Negro communities as they saw hordes of Southern whites imported into Detroit, provided with such housing as was available including tax-supported houses, apartments, and dormitories, speedily upgraded to the better paid jobs while Negroes who had lived in Detroit for many years were still shut out.

Morale and morals of Negroes were affected adversely as they saw the one agency which had been created to do away with discrimination emasculated. Those Negroes who were employed found themselves with money they could not spend for decent houses or other improvements in their living standards. Some invested in War Bonds and insurance; others threw away their money in riotous living because they had been robbed of hope.

Law Enforcement Agencies

. . . During the 30s especially when there was keen competition for jobs because of the depression, Southern whites sought and secured jobs on the police force in Detroit and in the courts. There was a period of years when cold-blooded killings of Negroes by policemen were a constant source of bitterness among Negroes. Eventually, protest by such organizations as the Detroit branch of the NAACP and other Negro and interracial groups led to a diminution and eventually a practical cessation of such killings. But a residue of distrust of the police remained. When the riot of June, 1943, broke forth, this suspicion of the police by Negroes was more than justified when 29 of the 35 killed were Negroes, 17 of them shot by police and a number of these shot in the back. . . .

The willful inefficiency of the Detroit police in its handling of the riot is one of the most disgraceful episodes in American history. When the riot broke out on Sunday night, June 20, following a dispute between a white and Negro motorist on the Belle Isle Bridge, an efficient police force armed with night sticks and fire hoses could have broken up the rioting on Woodward Avenue and broken the back of the insurrection, had the police been determined to do so. Instead, the police did little or nothing, though there were a few individual instances of courage by policemen which are commendable. . . .

The anti-Negro motivation of the Detroit police department is further illustrated by these facts and figures. It has already been pointed out that the Negro population of Detroit at the time of the riot was 200,000 or less, out of a total population of more than 2,000,000. The inevitable riot was the product of anti-Negro forces which had been allowed to operate without check or hindrance by the police over a period of many years. But 29 of the 35 persons who died during the riot were Negroes. An overwhelming majority of the more than 600 injured were Negroes. Of the 1,832 persons arrested for rioting, more than 85% were Negroes. And this in the face of the indisputable fact that the aggressors over a period of years were not Negroes but whites. . . .

National Aspects

The War Production Board on June 26 announced that more than one million man hours of production were lost forever during the riot. No figures are available of the man hours previously lost by work stoppages and slow down strikes to keep Negroes from being employed or upgraded. As the chief war production center of the country, the pattern of behavior there has affected and will continue to affect other war production centers. Failure to correct conditions similar to those in Detroit, or failure by federal, state, and municipal governments to act against those who, deliberately or unwittingly, foment similar racial and industrial clashes cannot but jeopardize the winning of the war. . . . Timorousness in attacking the problem and cowardice in surrender to the divisive forces of Detroit and other cities may conceivably cause the United States to lose the war or, most certainly, to prolong it unnecessarily at the sacrifice of the lives of American soldiers who would not otherwise die. One of the few bright spots of the Detroit riot has been the almost universal condemnation of the riot by Detroit members of the armed services.

6.3 Mississippi Congressman John Rankin Attacks the "Zoot Suiters," 1943[3]

The Zoot Suit Riots of 1943 are another example of resistance to the vast cultural, social, and economic changes wrought by World War II. Named for the high-waisted wool pants and baggy, long-tailed coats favored by Los Angeles's youth culture, the Zoot Suit Riots began in June 1943. The violence escalated over the next few days as a mob of white U.S. servicemen took to the streets in taxicabs to attack Mexican and Mexican American "zoot suiters." The mob also targeted other nonwhite groups, including African Americans and Filipinos. Remarkably, the violence did not result in any deaths. In the document that follows, Mississippi Representative John Rankin, one of the most virulent segregationists in Congress, blames the violence on the zoot suiters rather than their attackers. Rankin's speech suggests both the challenges the war posed to the "color line," and the determination of some, including members of Congress, to protect and defend white supremacy.

Zoot-Suiter Termites

Remarks of Hon. John E. Rankin of Mississippi in the House of Representatives, Tuesday, June 15, 1943

Mr. Rankin: Mr. Speaker, instead of criticizing and abusing our servicemen for tearing "zoot suits" off a bunch of marauding criminals throughout the country, we may find that we owe them a lasting debt of gratitude;

---

3. From Representative Rankin, speaking on "Zoot Suiter Termites," June 15, 1943, 78th Cong., 1st sess., *Congressional Record* 89, pt. 11:A3065.

and if they just keep it up until they obliterate this bunch of termites, we might be justified in giving to each one who renders such services a badge of distinction, an increase in pay, or an extra furlough home.

From an article appearing in last Sunday's *Washington Post*, one would think that a degenerate society and a lawless element in our armed forces are responsible for this whole trouble. That article ought to be encouraging, not only to the zoot-suit rapists our brave men in uniforms have been taking care of, but it should be doubly encouraging to our crackpot promoters of "social gains," whose inflammatory activities, speeches, and writings have encouraged these Negro rapists and their cohorts in the Black Dragon Society, to carry on their criminal activities.

This article tells us that—

> Everywhere the zoot-suiters are composed of underprivileged youngsters, or those who feel themselves to be such—a fact that must always be remembered in any attempt to deal with them.

This article also tells us that:

> The uniform of this (zoot-suit) movement is fascinating—

Now hold yourselves down, do not get excited; but listen to this: It goes on to say:

> The baggy trousers that narrow around the ankles give freedom of movement for jitterbugging—

Probably that is what is so fascinating
And—
The writer continues

> The tail of the long coat swirls like the girls' skirts during a pirouette. The outfit is very expensive, costing $100 or more.
> Chief features—

Says the writer—

> are the broad felt hat, the long key chain, the pocketknife of a certain size and shape.

While the writer did not describe the knife fully, it is described in another publication as having "a long blade on one end, a hook on the other."

Now when a red-blooded American soldier, sailor, or marine sees one of these "underprivileged" objects of "social gains," or a group of them—they usually go in groups—he no doubt feels justified in yielding to his natural, patriotic impulse to exterminate such termites, or, to use the words of his oath, to defend this country against all enemies "foreign and domestic."

But the truth is that these servicemen were being attacked by gangs of these "underprivileged" zoot-suiters, dressed in these $100 outfits, and armed with stilettoes, or knives, with "a very long blade on one end, a hook on the other." One of these gangs, composed largely of Negroes, would slip up on a serviceman out strolling with his girl, beat up the young man and then rape the girl; and probably murder both of them.

Of course, those service men resisted those savage brutes, and retaliated in no uncertain terms; and when the facts are known they will receive the plaudits of all decent patriotic Americans.

But this article in the *Washington Post* says:

> Let it be said at once that the gangsterism of our sailors in the Los Angeles area is no less alarming than the violent reactions of the zoot-suiters.

Is it "gangsterism" for our brave, patriotic soldiers, sailors, and marines to defend themselves and to defend innocent white girls from attacks at the hands of these brutal blacks and half-breeds?

It may seem so to one who is "fascinated" by a zoot suit, but red-blooded Americans who experience no such thrill of fascination will applaud our servicemen and thank them for the manhood and the courage they have displayed in stripping the masks, as well as the zoot suits, from these loathsome criminals and protecting innocent American girls from their beastly attacks.

6.4 Wartime and Postwar Conditions Affect Marriage, Divorce, and Birthrates, 1930–1950

World War II had the potential to restructure both the economy and women's role in it. Wartime labor shortages might have created new and lasting opportunities for women to work for wages outside the home and weakened sex segregation in industry. The war might also have led to the postponement of marriage and childbearing, just as the Depression had done in the 1930s. Yet none of this happened. Indeed, the war seems to have reaffirmed the primacy of the male breadwinner family and reinforced the social and cultural value of domesticity. The charts that follow show long-term trends in marriage, divorce, and fertility rates. What was happening to these indices before World War II? What trends to do you see in the decades after the war? How might we explain this?

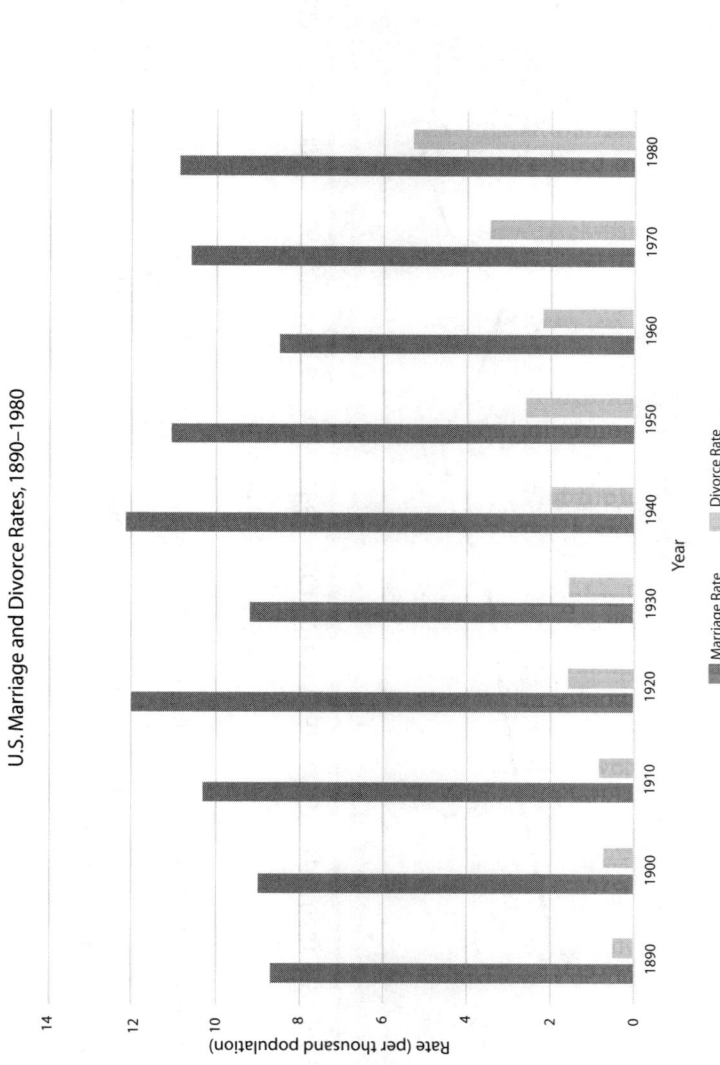

Sources: *Marriage and Divorce, 1887–1906*, Bulletin 96, Bureau of the Census, Department of Commerce and Labor, 1908; *Historical Statistics of the United States, Colonial Times to 1970*, Part 1, Bicentennial Edition, Bureau of the Census, U.S. Department of Commerce, 1975; *Statistical Abstract of the United States*, Bureau of the Census, U.S. Department of Commerce 1983. Note: Marriage and divorce rates are calculated per 1,000 population.

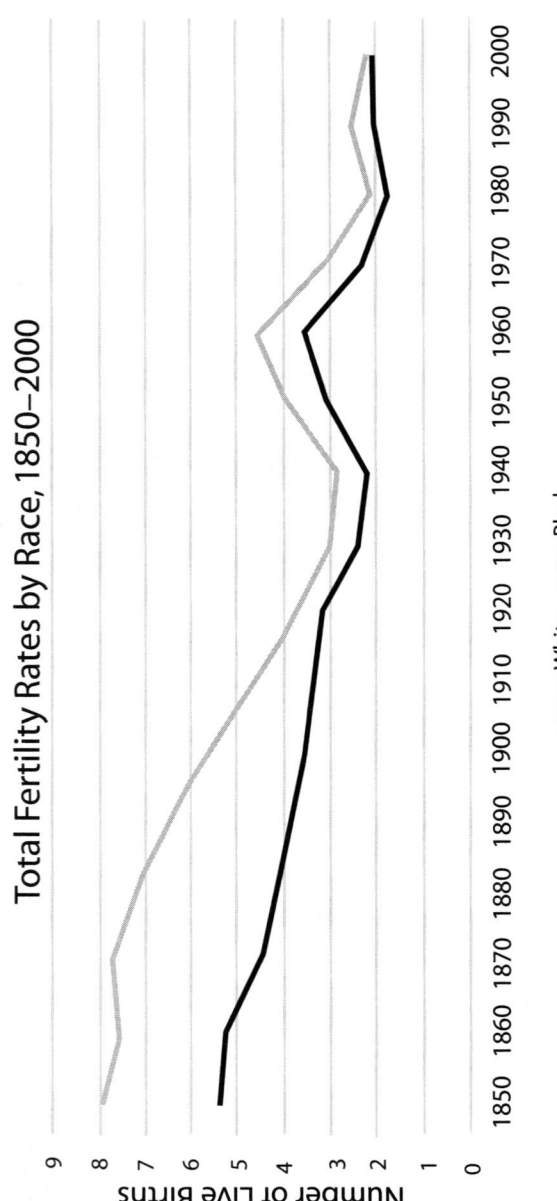

Total Fertility Rates by Race, 1850–2000

Source: Susan B. Carter, Scott Sigmund Gartner, Michael R. Haines, Alan L. Olmstead, Richard Sutch, and Gavin Wright, eds., *Historical Statistics of the United States, Millennial Edition (Online)*, Series Ab 1-10, "Fertility and Mortality by Race, 1800–2000." Note: The fertility rate estimates the number of children born to each woman were she to live to the end of her childbearing years. It is calculated by totaling age-specific fertility rates over five-year intervals.

6.5 *Ladies Home Journal* Tells You What to Do "If You're a War Bride," 1942[4]

World War II created both challenges and opportunities for American women. The war opened up new economic and social possibilities for women willing and able to take them. At the same time, the war disrupted many families and made planning for the future difficult, if not impossible. Popular culture, including mass-circulation magazines aimed at women, sought to make sense of these changes. This 1942 article from the *Ladies Home Journal* gives American "war brides" advice about such things as where to live, how to occupy themselves, and even whether to start a family. This article not only shows the challenges facing American women at home but also demonstrates how mass culture had begun to fashion a national identity that increasingly transcended, or at least competed with, older ethnic, religious, or regional identities.

It was a beautiful wedding on Easter afternoon. The church was over-flowed with flowers from the morning service. Everyone agreed that Melville looked handsome in his uniform, and that Marjorie was perfectly lovely. But in two weeks Melville was gone and Marjorie was obliged to make her plans for the future alone.

"I don't even know where he is," she explained, "except that he sailed from an Atlantic port and the Army issued tropical clothing, so I know he didn't go to Ireland. He might be in South America or Africa, Arabia or India—he's a ground man in aviation and they're needed everywhere. It's nearly two months since he left and I haven't had a word from him yet. It's a strange sort of marriage!"

"And a fairly common sort just now," I replied.

"Melville's parents were married in the same way, during the last war," she went on. "His mother was alone for only fourteen months, however. Melville was born while his father was in France. She didn't seem very anxious for us to marry, but when he heard that he was to be sent abroad and had two weeks' leave beforehand, we just felt we couldn't delay our wedding indefinitely. Now what am I to do?"

What is any bride to do in such circumstances? She faces three questions immediately: How shall she occupy herself? Where shall she live? What shall she plan for recreation? In many instances there is a fourth question: Shall she start a baby at once?

---

4. From Paul Popenoe, "If You're a War Bride," *Ladies Home Journal*, November 1942, 24.

The first question is the most difficult, since its answer will largely control the others. Not one war bride in a thousand can hope to be as fortunate as Helen, who married many months before Pearl Harbor. As an aviation instructor, her husband was assigned to a base near San Antonio. She got an apartment before rents went out of sight and they are living as comfortably and happily as anyone could desire.

For most women, war is not like that! Louise is staying at home with her parents and sympathizing with herself. She married with her eyes open—there is no reason why she should consider herself particularly abused, but she insists on feeling that way about it. Eleanor, Sandra and a dozen others whom I have been watching are taking almost as active a part in the war as are their husbands. Eleanor brushed up her acquaintance with foreign languages and is a censor for the post office; Sandra is a stenographer in a plant now making trucks for the Army; Gladys took a "defense course" and is already putting light rivets in airplanes.

"Every time I drive a rivet," she confessed to me, "I assert to myself that it is cutting the war short by one minute and bringing my husband home to me that much sooner. I'd hate to tell you how many thousand rivets I drive in a week! I feel that I'm working not merely for Uncle Sam but for my own future happiness. I'm putting most of my wages into War Savings Bonds and they'll help to carry us through the postwar disorganization, if necessary, or educate our children later on. I don't see how any war wife would want to loaf around home, these days."

Most of them don't want to loaf around home. Ruth is teaching, Genevieve is painting camouflage on tanks, Edith is filling shells in an arsenal, Gloria, at business college, is about to graduate as a mimeograph operator. Many others, including Marjorie herself, are busy in Red Cross or civilian-defense activities; but I know few war brides who are happier than those now working hard in some of the war industries. They feel that they are standing, in spirit, right beside their husbands in the fight for victory.

Where will you live? With your parents or his parents; alone or with other wives in similar situations? Happiness, usefulness, expense will all have to be considered. For many wives this is a good time to make the break with the old home and begin to be independent. They will be better prepared for homemaking when "he" returns than they will if they simply stay on with mother, who unconsciously tends to make all plans and decisions.

For most wives the attempt to live near a camp is ill-advised. I saw a good deal of this in the preceding war. David, for example, was assigned to a camp on the Mexican border. His wife came along, rented an unsatisfactory place at an exorbitant price, with two other Army wives. She was miserable most of the time and when her husband came home at night, tired and irritable himself, he found her in tears because of the way things had gone during the day. About the time their freight arrived from Nebraska, David was transferred from New Mexico to Alabama and they had to go through the same process again. They created patterns of unhappiness, which later wrecked their marriage completely. "Of course I can't tell my wife so," many a husband would confide to his friends, "but it would have been a whole lot better if she had stayed at home."

In the third place, what will you do for recreation? This requires unusual planning, because a young wife is cut off from so many activities just because she is a wife. Modern social life is built largely on couples, and she isn't a couple at the moment; yet because she is a wife she can't go around with other men, as she could a few years earlier. Unconsciously, her mental hygiene begins to suffer for lack of a normal recreational life, with damage to her marriage later on. She may find other war brides as associates, but that is not enough. One of the best things she can do is to take an active part in USO and other entertainment for men in uniform. Again she will feel that she is making a direct contribution to war effort; she will not merely be having someone entertain her but will be doing something for others—which is essential to morale; and she will learn more and more about men, which is a valuable education for any bride.

In the fourth place, what about a baby? For some wives, there is no room for argument on this subject. They will be guided by their own principles. Others feel that there is a great deal to be said on both sides and they want to weigh the arguments.

Marjorie, whom I introduced in the first paragraph, had hoped that she might become a mother as soon as possible. "After all, that's the way Melville was born," she argued. "If his mother hadn't been left with a baby, I might not have had a husband." It was no use to try to controvert such an argument—although his mother did not encourage Marjorie to follow her own example.

One day Marjorie brought Evelyn around to see me. They wanted to debate this particular issue. Evelyn's fiancé had been called in the spring draft. They were planning to marry before he went to camp, but did not want to start a family until the end of the war.

"But every woman has a natural desire to bear a child to the man she loves. She shouldn't frustrate that desire," Marjorie declared.

"That depends on the circumstances," Evelyn retorted. "Right now it would add too much to the husband's anxieties—financial as well as emotional."

"On the contrary, it would give him a greater interest—more to live for and look forward to. And think how much it adds to the wife's happiness during their separation."

Evelyn dissented again: "It would decrease my happiness as well as his, just at this time. You can afford it and we can't. I want to take a job and, in fact, I have to take a job."

"But the nation needs babies," Marjorie demurred. "And after all, we have to face the fact that our husbands might not return. I'd at least have his child to comfort my future years."

"A child shouldn't be brought up by one parent," Evelyn objected.

I thought it would be inappropriate to add the realistic suggestion that if the husband does not return, his widow will have a better chance to remarry if she does not have a child.

Marjorie and Evelyn did not bring in one argument that is sometimes offered. It is alleged that the existence of a child is more likely to hold the husband later. I do not think any war bride should attach importance to such an argument. The right kind of husband won't need a child to bring him back: the wrong kind won't be brought back by a child. There are plenty of things for war brides to do that will be more effective than pregnancy in ensuring the future success of the marriage.

One of these is to "keep on the job" as a wife, of course. Even if she has full-time work, she can still be making herself more efficient, matrimonially. Some women do not like to face the fact that their husbands admire efficiency—but it is a fact, nevertheless. If the bride has not been well educated as a homemaker, she can now make up for lost time before her husband has a chance to find her out. If she begins at once to practice on a budget, to study the whole profession of wifehood and motherhood as systematically as she would study the profession of social work or cosmetology, she will be making a matrimonial investment that will pay generous dividends as long as she lives.

At the same time, she should be taking every opportunity to become better acquainted with her husband's background if, as is often the case, she really knew little about it before marriage. She will need this information in order to correspond with him intelligently, in order to understand him now and when he returns. She can get it best from his own family, and this gives her as good a chance as possible to build up the right sort of relationship with her in-laws. They will always be ready to talk about the childhood of her hero. A firm bond established with them at this time will not only be profitable now but may be invaluable later. But she need not suppose that this bond will make them want to provide a home for her indefinitely when her own parents do not.

Correspondingly, she must keep her own family in line, if that is necessary; must see to it that they develop a helpful attitude toward her husband, especially if they were not too enthusiastic about her marriage to a man who was immediately going to leave her with nothing more substantial than the Government's small allowance to the wife of a private soldier. If she has an opportunity to visit him, as is likely during the first year of her husband's Army life, these visits will help to build up a solid foundation for the future. Weepers have only a nuisance value. Being a mere male, your husband will be more favorably impressed by the realization of how much you contribute to his happiness than by any argument you will be able to offer as to how great an obligation he has assumed to make you happy.

Visits will necessarily be few for most brides, so the task of building up a permanent and satisfying relationship will be largely a mail-order business. Even this may be infrequent. Men are being more and more shipped to places where mail days are weeks or even months apart. That means that each letter will be ten times as important as it would be if there were ten times as many letters. No one needs to study the art of correspondence so diligently as the war bride. Can you sit down today and write him a letter ten times as good as an average letter; or drop in the box a missive so cheerful, newsy and confident that for weeks it will make him feel a better man than before? If so, you are building solidly for the future.

After all, you won't actually lose your husband while he is in the Army. There is no place for him to go. You can hold him as long as he isn't with you! The critical time will be his return. There was a recognizable rise in the divorce rate in the early 1920s, when war romances began to encounter postwar realities. Your plans for the next few years will have that return in view.

Much of the breakdown of marriage comes from a lack of common interests; more from a lack of common sympathies. It is not necessary that husband and wife have the same aims and interests, but it is necessary that they have sympathy with each other's aims and interests. You are going to grow while he is in the Army. Will you grow toward him or away from him? You'll need to analyze this problem carefully every day from the point of view of your marriage. Are you building up interests in which you are sure that he will participate? Are you developing yourself along lines that mean a great deal to him? Or are you cultivating interests that will be foreign to him? In the last case, you may find that your new interests tend to separate you from your husband, or else that you will give them up reluctantly and feel aggrieved because he has required you to sacrifice them. Don't take up anything without weighing it from this point of view.

Bert and Josephine became engaged while they were seniors in high school. Bert insisted on enlisting in the Navy on graduation. They married and he went away a month later. Josephine decided that she would go on to college as a means of passing the time and of gratifying the ambition of her parents. She could spend four years in that way, and by that time Bert would surely be home. By and large, college is a good place to go. But in this instance, what will it mean to Bert? Does he admire college girls or is he afraid of them? Will he value Josephine all the more because she is so much more highly educated than he? Will she, four years hence, with a B.A., unconsciously begin to feel that she is superior to Bert, that it is a pity she didn't get a husband with more schooling? A college education may be just the thing for her, or it may end by wrecking her marriage. If I knew Bert I might make a more accurate prediction; but I advise her to think it over carefully. She can't ask him because knowing that her parents want her to go to college, he will hardly dare to say "I'd rather see you go to work right now." If she wants to take four years more of formal education, she must at all costs determine that she will make it an education that will fit her better, rather than worse, for marriage—not for marriage in general but for her marriage to her own husband.

These are some of the things that Marjorie and her friends and I talked over together. Finally, I urged, make up your mind to expect some personality changes. Your husband may not be, three or five years from now, at all the kind of man that he was—or you thought he was—when he took you to wife on Easter Sunday. You both will have changed, you will see things from new points of view; a lot of superficially romantic glamour will have evaporated. Let's assume, for the sake of argument, that like in the Army or Navy, life among the Brazilians, Persians or Australians, may have changed him for the worse in some ways, so far as you are concerned. Many a marriage was wrecked after the last war simply because neither husband nor wife had planned to meet these changes. Begin to do so today. Accustom yourself steadily to the idea. Assure yourself, in deadly earnest, that he won't seem so wonderful when he returns as he did when he went away. Make up your mind that he will come back with less than you expected, but that in the meanwhile you will make every effort to greet him with *more* than he expected. If you can do that, then any surprise is likely to be a pleasant one instead of a shocking one.

The success of any marriage requires a lot of effort. The success of a war marriage requires greater effort and one carried out on both sides under a much greater handicap than is usual.

6.6 Pinup Girls Remind American Soldiers Why They Fight

The "pinup girl" is one of the most ubiquitous images of World War II–era popular culture. During the war, the movie industry worked closely with government officials to produce and distribute millions of photographs of beautiful actresses to American servicemen at home and abroad. As the photo below shows, pinup girls decorated barracks walls, the bulkheads of ships and submarines, and the nosecones and fuselages of airplanes. Unlike the "naughty postcards" circulated among GIs during the First World War, WWII-era pinups received official sanction, and were even used in training exercises.

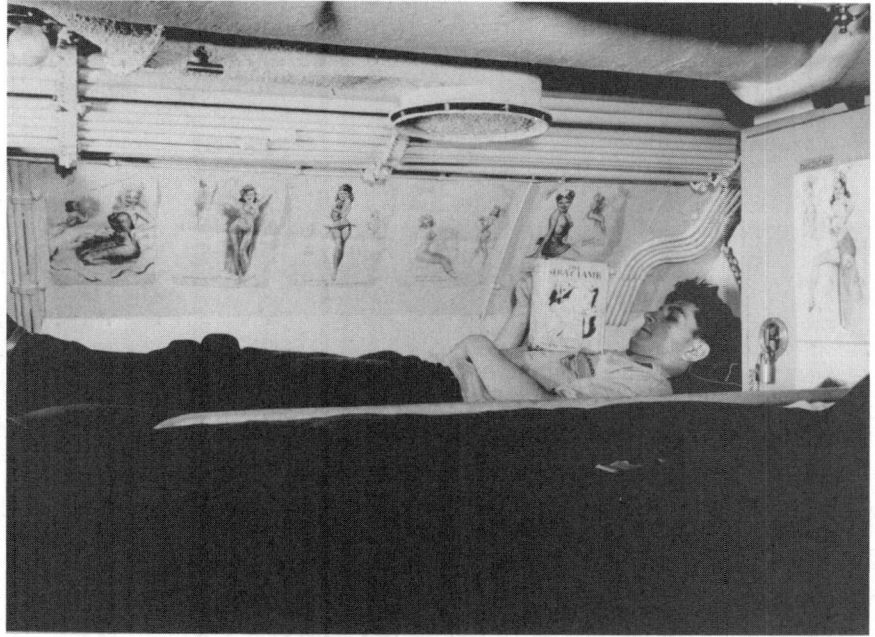

From Charles Fenno Jacobs, "Sailor in His Bunk Aboard USS Capelin in WWII," National Archives and Records Administration, ARC Identifier 520852; available at Wikimedia Commons, https://upload.wikimedia.org/wikipedia/commons/9/90/Sailor%27s_bunk_aboard_fleet_sub.jpg.

6.7 The Office of War Information Warns American Men about Venereal Diseases

Throughout the World War II period, American officials worried that venereal diseases posed a serious threat to the U.S. military. They had reason to do so. During the First World War, the U.S. Army had discharged more than 10,000 soldiers, and lost more than 7 million person-days due to sexually transmitted diseases. By the 1940s, the U.S. military had considerable experience in combatting the spread of these diseases through an extensive propaganda campaign that warned servicemen against the dangers posed by both "prostitutes" and "victory girls." This campaign relied on posters, such as the one shown here, that were remarkably frank for the era, addressing the topic in clinical language, ominous sexual imagery, and often a touch of jingoistic nationalism. The mass production of penicillin—which could cure most sexually transmitted infections—was not perfected until relatively late in the war (see Chapter 7), so the military relied largely on prevention, including the use of condoms, to contain the spread of these diseases.

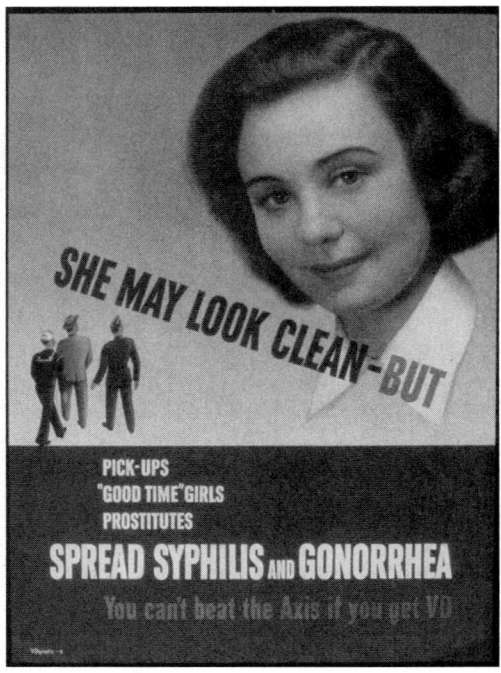

From Office of War Information, "She May Look Clean, But . . ." Poster, National Archives and Records Administration, available at Wikimedia Commons, https://upload.wikimedia.org/wikipedia/commons/4/4b/SHE_MAY_LOOK_CLEAN_-_BUT_-_NARA_-_513618.jpg.

6.8 An African American Woman Reflects on Her Experiences as a War Worker, 1943[5]

Some 600,000 African American women moved into paid employment during the Second World War. Black women had long worked for wages in greater proportion than their white counterparts, but the war changed the nature of that employment. The percentage of black women workers employed in domestic service dropped from about 60 percent to 45 percent; at the same time, the percentage of black women working in industry rose from 6.5 percent to 18 percent. Yet the experiences of these women were marked by persistent discrimination, prejudice, and job insecurity. Wartime surveys found that few employers were willing to hire black women workers and that even those that were tended to hire nonwhite women last. In the passage here, Hortense Johnson describes her experience as a war worker—the opportunities she saw, the challenges she faced, and the strategies she used to make the most of the war years.

Of course I'm vital to victory, just as millions of men and women who are fighting to save America's chances for Democracy, even if they never shoulder a gun nor bind a wound. It's true that my job isn't so exciting or complicated . . . I am an inspector in a war plant. For eight hours a day, six days a week, I stand in line with five other girls, performing a routine operation that is part of our production schedule. . . . Not much to that you say. Well that all depends on the way you look at it. A missing or projecting nail, a loose board or hinge . . . may mean injury for a fellow worker . . . with dozens of lives lost, or they might even spell disaster for American soldiers in a tight spot in North Africa. Did I say my job isn't exciting or complicated? I take that back. It may be a simple matter to inspect one box or a dozen, but it's different when you handle them by the hundreds. . . . It's exciting all right, and it's plenty complicated—in the same way that jungle warfare must be, hard and painstaking and monotonous—until something goes off with a bang!

And then when your shift is finished you stalk off stiffly to the washroom and hurry to get ready for the bus that brings you forty five miles back from the plant to your home in the city. . . .So when you get back home you're glad to jump into bed and die until morning—or until your alarm clock tells you it's morning, no matter how black it is. Then your two hour experience of traveling back to the job begins all over again. . . .

---

5. From Hortense Johnson, "What My Job Means to Me," *Opportunity: A Journal of Negro Life* 21 (1943): 553.

It never occurs to you to figure out how much money you're making because it isn't much anyhow—after you've had your victory tax deducted, paid for your war bond, set aside money for your bus commutation ticket. . . .

So, if it's as tough as all that—and it is!—why do you stick on the job? . . . Because it's not that easy to leave and it's not that tough to stay! Of course the work is hard and sometimes dangerous, but victory in this war isn't going to come the easy way without danger. And we brown women of America need victory so much, so desperately. America is a long way from perfect. We resent the racial injustices that we meet every day of our lives. But it's one thing to resent and fight against racial injustices; it's another thing to let them break your spirit, so that you quit this struggle and turn the country over to Hitler and the Talmadges and Dies who will run this country if Hitler wins. America can't win this war without all of us and we know it. We must prove it to white Americans as well—that our country can't get along without the labor and sacrifice of her brown daughters, can't win unless we all fight and work and save.

So the hardships of war work become willing sacrifices to victory, not to victory for Democracy, but to victory by a country that some day, please God, will win Democracy. . . . By doing my share today, I'm keeping a place for some brown woman tomorrow, and for the brown son of that woman the day after tomorrow. Sterling Brown once wrote, 'The strong men keep a-comin' on." And millions of those men have dark skins. There will be dark women marching by their side, and I like to think that I'm one of them.

6.9 President Franklin D. Roosevelt Talks to the Nation about Economic Sacrifice, 1942[6]

On April 28, 1942, President Franklin Roosevelt delivered a "fireside chat" on the necessity of economic sacrifice to enlist all Americans in the war effort. The language of "sacrifice" played a key role in the politics of the home front throughout the war. Public opinion polls found that the majority of Americans supported such wartime restrictions as wage freezes, no-strike pledges, rationing, and higher taxes. Yet the rhetoric of sacrifice, deployed so adeptly by Roosevelt in this address, belied public apathy and even antipathy toward wartime sacrifice. Mobilization agencies often despaired of the difficulties of

6. From Franklin D. Roosevelt, "Fireside Chat," April 28, 1942; available at *The American Presidency Project*, by Gerhard Peters and John T. Woolley, http://www.presidency.ucsb. edu/ws/?pid=16252.

transforming the public's stated willingness to sacrifice into action or to crack what one official called the "shell of public apathy." Roosevelt's "chat" raises questions about the role the language of sacrifice played on the home front, about the way the president—and other officials— can use rhetoric to shape the meaning of a military conflict, and about the relationship between that rhetoric and reality.

Franklin Roosevelt, Fireside Chat, April 28, 1942

My fellow Americans:

It is nearly five months since we were attacked at Pearl Harbor. For the two years prior to that attack this country had been gearing itself up to a high level of production of munitions. And yet our war efforts had done little to dislocate the normal lives of most of us.

Since then we have dispatched strong forces of our Army and Navy, several hundred thousand of them, to bases and battle fronts thousands of miles from home. We have stepped up our war production on a scale that is testing our industrial power, our engineering genius, and our economic structure to the utmost. We have had no illusions about the fact that this is a tough job—and a long one. . . .

. . . We went into this war fighting. We know what we are fighting for. We realize that the war has become what Hitler originally proclaimed it to be—a total war.

Not all of us can have the privilege of fighting our enemies in distant parts of the world.

Not all of us can have the privilege of working in a munitions factory or a shipyard, or on the farms or in oil fields or mines, producing the weapons or the raw materials that are needed by our armed forces.

But there is one front and one battle where everyone in the United States—every man, woman, and child—is in action, and will be privileged to remain in action throughout this war. That front is right here at home, in our daily lives, and in our daily tasks. Here at home everyone will have the privilege of making whatever self-denial is necessary, not only to supply our fighting men, but to keep the economic structure of our country fortified and secure during the war and after the war.

This will require, of course, the abandonment not only of luxuries but of many other creature comforts.

Every loyal American is aware of his individual responsibility. Whenever I hear anyone saying "The American people are complacent—they need to be aroused," I feel like asking him to come to Washington to read the mail that floods into the White House and into all departments of this Government. The one question that recurs through all these thousands of letters and messages is: What more can I do to help my country in winning this war?

To build the factories, to buy the materials, to pay the labor, to provide the transportation, to equip and feed and house the soldiers, sailors, and marines, and to do all the thousands of things necessary in a war—all cost a lot of money, more money than has ever been spent by any Nation at any time in the long history of the world.

We are now spending, solely for war purposes, the sum of about $100,000,000 every day in the week. But, before this year is over, that almost unbelievable rate of expenditure will be doubled.

All of this money has to be spent—and spent quickly—if we are to produce within the time now available the enormous quantities of weapons of war which we need. But the spending of these tremendous sums presents grave danger of disaster to our national economy.

When your Government continues to spend these unprecedented sums for munitions month by month and year by year, that money goes into the pocketbooks and bank accounts of the people of the United States. At the same time raw materials and many manufactured goods are necessarily taken away from civilian use; and machinery and factories are being converted to war production. . . .

. . . Yesterday I submitted to the Congress of the United States a seven-point program of general principles which taken together could be called the national economic policy for attaining the great objective of keeping the cost of living down. I repeat them now to you in substance:

First. We must, through heavier taxes, keep personal and corporate profits at a low reasonable rate.

Second. We must fix ceilings on prices and rents.

Third. We must stabilize wages.

Fourth. We must stabilize farm prices.

Fifth. We must put more billions into war bonds.

Sixth. We must ration all essential commodities which are scarce.

Seventh. We must discourage installment buying, and encourage paying off debts and mortgages. . . .

. . . The blunt fact is that every single person in the United States is going to be affected by this program. Some of you will be affected more directly by one or two of these restrictive measures, but all of you will be affected indirectly by all of them.

Are you a businessman, or do you own stock in a business corporation? Well, your profits are going to be cut down to a reasonably low level by taxation. Your income will be subject to higher taxes. Indeed in these days, when every available dollar should go to the war effort, I do not think that any American citizen should have a net income in excess of $25,000 per year after payment of taxes.

Are you a retailer or a wholesaler or a manufacturer or a farmer or a landlord? Ceilings are being placed on the prices at which you can sell your goods or rent your property.

Do you work for wages? You will have to forego higher wages for your particular job for the duration of the war.

All of us are used to spending money for things that we want, things, however, which are not absolutely essential. We will all have to forego that kind of spending. Because we must put every dime and every dollar we can possibly spare out of our earnings into war bonds and stamps. Because the demands of the war effort require the rationing of goods of which there are not enough to go around. Because the stopping of purchases of nonessentials will release thousands of workers who are needed in the war effort.

... [S]acrifice is not exactly the proper word with which to describe this program of self-denial. When, at the end of this great struggle, we shall have saved our free way of life, we shall have made no "sacrifice."

The price for civilization must be paid in hard work and sorrow and blood. The price is not too high. If you doubt it, ask those millions who live today under the tyranny of Hitlerisms. ...

... We do not have to ask them. They have already given us their agonized answers.

... Never in the memory of man has there been a war in which the courage, the endurance, and the loyalty of civilians played so vital a part. ...

... As we here at home contemplate our own duties, our own responsibilities, let us think and think hard of the example which is being set for us by our fighting men.

Our soldiers and sailors are members of well-disciplined units. But they are still and forever individuals—free individuals. They are farmers, and workers, businessmen, professional men, artists, clerks. They are the United States of America. That is why they fight. We too are the United States of America. That is why we must work and sacrifice. It is for them. It is for us. It is for victory.

CHAPTER 7

THE MANHATTAN PROJECT AND BEYOND: THE ROLE OF SCIENCE, MEDICINE, AND TECHNOLOGY IN THE AMERICAN WAR EFFORT

World War II spurred significant advances in science and technology. Scientific and technological innovations in turn played a key role in the Allied victory. The atomic bomb is only the best known of the era's discoveries in these fields. World War II also produced significant advances in medicine, including the mass production of penicillin and sulfa drugs; improvements in radar and other communications technologies; and major innovations in aviation, rocketry, and other military technologies. Scientists and engineers also contributed to the war effort by building new machines to intercept and decode enemy communications. These contributions are discussed in the next chapter. The Allies' success in harnessing the power of science and technology to military strategy proved critical to their eventual victory.

The British government led the way in coordinating scientific research with potential military applications. Indeed, the British understood the importance of scientific and technological research well before their American allies. In 1934, the British government established the Committee for the Scientific Survey of Air Defense (CSSAD). Under the leadership of Sir Henry Tizard, the CSSAD produced major improvements in radar technology. In 1940, as the Battle of Britain raged, Tizard traveled to the United States to secure American assistance and cooperation in developing new military technologies. The "Tizard Mission" provided U.S. officials with top-secret information on some of the most significant scientific advances of the twentieth century, including improved technology for radar, details of a new jet engine design, and the "Frisch-Peierls memorandum" on the feasibility of the atomic bomb. Tizard's mission succeeded; the United States and Great Britain cooperated throughout the war.

Vannevar Bush deserves much of the credit for coordinating U.S. scientific research during the war. Convinced that American scientific efforts were haphazard at best, Bush, an MIT-trained electrical engineer, persuaded President Roosevelt to establish a new agency devoted to military research. Like much of the U.S. mobilization effort, the National Defense Research Committee (NDRC) and later the Office of Scientific Research and Development (OSRD) relied on both public and private resources. Rather than build new laboratories, the federal government used contracts to mobilize scientists for the "defense effort in their own laboratories." This approach produced major breakthroughs. The Radiation Lab at MIT, for example, working with cavity magnetrons produced by Bell Labs in New York, led the way in improving radar technology for the Allies. This technology played a key role both in the Battle of Britain and in Allied victory over German U-boats in the Battle of the Atlantic.

Important improvements in medical care also proved vital to Allied success. Of particular importance was the mass production of penicillin. Although the effort was at first slow going, by 1943 British scientists were collaborating with their American counterparts and with the American pharmaceutical industry to produce significant quantities of the lifesaving drug. As a result of penicillin, as well as the increasing use of antiseptic sulfonamide drugs and the development of pesticides to fight the spread of tropical, mosquito-borne diseases, the number of nonbattle fatalities declined significantly. Indeed, World War II is the first conflict in which more Americans died on the battlefield than from illness, disease, or other nonbattle-related causes.

The development of an atomic bomb is, of course, the most well-known scientific advance of World War II. In June of 1940, after receiving a letter from renowned physicist Albert Einstein about a German "super bomb" based on the principles of atomic fission, Roosevelt authorized research into the "possible relationship to national defense of recent discoveries in the field . . . [of] the fusion of uranium." But it was not until 1942, after the United States had entered the war, that Roosevelt authorized a real atomic bomb development project. The effort, known as the Manhattan Project, was a joint American and British undertaking that ultimately cost $2 billion (about $26 billion in 2016 dollars) and employed nearly 130,000 people. Brigadier General Leslie Groves, the U.S. military's "builder in chief," worked with University of California, Berkeley physicist J. Robert Oppenheimer to oversee the construction of a massive research facility in the New Mexico desert on the site of the old Los Alamos Ranch School. By 1945, more than 4,000 people—mostly scientists and their families—lived and worked at the Los Alamos facility.

Massive facilities at Oakridge, Tennessee, and Hanford, Washington, which specialized in the production of fissionable material (uranium and plutonium, respectively), as well as research done at university and industry labs across the country, also played key roles in the Manhattan Project. In the summer of 1945, the success of Trinity, the first nuclear weapon test, led to hope for a quick end to the ongoing Pacific War, although historians have since debated the role that the bomb played in ending the conflict (see Chapter 12). Nevertheless, war-weary Americans were quick to credit the new weapon with bringing the war to a speedy conclusion. As President Harry Truman noted in his address to the American people after the bombing of Hiroshima: "We have spent nearly $2 billion on the greatest scientific gamble in history, and we have won."

World War II fundamentally transformed the relationship between the scientific community and the federal government, as scientists became increasingly dependent on federal monies in the postwar period. The "military-industrial complex" of the Cold War period might more accurately be termed the "military-industrial-scientific complex," as the federal government has underwritten scientific research both directly at government facilities and indirectly through grants to universities or individual researchers or purchases of technology manufactured by private corporations. Scientific discoveries made during the war also transformed life after it. The Manhattan Project introduced the world to the potential and the horrors of atomic power, penicillin and other antibiotic drugs significantly reduced mortality rates, and advances in jet technology made by the Nazis made space travel possible. New technologies also transformed daily life. Plastic wrap, cardboard milk and juice containers, polyester and other synthetics, all had their roots in the era of World War II.

The documents in this chapter raise questions about the organization and importance of science and technology during the Second World War. How did science and technology change the nature of war itself? How did governments harness the energies of scientists and direct them to military purposes? Why were the Allies more successful in translating scientific advances into military gains? What consequences did wartime science and scientific organization have on the postwar world? What are the benefits of the tight relationship between the state and science? What are the possible dangers?

* * * *

7.1 Office of Scientific Research and Development Director Dr. Vannevar Bush Reports to the White House on the Importance of Science during and after the War[1]

During World War II, Dr. Vannevar Bush, an American inventor and engineer, served as the director of the U.S. Office of Scientific Research and Development (OSRD). Under Bush's leadership, the OSRD played

---

1. From Vannevar Bush, *Science: The Endless Frontier: A Report to the President* (Washington, DC: U.S. Government Printing Office, 1945), 1–4.

a key role in the initiation and early administration of the Manhattan Project. The OSRD also invested in medical research and was in large part responsible for the successful mass production of penicillin and other lifesaving drugs during the war years. After the war, Bush argued that the federal government must take on "new responsibilities for promoting the flow of new scientific research." Bush's report laid the groundwork for continued federal investment in scientific research and for the creation of the National Science Foundation in 1950.

Scientific Progress Is Essential

Progress in the war against disease depends upon a flow of new scientific knowledge. New products, new industries, and more jobs require continuous additions to knowledge of the laws of nature, and the application of that knowledge to practical purposes. Similarly, our defense against aggression demands new knowledge so that we can develop new and improved weapons. This essential, new knowledge can be obtained only through basic scientific research.

Science can be effective in the national welfare only as a member of a team, whether the conditions be peace or war. But without scientific progress no amount of achievement in other directions can insure our health, prosperity, and security as a nation in the modern world.

For the War against Disease.   We have taken great strides in the war against disease. The death rate for all diseases in the Army, including overseas forces, has been reduced from 14.1 per thousand in the last war to 0.6 per thousand in this war. In the last 40 years life expectancy has increased from 49 to 65 years, largely as a consequence of the reduction in the death rates of infants and children. But we are far from the goal. . . .

The responsibility for basic research in medicine and the underlying sciences, so essential to progress in the war against disease, falls primarily upon the medical schools and universities. Yet we find that the traditional sources of support for medical research in the medical schools and universities, largely endowment income, foundation grants, and private donations, are diminishing and there is no immediate prospect of a change in this trend. Meanwhile, the cost of medical research has been rising. If we are able to maintain the progress in medicine which has marked the last 25 years, the Government should extend financial support to basic medical research in the medical schools and in universities.

For Our National Security.   The bitter and dangerous battle against the U-boat was a battle of scientific techniques—and our margin of success was dangerously small. The new eyes which radar has supplied can some-times be blinded by new scientific developments. V-2 was countered only by capture of the launching sites.

We cannot again rely on our allies to hold off the enemy while we struggle to catch up. There must be more—and more adequate—military research in peacetime. It is essential that the civilian scientists continue in peacetime some portion of those contributions to national security which they have made so effectively during the war. This can best be done through a civilian-controlled organization with close liaison with the Army and Navy, but with funds direct from Congress, and the clear power to initiate military research which will supplement and strengthen that carried on directly under the control of the Army and Navy.

And for the Public Welfare.   One of our hopes is that after the war there will be full employment. To reach that goal the full creative and productive energies of the American people must be released. To create more jobs we must make new and better and cheaper products. We want plenty of new, vigorous enterprises. But new products and processes are not born full-grown. They are founded on new principles and new con-ceptions which in turn result from basic scientific research. Basic scientific research is scientific capital. Moreover, we cannot any longer depend upon Europe as a major source of this scientific capital. Clearly, more and better scientific research is one essential to the achievement of our goal of full employment.

How do we increase this scientific capital? First, we must have plenty of men and women trained in science, for upon them depends both the creation of new knowledge and its application to practical purposes. Sec-ond, we must strengthen the centers of basic research which are princi-pally the colleges, universities, and research institutes. These institutions provide the environment which is most conducive to the creation of new scientific knowledge and least under pressure for immediate, tangible results. With some notable exceptions, most research in industry and in Government involves application of existing scientific knowledge to practical problems. It is only the colleges, universities, and a few research institutes that devote most of their research efforts to expanding the fron-tiers of knowledge.

Expenditures for scientific research by industry and Government increased from $140,000,000 in 1930 to $309,000,000 in 1940. Those for the colleges and universities increased from $20,000,000 to $31,000,000, while those for the research institutes declined from $5,200,000 to $4,500,000 during the same period. If the colleges, universities, and research institutes are to meet the rapidly increasing demands of industry and Government for new scientific knowledge, their basic research should be strengthened by use of public funds. . . .

The most important ways in which the Government can promote industrial research are to increase the flow of new scientific knowledge through support of basic research, and to aid in the development of scientific talent. In addition, the Government should provide suitable incentives to industry to conduct research. . . .

A Program for Action

The Government should accept new responsibilities for promoting the flow of new scientific knowledge and the development of scientific talent in our youth. These responsibilities are the proper concern of the Government, for they vitally affect our health, our jobs, and our national security. It is in keeping also with basic United States policy that the Government should foster the opening of new frontiers and this is the modern way to do it. For many years the Government has wisely supported research in the agricultural colleges and the benefits have been great. The time has come when such support should be extended to other fields.

The effective discharge of these new responsibilities will require the full attention of some over-all agency devoted to that purpose. There is not now in the permanent Governmental structure receiving its funds from Congress an agency adapted to supplementing the support of basic research in the colleges, universities, and research institutes, both in medicine and the natural sciences, adapted to supporting research on new weapons for both Services, or adapted to administering a program of science scholarships and fellowships.

Therefore I recommend that a new agency for these purposes be established. Such an agency should be composed of persons of broad interest and experience, having an understanding of the peculiarities of scientific research and scientific education. It should have stability of funds so that long-range programs may be undertaken. It should recognize that freedom of inquiry must be preserved and should leave internal control of policy, personnel, and the method and scope of research to the institutions in which it is carried on. It should be fully responsible to the President and through him to the Congress for its program.

Early action on these recommendations is imperative if this nation is to meet the challenge of science in the crucial years ahead. On the wisdom with which we bring science to bear in the war against disease, in the creation of new industries, and in the strengthening of our Armed Forces depends in large measure our future as a nation.

7.2 Mass-Produced Penicillin Saves Countless Lives[2]

Alexander Fleming, a Scottish biologist, pharmacologist, and botanist, discovered the bacteria-killing properties of penicillin in 1928. It took more than a decade, however, to transform Fleming's "mold juice" into medicine. Military officials on both sides of the Atlantic recognized the significance of the new drug, and hurried to develop the technology to produce large quantities of the miracle mold. Through a process of trial and error, a joint British-American research team, with the assistance of the OSRD and the American pharmaceutical industry, finally figured out how to manufacture large quantities of the lifesaving drug. By the end of the war, American drug companies were producing 650 billion units of penicillin every month. The new drug saved countless lives. Indeed, as Document 7.3 shows, World War II was the first war in which more Americans died on the battlefield than of disease or infection.

In the document reproduced here, Representative George Mahon of Texas traces the history of the "wonder drug," and its importance in improving the health of the American military.

Penicillin, the Magic Drug: Extension of Remarks of Hon. George H. Mahon of Texas in the House of Representatives, Monday, November 15, 1943

In May 1940 penicillin was first used in this country in the treatment of a case. Penicillin is very difficult to manufacture and it was May 1942 before many cases were treated by the use of this drug. It was found especially useful in the treatment of infections.

In July 1943 the War Production Board took over the direction of the production of penicillin. About 19 companies are manufacturing, or soon will be manufacturing, penicillin. Officials of the War Production Board estimate that by February 1944 it will be possible to meet all Army and Navy requirements and that within a few more months—possibly by July 1, 1944—it will be possible to take care of all pressing civilian demands. This is good news, and it is to be hoped that the estimate is not too optimistic. It will mean the saving of many thousands of lives of soldiers, sailors, and civilians. By November 1 of this year the drug had been used in 794 civilian cases, and the results were amazingly effective, according to official reports. This is only the beginning of the use of one of the greatest medical discoveries of all time.

---

2. From Representative Mahon, "Penicillin the Magic Drug," November 15, 1943, 78th Cong., 1st sess., *Congressional Record* 89, pt. 12:A4868.

About 25 percent of the drug which has been produced in recent months has been used in treating civilians. A much larger portion has been allocated to the Army for use in Army hospitals. The Navy gets one-third as much as the Army.

Prior to October 1 the Army was using the drug experimentally in 20 Army hospitals. The drug was used by the Army in about 2,000 cases. It was used in 3 general types of cases. The first type involved the treatment of bone infections. The second type had to do with the treatment of certain venereal diseases where the patient did not respond favorably to the sulfa drug. The third class of cases involved the treatment of such diseases as pneumonia, meningitis, and blood-stream infections. The results were highly satisfactory, especially in the first 2 classes of cases.

Experimental treatments proved so highly successful the Army began last month to allocate the bulk of its quota for use in treating soldiers overseas. We cannot foresee what our casualties may be in the coming months. This much is certain. The availability of penicillin to the Army and Navy will mean that many American boys will live who otherwise would have had no chance of recovery. The Army is now losing less than 3 percent of the boys who are hospitalized, as compared with 15 percent in World War No. 1. The use of the new magic drug should now enable the Army to make even a better record.

7.3 Advances in Medicine Save Soldiers from Disease and Death

Until the Second World War, more American soldiers died from disease than from wounds received in battle. During the Civil War, for example, only 38 percent of Union deaths were the direct result of battlefield wounds. New medical advances, including the discovery of germ theory and the development of antiseptics, improved military medical care, but not by much. Even during World War I, more American soldiers died of disease and other nonbattle causes than from battlefield wounds. Improvements in medical technology, namely the discovery and mass production of penicillin, saved countless lives during World War II.

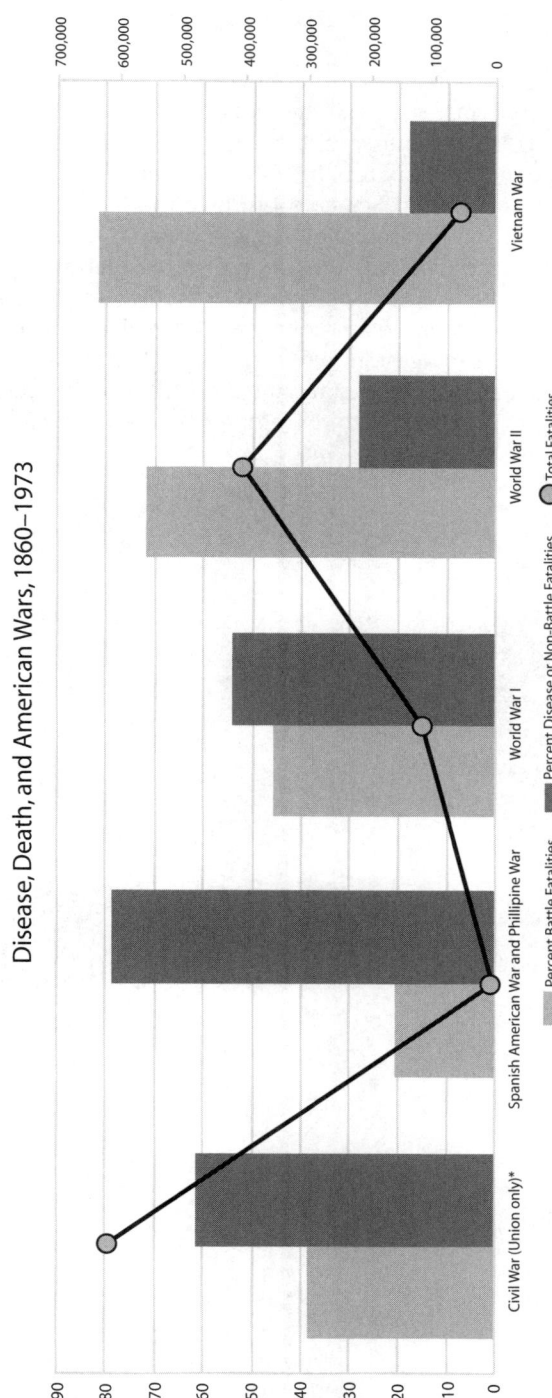

Disease, Death, and American Wars, 1860–1973

Because reliable numbers for the reasons for Confederate deaths are unavailable, this chart compares only Union battle deaths and Union deaths due to disease and other causes. However, because using only total deaths would understate the enormous human cost of the Civil War, this chart includes the total number of American soldiers killed during the Civil War in the "Total Fatalities" category. Even so, this chart probably understates the number of deaths during the Civil War, which have recently been revised to between 650,000 and 850,000 dead. Source: John Whiteclay Chambers, et al., eds. *The Oxford Companion to American Military History* (New York: Oxford University Press, 1999), 849.

7.4 Radar Helps the Allies to Victory[3]

Radar uses radio waves to detect distant moving objects like planes, ships, and weather formations. The basic technology had been available since the end of the 19th century, but it was not until the 1930s that radar was developed for military use. In 1940, the United Kingdom secretly partnered with the United States to produce the large cavity magnetrons necessary to improve the effectiveness of radar detection systems. Although the Axis powers also invested in radar technology, German and Japanese systems were less effective than those developed by the Allies. Superior radar technology gave the Allies a meaningful edge in the war. The images shown here are of the SCR-270, one of the first operational early warning radar systems. These devices, which detected the Pearl Harbor raid thirty minutes before the attack, remained in use for the duration of the war.

 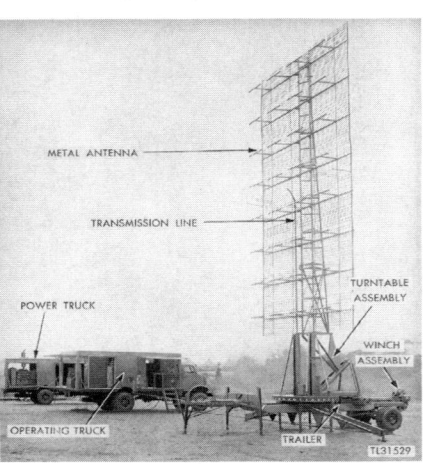

---

3. From Harold Zahl, Army Air Corps, photographs, available at Wikimedia Commons, https://upload.wikimedia.org/wikipedia/commons/a/a6/SCR-270-set-up.jpg, and https://upload.wikimedia.org/wikipedia/commons/c/c5/SCR-270-in-k-30-truck-300.jpg.

7.5 Physicist Leo Szilard Issues a Warning about the Atomic Bomb, 1939[4]

Leo Szilard was born in 1898 in Budapest in what was then the King-dom of Hungary to middle-class Jewish parents. In 1919, after serv-ing in World War I, Szilard left Hungary for Austria, where he studied physics at Friedrich Wilhelm University. Szilard's 1922 dissertation on thermodynamic fluctuations brought Szilard to the attention of the international scientific community, including Albert Einstein. Szilard moved to Berlin in 1924 and received German citizenship in 1930. However, the scientist fled Germany for England soon after Adolf Hit-ler seized power in 1933. While in England, Szilard hypothesized that a nuclear chain reaction might be possible, but it was not until 1938 that two German scientists, Otto Hahn and Fritz Strassman, discov-ered nuclear fission. It was this discovery that led Szilard to write to businessman and philanthropist Lewis Strauss regarding his worries about how Hahn and Strassman's discovery could lead to a deadly new weapon.

Hotel King's Crown
Opposite Columbia University
420 West 116th Street
New York City
January 25th, 1939

Mr. Lewis L. Strauss
c/o Kuhn, Loeb & Co.
52 William Street
New York City

Dear Mr. Strauss:

I feel that I ought to let you know of a very sensational new devel-opment in nuclear physics. In a paper in the *Naturwissenschaften* Hahn reports that he finds when bombarding uranium with neutrons the ura-nium breaking up into two halves giving elements of about half the atomic weight of uranium. This is entirely unexpected and exciting news for the average physicist. The Department of Physics at Princeton, where I spent the last few days, was like a stirred-up ant heap. Apart from the purely scientific interest there may be another aspect of this discovery, which so

---

4. From Leo Szilard to Leo Strauss, January 25, 1939, NuclearFiles.org, Nuclear Age Peace Foundation, http://www.nuclearfiles.org/menu/library/correspondence/szilard-leo/corr_szilard_1939-01-25.htm.

far does not seem to have caught the attention of those to whom I spoke. First of all it is obvious that the energy released in this new reaction must be very much higher than in all previously known cases. It may be 200 million (electron-) volts instead of the usual 3–10 million volts. This in itself might make it possible to produce power by means of nuclear energy, but I do not think that this possibility is very exciting, for if the energy output is only two or three times the energy input, the cost of investment would probably be too high to make the process worthwhile.

Unfortunately, most of the energy is released in the form of heat and not in the form of radioactivity.

I see, however, in connection with this new discovery potential possibilities in another direction. These might lead to a large-scale production of energy and radioactive elements, unfortunately also perhaps to atomic bombs. This new discovery revives all the hopes and fears in this respect which I had in 1934 and 1935, and which I have as good as abandoned in the course of the last two years. At present I am running a high temperature and am therefore confined to my four walls, but perhaps I can tell you more about these new developments some other time. Meanwhile you may look out for a paper in "Nature" by Frisch and Meitner which will soon appear and which might give you some information about this new discovery.

With best wishes,
Yours sincerely,
Leo Szilard

7.6 Albert Einstein Informs President Franklin D. Roosevelt of the Potential for the Atomic Bomb, 1939[5]

On August 2, 1939, Leo Szilard met with Albert Einstein to discuss the possibility that Hitler's Germany was trying to build an atomic bomb. Evidence was mounting that the Nazis were working to develop a weapon of unprecedented force. In 1939, the Nazi government had banned the export of uranium from Greater Germany, including that from Czechoslovakia's rich Joachimsthal mines. At the urging of Alexander Sachs, President Roosevelt's science advisor, Szilard and Einstein wrote a letter to the president warning that Germany might produce

5. From Franklin D. Roosevelt Papers, President's Secretary's File, Roosevelt Library, Hyde Park, NY; repr. in Michael B. Stoff, Jonathan Fanton, and R. Hal Williams, eds., *The Manhattan Project: A Documentary Introduction to the Atomic Age* (New York: McGraw Hill, 1991), 18–19.

"extremely powerful bombs" capable of destroying a "whole port together with some of the surrounding territory." The letter, signed only by Einstein whose status and fame ensured presidential attention, urged Roosevelt to meet the German threat with an American atomic bomb project. This letter offers an early blueprint of what would become the Manhattan Project.

Albert Einstein
Old Grove Road
Peconic, Long Island
August 2nd, 1939

F. D. Roosevelt
President of the United States
White House
Washington, D.C.

Sir:

Some recent work by E. Fermi and L. Szilard, which has been communicated to me in manuscript, leads me to expect that the element uranium may be turned into a new and important source of energy in the immediate future. Certain aspects of the situation which has arisen seem to call for watchfulness and if necessary, quick action on the part of the Administration. I believe therefore that it is my duty to bring to your attention the following facts and recommendations.

In the course of the last four months it has been made probable through the work of Joliot in France as well as Fermi and Szilard in America— that it may be possible to set up a nuclear chain reaction in a large mass of uranium, by which vast amounts of power and large quantities of new radium-like elements would be generated. Now it appears almost certain that this could be achieved in the immediate future.

This new phenomenon would also lead to the construction of bombs, and it is conceivable—though much less certain—that extremely powerful bombs of this type may thus be constructed. A single bomb of this type, carried by boat and exploded in a port, might very well destroy the whole port together with some of the surrounding territory. However, such bombs might very well prove too heavy for transportation by air.

The United States has only very poor ores of uranium in moderate quantities. There is some good ore in Canada and former Czechoslovakia, while the most important source of uranium is in the Belgian Congo.

In view of this situation you may think it desirable to have some permanent contact maintained between the Administration and the group of physicists working on chain reactions in America. One possible way of achieving this might be for you to entrust the task with a person who has your confidence and who could perhaps serve in an unofficial capacity. His task might comprise the following:

a) to approach Government Departments, keep them informed of the further development, and put forward recommendations for Government action, giving particular attention to the problem of securing a supply of uranium ore for the United States.

b) to speed up the experimental work, which is at present being carried on within the limits of the budgets of University laboratories, by providing funds, if such funds be required, through his contacts with private persons who are willing to make contributions for this cause, and perhaps also by obtaining co-operation of industrial laboratories which have necessary equipment.

I understand that Germany has actually stopped the sale of uranium from the Czechoslovakian mines which she has taken over. That she should have taken such early action might perhaps be understood on the ground that the son of the German Under-Secretary of State, von Weizsacker, is attached to the Kaiser-Wilhelm Institute in Berlin, where some of the American work on uranium is now being repeated.

Yours very truly,
/s/ Albert Einstein

7.7 The Manhattan Project Spans the Country[6]

The Manhattan Project was a serious undertaking that required the cooperation of the military, industry, civilian scientists, and university research labs. In addition to the facility at Los Alamos, the federal government also built massive installations in Tennessee and Washington State to produce fissionable materials. The project also relied on research being done at university research labs, including the Metallurgical Lab at the University of Chicago, the Ames Laboratory at Iowa State University, and the Pupin Hall Cyclotron at Columbia University. All told, the Manhattan Project employed some 130,000 people at thirty-seven separate facilities in thirteen states.

---

6. Fallschirmajr, Major Sites in the U.S. and Canada involved in the Manhattan Project, 30 June 2011, available via Wikimedia Commons at https://en.wikipedia.org/wiki/File:Manhattan_Project_US_Canada_Map_2.svg#file

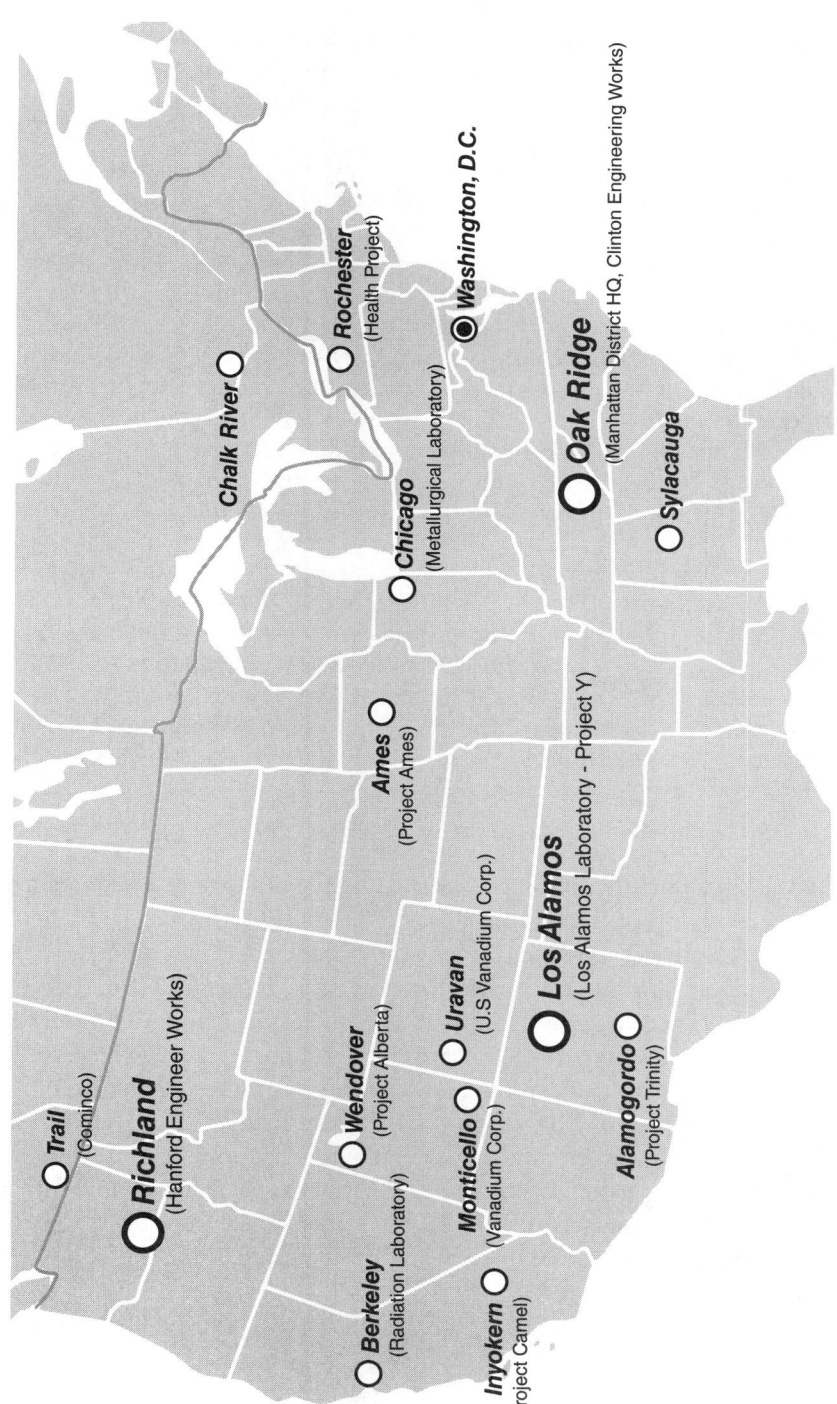

Trail
(Cominco)

Richland
(Hanford Engineer Works)

Berkeley
(Radiation Laboratory)

Inyokern
(Project Camel)

Wendover
(Project Alberta)

Monticello
(Vanadium Corp.)

Uravan
(U.S Vanadium Corp.)

Alamogordo
(Project Trinity)

Los Alamos
(Los Alamos Laboratory - Project Y)

Ames
(Project Ames)

Chalk River

Rochester
(Health Project)

Chicago
(Metallurgical Laboratory)

Washington, D.C.

Oak Ridge
(Manhattan District HQ, Clinton Engineering Works)

Sylacauga

7.8 Physicist J. Robert Oppenheimer Later Explains the Establishment of the Atomic Bomb Laboratory at Los Alamos, New Mexico, 1954[7]

J. Robert Oppenheimer was a theoretical physicist and professor at the University of California. Oppenheimer's work on calculating what needed to be done to make a working atomic weapon so impressed General Leslie Groves that he asked the scientist to direct the Manhattan Project. Oppenheimer proved an inspired choice, and quickly learned the art of large-scale administration. The Manhattan Project was a massive endeavor that required not only scientific knowledge but also the ability to manage large groups of people, negotiate the requirements of secrecy, and control the inevitable conflicts between the military, civilian, and scientific communities forced together at Los Alamos.

After the war, Oppenheimer became an internationally recognized spokesman for science and a key advocate for international nuclear control. Oppenheimer also battled publicly with his colleague Edward Teller over the feasibility of a hydrogen bomb. Thanks in part to these conflicts, Oppenheimer came under scrutiny by the Atomic Energy Commission (AEC) during the 1950s for his left-wing politics. In 1954, the AEC stripped Oppenheimer of his security clearance. The passage that follows is taken from Oppenheimer's testimony before the AEC, in which he describes his role in the Manhattan Project and the establishment of the Los Alamos laboratory.

. . . Beginning in late 1936, my interests began to change. These changes did not alter my earlier friendships, my relations to my students, or my devotion to physics; but they added something new. I can discern in retrospect more than one reason for these changes. I had had a continuing, smoldering fury about the treatment of Jews in Germany. I had relatives there, and was later to help in extricating them and bringing them to this country. I saw what the depression was doing to my students. Often they could get no jobs, or jobs which were wholly inadequate. And through them, I began to understand how deeply political and economic events could affect men's lives. I began to feel the need to participate more fully in the life of the community. But I had no framework of political conviction or experience to give me perspective in these matters. . . .

---

7. From "Oppenheimer's Autobiographical Sketch for the Personal Security Board," repr. in Michael B. Stoff, Jonathan F. Fanton, and R. Hal Williams, eds., *The Manhattan Project: A Documentary Introduction to the Atomic Age* (New York: McGraw Hill, 1991), 29–32.

Ever since the discovery of nuclear fission, the possibility of powerful explosives based on it had been very much in my mind, as it had in that of many other physicists. We had some understanding of what this might do for us in the war, and how much it might change the course of history. In the autumn of 1941, a special committee was set up by the National Academy of Sciences under the chairmanship of Arthur Compton to review the prospects and feasibility of the different uses of atomic energy for military purposes. I attended a meeting of this committee; this was my first official connection with the atomic-energy program.

After the academy meeting, I spent some time in preliminary calculations about the consumption and performance of atomic bombs, and became increasingly excited at the prospects. At the same time I still had a quite heavy burden of academic work with courses and graduate students. I also began to consult, more or less regularly, with the staff of the Radiation Laboratory in Berkeley on their program for the electromagnetic separation of uranium isotopes. I was never a member or employee of the laboratory; but I attended many of its staff and policy meetings. With the help of two of my graduate students, I developed an invention which was embodied in the production plants at Oak Ridge. I attended the conference in Chicago at which the Metallurgical Laboratory (to produce plutonium) was established and its initial program projected.

In the spring of 1942, Compton called me to Chicago to discuss the state of work on the bomb itself. During this meeting Compton asked me to take the responsibility for this work, which at that time consisted of numerous scattered experimental projects. Although I had no administrative experience and was not an experimental physicist, I felt sufficiently informed and challenged by the problem to be glad to accept. At this time I became an employee of the Metallurgical Laboratory. . . .

In later summer, after a review of the experimental work, I became convinced, as did others, that a major change was called for in the work on the bomb itself. We needed a central laboratory devoted wholly to this purpose, where people could talk freely with each other, where theoretical ideas and experimental findings could affect each other, where the waste and frustration and error of the many compartmentalized experimental studies could be eliminated, where we could begin to come to grips with chemical, metallurgical, engineering, and ordnance problems that had so far received no consideration. We therefore sought to establish this laboratory for a direct attack on all the problems inherent in the most rapid possible development and production of atomic bombs.

In the autumn of 1942 General Groves assumed charge of the Manhattan Engineer District. I discussed with him the need for an atomic laboratory. There had been some thought of making this laboratory a part of Oak Ridge. For a time there was support for making it a Military Establishment in which key personnel would be commissioned as officers; and in preparation for this course I once went to the Presidio to take the initial steps toward obtaining a commission. After a good deal of discussion with the personnel who would be needed at Los Alamos and with General Groves and his advisers, it was decided that the laboratory should, at least initially, be a civilian establishment in a military post. While this consideration was going on, I had showed General Groves Los Alamos; and he almost immediately took steps to acquire the site.

In early 1943, I received a letter signed by General Groves and Dr. Conant, appointing me director of the laboratory, and outlining their conception of how it was to be organized and administered. The necessary construction and assembling of the needed facilities were begun. All of us worked in close collaboration with the engineers of the Manhattan District.

The site of Los Alamos was selected in part at least because it enabled those responsible to balance the obvious need for security with the equally important need of free communication among those engaged in the work. Security, it was hoped, would be achieved by removing the laboratory to a remote area, fenced and patrolled, where communication with the outside was extremely limited. Telephone calls were monitored, mail was censored, and personnel who left the area—something permitted only for the clearest of causes—knew that their movements might be under surveillance. On the other hand, for those within the community, fullest exposition and discussion among those competent to use the information was encouraged.

The last months of 1942 and early 1943 had hardly hours enough to get Los Alamos established. The real problem had to do with getting to Los Alamos the men who would make a success of the undertaking. For this we needed to understand as clearly as we then could what our technical program would be, what men we would need, what facilities, what organization, what plan.

The program of recruitment was massive. Even though we then underestimated the ultimate size of the laboratory, which was to have almost 4,000 members by the spring of 1945, and even though we did not at that time see clearly some of the difficulties which were to bedevil and threaten the enterprise, we knew that it was a big, complex, and diverse job. Even the initial plan of the laboratory called for a start with more than 100 highly qualified and trained scientists, to say nothing of the technicians, staff, and mechanics who would be required for their support, and of the equipment that we would have to beg and borrow since there would be no time to build it from scratch. We had to recruit at a time when the country was fully engaged in war and almost every competent scientist was already involved in the military effort.

The primary burden of this fell on me. To recruit staff I traveled all over the country talking with people who had been working on one or another aspect of the atomic-energy enterprise, and people in radar work, for example, and underwater sound, telling them about the job, the place that we were going to, and enlisting their enthusiasm.

In order to bring responsible scientists to Los Alamos, I had to rely on their sense of the interest, urgency, and feasibility of the Los Alamos mission. I had to tell them enough of what the job was, and give strong enough assurance that it might be successfully accomplished in time to affect the outcome of the war, to make it clear that they were justified in their leaving other work to come to this job.

The prospect of coming to Los Alamos aroused great misgivings. It was to be a military post; men were asked to sign up more or less for the duration; restrictions on travel and on the freedom of families to move about to be severe; and no one could be sure of the extent to which the necessary technical freedom of action could actually be maintained by the laboratory. The notion of disappearing into the New Mexico desert for an indeterminate period and under quasi military auspices disturbed a good many scientists, and the families of many more. But there was another side to it. Almost everyone realized that this was a great undertaking. Almost everyone knew that if it were completed successfully and rapidly enough, it might determine the outcome of the war. Almost everyone knew that it was an unparalleled opportunity to bring to bear the basic knowledge and art of science for the benefit of his country. Almost everyone knew that this job, if it were achieved, would be a part of history. This sense of excitement, of devotion and of patriotism in the end prevailed. Most of those with whom I talked came to Los Alamos. Once they came, confidence in the enterprise grew as men learned more of the technical status of the work; and though the laboratory was to double and redouble its size many times before the end, once it had started it was on the road to success.

We had information in those days of German activity in the field of nuclear fission. We were aware of what it might mean if they beat us to the draw in the development of atomic bombs. The consensus of all our opinions, and every directive that I had, stressed the extreme urgency of our work, as well as the need for guarding all knowledge of it from our enemies. . . .

The story of Los Alamos is so long and complex. Part of it is public history. For me it was a time so filled with work, with the need for decision and action and consultation, that there was room for little else. I lived with my family in the community which was Los Alamos. It was a remarkable community, inspired by a high sense of mission, of duty and of destiny, coherent, dedicated, and remarkably selfless. There was plenty in the life of Los Alamos to cause irritation; the security restrictions, many of my own devising, the inadequacies and inevitable fumblings of a military post unlike any that had ever existed before, shortages, inequities, and in the laboratory itself the shifting emphasis on different aspects of the technical work as the program moved forward; but I have never known a group more understanding and more devoted to a common purpose, more willing to lay aside personal convenience and prestige, more understanding of the role that they were playing in their country's history. Time and again we had in the technical work almost paralyzing crises. Time and again the laboratory drew itself together and faced the new problems and got on with the work. We worked by night and by day; and in the end the many jobs were done.

7.9 Manhattan Project Commanding General Leslie Groves Reports the Results of the Alamogordo Test, 1945[8]

On the morning of July 16, 1945, the U.S. Army successfully detonated the first atomic bomb. Code-named "Trinity," the test was conducted in the Jornada del Muerto desert about thirty-five miles outside of Socorro, New Mexico. General Leslie Groves, the head of the Manhattan Project, informed Secretary of War Henry Stimson who was in Germany for the Potsdam Conference, of the test results via telegram.

The Commanding General, Manhattan District Project (Groves) to the Secretary of War (Stimson)

TOP SECRET

Washington, 18 July 1945

Memorandum for the Secretary of War
Subject: The Test.

. . . 2. At 0530, 16 July 1945, in a remote section of the Alamogordo Air Base, New Mexico, the first full scale test was made of the implosion type atomic fission bomb. For the first time in history there was a nuclear explosion. And what an explosion! . . . The bomb was not dropped from

---

8. From Manhattan Engineer District Records, National Archives, Washington D.C., repr. in Michael B. Stoff, Jonathan F. Fanton, and R. Hal Williams, eds., *The Manhattan Project: An Introduction to the Atomic Age* (New York: McGraw Hill, 1991), 188–91.

an airplane but was exploded on a platform on top of a 100-foot high steel tower.

3. The test was successful beyond the most optimistic expectations of anyone. Based on the data which it has been possible to work up to date, I estimate the energy generated to be in excess of the equivalent of 15,000 to 20,000 tons of TNT; and this is a conservative estimate. Data based on measurements which we have not yet been able to reconcile would make the energy release several times the conservative figure. There were tremendous blast effects. For a brief period there was a lighting effect within a radius of 20 miles equal to several suns in midday; a huge ball of fire was formed which lasted for several seconds. This ball mushroomed and rose to a height of over ten thousand feet before it dimmed. The light from the explosion was seen clearly at Albuquerque, Santa Fe, Silver City, El Paso and other points generally to about 180 miles away. The sound was heard to the same distance in a few instances but generally to about 100 miles. Only a few windows were broken although one was some 125 miles away. A massive cloud was formed which surged and billowed upward with tremendous power, reaching the substratosphere at an elevation of 41,000 feet, 36,000 feet above the ground, in about five minutes, breaking without interruption through a temperature inversion at 17,000 feet which most of the scientists thought would stop it. Two supplementary explosions occurred in the cloud shortly after the main explosion. The cloud contained several thousand tons of dust picked up from the ground and a considerable amount of iron in the gaseous form. Our present thought is that this iron ignited when it mixed with the oxygen in the air to cause these supplementary explosions. Huge concentrations of highly radioactive materials resulted from the fission and were contained in this cloud.

4. A crater from which all vegetation had vanished, with a diameter of 1200 feet and a slight slope toward the center, was formed. In the center was a shallow bowl 130 feet in diameter and 6 feet in depth. The material within the crater was deeply pulverized dirt. The material within the outer circle is greenish and can be distinctly seen from as much as 5 miles away. The steel from the tower was evaporated. 1500 feet away there was a four-inch iron pipe 16 feet high set in concrete and strongly guyed. It disappeared completely.

5. One-half mile from the explosion there was a massive steel test cylinder weighing 220 tons. The base of the cylinder was solidly encased in concrete. Surrounding the cylinder was a strong steel tower 70 feet high, firmly anchored to concrete foundations. This tower is comparable to a steel building bay that would be found in typical 15 or 20 story skyscraper or in warehouse construction. . . . The blast tore the tower from its foundations, twisted it, ripped it apart and left it flat on the ground. The effects

on the tower indicate that, at that distance, unshielded permanent steel and masonry buildings would have been destroyed. I no longer consider the Pentagon a safe shelter from such a bomb. . . .

6. The cloud traveled to a great height first in the form of a ball, then mushroomed, then changed into a long trailing chimney-shaped column and finally was sent in several directions by the variable winds at the different elevations. It deposited its dust and radioactive materials over a wide area. It was followed and monitored by medical doctors and scientists with instruments to check its radioactive effects. While here and there the activity on the ground was fairly high, at no place did it reach a concentration which required evacuation of the population. Radioactive material in small quantities was located as much as 120 miles away. The measurements are being continued in order to have adequate data with which to protect the Government's interests in case of future claims. For a few hours I was none too comfortable about the situation. . . .

10. Just before 1100 the news stories from all over the state started to flow into the Albuquerque Associated Press. I then directed the issuance by the Commanding Officer, Alamogordo Air Base of a news release as shown on the enclosure. With the assistance of the Office of Censorship we were able to limit the news stories to the approved release supplemented in the local papers by brief stories from the many eyewitnesses not connected with our project. One of these was a blind woman who saw the light.

11. Brigadier General Thomas F. Farrell was at the control shelter located 10,000 yards south of the point of explosion. His impressions are given below:

> "The scene inside the shelter was dramatic beyond words. In and around the shelter were some twenty-odd people concerned with last minute arrangements prior to firing the shot. Included were: Dr. Oppenheimer, the Director who had borne the great scientific burden of developing the weapon from the raw materials made in Tennessee and Washington and a dozen of his key assistants—Dr. Kistiakowsky, who developed the highly special explosives; Dr. Bainbridge, who supervised all the detailed arrangements for the test; D. Hubbard, the weather expert, and several others. Besides these, there were a handful of soldiers, two or three Army officers and one Naval officer. The shelter was cluttered with a great variety of instruments and radios.
>
> "For some hectic two hours preceding the blast, General Groves stayed with the Director, walking with him and steadying his tense excitement. Every time the Director would be about to explode because of some untoward happening, General Groves would take him off and walk with him in the rain, counselling with him and reassuring him that everything would be all right. At twenty minutes before zero hour, General Groves left for his

station at the base camp, first because it provided a better observation point and second, because of our rule that he and I must not be together in situations where there is an element of danger, which existed at both points.

"Just after General Groves left, announcements began to be broadcast of the interval remaining before the blast. They were sent by radio to the other groups participating in and observing the test. As the time interval grew smaller and changed from minutes to seconds, the tension increased by leaps and bounds. Everyone in that room knew the awful potentialities of the thing that they thought was about to happen. The scientists felt that their figuring must be right and that the bomb had to go off but there was in everyone's mind a strong measure of doubt. The feeling of many could be expressed by 'Lord, I believe; help Thou mine unbelief.' We were reaching into the unknown and we did not know what might come of it. It can be safely said that most of those present—Christian, Jew, and Atheist—were praying and praying harder than they had ever prayed before. If the shot were successful, it was a justification of the several years of intensive effort of tens of thousands of people—statesmen, scientists, engineers, manufacturers, soldiers, and many others in every walk of life.

"In that brief instant in the remote New Mexico desert the tremendous effort of the brains and brawn of all these people came suddenly and startlingly to the fullest fruition. Dr. Oppenheimer, on whom had rested a very heavy burden, grew tenser as the last seconds ticked off. He scarcely breathed. He held on to a post to steady himself. For the last few seconds, he stared directly ahead and then when the announcer shouted 'Now!' and there came this tremendous burst of light followed shortly thereafter by the deep growling roar of the explosion, his face relaxed into an expression of tremendous relief. Several of the observers standing back of the shelter to watch the lighting effects were knocked flat by the blast.

"The tension in the room let up and all started congratulating each other. Everyone sensed 'This is it!' No matter what might happen now all knew that the impossible scientific job had been done. Atomic fission would no longer be hidden in the cloisters of the theoretical physicists' dreams. It was almost full grown at birth. It was a great new force to be used for good or for evil. There was a feeling in that shelter that those concerned with its nativity should dedicate their lives to the mission that it would always be used for good and never for evil.

"Dr. Kistiakowsky, the impulsive Russian, threw his arms around Dr. Oppenheimer and embraced him with shouts of glee. Others were equally enthusiastic. All the pent-up emotions were released in those few minutes and all seemed to sense immediately that the explosion had far exceeded the most optimistic expectations and wildest hopes of the scientists. All seemed to feel that they had been present at the birth of a new age—The Age of Atomic Energy—and felt their profound responsibility to help in guiding into right channels the tremendous forces which had been unlocked for the first time in history.

"As to the present war, there was a feeling that no matter what else might happen, we now had the means to insure its speedy conclusion and save thousands of American lives. As to the future, there had been brought into being something big and something new that would prove to be immeasurably more important than the discovery of electricity or any of the other great discoveries which have so affected our existence.

"The effects could well be called unprecedented, magnificent, beautiful, stupendous and terrifying. No man-made phenomenon of such tremendous power had ever occurred before. The lighting effects beggared description. The whole country was lighted by a searing light with the intensity many times that of the midday sun. It was golden, purple, violet, gray and blue. It lighted every peak, crevasse and ridge of the nearby mountain range with a clarity and beauty that cannot be described but must be seen to be imagined. It was that beauty the great poets dream about but describe most poorly and inadequately. Thirty seconds after the explosion came first, the air blast pressing hard against the people and things, to be followed almost immediately by the strong, sustained, awesome roar which warned of doomsday and made us feel that we puny things were blasphemous to dare tamper with the forces heretofore reserved to The Almighty. Words are inadequate tools for the job of acquainting those not present with the physical, mental and psychological effects. It had to be witnessed to be realized."

CHAPTER 8

THE INTELLIGENCE WAR: CODE BREAKING, CRYPTOGRAPHY, INTELLIGENCE GATHERING, AND ALLIED VICTORY

The intelligence services played a significant role in World War II. Allied and Axis powers depended on spies to provide critical information about their enemies and friends alike. The war also led to the reorganization of American intelligence operations. In June 1942, President Franklin Roosevelt issued a military executive order establishing the Office of Strategic Services (OSS), a brand new intelligence organization reporting directly to the Joint Chiefs of Staff. Developed with British assistance, the OSS performed a number of duties, including spying, performing acts of sabotage, conducting disinformation campaigns, assisting anti-Nazi resistance groups, and providing help to anti-Japanese guerillas in Asia. At its height, the OSS employed as many as 24,000 people.

Individual spies played a critical role in gathering and using intelligence. Some of the most important intelligence, however, came not from the work of ordinary spies, but from revolutionary developments in the field of cryptography. Allied success in breaking German and Japanese codes not only proved critical in the war's outcome but also stimulated the development of new technologies that would revolutionize life in the postwar period. Indeed, some of the most significant technological and scientific breakthroughs of the war—including the world's first programmable computer—came in the field of cryptanalysis.

Throughout the war, Allied intelligence services intercepted, decoded, and read significant portions of top secret military and diplomatic radio traffic from the Axis powers. Many of the Axis codes were enciphered using new encryption machines. The Germans, for example, developed a sophisticated enciphering machine known as Enigma. In 1929, one of these machines fell into the hands of Polish counterintelligence agents, who built an exact replica before sending the original on to its destination. Polish intelligence services used the replica Enigma machine to break the German cipher by 1932. After the Nazi invasion of Poland in 1939, many Polish cryptanalysts escaped to the West; some even brought Enigma machines with them. By 1941, cryptanalysts at the British Government

Code and Cypher School (GCCS) at Bletchley Park—a team that included British mathematician and logician Alan Turing—had success-fully cracked the Enigma code.

The intelligence produced from those intercepts was code-named Ultra and proved vital to Allied strategy. Indeed, when the German Navy switched to the new Triton code in 1942—simultaneously adding an addi-tional coding wheel to the Enigma machine—the Allies temporarily lost the ability to read German naval transmissions and suffered significant setbacks in the Battle of the Atlantic. Only after British code breakers had figured out Triton did the Allies regain the upper hand against German U-boats.

The Allied powers also had success breaking Japanese military and diplomatic codes. The Empire of Japan used a number of different codes and enciphering methods. Japanese diplomatic radio traffic, for example, was enciphered using a device similar to the German Enigma machine. American intelligence officials broke this code before Pearl Harbor, and the information produced was code-named Magic. It was not until after the war began, however, that the Americans successfully decoded Japa-nese military transmissions. The Japanese navy and army each used totally different encryption methods than the diplomatic corps. The main naval code, JN-25, for example, used a five-digit manual cipher; the Army, on the other hand, relied on a four-digit manual cipher. These codes were cracked in 1942 and 1943, providing American military officials with vital infor-mation about Japanese military operations. In 1942, for example, infor-mation gleaned from Japanese naval communications allowed American forces to expect, and then defeat, Japanese forces at the Battle of Midway. This proved a significant turning point in the Pacific War.

Allied victory often relied both on information learned from these intercepts and from the everyday work done by the men and women of the Allied intelligence services. For example, the Allied invasion of Normandy in 1944 depended on the success of a plan—code-named Bodyguard—to mislead the Germans about both the location of the planned invasion and its timing. This deception campaign used German double agents to feed their Nazi handlers a steady stream of disinformation about the Allies' plans. British and American access to Ultra information could be used to confirm the success or failure of these misinformation campaigns.

Code-breaking efforts also led to significant breakthroughs in the field of mathematics and computer science. In 1942, GCCS code breakers began the arduous process of breaking what were known as the German "Fish" codes. Taking advantage of an operator error, GCCS engineers were able to reverse engineer a replica of the enciphering device, a twelve-wheel teletype cipher attachment manufactured by the Lorenz company.

In keeping with the fish theme, the GCCS code-named this device—and the intelligence it produced—Tunny. To make the complicated calculations necessary to break the code, GCCS engineers designed a machine known as the Colossus to perform Boolean and counting operations. Programmed by switches and plugs, rather than a stored program, Colossus is nevertheless regarded as the world's first programmable, electronic, digital computer.

Most of these technological breakthroughs remained secret until the 1970s. Revelations around both Colossus and Ultra led to the creation of a new field in World War II history—Signals Intelligence or SIGINT—and to major reassessments of the diplomatic and military history of the war. These discoveries also led to new questions. For example, given the significance of the Ultra information, why did it take so long to defeat the Axis powers? Why were the Axis nations less successful at breaking Allied codes and making good use of such information? More broadly, what impact did science and technology have not only on intelligence gathering but also on the outcome of the war itself? How did these wartime developments affect the postwar world?

* * * *

8.1 A Congressional Committee Assesses Blame for the Pearl Harbor Disaster, 1945[1]

The attack on Pearl Harbor, which cost more than 2,400 Americans their lives and inflicted significant losses on the Pacific Fleet, was one of the greatest intelligence failures in American history. After Japan's surrender in September 1945, Congress appointed a joint committee to investigate the "facts relating to the events and circumstances leading up to or following the attack made by Japanese armed forces upon Pearl Harbor." The final report was issued in 1946. Eight members of the ten-person committee signed a majority report that assigned Japan the "ultimate responsibility for the attack" and placed primary blame for the disaster on the army and navy commanders in Hawaii, General Walter C. Short and Admiral Husband E. Kimmel. The majority rejected any claims that Roosevelt or top administration officials "tricked, provoked, incited, cajoled, or coerced Japan" into attacking

1. From *Report of the Joint Committee on the Investigation of the Pearl Harbor Attack*, July 29 (legislative date July 5), 1946, 79th Cong., 2nd sess., *Congressional Record* 27, 251–52, 493, 504–5.

the United States. A minority report, signed by Republican Senators Homer Ferguson (Michigan) and Owen Brewster (Maine) dismissed the majority's findings as "illogical and unsupported by the preponderance of evidence before the Committee."

Majority Report

. . . 2. The ultimate responsibility for the attack and its results rests upon Japan, an attack that was well planned and skillfully executed. Contributing to the effectiveness of the attack was a powerful striking force, much more powerful than it had been thought the Japanese were able to employ in a single tactical venture at such distance and under such circumstances. . . .

4. The committee has found no evidence to support the charges, made before and during the hearings, that the President, the Secretary of State, the Secretary of War, or the Secretary of Navy tricked, provoked, incited, cajoled, or coerced Japan into attacking this Nation in order that a declaration of war might be more easily obtained from Congress. On the contrary, all evidence conclusively points to the fact that they discharged their responsibilities with distinction, ability, and foresight and in keeping with the highest traditions of our fundamental foreign policy.

5. The President, the Secretary of State, and high Government officials made every possible effort, without sacrificing our national honor and endangering our security, to avert war with Japan.

6. The disaster of Pearl Harbor was the failure, with attendant increase in personnel and material losses, of the Army and the Navy to institute measures designed to detect an approaching hostile force, to effect a state of readiness commensurate with the realization that war was at hand, and to employ every facility at their command in repelling the Japanese.

7. Virtually everyone was surprised that Japan struck the Fleet at Pearl Harbor at the time that she did. Yet officers, both in Washington and Hawaii, were fully conscious of the danger from air attack; they realized this form of attack on Pearl Harbor by Japan was at least a possibility; and they were adequately informed of the imminence of war.

8. Specifically, the Hawaiian commands failed—

(*a*) to discharge their responsibilities in the light of the warning received from Washington, other information possessed by them, and the principle of command by mutual cooperation.

(*b*) To integrate and coordinate their facilities for defense and to alert properly the Army and Navy establishments in Hawaii, particularly in the light of the warnings and intelligence available to them during the period November 27 to December 7, 1941.

(*c*) To effect liaison on a basis designed to acquaint each of them with the operations of the other, which was necessary to their joint security, and to exchange fully all significant intelligence.

(*d*) To maintain a more effective reconnaissance within the limits of their equipment.

(*e*) To effect a state of readiness throughout the Army and Navy establishments designed to meet all possible attacks.

(*f*) To employ the facilities, material, and personnel at their command, which were adequate at least to have greatly minimized the effects of the attack, in repelling the Japanese raiders.

(*g*) To appreciate the significance of intelligence and other information available to them.

9. The errors made by the Hawaiian commands were errors of judgment and not derelictions of duty.

10. The War Plans Division of the War Department failed to discharge its direct responsibility to advise the commanding general he had not properly alerted the Hawaiian Department when the latter, pursuant to instructions, had reported action taken in a message that was not satisfactorily responsive to the original directive. . . .

12. Notwithstanding the fact that there were officers on twenty-four hour watch, the Committee believes that under all of the evidence the War and Navy Departments were not sufficiently alerted on December 6 and 7, 1941, in view of the imminence of war. . . .

Minority Report

We, the undersigned, find it impossible to concur with the findings and conclusions of the Committee's report because they are illogical, and unsupported by the preponderance of the evidence before the Committee. The conclusions of the diplomatic aspects are based upon incomplete evidence.

We, therefore, find it necessary to file a report setting forth the conclusions which we believe are properly sustained by evidence before the Committee.

Homer Ferguson.
Owen Brewster.

. . . 8. Judging by the military and naval history of Japan, high authorities in Washington and the Commanders in Hawaii had good grounds for expecting that in starting war the Japanese Government would make a surprise attack on the United States.

9. Neither the diplomatic negotiations nor the intercepts and other information respecting Japanese designs and operations in the hands of the United States authorities warranted those authorities in excluding from defense measures or from orders to the Hawaiian commanders the probability of an attack on Hawaii. On the contrary, there is evidence to the effect that such an attack was, in terms of strategy, necessary from the Japanese point of view and in fact highly probable, and that President Roosevelt was taking the probability into account—before December 7. . . .

11. The decision of the President, in view of the Constitution, to await the Japanese attack rather than ask for a declaration of war by Congress increased the responsibility of high authorities in Washington to use the utmost care in putting the commanders at Pearl Harbor on a full alert for defensive actions before the Japanese attack on December 7, 1941. . . .

13. The messages sent to General Short and Admiral Kimmel [Hawaiian commanders] by high authorities in Washington during November were couched in such conflicting and imprecise language that they failed to convey to the commanders definite information on the state of diplomatic relations with Japan and on Japanese war designs and positive orders respecting the particular actions to be taken—orders that were beyond all reasonable doubts as to the need for an all-out alert. In this regard the said high authorities failed to discharge their full duty.

14. High authorities in Washington failed in giving proper weight to the evidence before them respecting Japanese designs and operations which indicated that an attack on Pearl Harbor was highly probable and they failed also to emphasize this probability in messages to the Hawaiian commanders.

15. The failure of Washington authorities to act promptly and consistently in translating intercepts, evaluating information, and sending appropriate instructions to the Hawaiian commanders was in considerable measure due to delays, mismanagement, noncooperation, unpreparedness, confusion, and negligence on the part of officers in Washington.

8.2 Bletchley Park Cryptologist and Historian Peter Calvocoressi Explains How Enigma Worked during the War[2]

Arthur Scherbius invented the Enigma machine in the early 1920s. Although Scherbius hoped the encoding device would have commercial

---

2. From Peter Calvocoressi, *Top Secret Ultra* (New York: Pantheon, 1980), 23–29. Copyright Pantheon Books, a division of Random House, Inc.

applications, the German military soon developed its own version of the encrypting device. Enigma allowed users to type in a message, and then encode it using three to five notched rotors. To decode the message, the receiver needed to know how those wheels were set on that date. The British knew about the Enigma machine as early as 1931, but made little headway toward breaking its cipher until 1939. With the help of Polish code breakers, who had managed to reconstruct an Enigma machine, and early computers known as "bombes," British cryptologists at Bletchley Park managed to break the Germans' "unbreakable" code. All information gleaned from the Enigma transmissions was code-named Ultra. In the document that follows British cryptologist and historian Peter Calvocoressi explains how Enigma worked during the war.

Essentially Enigma was a transposition machine. That is to say, it turned every letter in a message into some other letter. The message stayed the same length but instead of being in German it became gobbledegook: it was garbled. That the Enigma machine did this was obvious. The problem was to find out how it performed its tricks. Only if its hidden workings were known, could a decypherer or cryptographer even begin to turn the gobbledegook back into German.

Even when he had got as far as to understand how Enigma worked the cryptographer was still no more than half way to decyphering any particular message. This was because the machine had a number of manually adjustable parts and the cryptographer needed to know not only how the machine was constructed and how it worked but also how these various movable parts were set by the operator at the moment when he began transmitting each particular message. These parts were adjusted every so often—in peace time once a month, later once every 24 hours, and from September 1942 some of them every 8 hours. In addition some parts moved automatically minute by minute when the machine was in use. And, the final complication, each separate message contained its own, individual key and this key was randomly selected. . . .

At first glance the Enigma machine looked like a typewriter but a peculiarly complicated one. It had a keyboard like the standard three-row keyboard of an ordinary typewriter but without numerals, punctuation marks or other extras. . . .

Behind the keyboard the alphabet was repeated in another three rows and in the same order, but this time the letters were not on keys but in small round glass holes which were set in a flat rectangular plate and could light up one at a time. When the operator struck a key one of these letters lit up. But it was never the same letter. By striking P the operator might, for example, cause L to appear; and next time he struck P he would get neither P nor L but something entirely different.

This operator called out the letters as they appeared in lights and a second operator sitting alongside him noted them down. This sequence was then transmitted by wireless in the usual Morse code and was picked up by whoever was supposed to be listening for it. It could also be picked up by an eavesdropper. The Germans experimented with a version of the machine which, by transmitting automatically as the message was encyphered, did away with the need for the second operator, but they never brought this version into use.

The legitimate recipient took the gobbledegook which had been transmitted to him and tapped it out on his machine. Provided he got the drill right the message turned itself back into German. The drill consisted in putting the parts of his machine in the same order as those of the sender's machine. This was no problem since he had a handbook or manual which told him what he had to do each day. In addition, the message which he had just received contained within itself the special key to that message.

The eavesdropper on the other hand had to work all this out for himself. Even assuming he had an Enigma machine in full working order it was no good to him unless he could discover how to arrange its parts—the gadgets which it had in addition to its keyboard. These were the mechanisms which caused L to appear when the operator struck P.

These parts or gadgets consisted of a set of wheels or drums and a set of plugs. Their purpose was not simply to turn P into L but to do so in so complex a manner that it was virtually impossible for an eavesdropper to find out what had gone on inside the machine in each case. And, furthermore, to ensure that if P became L this time it would become something else next time. It is quite easy to construct a machine that will always turn P into L but it is then comparatively easy to find out that L always means P: a simple substitution of this kind is inadequate for specially secret traffic.

The eavesdropper's basic task was to set his machine in exactly the same way as the legitimate recipient of the message had set his, since the eavesdropper would then be able to read the message with no more difficulty than the legitimate recipient. The more complex the machine and its internal workings, the more difficult and more time-consuming was it for the eavesdropper to solve this problem.

The Enigma machine fitted compactly into a wooden box which measured about 7 × 11 × 13 inches.

As the operator sat at his machine he had in front of him, first, the rows of keys, then the space for the letters to appear illuminated, and beyond these again and in the far left-hand corner of the machine three slots to take three wheels or drums. Each wheel was about three inches in diameter. The wheels were not much more than half embedded in the machine and end-on to the operator. They were covered by a lid and when this lid was closed the operator could see only the tops of them. He could easily lift them out and replace them.

Although there were three slots for three wheels, there were by 1939 five wheels. The operator had to use three of his set of five. He had to select the correct three and then place them in a prescribed order. This was crucial because the wheels, although outwardly identical, were different inside.

The German navy introduced a four-wheel machine at the beginning of March 1942. At this point the naval operator had six wheels for four slots but the new wheel had distinct limitations: it had to go to the left of the other three and it did not rotate, so that the number of permutations, though much increased by this innovation, was not nearly as large as it would have been if the four wheels had been as freely interchangeable as the three and if all four had rotated. In July of the same year a seventh wheel and fifth slot were added to the naval kit. The greater flexibility and inventiveness of the navy, which was still in evidence at the end of the war, may be ascribed to the fact that it used far fewer machines than either the army or the Luftwaffe. They could therefore be more easily replaced. Most of them moreover were static either in naval HQs shore or in fleet units. In this context a ship, even when at sea, provides a static home for its machinery in a way which is impossible for an army division or an air squadron, for which moving means considerably more upheaval.

Finally, there were besides the wheels the plugs (in German *Stecker*). These were in pairs. They looked like the plugs on a telephone switchboard. . . . There was one plughole for every letter of the alphabet. Each pair of plugs coupled a pair of letters. Putting them in and taking them out to change the couplings was the work of a moment. The number of pairings varied from 5 to 10. In theory there could be 13 pairings of 26 letters but there never were, and for some mathematical reason which I do not understand the maximum number of permutations is obtained when 10 pairings are used. . . .

The Enigma machine ran on an electric battery. When the operator of an ordinary typewriter strikes P on his keyboard he mechanically and immediately produces P on the paper in his machine. When an Enigma operator struck his P the effect, though all but instantaneous, was neither mechanical nor immediate. The operator's touch did not move a key and there was of course no paper in his machine. What he did by his touch was to release an electric pulse and this pulse went on a tortuous journey round the machine before returning to illumine not P but L. The electric current passed through the plug system; then through each of the three removable wheels from right to left, entering each in turn and leaving each of them by any one of 26 different points of entry and exit; and then—after bounding off a fixed wheel or reflector to the left of these removable three wheels— back from left to right by a different and equally multifarious route, back through the plug system again by a different route, and so to the light for L. The variety and unpredictability of each of these journeyings every time a key was struck were the inventor's pride and the cryptographer's headache.

Each journey from key to light—such was the complexity of Enigma's entrails—might take any one of an astronomical number of routes. The outcome, as shown in the row of lights, was not so multifarious. P could turn into one only of 25 different letters, i.e. 26 minus one. But that was not the point. The point was not what happened at the end of the journey but how it happened. What the cryptographer needed to know was the route, for without being able to establish and repeat the route he could not discover the journey's end.

Enigma, in the form in service when the war began, multiplied its permutations in various ways. First, there was the wheel-order. When there were just three different wheels to place in three slots the number of possible wheel-orders was six. Call the wheels A, B and C: the possible wheel-orders are ABC, ACB, BAC, BCA, CAB, CBA. But when the Germans added a fourth and a fifth wheel for the three slots, the number of possible three-wheel-orders rose from six to sixty.

But that was only the beginning. Not only were the wheels not identical; they were not stationary. They rotated. Each had a rotatable rim with 26 different contact points on either side. So each, independently of its fellows, could be set in any one of 26 different positions. And furthermore, every time the operator touched a key the right-hand wheel moved itself on by one notch. When it had done this 26 times the middle wheel began to behave likewise: and ultimately the left-hand wheel too. These shifts vastly raised the number of permutations—the number of different states in which the machine might be at a given moment.

Finally, the extra changes introduced by the plug couplings raised the total to an astronomical figure which, when laid out in full, had 88 digits.

All this sounds horribly complicated and so in one sense it was. But not in another. Although the Enigma machine was a highly complex piece of electrical machinery it was easy to operate. . . . [T]he essential difference between the legitimate recipient of an Enigma message and an enemy cryptographer was that, although both possessed and understood the machine, only the former had the handbook which told how the machine's parts were to be arranged each day.

8.3 WRNS Tends the Colossus Code-Breaking Computer, 1943

In 1944, members of the British Government Code and Cypher School (GCCS) unveiled the world's first electronic computer. Named the Colossus, the machine was the first computing device with a substantial electronic memory, programmable with switches and patch cords. Colossus allowed Allied code breakers to break the German teleprinter cypher known as Tunny. Members of the Women's Royal Navy Service, or WRNS, tended to the massive machine, which included 1,500–2,500 vacuum tubes.

Colossus II, photograph from the National Archives (United Kingdom), available at Wikimedia Commons, http://en.wikipedia.org/wiki/Colossus_computer#mediaviewer/File:Colossus.jpg.

8.4 Americans Decode and Translate a Japanese Encrypted Message, 1944[3]

The Empire of Japan used separate enciphering methods for diplomatic, naval, and army codes. The Imperial Army message reproduced here was enciphered using a three-step, book-based, manual enciphering method. While U.S. intelligence services were able to break the Japanese diplomatic code in 1940 and the naval code in 1942, they did not break the Japanese army code until 1943. By the winter of 1944, however, U.S. cryptanalysts were able to decipher upward of 20,000 Japanese army codes each month.

A Japanese Army Message Enciphered for Transmission

57[a]		491[b]		48[c]		12022240[d]			
1887	1773	3972[e]							
DD 6635 = 4761[f]									
2345[g]	6966[h]	2803	6249	4481	2424	8376	6135	7994	9570
1115	0312	2284	6870	6683	5207	1397	3689	7290	1861
8944	1980	3848	8428	9292	7802	1864	7499	3588	8585
1199	6952	9659	3102	1750	0646	7871	5765	6085	9415
1489	8410	4835	5340	9436	3943	0900	6249		

[a]Circuit number
[b]Originating message center number (Army Operations Department, IGHQ)
[c]Group count (forty-eight four-digit groups of numbers in the message)
[d]File date and time (December 2/10:40 p.m. Tokyo time)
[e]Disguised address (Second Area Army, Chief of Staff)
[f]Disguised points of origin and destination (DD = *den'dai* or telegraph address) (Tokyo = Davao)
[g]Discriminant code (3155 when converted from substitution table)
[h]Key indicator (299 when converted from substitution table)

---

3. From Edward J. Drea, *MacArthur's Ultra: Codebreaking and the War against Japan, 1942–1945* (Lawrence: University Press of Kansas, 1992), 4, 6–7. Copyright University Press of Kansas 1992.

The Japanese Army Message Transmitted in Morse Code

(RONSE/RONSE)[a]

7190/6720[b]		12022343[c]	(A)[d]	US00298367[e]
MA[f]	57[g]	MVN[h]	MW[i]	NZ/ZZMO[j]

NWWR   NRRS   SVRZ[k]

DD 6635 = 4767[l]

[m]ZSMA   TVTT   ZWOM   TZMV   MMWN   ZMZN   WSRT   TNSA
RVVM   VARO   NNNA   OSNZ   ZZWM   TWRO   TAWS   AZOR
NSVR   STWV   RZVO   NWTN   WBMM   NVWO   SWMW   WMZW
RWPZ   NWTM   RMVV   SAWW   WAWA   NNVV   TVAZ   VRAV
SZON   ZRAO   OTMT   RWRN   ARTA   TOWA   VMNA   NMWV
WMNO   MWSA   ASMO   VSMT   SVMS   OOVO   TZMV   VE[n]

---

[a]Circuit call between Tokyo and Manila
[b]Kilocycles to 7190 kilocycles from 6720
[c]Day, month, and hour of interception (Tokyo time)
[d]Classification of quality of intercept
[e]Intercept station number and teletype transmission number
[f]Routing instruction indicating relay
[g]Circuit number
[h]Originating message center number
[i]Group count
[j]File date and time
[k]Enciphered address
[l]Geographic code indicating point of origin and destination
[m]Text of message including discriminant and key cipher groups
[n]Procedure signal indicating end of message

Transliteration into Roman Letters

DAI ICHI. DAI JU YON SHIDAN WO DAI SAN HOMEN GUN NOO HENSO YORI WO NOZOKU DAI NI GUN SENTO JORETSU HENNYU SHI DAI NIJU KU SHIDAN WO KANTOGUN HENSO YORI WO NOZUKU DAI HACHI HOMEN GUN SENTO JORETSU HENNYU SHI.

Translation

Paragraph 1. The 14th Division is deleted from the Third Area Army Order of Battle and enrolled in the Second Area Army Order of Battle. Paragraph 2. The 29th Division is removed from the Kwantung Army Order of Battle and enrolled in the Eighth Area Army Order of Battle.

8.5 The Navajo Language Becomes an Unbreakable American Code, 1942[4]

During the Second World War, some 500 Native Americans served in the U.S. Marine Corps (USMC) as "code talkers," whose job it was to transmit tactical messages using ciphers based on their native languages. The Navajo language was a good cipher because it had a very complex grammar and was spoken only by a very small group of people. In 1942, the USMC developed a formal code substituting Navajo words for English letters (similar to the Army and Navy's shared Phonetic Alphabet that uses English words to represent letters). Although the Navajo were the most famous World War II–era code talkers, the U.S. military also used members of the Lakota, Meskwaki, and Comanche nations, as well as soldiers who spoke Basque.

ALPHABET	NAVAJO WORD	LITERAL TRANSLATION
A	WOL-LA-CHEE	ANT
A	BE-LA-SANA	APPLE
A	TSE-NILL	AXE
B	NA-HASH-CHID	BADGER
B	SHUSH	BEAR
B	TOISH-JEH	BARREL
C	MOASI	CAT
C	TLA-GIN	COAL
C	BA-GOSHI	COW
D	BE	DEER
D	CHINDI	DEVIL
D	LHA-CHA-EH	DOG
E	AH-JAH	EAR
E	DZEH	ELK
E	AH-NAH	EYE
F	CHUO	FIR
F	TSA-E-DONIN-EE	FLY
F	MA-E	FOX
G	AH-TAD	GIRL
G	KLIZZIE	GOAT
G	JEHA	GUM
H	TSE-GAH	HAIR
H	CHA	HAT
H	LIN	HORSE
I	TKIN	ICE
I	YEH-HES	ITCH
I	A-CHI	INTESTINE

---

4. From U.S. Naval Historical Center, http://www.history.navy.mil/faqs/faq61-4.htm.

J	TKELE-CHO-G	JACKASS
J	AH-YA-TSINNE	JAW
J	YIL-DOI	JERK
K	JAD-HO-LONI	KETTLE
K	BA-AH-NE-DI-TININ	KEY
K	KLIZZIE-YAZZIE	KID
L	DIBEH-YAZZIE	LAMB
L	AH-JAD	LEG
L	NASH-DOIE-TSO	LION
M	TSIN-TLITI	MATCH
M	BE-TAS-TNI	MIRROR
M	NA-AS-TSO-SI	MOUSE
N	TSAH	NEEDLE
N	A-CHIN	NOSE
O	A-KHA	OIL
O	TLO-CHIN	ONION
O	NE-AHS-JAH	OWL
P	CLA-GI-AIH	PANT
P	BI-SO-DIH	PIG
P	NE-ZHONI	PRETTY
Q	CA-YEILTH	QUIVER
R	GAH	RABBIT
R	DAH-NES-TSA	RAM
R	AH-LOSZ	RICE
S	DIBEH	SHEEP
S	KLESH	SNAKE
T	D-AH	TEA
T	A-WOH	TOOTH
T	THAN-ZIE	TURKEY
U	SHI-DA	UNCLE
U	NO-DA-IH	UTE
V	A-KEH-DI-GLINI	VICTOR
W	GLOE-IH	WEASEL
X	AL-NA-AS-DZOH	CROSS
Y	TSAH-AS-ZIH	YUCCA
Z	BESH-DO-TLIZ	ZINC

NAMES OF COUNTRIES	NAVAJO WORD	LITERAL TRANSLATION
AMERICA	NE-HE-MAH	OUR MOTHER
BRITAIN	TOH-TA	BETWEEN WATERS
GERMANY	BESH-BE-CHA-HE	IRON HAT
JAPAN	BEH-NA-ALI-TSOSIE	SLANT EYE

NAMES OF AIRPLANES	NAVAJO WORD	LITERAL TRANSLATION
PLANES	WO-TAJH-DE-NE-IH	AIR FORCE
DIVE BOMBER	GINI	CHICKEN HAWK
TORPEDO PLANE	TAS-CHIZZIE	SWALLOW

OBS. PLANE	NE-AS-JAH	OWL
FIGHTER PLANE	DA-HE-TIH-HI	HUMMING BIRD
BOMBER PLANE	JAY-SHO	BUZZARD
PATROL PLANE	GA-CIH	CROW
TRANSPORT	ATSAH	EAGLE

NAMES OF SHIPS	NAVAJO WORD	LITERAL TRANSLATION
SHIPS	TOH-DINEH-IH	SEA FORCE
BATTLESHIP	LO-TSO	WHALE
AIRCRAFT	TSIDI-MOFFA-YE-HI	BIRD CARRIER
SUBMARINE	BESH-LO	IRON FISH
MINE SWEEPER	CHA	BEAVER
DESTROYER	CA-LO	SHARK
TRANSPORT	DINEH-NAY-YE-HI	MAN CARRIER
CRUISER	LO-TSO-YAZZIE	SMALL WHALE
MOSQUITO BOAT	TSE-E	MOSQUITO

VOCABULARY WORD	NAVAJO WORD	LITERAL TRANSLATION
ALLIES	NIH-HI-CHO	ALLIES
BOMB	A-YE-SHI	EGGS
COAST GUARD	TA-BAS-DSISSI	SHORE RUNNER
COMMUNICATION	HA-NEH-AL-ENJI	MAKING TALK
DETONATOR	AH-DEEL-TAHI (OR)	BLOWN UP
EXPLOSIVE	AH-DEL-TAHI (E)	EXPLOSIVE
HOSPITAL	A-ZEY-AL-H	PLACE OF MEDICINE
PYROTECHNIC	COH-NA-CHANH	FANCY FIRE
SABOTAGE	A-TKEL-YAH	HINDERED
SUBMERGE	TKAL-CLA-YI-YAH	WENT UNDER WATER

8.6 Office of Strategic Services Official Allen Dulles Explains His Wartime Intelligence Activities, 1941–1945[5]

Spies played a key role in supplying both the Allied and Axis powers with information about their enemies and friends. These clandestine operatives also spread disinformation designed to confuse the other side, and lent support to underground groups "behind enemy lines." In the United States, such activities were the purview of the newly formed Office of Strategic Services (OSS). Established in 1942 to "collect and

---

5. From Allen W. Dulles, *The Craft of Intelligence* (New York: Harper & Row, 1963; repr. Boulder, CO: Westview Press, 1985), 41–43. Copyright HarperCollins Publishers, Inc., 1963.

analyze strategic information and to plan and operate special services," the OSS was the precursor to the modern Central Intelligence Agency (CIA). As the director of the OSS in Switzerland, Alan Dulles cultivated contacts with high-ranking German generals, as well German exiles, members of the resistance, and anti-Nazis of all stripes. In the document that follows, Dulles describes his work and his part in Operation Sunrise, a secret 1945 mission to arrange a local surrender of German forces in Northern Italy.

The Craft of Intelligence

It was only in World War II, and particularly after the Pearl Harbor attack, that we began to develop, side by side with our military intelligence organizations, an agency for secret intelligence collection and operations. . . . The origin of this agency was a summons by President Franklin D. Roosevelt to William J. Donovan in 1941 to come down to Washington and work on this problem.

Colonel (later Major General) Donovan was eminently qualified for the job. A distinguished lawyer, a veteran of World War I who had won the Medal of Honor, he had divided his busy life in peacetime between the law, government service and politics. He knew the world, having traveled widely. He understood people. He had a flair for the unusual and for the dangerous, tempered with judgment. In short, he had the qualities to be desired in an intelligence officer.

The Japanese sneak attack on Pearl Harbor and our entry into the war naturally stimulated the rapid growth of the OSS and its intelligence operations.

It had begun, overtly, as a research and analysis organization, manned by a hand-picked group of some of the best historians and other scholars available in this country. By June, 1942, the COI (Coordinator of Information), as Donovan's organization had been called at first, was renamed the Office of Strategic Services (OSS) and told "to collect and analyze strategic information and to plan and operate special services."

By this time the OSS was already deep in the task of "special services," a cover designation for secret intelligence and secret operations of all kinds and character, particularly the support of various anti-Nazi underground groups behind the enemy lines and covert preparations for the invasion of North Africa.

During 1943, elements of the OSS were at work on a world-wide basis, except for Latin America, where the FBI was operating, and parts of the Far Eastern Command, which General MacArthur had already pre-empted.

Its guerrilla and resistance branch, modeled on the now well-publicized British Special Operations Executive (SOE) and working closely with the latter in the European Theater, had already begun to drop teams of men and women into France, Italy and Yugoslavia and in the China-Burma-India Theater of war. The key idea behind these operations was to support, train and supply already existing resistance movements or, where there were none, to organize willing partisans into effective guerrillas. The Jedburghs, as they were called, who dropped into France, and Detachment 101, the unit in Burma, were among the most famous of these groups. Later the OSS developed special units for the creation and dissemination of black propaganda, for counterespionage, and for certain sabotage and resistance tasks that require unusual talents, such as underwater demolitions or technical functions in support of regular intelligence tasks. In conjunction with all these undertakings, it had to develop its own training schools.

Toward the end of the war, as our armies swept over Germany, it created special units for the apprehension of war criminals and the recovery of looted art treasures as well as for tracking down the movements of funds which, it was thought, the Nazi leaders would take into hiding in order to make a comeback at a later date. There was little that it did not attempt to do at some time or place between 1942 and the war's end. . . .

The Secret Surrender

Unknown to the outside world, since the end of February, 1945, emissaries and messages had been passing secretly between the OSS mission in Switzerland, of which I was in charge, and German generals in Italy. For two crucial months the commanders of contending armies locked in battle had maintained secret communications through my office in Bern seeking the means to end the fighting on the front in Italy, hoping that a Nazi surrender there would bring in its wake a general surrender in Europe. We had given the code name "Sunrise" to this operation to facilitate speed and secrecy in the handling of our messages. We did not know until later that Winston Churchill, who was closely following the proceedings, had already named the operation "Crossword."

What prevented our early success was the stubborn and insane policy of one man, Adolf Hitler. Despite the hopeless position of his armies, he would not countenance any surrender anywhere. His generals had good reason to fear that they would pay with their lives for any unauthorized attempt to stop the fighting. This meant there could be no parliamentarians crossing enemy lines with white flags, no public parleys, no formalized negotiations. Instead, a secret intelligence organization took over the unusual function of establishing the first contact and actively pursuing the negotiations with the enemy until the surrender was ready to be signed. We became, in agreement with Field Marshal Alexander, the channel through which communications between the Allied and the German High Commands were maintained. . . .

Against Germany it was obvious from the start that our work would have to be of another sort. There were certain high-level resistance groups in Germany but no partisan activities of the kind we supported in France and Italy. Our best intelligence source on Germany materialized in the summer of 1943, in the person of a diplomat, one who had the kind of access which is the intelligence officer's dream. George Wood (our code name for him) was not only our best source on Germany but undoubtedly one of the best secret agents any intelligence service has ever had. He was an official in the German Foreign Office in Berlin and his job there was to screen and distribute for action the cable traffic between the Foreign Office and German diplomatic posts all over the world. Since the messages to and from German military and air attaches in Tokyo were also generally sent through Foreign Office channels, he saw these, too, and they became of great value as the war in the Far East was still to be fought out. He was frequently sent by the Foreign Office as a courier to Switzerland as well as to other posts, and it was on one of his courier trips to Switzerland that he succeeded in making contact with us, having convinced himself that in this way he could contribute to the fall of the Nazis, whom he hated.

While at his post in Berlin, he would scour the files of official cables and copy or photograph (microfilm) for us everything he thought of importance. He would then bring the copies out in his locked diplomatic bag along with the material he was delivering to the German Legation in Bern or mail them to us by secret channels. It is impossible here to describe fully his coverage. He turned in to us some of the best technical and tactical information on the V-weapons, on the effects of Allied bombings, on German planning, on the gradually weakening fabric of the whole Nazi regime. General Donovan thought highly enough of this material to pass much of it on directly to President Roosevelt. . . .

Of direct practical value of the very highest kind among Wood's contributions was a copy of a cable in which the German Ambassador in Turkey, von Papen, proudly reported to Berlin (in November, 1943) the acquisition of top-secret documents from the British Embassy in Ankara through "an important German agent." This was, of course, the famous Cicero, the valet of the British Ambassador who had managed to procure the keys to the Ambassador's private safe and to photograph its contents. I immediately passed word of this to my British colleagues, and a couple of British security inspectors immediately went over to the British Embassy in Ankara and changed the safes and their combinations, thus putting Cicero out of business. Neither the Germans nor Cicero ever knew what was behind the security visit, which was, of course, made to appear routine and normal. Thus our rifling of the German Foreign Office safes in Berlin through an agent reporting to the Americans in Switzerland, put an end to the rifling of the British Ambassador's safe by a German agent in Turkey.

8.7 Historian and OSS Official William Langer Describes the Contribution of Scholars to the Intelligence War, 1943–1946[6]

The OSS included five separate branches. The Research and Analysis Branch (R&A) was responsible for analyzing open sources, like libraries, newspaper reports, and government information, to discover Axis strengths and weaknesses. The group played a key role in designing the Allied powers 1944 bombing campaign against German industry when a group of R&A economists posted in London identified oil production as a major German vulnerability. William Langer, a Harvard historian, was the R&A's second director. The R&A branch attracted the "best and the brightest" of American academics and intellectuals. Veterans of the branch included future presidents of the American Historical Association and the American Economic Association, as well as two Nobel laureates.

As the war progressed, the Joint Chiefs of Staff assigned more and, indeed, even more difficult operational assignments to the OSS. These fascinated [OSS Chief William J.] Donovan and gave full scope to his imagination. More and more of this attention was focused on these tasks, many of which required him to be abroad. Compared to plans for sabotage of enemy installations, aid and supplies to resistance groups, the penetration of enemy positions, etc., the work of the R and A [Research and Analysis] lacked drama and excitement. Hence, the books that have been written on the OSS have little to say of it and devote themselves to the narrative of adventure and heroism. But Donovan never lost his interest in R and A and its work. On the contrary, he rated it highly and interfered little, though he never failed to have visiting notables shown around, if only to see men and women busy at desks or typewriters.

---

6. From William Langer, *In and Out of the Ivory Tower* (New York: Neale Watson Academic Publications, 1977), 187–88, 190–92.

The work of the R and A was so varied and so conditioned by the requirements of the war that it is extremely difficult to give a coherent account of it. At first we were ignored, if not opposed, by other agencies, and most of our reports were unsolicited. Our Projects Committee decided which problems were important or apt to become so, and directed and criticized the product. . . .

In the planning of the invasion of North Africa, all sorts of abstruse information was required and the contributions of our African section, headed by Sherman Kent, who for many years was to play a key role in foreign intelligence work and actually wrote a book on the subject, were gratefully received. The landing in Sicily and the Italian campaign were to tax our Italian section, and here, if I am not mistaken, we first began to make careful target studies for Air Force bombardment. . . .

. . . Almost anyone would admit that the outcome of the war hinged largely on the success or failure of the Russian forces, which in turn depended largely on the availability not only of tanks, airplanes, and trucks, but also of munitions. How were we to form an independent judgment on Russian capabilities and needs? Very few of our economists, even among the ablest, had any knowledge of the organization and workings of either the Soviet or the Nazi economy. The economics of the New Deal, which had brought many of them to Washington, were too fascinating and immediately important to study the functioning of the dictatorships.

Our economics section, headed by my distinguished colleague and lifelong friend Edward S. Mason, was extraordinarily able, imaginative, and dynamic, staffed by a number of brilliant young scholars, who were for many later years to play important roles in Washington. They had no difficulty in recognizing the problems and mapping out approaches to their solution. There was only one serious obstacle—ignorance of the Russian language and hence inability to read many of the crucial materials.

According to Geroid T. Robinson, professor of Russian history at Columbia and author of a well-known study, *Rural Russia under the Old Regime* (based on two years of archival work in Russia in the 1930s), ignorance of the language vitiated the value of the reports on Russian affairs produced by the economics section. The latter replied that such work could not be abandoned to the Russian section because it knew no economics. Actually, I think Robinson and some of his staff knew more of Russian economics than the economics section knew of the Russian language; but fortunately, it never became necessary to rule apodictically on this important issue. Both Mason and Robinson were outstanding men, whose prime interest was in getting the work well done. It was soon arranged that on Russian problems appropriate members of each section should work together. This was the natural and successful solution. The R and A studies on Russian needs and productive capabilities were among the most effective of our products. Towards the end of the conflict, various sections working together produced an extended analysis of Soviet capabilities and intentions that may justly be called the first national intelligence estimate. In the budding "cold war," it was highly regarded by General Embick and the Joint Chiefs of Staff and may well be described as the very acme of intelligence analysis.

Before leaving the economics section, more than mere mention must be made of its contributions on the German side, where the economists had a better command of the language and where, too, close collaboration with the German section was gradually established. Using captured Nazi material, the economists discovered the key to the serial numbers of captured truck tires, engines, and other Nazi industrial products. Presently they could tell with astonishing accuracy which factory was producing what amount of what product, where the bottlenecks were (as with ball bearings), and which plants it was urgently necessary to destroy by bombardment. Similarly, by the careful analysis of the local Nazi press (collected in Stockholm), it became possible to determine, through the officer obituaries, where different Nazi units were and sometimes what their losses were in recent engagements. I submit that these items were military intelligence of the highest order, attained by altogether new and ingenious methods. No other nation during the war was, or so far as I know, has since been able to bring such concentrated intellectual power to bear on wartime problems as did Donovan's R and A.

During the concluding year of the war, the German section had the crucial role of studying for the occupation and military governments of territories conquered from the enemy. This section was peculiarly fitted for this assignment because it had on its staff a number of German refugees with considerable firsthand knowledge about conditions and procedures. I think here of the late Hajo Holborn, professor of history at Yale, the late Franz Neumann, of the New School for Social Research, and Herbert Marcuse, whose later revolutionary role was then indiscernible. These senior scholars were supported by younger men, almost all of whom were eventually to fill chairs at our major universities. To mention Franklin L. Ford, Carl E. Schorske, Robert L. Wolff, H. Stuart Hughes, and Paul Sweet is only to cite those whom I knew best. Holborn was later to write an excellent book on occupation policies and military government, and all that need be said here is that by dint of hard and sustained work the R and A was able to make a major contribution in a difficult and troublesome field.

CHAPTER 9

THE UNITED STATES AND THE HOLOCAUST

Unlike in World War I, a majority of the deaths in World War II were civilian rather than military. Indeed, the concept of "civilian" virtually disappeared during this total war. Partially this resulted from new weapons and doctrines on their use that targeted civilians, most notably the strategic bombing of cities (see Chapter 4). But it was also due to the fact that in many theaters a vicious race war on civilian noncombatants as well as uniformed combatants took place. In Asia, Japanese soldiers murdered hundreds of thousands, if not millions, of Chinese civilians—most notably but far from exclusively in the notorious 1937–1938 "Rape of Nanking." In the Pacific, U.S. and Japanese forces often fought without quarter in what historian John Dower aptly labeled a "war without mercy." Nazi-occupied Europe, however, witnessed the most widespread, destructive, and notorious race war.

Racism was a central component in Nazi ideology and Hitler's thinking. In his racial hierarchy most of the peoples of Europe were biologically inferior to the "Aryan" Germans and were to be not only conquered but also deprived of their property and often murdered. Indeed, one of Hitler's key aims in Eastern Europe was to obtain *lebensraum*, or "living space" for the growing German population by forcing out, enslaving, and/or killing the millions of Slavic peoples who lived there. More than 25 million Russians and other Soviet citizens consequently perished during the war, the majority of them civilians. While the raw numbers were lower in Poland, the actual percentage of the prewar Polish population to die during the war was even higher than in the USSR.

In Nazi racial thinking, the Jews of Europe constituted a separate category and were demonized as the source of all evil. Prior to World War II, Hitler tried to isolate, expropriate, and force out all Jews so as to make Germany "Jew free." His 1935 Nuremberg racial laws began the process by defining German Jews and depriving them of their rights. The ensuing persecution of Jews before war began culminated in the 1938 *Kristallnacht*, or "Night of Broken Glass," during which German Jews, their businesses, and their synagogues were savagely attacked in a government-sponsored assault. As a result, thousands of Jews did leave Germany, but Nazi territorial acquisitions from 1938 to 1942 brought millions more into the

German Reich. Nazi policy consequently changed from expulsion of Jews to outright mass murder as the way to make their empire free of all Jews. This policy began with the 1939 conquest of Poland, accelerated with the 1941 invasion of the Soviet Union, and was codified in early 1942 as the notorious "Final Solution" to what the Nazis called their "Jewish problem." Death camps such as Auschwitz II/Birkenau and Treblinka were created in German-occupied Poland to exterminate all the Jews of Europe, as well as other "undesirables" including gay men and women and the Romani people. Extermination also took place at many of the concentration camps that the Nazis had previously established and in the field, as special death squads known as *Einsatzgruppen* accompanied the German army into the Soviet Union.

The American response to this attempted extermination of European Jewry has been the subject of much discussion and debate. The government did little if anything to help the refugees fleeing Germany during the 1930s nor the millions being systematically murdered during the war. President Roosevelt was extremely popular with American Jews and spoke out against Nazi actions on numerous occasions; he also called in 1938 for an international conference to deal with the refugees and in 1944 established the War Refugee Board, which has been credited with saving the lives of tens of thousands of Jews. But he would not challenge the existing U.S. immigration laws that sharply limited the number of people allowed into the country—especially from East European countries containing the largest number of Jews. Nor were the Congress and American people willing to modify those laws. To make matter worse, State Department officials insisted on interpreting them in a very rigid manner. During the war the Allies did condemn Nazi war crimes and promise postwar punishment of the perpetrators. But no effort was made to bomb the extermination camps or in other ways halt the extermination process. To the contrary, the State Department acted to suppress knowledge of and information about what we now call the Holocaust.

This American behavior has led to much historical controversy—especially but far from exclusively regarding Roosevelt. In general, his critics emphasize what they consider his callousness if not cowardice and his inaction in the face of this horror. They also condemn State Department officials—especially Assistant Secretary of State Breckenridge Long—for anti-Semitism, for opposing efforts to modify existing immigration laws and allow persecuted European Jews to enter the country, and for interpreting those laws in an extremely rigid manner. These attacks began in the 1960s and peaked in the 1980s. Since then, however, Roosevelt's defenders have emphasized the severe limits under which he had to work, including the anti-immigrant and anti-Semitic beliefs of the Congress and general public as well as the State Department. They have also emphasized the other priorities the president had during this time period and what he actually did accomplish compared to others, and they have accused the attackers of ignoring all these factors and incorrectly project-ing contemporary values and knowledge onto the past.

This controversy raises numerous questions for you to consider. What, if anything, was done to aid the Jews of Europe? What could have been done that was not done, and why? Why was Congress unwilling to modify its harsh immigration laws, and why did the State Department interpret them so rigidly and seek to suppress information about the Holocaust? Why was Roosevelt unwilling to challenge such behavior or call for modi-fication of the country's immigration laws? Why were the extermination camps not bombed? Were there other measures that could have been tried but were not? If so, why?

* * * *

9.1 The National Origins Act Restricts Immigration, 1924[1]

In the aftermath of World War I, American public opinion turned deci-sively against immigrants, whom many Americans blamed for dragging the United States into that war and for the wave of labor radicalism that swept the country in 1918 and 1919. This xenophobia influenced U.S. immigration policy. The National Origins Act of 1924, key portions of which are reproduced here, established strict quotas that limited the number of immigrants especially from Eastern and Southern Europe. This law remained the basis of U.S. immigration policy both before and during World War II. What effect might this law have had on Jews who wished to come to the United States in the 1930s and 1940s?

Section 11

(a) The annual quota of any nationality shall be 2 per centum of the num-ber of foreign-born individuals of such nationality resident in continental United States as determined by the United States census of 1890, but the minimum quota of any nationality shall be 100.

(b) The annual quota of any nationality for the fiscal year beginning July 1, 1927, and for each fiscal year thereafter, shall be a number which

---

1. From Public Law 139, Chapter 190, *United States Statutes at Large* 43 (1925): 153.

bears the same ratio to 150,000 as the number of inhabitants in continental United States in 1920 having that national origin (ascertained as
hereinafter provided in this section) bears to the number of inhabitants in
continental United States in 1920, but the minimum quota of any nationality shall be 100.

9.2 Henry Ford's *Dearborn Independent* Reveals American Anti-Semitism, 1921–1922[2]

Anti-Semitism was by no means limited to Germany. Reproduced here
is a sample of the published anti-Semitic writings of the famous American automaker Henry Ford.

The international Jewish banker who has no country but plays them all
against one another, and the International Jewish proletariat that roams
from land to land in search of a peculiar type of economic opportunity, are
not figments of the imagination except to the non-Jew who prefers a lazy
laxity of mind.

Of these classes of Jews, one or both are at the heart of the problems
that disturb the world today. The immigration problem is Jewish. The
money question is Jewish. The tie-up of world politics is Jewish. The terms
of the Peace Treaty are Jewish. The diplomacy of the world is Jewish. The
moral question in movies and theaters is Jewish. The mystery of the illicit
liquor business is Jewish.

These facts are unfortunate as well as unpleasant for the Jew, and it is
squarely up to him to deal with the facts, and not waste time in trying to
destroy those who define the facts. . . .

To say that the immigration problem is Jewish does not mean that Jews
must be prohibited entry to any country; it means that they must become
rooted to a country in loyal citizenship, as no doubt some are, and as no
doubt most are not. To say that the money question is Jewish does not
mean the Jews must get out of finance; it means that they must rid finance
of the Jewish idea which has always been to use money to get a stranglehold on men and business concerns, instead of using finance to help general business. . . .

---

2. From Henry Ford, *The International Jew: The World's Foremost Problem*, vol. 3, *Jewish Influences on American Life*, and vol. 4, *Aspects of Jewish Power in the United States* (Dearborn, MI: Dearborn Publishing, 1921 and 1922), 3:243–44; 4:41–44, 47–48, 50–51, 53. Reprints of third and fourth selections from articles appearing in the *Dearborn Independent*.

It is not the true Jewishness of the Jew, nor yet the nationalism of the Jew that is on trial, but his anti-national internationalism. A true Mosaic Jew—not a Talmud Jew—would be a good citizen. A nationalist Jew would at least be logical. But an international Jew has proved an abomination, because his internationalism is focused on his own racial nationalism which in turn is founded on his ingrained belief that the rest of humanity is inferior to him and by right his prey. Jewish leaders may indulge in all the platitudes they possess, the fact which they cannot deny is that the Jew has for centuries regarded the "goyim" as beneath him and legitimately his spoil.

The internationalism of the Jew is confessed everywhere by him. Listen to a German banker: imagine the slow, oily voice in which he said:

"We are international bankers. Germany lost the war?—what of it?—that is an affair of the army. We are international bankers."

And that was the attitude of every international Jewish banker during the war. . . .

The Jewish Question is not in the number of Jews who here reside, not in the American's jealousy of the Jew's success, certainly not in any objection to the Jew's entirely unobjectionable Mosaic religion; it is in something else, and that something else is the fact of Jewish influence on the life of the country where Jews dwell; in the United States it is *the Jewish influence on American life.* . . .

The essence of the Jewish Idea *in its influence on the labor world* is the same as in all other departments—the destruction of real values in favor of fictitious values. The Jewish philosophy of money is not to "make money," but to "get money." The distinction between these two is fundamental. That explains Jews being "financiers" instead of "captains of industry." It is the difference between "getting" and "making."

The creative, constructive type of mind has an affection for the thing it is doing. The non-Jewish worker formerly chose the work he liked best. He did not change employment easily, because there was a bond between him and the kind of work he had chosen. Nothing else was so attractive to him. He would rather draw a little less money and do what he liked to do, than a little more and do what irked him. The "maker" is always thus influenced by his liking.

Not so the "getter." It doesn't matter what he does, so long as the income is satisfactory. He has no illusions, sentiments or affections on the side of work. It is the "geld" that counts. He has no attachment for the things he makes, for he doesn't make any; he deals in the things which other men make and regards them solely on the side of their money-drawing value. "The joy of creative labor" is nothing to him, not even an intelligible saying. . . .

The idea of "get" is a vicious, anti-social and destructive idea *when held alone*; but when held in company with "make" and as second in importance, it is legitimate and constructive. As soon as a man or a class is inoculated with the strictly Jewish Idea of "getting"—("getting mine"; "getting while the getting is good"; "honestly if you can, dishonestly if you must, but *get* it"—all of which are notes of this treasonable philosophy), the very cement of society loses its adhesiveness and begins to crumble. . . .

Jewish influence on the thought of the workingmen of the United States, as well as on the thought of business and professional men has been bad, thoroughly bad. This is not manifested in a division between "capital" and "labor," for there are no such separate elements; there is only the executive and operating departments of American business. The real division is between the Jewish idea of "get" and the Anglo-Saxon idea of "make," and at the present time the Jewish idea has been successful enough to have caused an upset.

All over the United States, in many branches of trade, Communist colleges are maintained, officered and taught by Jews. These so-called colleges exist in Chicago, Detroit, Cleveland, Rochester, Pittsburgh, New York, Philadelphia and other cities, the whole intent being to put all American labor on a "get" basis, which must prove the economic damnation of the country. And that, apparently, is the end sought, as in Russia.

Until Jews can show that the infiltration of foreign Jews and the Jewish Idea into the American labor movement has made for the betterment in character and estate, in citizenship and economic statesmanship, of the American workingman, the charge of being an alien, destructive and treasonable influence will have to stand. . . .

Colleges are being constantly invaded by the Jewish Idea. . . . Young men in the first exhilarating months of intellectual freedom are being seized with promissory doctrines, the source and consequences of which they do not see. There is a natural rebelliousness of youth, which promises progress; there is a natural venturesomeness to play free with ancient faiths; both of which are ebullitions of the spirit and significant of dawning mental virility. It is during the periods when these adolescent expansions are in process that the youth is captured by influences which deliberately lie in wait for him in the colleges. True, in after years a large proportion come to their senses sufficiently to be able "to sit on the fence and see themselves go by," and they come back to sanity. They find that "free love" doctrines make exhilarating club topics, but that the Family—the old-fashioned loyalty of one man and one woman to each other and their children—is the basis, not only of society, but of all personal character and progress. They find that Revolution, while a delightful subject for fiery debates and an excellent stimulant to the feeling of supermanlikeness, is nevertheless not the process of progress.

And, too, they come at length to see that the Stars and Stripes and the Free Republic are better than the Red Star and Soviet sordidness. . . .

The only absolute antidote to the Jewish influence is to call college students back to a pride of race. We often speak of the Fathers as if they were the few who happened to affix their signatures to a great document which marked a new era of liberty. The Fathers were the men of the Anglo-Saxon Celtic race. The men who came across Europe with civilization in their blood and in their destiny; the men who crossed the Atlantic and set up civilization on a bleak and rock-bound coast; the men who drove west to California and north to Alaska; the men who peopled Australia and seized the gates of the world at Suez, Gibraltar and Panama; the men who opened the tropics and subdued the arctics—Anglo-Saxon men, who have given form to every government and a livelihood to every people and an ideal to every century. They got neither their God nor their religion from Judah, nor yet their speech nor their creative genius—they are the Ruling People, Chosen throughout the centuries to Master the world, by Building it ever better and better and not by breaking it down.

Into the camp of this race, among the sons of the rules, comes a people that has no civilization to point to, no aspiring religion, no universal speech, no great achievement in any realm but the realm of "get," cast out of every land that gave them hospitality, and these people endeavor to tell the sons of the Saxons what is needed to make the world what it ought to be. . . .

Judah has begun the struggle. Judah has made the invasion. Let it come. Let no man fear it. But let every man insist that the fight be fair. Let college students and leaders of thought know that the objective is the regnancy of the ideas and the race that have built all the civilization we see and that promise all the civilization of the future; let them also know that the attacking force is Jewish.

9.3 The United States Supreme Court Finds the Sterilization of "Defectives" Constitutional, 1927[3]

Immigration restrictions flowed logically not only from Ford's anti-Semitism but also from the broader "scientific racism" popular in the United States at this time—and from the related field of eugenics that sought to preserve and improve the American gene pool by restricting

---

3. From *Buck v. Bell*, 274 U.S. 200.

if not halting the influx of "inferior" races, outlawing racial intermarriage, and implementing compulsory sterilization of mental and racial "defectives." In the 1927 case of *Buck v. Bell*, the Supreme Court ruled that such compulsory sterilization was constitutional, with the court's opinion written by Justice Oliver Wendell Holmes.

Mr. JUSTICE HOLMES delivered the opinion of the Court.

This is a writ of error to review a judgment of the Supreme Court of Appeals of the State of Virginia affirming a judgment of the Circuit Court of Amherst County by which the defendant in error, the superintendent of the State Colony for Epileptics and Feeble Minded, was ordered to perform the operation of salpingectomy upon Carrie Buck, the plaintiff in error, for the purpose of making her sterile. The case comes here upon the contention that the statute authorizing the judgment is void under the Fourteenth Amendment as denying to the plaintiff in error due process of law and the equal protection of the laws.

Carrie Buck is a feeble minded white woman who was committed to the State Colony above mentioned in due form. She is the daughter of a feeble minded mother in the same institution, and the mother of an illegitimate feeble minded child. She was eighteen years old at the time of the trial of her case in the Circuit Court, in the latter part of 1924. An Act of Virginia, approved March 20, 1924, recites that the health of the patient and the welfare of society may be promoted in certain cases by the sterilization of mental defectives, under careful safeguard, &c.; that the sterilization may be effected in males by vasectomy and in females by salpingectomy, without serious pain or substantial danger to life; that the Commonwealth is supporting in various institutions many defective persons who, if now discharged, would become a menace, but, if incapable of procreating, might be discharged with safety and become self-supporting with benefit to themselves and to society, and that experience has shown that heredity plays an important part in the transmission of insanity, imbecility, &c. The statute then enacts that, whenever the superintendent of certain institutions, including the above-named State Colony, shall be of opinion that it is for the best interests of the patients and of society that an inmate under his care should be sexually sterilized, he may have the operation performed upon any patient afflicted with hereditary forms of insanity, imbecility, &c., on complying with the very careful provisions by which the act protects the patients from possible abuse.

The superintendent first presents a petition to the special board of directors of his hospital or colony, stating the facts and the grounds for his opinion, verified by affidavit. Notice of the petition and of the time and place of the hearing in the institution is to be served upon the inmate, and also upon his guardian, and if there is no guardian, the superintendent is to apply to the Circuit Court of the County to appoint one. If the inmate is a minor, notice also is to be given to his parents, if any, with a copy of the petition. The board is to see to it that the inmate may attend the hearings if desired by him or his guardian. The evidence is all to be reduced to writing, and, after the board has made its order for or against the operation, the superintendent, or the inmate, or his guardian, may appeal to the Circuit Court of the County. The Circuit Court may consider the record of the board and the evidence before it and such other admissible evidence as may be offered, and may affirm, revise, or reverse the order of the board and enter such order as it deems just. Finally any party may apply to the Supreme Court of Appeals, which, if it grants the appeal, is to hear the case upon the record of the trial in the Circuit Court, and may enter such order as it thinks the Circuit Court should have entered. There can be no doubt that, so far as procedure is concerned, the rights of the patient are most carefully considered, and, as every step in this case was taken in scrupulous compliance with the statute and after months of observation, there is no doubt that, in that respect, the plaintiff in error has had due process of law.

The attack is not upon the procedure, but upon the substantive law. It seems to be contended that in no circumstances could such an order be justified. It certainly is contended that the order cannot be justified upon the existing grounds. The judgment finds the facts that have been recited, and that Carrie Buck is the probable potential parent of socially inadequate offspring, likewise afflicted, that she may be sexually sterilized without detriment to her general health, and that her welfare and that of society will be promoted by her sterilization, and thereupon makes the order. In view of the general declarations of the legislature and the specific findings of the Court, obviously we cannot say as matter of law that the grounds do not exist, and, if they exist, they justify the result. We have seen more than once that the public welfare may call upon the best citizens for their lives. It would be strange if it could not call upon those who already sap the strength of the State for these lesser sacrifices, often not felt to be such by those concerned, in order to prevent our being swamped with incompetence. It is better for all the world if, instead of waiting to execute degenerate offspring for crime or to let them starve for their imbecility, society can prevent those who are manifestly unfit from continuing their kind. The principle that sustains compulsory vaccination is broad enough to cover cutting the Fallopian tubes.

Three generations of imbeciles are enough.

But, it is said, however it might be if this reasoning were applied generally, it fails when it is confined to the small number who are in the institutions named and is not applied to the multitudes outside. It is the usual last resort of constitutional arguments to point out shortcomings of this sort. But the answer is that the law does all that is needed when it does all that it can, indicates a policy, applies it to all within the lines, and seeks to bring within the lines all similarly situated so far and so fast as its means allow. Of course, so far as the operations enable those who otherwise must be kept confined to be returned to the world, and thus open the asylum to others, the equality aimed at will be more nearly reached.

Judgment affirmed.

9.4 Public Opinion Polls Reveal American Attitudes about Jews in Europe, Refugees, and Immigration, 1938–1945[4]

These public opinion polls illustrate American views not only about Jews but also about refugees and immigration both before and during World War II. What were those views, and what do you think accounts for them?

Refugees

(US July '38) What is your attitude toward allowing German, Austrian, and other political refugees to come into the United States?

We should encourage them to come even if we have to
    raise our immigration quotas. 4.9%
We should allow them to come but not raise immigration quotas. . . 18.2
With conditions as they are, we should try to keep them out 67.4
Don't know 9.5

Colonization

(US Nov. 22 '38) Should we allow a larger number of Jewish exiles from Germany to come to the United States to live?

Yes   23%   NO   77%

---

4. From Hadley Cantril, *Public Opinion, 1935–1946* (Princeton, NJ: Princeton University Press, 1951), 382–85, 1150.

Jewish Questions

(US Nov. '38) Do you believe that in this country there is very little hostility toward the Jewish people or that there is a growing hostility toward them?

	Little hostility	*Growing hostility*	*Don't know*
National total.	52.5%	32.5%	15.0%

BY EXTREMES IN SIZE OF COMMUNITY

Cities over 1,000,000.	44.1%	46.7%	9.2%
Towns under 2,500	55.9%	22.0%	22.1%

BY RELIGION

Jewish	50.3%	41.7%	8.0%
Catholic.	51.3%	35.3%	13.4%
Protestant	53.0%	31.0%	16.0%
None	50.0%	30.0%	20.0%

(US Apr. '38) What do you feel is the reason for hostility toward Jewish people here or abroad?

Reasons favorable to Jews	*National total*	*Jewish people*
People are jealous and envious of Jews' accomplishments.	5.5%	17.2%
Jews too clever and successful, have too much ability to make money.	4.7	2.5
People who are against Jews are mean, narrow-minded, ignorant, crazy	1.5	10.8
Other favorable to Jews.	1.1	5.1
	12.8%	35.6%

	National total	*Jewish people*
Reasons unfavorable to Jews		
Jews control and monopolize enterprise, hoard money, have too much power	13.0%	8.9%
Unfair and dishonest in business; they cheat and swindle	6.4	1.3
Too grasping, covetous, avaricious, cheap . . .	5.6	—
Their own fault; their manners, characteristics, and attitudes cause people to resent them. .	4.9	3.2
They're clannish, nonmixers, not good citizens, interested only in race	4.4	1.3
Aggressive, energetic; too aggressive	2.6	2.5
Overbearing; forward; noisy	1.9	—
Lazy; parasitic; won't do manual labor or pioneer	1.1	—
Other unfavorable	2.4	1.9
	42.3%	19.1%
External and neutral reasons		
Religious and racial prejudice	3.7%	3.2%
Germans; Hitler; dictatorship	2.6%	5.1
Biblical prophecy being fulfilled; will of God—persecuted race.	2.1	.6
Financial status of Germany; needs Jewish money to carry on	2.0	8.3
Propaganda; agitation	2.0	11.5
Political move; Jews made scapegoat to divert attention from defects of Nazism	1.1	7.6
Subjugation of minorities; fear of overthrow; desire for sole control	.6	1.9
Other; general reasons.	2.0	6.4
	16.1	44.6
Don't know	43.3	22.9
	114.5%*	122.2%*

BY OPINIONS ON IMMIGRATION

	Let immi-grants in	*Keep immi-grants out*
Reasons unfavorable to the Jews	26.0%	46.1%
Reasons favorable	21.8	12.4
Reasons neutral or external	29.0	15.2
Don't know	38.1	41.0
	114.9%	114.7%

BY OPINIONS ON ANTI-SEMITISM

	Anti-Semitism not growing	*Anti-Semitism growing*
Reasons unfavorable to Jews	33.9%	67.7%
Reasons favorable	17.8	11.0
Reasons neutral or external	19.8	16.3
Don't know	42.5	25.4
	114.0%*	120.4%*

*Percentages add to more than 100 because some respondents gave more than one answer.

(US July '39) Which of the following statements most nearly represents your general opinion on the Jewish question?

In the United States the Jews have the same standing as any other peoples and they should be treated in all ways exactly as any other Americans	38.9%
Jews are in some ways distinct from other Americans, but they make respected and useful citizens so long as they don't try to mingle socially where they are not wanted	10.8
Jews have some different business methods and, therefore, some measures should be taken to prevent Jews from getting too much power in the business world	31.8
We should make it a policy to deport Jews from this country to some new homeland as fast as it can be done without inhumanity . . .	10.1
Don't know	6.5
Refused to answer	3.0
	101.1%

*Percentages add to more than 100 because some respondents gave more than one answer.

(US July 15 '42) Do you think the Jews have too much power and influence in this country?

Yes   44%   No   41%   No opinion and no answer   15%

(US Jan. '43, Dec. '44, Nov. '45) Do you think that Jewish people in the United States have too much influence in the business world, not enough influence, or about the amount of influence they should have?

	Too much	Not enough	About right	Don't know	Qualified answers
Jan. '43	49.7%	2.0%	33.4%	13.3%	1.6%
Dec. '44	57	2	29	11	1
Nov. '45	58	1	30	11	*

 *Less than 0.5%

(US Jan. 7 '43) It is said that two million Jews have been killed in Europe since the war began. Do you think this is true or just a rumor?

True[a]   47%   Rumor[a]   29%   No opinion[a]   24%

(Germany Oct. 26 '45) Which of these statements do you consider as generally true—(1) the treatment the Jews received under Hitler was just what they deserved. (2) Hitler went too far in his treatment of the Jews, but something had to be done to keep them within bounds. (3) The anti-Jewish measure were absolutely unjustified.

Statement 1 . . . . . . —
Statement 2 . . . . . . 19%
Statement 3 77
No opinion 3
Other 1

9.5 Jan Karski of the Polish Underground Gives an Eyewitness Account of the Final Solution, 1942–1944[5]

Jan Karski was a member of the Polish Underground and one of the first eyewitnesses to the German extermination of European Jews. In this

5. From Jan Karski, "Polish Death Camp," *Collier's*, October 14, 1944, 18–19, 60–61. Copyright *Colliers*, 1944.

1944 article he describes his 1942 visit, in disguise and accompanied by a Nazi militiaman, to a camp in Eastern Poland serving as a transit point for Jews being sent to the Belzec death camp.

As we approached to within a few hundred yards of the camp, the shouts, cries, and shots cut off further conversation. I noticed an unpleasant stench that seemed to have come from decomposing bodies mixed with horse manure. This may have been an illusion. [My guide] was, in any case, completely impervious to it. He even began to hum some sort of folk tune to himself. We passed through a small grove of decrepit-looking trees and emerged directly in front of the loud, sobbing, reeking camp of death.

It was on a large, flat plain and occupied about a square mile. It was surrounded on all sides by a formidable barbed-wire fence, nearly two yards in height and in good repair. Inside the fence, at intervals of about fifteen yards, guards were standing, holding rifles with bayonets ready for use. Around the outside of the fence, militiamen circulated on constant patrol. The camp itself contained a few small sheds or barracks. The rest of the area was completely covered by a dense, pulsating, throbbing, noisy human mass—starved, stinking, gesticulating, insane human beings in constant agitated motion. Through them, forcing paths if necessary with their rifle butts, walked the German police and militiamen. They walked in silence, their faces bored and indifferent. They looked like shepherds bringing in a flock to the market. They had the tired, vaguely disgusted appearance of men doing a routine, tedious job. . . .

The Jewish mass vibrated, trembled, and moved to and fro as if united in a single, insane rhythmic trance. They waved their hands, shouted, quarreled, cursed, and spat at one another. Hunger, thirst, fear, and exhaustion had driven them all insane. I had been told that they were usually left in the camp for three or four days without food or a drop of water. . . .

The chaos, the squalor, the hideousness of it all were simply indescribable. There was a suffocating stench of sweat, filth, decay, damp straw, and excrement. To get to my post we had to squeeze our way through this mob. It was a ghastly ordeal. I had to push foot by foot through the crowd and step over the limbs of those who were lying prone. It was like forcing my way through a mass of death and decomposition made even more horrible by its agonized pulsations. My companion had the skill of long practice, evading the bodies on the ground and winding his way through the mass with the ease of a contortionist. Distracted and clumsy, I would brush against people or step on a figure that reacted like an animal; quickly, often with a moan or a yelp. Each time this occurred I would be seized by a fit of nausea and come to a stop. But my guide kept urging and hustling me along.

In this way we crossed the entire camp and finally stopped about twenty yards from the gate which opened on the passage leading to the train. It was a comparatively uncrowded spot. I felt immeasurably relieved at having finished my stumbling, sweating journey. . . .

I remained there perhaps half an hour, watching this spectacle of human misery. At each moment I felt the impulse to run and flee. I had to force myself to remain indifferent, to practice stratagems to convince myself that I was not one of the condemned. Finally, I noticed a change in the motion of the guards. They walked less and they all seemed to be glancing in the same direction—at the passage to the track which was quite close to me.

I turned toward it myself. Two German policemen came to the gate with a tall, bulky SS man. He barked out an order and they began to open the gate. It was very heavy. He shouted at them impatiently. They worked at it frantically and finally shoved it open. They dashed down the passage as though they were afraid the SS man might come after them, and took up their positions where the passage ended. The whole system had been worked out with crude effectiveness. The outlet of the passage was blocked off by two cars of the freight train, so that any attempt on the part of one of the Jews to break out of the mob would have been completely impossible.

The SS man turned to the crowd, planted himself with his feet wide apart and his hands on his hips, and loosed a roar that must have actually hurt his ribs. It could be heard far above the hellish babble that came from the crowd:

"*Ruhu, ruhe!* Quiet, quiet! All Jews will board this train to be taken to a place where work awaits them. Keep order. Do not push. Anyone who attempts to resist or create a panic will be shot."

He stopped speaking and looked challengingly at the helpless mob that hardly seemed to know what was happening. Suddenly, accompanying the movement with a loud, hearty laugh, he yanked out his gun and fired three random shots into the crowd. A single, stricken groan answered him. He replaced the gun in his holster, smiled, and set himself for another roar:

"*Alle Juden, 'rause—'rause!*"

For a moment the crowd was silent. Those nearest the SS man recoiled from the shots and tried to dodge, panic-stricken, toward the rear. But this was resisted by the mob as a volley of shots from the rear sent the whole mass surging forward madly, screaming in pain and fear. The shots continued without letup from the rear and now from the sides, too, narrowing the mob down and driving it in a savage scramble onto the passageway. In utter panic they rushed down the passageway, trampling it so furiously that it threatened to fall apart.

Then new shots were heard. The two policemen at the entrance to the train were now firing into the oncoming throng corralled in the passageway, in order to slow them down and prevent them from demolishing the flimsy structure. The SS man added his roar to the bedlam.

"*Ordnung, ordnung!*" He bellowed like a madman.

"Order, order!" The two policemen echoed him hoarsely, firing straight into the faces of the Jews running to the trains. Impelled and controlled by this ring of fire, they filled the two cars quickly.

And now came the most horrible episode of all. The military rule stipulates that a freight car may carry eight horses or forty soldiers. Without any baggage at all, a maximum of a hundred passengers pressing against one another could be crowded into a car. The Germans had simply issued orders that 120 to 130 Jews had to enter each car. Those orders were now being carried out. Alternately swinging and firing their rifles, the policemen were forcing still more people into the two cars which were already overfull. The shots continued to ring out in the rear, and the driven mob surged forward, exerting an irresistible pressure against those nearest the train. These unfortunates, crazed by what they had been through, scourged by the policemen, and shoved forward by the milling mob, then began to climb on the heads and shoulders of those in the trains.

These latter were helpless since they had the weight of the entire advancing throng against them. They howled with anguish at those who, clutching at their hair and clothes for support; trampling on necks, faces, and shoulders; breaking bones; and shouting with insensate fury, attempted to clamber over them. More than another score of men, women, and children crushed into the cars in this fashion. Then the policemen slammed the doors across the arms and legs that still protruded, and pushed the iron bars in place.

The two cars were now crammed to bursting with tightly packed human flesh. All this while the entire camp reverberated with a tremendous volume of sound in which groans and screams mingled with shots, curses, and bellowed commands.

Nor was this all. I know that many people will not believe me, but I saw it, and it is not exaggerated. I have no other proofs, no photographs. All I can say is that I saw it, and it is the truth.

The floors of the car had been covered with a thick, white powder. It was quicklime. Quicklime is simply unslaked lime or calcium oxide that has been dehydrated. Anyone who has seen cement being mixed knows what occurs when water is poured on lime. The mixture bubbles and steams as the powder combines with the water, generating a searing heat.

The lime served a double purpose in the Nazi economy of brutality: The moist flesh coming in contact with the lime is quickly dehydrated and burned. The occupants of the cars would be literally burned to death before long, the flesh eaten from their bones. Thus the Jews would "die in agony," fulfilling the promise Himmler had issued "in accord with the will of the Fuehrer," in Warsaw in 1942. Secondly, the lime would prevent the decomposing bodies from spreading disease. It was efficient and inexpensive—a perfectly chosen agent for its purpose.

It took three hours to fill up the entire train. It was twilight when the forty-six cars were packed. From one end to the other the train, with its quivering cargo of flesh, seemed to throb, vibrate, rock, and jump as if bewitched. There would be a strangely uniform momentary lull and then the train would begin to moan and sob, wail and howl. Inside the camp a few score dead bodies and a few in the final throes of death remained. German policemen walked around at leisure with smoking guns, pumping bullets into anything that moaned or moved. Soon none were left alive. In the now quiet camp the only sounds were the inhuman screams that echoed from the moving train. Then these, too, ceased. All that was now left was the stench of excrement and rotting straw and a queer, sickening, acidulous odor which, I thought, may have come from the quantities of blood that had stained the ground.

The Last Incredible Journey

As I listened to the dwindling outcries from the train I thought of the destination toward which it was speeding. My informants had minutely described the entire journey. The train would travel about eight miles and finally come to a halt in an empty, barren field. Then nothing at all would happen. The train would stand stock-still, patiently waiting while death penetrated into every corner of its interior. This would take from two to four days.

When quicklime, asphyxiation, and injuries had silenced every outcry, a group of men would appear. They would be young, strong Jews, assigned to the task of cleaning out these cars until their own turn to ride in them should arrive. Under a strong guard they would unseal the cars and expel the heaps of decomposing bodies. The mounds of flesh that they piled up would then be burned and the remnants buried in a single huge hole. The cleaning, burning, and burial would consume one or two full days.

The entire process of disposal would take, then, from three to six days. During this period the camp would have recruited new victims. The train would return and the whole cycle would be repeated. . . .

. . . I walked to the store as quickly as I could, running when there was no one about to see me. I reached the grocery store so breathless that the owner became alarmed. I reassured him while I threw off my uniform, boots, stockings, and underwear. I ran into the kitchen and locked the door. In a little while my bewildered and worried host called out to me:

"Hey, what are you doing in there?"

"Don't worry. I'll be right out."

When I came out, he promptly entered the kitchen and called back in despair:

"What the devil have you been doing? The whole kitchen is flooded?"

"I washed myself," I replied, "that is all. I was very dirty."

Then I collapsed. I was completely, violently, rackingly sick. Even today, when I remember those scenes, I become nauseated.

9.6 The State Department Receives and Suppresses News of the Final Solution, 1942[6]

State Department officials were informed in 1942 of Nazi plans to exterminate European Jews but, as this document reveals, they sought to suppress this information.

August 8, 1942

MEMORANDUM

Subject: Conversation with Mr. Gerhart
M. RIEGNER, Secretary of World
Jewish Congress

This morning Mr. Gerhardt M. RIEGNER, Secretary of the World Jewish Congress in Geneva, called in great agitation. He stated that he had just received a report from a German business man of considerable prominence, who is said to have excellent political and military connections in Germany and from whom reliable and important political information has been obtained on two previous occasions, to the effect that there has been and is being considered in Hitler's headquarters a plan to exterminate all Jews from Germany and German controlled areas in Europe after they have been concentrated in the east (presumably Poland). The number involved is said to be between three-and-a-half and four millions and the

6. From State Department Files, Record Group 59, National Archives, Washington, DC; repr. in *America in the Holocaust*, vol. 1, ed. David S. Wyman (New York: Garland, 1990), 187, 191–94.

object is to permanently settle the Jewish question in Europe. The mass execution if decided upon would allegedly take place this fall.

Riegner stated that according to his informant the use of prussic acid was mentioned as a means of accomplishing the executions. When I mentioned that this report seemed fantastic to me, Riegner said that it had struck him in the same way but that from the fact that mass deportation had been taking place since July 16 as confirmed by reports received from him from Paris, Holland, Berlin, Vienna, and Prague it was always conceivable that such a diabolical plan was actually being considered by Hitler as a corollary.

According to Riegner, 14,000 Jews have already been deported from occupied France and 10,000 more are to be handed over from occupied France in the course of the next few days. Similarly from German sources 56,000 Jews have already been deported from the Protectorate together with unspecified numbers from Germany and other occupied countries.

Riegner said this report was so serious and alarming that he felt it his duty to make the following requests: (1) that the American and other Allied Governments be informed with regard thereto at once; (2) that they be asked to try by every means to obtain confirmation or denial; (3) that Dr. Stephen Wise, the president of his organization, be informed of the report.

I told Riegner that the information would be passed on to the Legation at once but that I was not in a position to inform him as to what action, if any, the Legation might take. He hoped that he might be informed in due course that the information had been transmitted to Washington.

For what it is worth, my personal opinion is that Riegner is a serious and balanced individual and that he would never have come to the Consulate with the above report if he had not had confidence in his informant's reliability and if he did not seriously consider that the report might well contain an element of truth. Again it is my opinion that the report should be passed on to the Department for what it is worth.

There is attached a draft of a telegram prepared by Riegner giving in his own words a telegraphic summary of his statements to me.

Howard Elting, Jr.
American Vice Consul
[Geneva, Switzerland]

Copy

Dr. Stephen Wise President American Jewish Congress
330 West 42nd Street Room 809
New York

RECEIVED ALARMING REPORT STATING THAT IN FUEH-RERS HEADQUARTERS A PLAN HAS BEEN DISCUSSED AND BEING UNDER CONSIDERATION ACCORDING WHICH TOTAL OF JEWS IN COUNTRIES OCCUPIED CONTROLLED BY GERMANY NUMBERING THREE-AND-HALF TO FOUR MILLIONS SHOULD AFTER DEPORTATION AND CONCEN-TRATED IN EAST BE AT ONE BLOW EXTERMINATED IN ORDER RESOLVE ONCE FOR ALL JEWISH QUESTION IN EUROPE STOP ACTION IS REPORTED TO BE PLANNED FOR AUTUMN WAYS OF EXECUTION STILL DISCUSSED STOP IT HAS BEEN SPOKEN OF PRUSSIC ACID STOP IN TRANSMITTING INFORMATION WITH ALL NECESSARY RESERVATION AS EXACTITUDE CANNOT BE CONTROLLED BY US BEG TO STATE THAT INFORMER IS REPORTED HAVE CLOSE CONNECTIONS WITH HIGHEST GERMAN AUTHOR-ITIES AND HIS REPORTS TO BE GENERALLY RELIABLE
WORLD JEWISH CONGRESS
GERARD RIEGNER

ADDRESS OFFICIAL COMMUNICATIONS TO
THE SECRETARY OF STATE
WASHINGTON, D. C.

DEPARTMENT OF STATE
WASHINGTON

Don't send

In reply refer to
En:862.4016/2233

My dear Dr. Wise:

The following message, in paraphrase, has been received from the American Legation at Bern. It was sent
at the request of Mr. Gerhardt M. Riegner, Secretary of
the World Jewish Congress at Geneva.

In Hitler's headquarters a plan is being considered to wipe out at one blow from 3,500,000 to
4,000,000 Jews this autumn, following their expulsion from countries controlled or occupied by Germany and their concentration in the East, according to a report from a person whose previous reports have been generally reliable and who is alleged to have intimate connections among the highest German officials. Prussic acid has been contemplated but the manner of extermination has not
yet been determined. The correctness of the report
cannot be confirmed and the information is therefore
sent with reservation.

The Legation at Bern has no information which would
confirm this rumor and believes it is one of the many un-
reliable war rumors circulating in Europe today.

Sincerely yours,

For the Secretary of State:

Paul T. Culbertson

Paul T. Culbertson,
Assistant Chief, Division of
European Affairs.

Dr. Stephen S. Wise,
    President, American Jewish Congress,
        330 West 42nd Street,
            New York, New York.

FOR DEFENSE
BUY
UNITED
STATES
SAVINGS
BONDS
AND STAMPS

Department of State
Division of European Affairs

MEMORANDUM

August 13, 1942

With reference to Bern's telegram no. 3697 [862.4016/2233] August 11,
3 p.m. transmitting information from Mr. Gerhardt M. Riegner, Secretary

of the World Jewish Congress, Geneva, regarding the alleged plan of the Nazis to exterminate three and a half to four million Jews, it does not appear advisable in view of the Legation's comments, the fantastic nature of the allegation, and the impossibility of our being of any assistance if such action were taken, to transmit the information to Dr. Stephen Wise as suggested.

[Elbridge Durbrow]

9.7 The Moscow Declaration on War Crimes, 1943[7]

Nazi atrocities were by no means limited to the attempted extermination of all European Jews. The horrors the Germans inflicted on those they conquered led to this Allied warning and promise of punishment for the perpetrators, issued at the October 1943 Moscow Foreign Ministers Conference.

Statement on Atrocities
Moscow Conference
October, 1943

The United Kingdom, the United States, and the Soviet Union have received from many quarters evidence of atrocities, massacres and cold-blooded mass executions which are being perpetrated by Hitlerite forces in many of the countries they have overrun and from which they are now being steadily expelled. The brutalities of Nazi domination are no new thing, and all peoples or territories in their grip have suffered from the worst form of government by terror. What is new is that many of the territories are now being redeemed by the advancing armies of the liberating powers, and that in their desperation the recoiling Hitlerites and Huns are redoubling their ruthless cruelties. This is now evidenced with particular clearness by monstrous crimes on the territory of the Soviet Union which is being liberated from Hitlerites, and on French and Italian territory.

Accordingly, the aforesaid three Allied powers, speaking in the interest of the thirty-two United Nations, hereby solemnly declare and give full warning of their declaration as follows:

---

7. From Senate Committee on Foreign Relations and Department of State, *A Decade of American Foreign Policy: Basic Documents, 1941–49* (Washington, DC: Government Printing Office, 1950), 13–14. http://avalon.law.yale.edu/wwii/moscow.asp.

At the time of granting of any armistice to any government which may be set up in Germany, those German officers and men and members of the Nazi party who have been responsible for or have taken a consenting part in the above atrocities, massacres and executions will be sent back to the countries in which their abominable deeds were done in order that they may be judged and punished according to the laws of these liberated countries and of free governments which will be erected therein. Lists will be compiled in all possible detail from all these countries having regard especially to invaded parts of the Soviet Union, to Poland and Czechoslovakia, to Yugoslavia and Greece including Crete and other islands, to Norway, Denmark, Netherlands, Belgium, Luxembourg, France and Italy.

Thus, Germans who take part in wholesale shooting of Polish officers or in the execution of French, Dutch, Belgian or Norwegian hostages of Cretan peasants, or who have shared in slaughters inflicted on the people of Poland or in territories of the Soviet Union which are now being swept clear of the enemy, will know they will be brought back to the scene of their crimes and judged on the spot by the peoples whom they have outraged.

Let those who have hitherto not imbued their hands with innocent blood beware lest they join the ranks of the guilty, for most assuredly the three Allied powers will pursue them to the uttermost ends of the earth and will deliver them to their accusors [sic] in order that justice may be done.

The above declaration is without prejudice to the case of German criminals whose offenses have no particular geographical localization and who will be punished by joint decision of the government of the Allies.

Signatories:
President Roosevelt
Prime Minister Churchill
Premier Stalin

9.8 Secretary of the Treasury Henry Morgenthau Jr. Denounces State Department Behavior to President Franklin D. Roosevelt, 1944[8]

State Department suppression of news regarding the German extermination of Jews did not go unchallenged within the Roosevelt

---

8. From Henry Morgenthau Jr. diaries, Franklin D. Roosevelt Library, Hyde Park, NY; repr. in *America and the Holocaust*, vol. 8, ed. David S. Wyman (New York: Garland, 1990), 498–506.

administration. Reproduced here is Secretary of the Treasury Henry Morgenthau's January 1944 letter to the president denouncing State Department behavior and calling for action. Roosevelt responded by creating the War Refugee Board, which has been credited with helping to save tens of thousands of Jews.

Personal Report to the President

One of the greatest crimes in history, the slaughter of the Jewish people in Europe, is continuing unabated.

This Government has for a long time maintained that its policy is to work out programs to save those Jews and other persecuted minorities of Europe who could be saved.

You are probably not as familiar as I with the utter failure of certain officials in our State Department, who are charged with actually carrying out this policy, to take any effective action to prevent the extermination of the Jews in German-controlled Europe.

The public record, let alone the facts which have not yet been made public, reveals the gross procrastination of these officials. It is well known that since the time when it became clear that Hitler was determined to carry out a policy of exterminating the Jews in Europe, the State Department officials have failed to take any positive steps reasonably calculated to save any of these people. Although they have used devices such as setting up intergovernmental organizations to survey the whole refugee problem, and calling conferences such as the Bermuda Conference to explore the whole refugee problem, making it appear that positive action could be expected, in fact nothing has been accomplished.

The best summary of the whole situation is contained in one sentence of a report submitted on December 20, 1943, by the Committee on Foreign Relations of the Senate, recommending the passage of a Resolution (S.R. 203), favoring the appointment of a commission to formulate plans to save the Jews of Europe from extinction by Nazi Germany. . . .

> "We have talked; we have sympathized; we have expressed our horror; the time to act is long past due."

Whether one views this failure as being deliberate on the part of those officials handling the matter, or merely due to their incompetence, is not too important from my point of view. However, there is a growing number of responsible people and organizations today who have ceased to view our failure as the product of simple incompetence on the part of those officials in the State Department charged with handling this problem. They see plain Anti-Semitism motivating the actions of these State Department officials and, rightly or wrongly, it will require little more in the way of proof for this suspicion to explode into a nasty scandal. . . .

The facts I have detailed in this report, Mr. President, came to the Treasury's attention as a part of our routine investigation of the licensing of the financial phases of the proposal of the World Jewish Congress for the evacuation of Jews from France and Rumania. The facts may thus be said to have come to light through accident. How many others of the same character are buried in State Department files is a matter I would have no way of knowing. Judging from the almost complete failure of the State Department to achieve any results, the strong suspicion must be that they are not few.

This much is certain, however. The matter of rescuing the Jews from extermination is a trust too great to remain in the hands of men who are indifferent, callous, and perhaps even hostile. The task is filled with difficulties. Only a fervent will to accomplish, backed by persistent and untiring effort can succeed where time is so precious.

[Henry Morgenthau, Jr.
Jan. 16, 1944.]

9.9 U.S. Soldier Clinton C. Gardner Remembers the Liberation of the Buchenwald Concentration Camp, 1945[9]

In 1945, the advancing Allied armies liberated numerous concentration camps and saw for the first time the full extent of what the Nazis had done. Reproduced here are the 1946 recollections of Clinton C. Gardner, who as a U.S. soldier participated in the liberation of the Buchenwald camp.

Clinton Gardner's report of the liberation of Buchenwald appears here as it did originally in The Dartmouth *on 15, 17, and 19 April 1946—except that a few misprints have been corrected. It reflects the time in which it was written, as well as the events of April 1945.*

---

9. From *The Dartmouth*, April 15, 17, and 19, 1946; repr. with misprints in David Scrase and Wolfgang Mieder, eds., *The Holocaust: Personal Accounts* (Burlington: Center for Holocaust Studies at the University of Vermont, 2001), 238–42.

. . . As you go north from Weimar the road climbs a long well-forested hill. The trees whose arched limbs frame the way are beech, which is how the forest got its name: Buchenwald. It is an annoying, rutted road that you follow for a few kilometers, but at the top of the hill, where this road continues straight, there on your left is a broad, new concrete highway. When you take this left, as some three hundred thousand Europeans have done before you, you will find that you are on a one way road and there are no more turns.

A few more kilometers and the road bursts out into a huge clearing on the hill's north side. The view is breath-taking: thirty miles of patchwork scenery, brilliant green farmland and velvety purple forests. But to enjoy this view is uncommon. The hill is a bad place for weather; in winter it is one of the coldest, most bitter places in Germany.

Let your eyes drop from the view and focus on the clearing. On each side of the road are bombed-out factory buildings, junk heaps of brick and steel. To the left, a quarter of a mile away are twenty four-story brick barracks, the SS soldiers' garrison. Four thousand elite, black-uniformed Nazis lived here. Just to the right of the barracks begins another built-up area: neat rows of one-story wooden buildings and a few rows of two-story brick. These make up a compact block, five rows wide, eleven buildings to a row. The square thus formed is about three hundred yards on a side. In it, surrounded by an electrified, fifteen foot barbed wire fence, existed at one time forty-eight thousand human beings. That is the concentration camp—*Konzentrationslager Buchenwald*. . . .

There were twenty thousand prisoners left when we liberated the camp. A few days before another twenty thousand had been evacuated eastward. More than a thousand of these were found dead on the train at Dachau. No women stayed at Buchenwald; when families arrived the women were sent north to Bergen-Belsen. But children stayed behind. There were eight hundred children under fourteen kept behind the wire. Every nation in Europe was represented. Our first census showed: 4,000 Russians, 3,000 French, 3,000 Poles, 2,000 Germans, and 2,000 Czechs; many hundreds of Belgians, Dutch, Austrians, Yugoslavs, Spaniards and Italians; some Greeks, Norwegians, ex-Swedes, ex-Swiss, and ex-Americans.

The first thing we went to see inside the camp was the crematory. It was not far from the entrance gate and easy to find because it was stone and stood out from the flimsy wooden barracks. Its smokestack was tall, a sort of monument visible from all over the camp. There were lots of our soldiers waiting to see the crematory yard. You could easily smell what they were waiting to see. Dead bodies in the sun have a smell that is peculiarly indescribable. The sight of them, however, was far more powerful. It crystallized many a thought you had had on man's inhumanity to man. Now these men were only dust, but to the Nazis they had been dust long before their death. The four hundred bodies there were waiting to be burned, waiting to join the *fifty-one* thousand that had gone before them there.

They lay there because in the last few weeks there had been no coal. In fact two thousand others had collected in those few weeks and the SS had had to throw them into a huge natural pit up on the very top of the Buchenwald hill. . . .

Buchenwald is generally considered by the American public to have been the worst or at least one of the worst Nazi concentration camps. This is not true. Of the ten biggest, Buchenwald was the "best."

The probable reason for its reputation is that it received more publicity. First Army headquarters was at Weimar and with it, of course, was the press. It was very convenient for the reporters to hop into a jeep and go the few kilometers to Buchenwald for the horror story of the year.

Had they gone to Nordhausen, fifty miles north, they would have seen a camp whose name was whispered in awe at Buchenwald. At this camp, where V-2s were made, there were about ten thousand prisoners, with a monthly death rate of one thousand—usually due to a combination of starvation and overwork.

Even more deadly than Nordhausen were the annihilation camps (*Vernichtungslager*). The best known of these are Auschwitz at Kraków and Majdanek at Lublin, Poland. Buchenwald was a health resort compared to these. It had its factories and stone quarries to run. Deaths were not its mission. Indeed they were not particularly sought after. If they occurred, it had to be charged up to operating expenses. After all, only fifty-one thousand died there. At Majdanek well over a million were gassed, shot and burned.

In that light, knowing that the prisoners preferred Buchenwald to the others (many of which they had passed through), it is perhaps even more significant to see what a "good" concentration camp was like.

A sharp distinction should be made at this point between what were called the Big and the Little Camps at Buchenwald. The Big Camp provided workers for the factories that made such things as artillery caissons, truck parts, and optical instruments. But men in the Little Camp had no work to do. They just had to exist, just had to wait.

Before 1943 the Little Camp had been a quarantine area. Newly arrived prisoners spent their first six weeks there. They slept on triple-decker plain wood shelves sixteen men to twelve feet of shelf space, two feet of headroom between shelves. Rations were soup twice a day, bread occasionally, but less of both than in the Big Camp where they were nominally the same. Most men lost forty per cent of their weight in those first six weeks. Often they didn't last. One night in 1941 seventy men went mad and had to be killed by the camp doctors.

When the Little Camp hospital got overcrowded the doctors took the same measures. Shortly after we liberated the camp we captured two Poles who, when they realized that we had found out about it, admitted to having helped in this hospital clearance. They had disposed of a thousand patients. One held the man while the other gave him an injection of carbolic acid in the base of the brain.

At the end of their six weeks initiation period a prisoner was supposed to graduate to the Big Camp. If he was a Jew, he seldom did. And after perhaps a year in the Big Camp, if a man got sick or feeble, he was sent back to the Little Camp. After all, if he was sick he was of no more use. By the winter of 1944–45 starvation was causing one hundred deaths a day in the Little Camp.

CHAPTER 10

PLANNING AND PREPARING FOR THE PEACE AT HOME

Most Americans were well aware that World War II would change both the world and the United States' role in it. In 1943, New Dealer and poet laureate Archibald MacLeish captured this feeling in a commencement address to students at the University of California at Berkeley. "We know," MacLeish told the crowd, "that whatever the world will be when the war ends, it will be different." Indeed, mobilization, both military and economic, had transformed American society, revived the American economy, empowered both labor and business, and vastly expanded the power of the federal government. Many Americans looked with hope toward what publisher Henry Luce termed the "American Century."

But hope mingled with anxiety and unanswered questions. How might the return to peace affect these and other elements of American life? How could the nation plan for the peace, while still doing all it could to win the war?

Foremost in the minds of many Americans were the economic consequences of the return to peace. Mobilization in 1940 and 1941 had done what the New Deal could not: end the Great Depression. The transformation of the United States into the great "arsenal of democracy" had pushed the national economy to new levels of production (see Chapter 2). Businesses, and especially big businesses, had taken advantage of generous military contracts to invest in new production capacity. By 1944, the government had sunk $16 billion into new industrial facilities. What would happen to all the new capacity—not to mention jobs—created by the wartime boom? The specter of the Great Depression hung over these discussions, and many Americans feared that the end of the war would bring economic collapse.

The cancellation of certain large military contracts in 1943 lent credence to these fears. As factories closed, workers lost their jobs. Some found new ones close to home. Others moved. Still others fell out of the workforce. This was particularly true for women, many of whom had moved into industrial production for the first time during the war. Bound by familial obligations, female workers tended to be less mobile than their male counterparts, and thus less able to go where the jobs were. As *Time* magazine reported in 1944, women began dropping out of the workforce in greater numbers as the war drew to a close. For many American women, "reconversion" meant the withdrawal—voluntary or otherwise—from paid labor and the embrace of the domestic ideal. Nevertheless, American women's wartime experiences would have lasting consequences (see Chapter 6).

As early as 1943, federal officials, the military, labor representatives, and business leaders began to debate the question of "reconversion" and what Roosevelt, in a July 1943 radio broadcast, called the "transition to peace." New Dealers in and outside of the Roosevelt administration hoped to translate the lessons of the wartime experience to build a better economy and society after the war. In 1944, President Roosevelt promised a new "economic bill of rights" for all Americans. Like many progressives, Vice President Henry Wallace hoped to undertake a "third New Deal" once the war had been won.

The reconversion plans laid out by the War Production Board (WPB) and the National Resources Planning Board (NRPB), among others, contained the outlines of a liberal vision for the postwar period. The federal government could work with the private market using tax and spending policies to create a growing economy that would offer both security and mobility to the majority of Americans. Conservatives, on the other hand, wanted to return to the prewar status quo, and did all they could—including defunding organizations like the NRPB—to limit long-term changes in the American economy and American governance. These conservatives shared with a wide swath of the American people a distrust of the new forms of government regulation that had first cropped up during the New Deal, but had grown by leaps and bounds during the war. Labor and business likewise nurtured starkly different visions of what the postwar world would look like.

The Servicemen's Readjustment Act of 1944—better known as the GI Bill of Rights—played a critical role in the reconversion process. More than 16 million Americans—mostly men—joined the armed forces during the war. The GI Bill of Rights sought to reward this service—and to stimulate the national economy—by providing the vast majority of returning veterans with generous health, education, and financial benefits. President Roosevelt first proposed legislation to allow "our gallant men and women in the armed services" to return to "civilian life" in the summer of 1943, but it was the American Legion that crafted the legislation adopted by Congress and signed into law by the president the following year. The bill provided veterans with unemployment and pension benefits, with help finding a job, with cheap loans to buy a house or farm or start a business, and with educational assistance for college or technical school. The program, which passed Congress by a wide margin, was remarkably generous. By 1949, the GI Bill had cost nearly $3.7 billion.

By helping GIs buy homes, start businesses, get their degrees, or learn a skill, the law played a key role in creating the postwar middle class. According to some scholars the bill also engendered civic engagement by, in Suzanne Mettler's terms, transforming soldiers into citizens. But others have pointed out that the bill's benefits were unequally distributed, particularly along racial lines. Scholars like Ira Katznelson have argued that African American veterans had a harder time taking advantage of the bill's provisions than their white counterparts. Black veterans, for example, often found it difficult to use their educational benefits because few institutions were willing to accept nonwhite students. Likewise, African American GIs regularly faced discrimination from banks when they applied for mortgages and often violent resistance from white homeowners when they sought to buy homes in white neighborhoods. These debates about the racial impact of the GI Bill among scholars echo the debates that took place within the African American community itself at the time of the bill's passage.

The documents in this chapter aim to introduce readers to the multiple problems policy makers and ordinary citizens alike faced with regard to reconversion from war to peace. What "visions" did World War II–era Americans have for the postwar world? What alternatives did policy makers face regarding the reconversion of the economy and of society? Why did they make the choices they did? How did labor and business see the perils and opportunities of reconversion? Where did they agree? What were the long-term consequences of reconversion policies for American politics, for the economy, and for American society?

* * * *

10.1 The National Resources Planning Board Looks Forward, 1943[1]

The National Resources Planning Board (NRPB) was a government agency founded in 1939 to study the nation's economy and make recommendations. In late 1941—just three days before Pearl Harbor—the board completed work on a massive three-part report on the status of and prospects for the nation's economic security programs. Released to the public more than a year later, the Board's report, entitled *Postwar*

---

1. From National Resources Planning Board, *National Resources Development Report for 1943: Part 1, Postwar Plan and Program* (Washington, DC: U.S. Government Printing Office, 1943).

Plan and Program, detailed recommendations for a set of public polices to ensure postwar prosperity, a "dynamic expanding economy," and "higher standards of living" for all Americans. The Roosevelt administration did little to promote the report and the increasingly anti-New Deal Congress terminated the NRPB in 1943. Nevertheless, the NRPB's vision of a mixed public-private economy of abundance shaped economic and social policy in the postwar period.

The National Resources Planning Board believes that it should be the declared policy of the United States Government to promote and maintain a high level of national production and consumption by all appropriate measures necessary for this purpose. The Board further believes that it should be the declared policy of the United States Government:

> To underwrite full employment for the employables;
>
> To guarantee a job for every man released from the armed forces and the war industries at the close of the war, with fair pay and working conditions;
>
> To guarantee and, when necessary, underwrite:
> Equal access to security,
> Equal access to education for all,
> Equal access to health and nutrition for all, and
> Wholesome housing conditions for all.

This policy grows directly out of the Board's statement concerning which the President has said, "All of the free peoples must plan, work, and fight together for the maintenance and development of 'Our Freedoms and Rights'."

. . . Extensive post-war plans are being made now in every country of the world, both by the United Nations and the Axis. The governments of the world are expending for this purpose large amounts of time and money in the midst of fighting. . . .

The National Resources Planning Board, in presenting to the President a series of recommendations for post-war planning, at the outset states the general policy underlying its plans and programs.

We look to and plan for:

I. The fullest possible development of the human personality, in relation to the common good, in a framework of freedoms and rights, of justice, liberty, equality, and the consent of the governed.

As a means of protecting justice, freedom, and democracy:

II. The fullest possible development of the productive potential of all our resources, material and human, with full employment, continuity of income, equal access to minimum security and living standards, and a balance between economic stability and social adventure.

As a means of insuring the peaceful pursuit of life, liberty, and happiness:

III. An effective jural order of the world outlawing violence and imperialism, old or new fashioned, in international relations; and permitting and energizing the fullest development of resources and rights everywhere.

The three factors—democracy, dynamic economy, and peace—never in the history of mankind have been united in a political system. The development of a society combining these three factors means a dynamic economy with fair distribution of the resulting gains throughout the community, the organization of this economy upon the basis of democratic controls and cooperation, the organization of a jural order of the world within which societies can live in peace and freedom. This is a novel combination never before attempted as a whole, although tried in part, nor ever before possible in man's history until the present time.

Experience clearly shows that it is impossible to maintain high standards of living without a dynamic economy; that it is impossible to live in peace without some effective force of world concert and order; that only under the fraternal influence of a democratic society can there be any security either for peace or prosperity, liberty and justice, or the continuing advancement of the spiritual ideals we cherish above material gains. . . .

A Dynamic Expanding Economy

How can these aims be realized in practice? We know that the road to the new democracy runs along the highway of a dynamic economy, to the full use of our national resources, to full employment, and increasingly higher standards of living. This goal is within our reach if we plan to meet the challenge of our times. . . .

All necessary physical things exist to supply all reasonable wants of all the people of the civilized world, and especially of the United States. . . .

But the mere existence of plenty of labor, raw materials, capital, and organizing skill is no guarantee that all reasonable wants will be supplied—or that wealth will actually be produced. . . . Regardless of the existence of plant, labor, capital, and raw material, actual production of goods and services and the size of the national income will depend on effective consumer demand and effective organization. . . .

Peacetime activities can be found big enough to keep people employed to the extent necessary, both to create the market—through effective demand—and create the goods and services to maintain national income at a one hundred billion level or higher. With the will to act, it is possible to reach this peacetime goal with no great departure from the pattern of life and enterprise that we have enjoyed. Government can and should underwrite effective demand for goods and services. The methods to accomplish this purpose are several. No one alone is adequate. No list is final, for times and conditions change.

One of the most important economic facts we have learned in the past decade is that fiscal and monetary policy can be and should be used to foster an expanding economy. We need not be afraid of our monetary system and our production machinery. We have begun to master the tools of resource management in a changing world. . . . We have begun to understand the place private business plays in creating inflationary as well as deflationary currents in the national economic life. We have begun to see the place which public finance, municipal, state, and national, plays in maintaining economic activity.

Accordingly we plan for a dynamic expanding economy on the order of 100 to 125 billions national income. It has taken total war to reveal to us the capacity of our production machine, once it is fully energized. We know now that the American national income which was 40 billion in 1932 leaped to 75 billion in 1940. It has now reached the figure of over 100 billion (1940 dollars). Little vision is required to see that our production machine can be made to produce plenty for peace as well as plenty for war. . . .

The government need not and should not alone undertake the attainment of such high national production, but can underwrite it and cooperate in its attainment. It must see to it that the people are not let down by failure to stabilize employment and investment. With adequate post-war policy and planning, involving the cooperation of private industry—business, labor, agriculture—with government, new levels can be reached far beyond anything yet attained.

We stand on the threshold of an economy of abundance. This generation has it within its power not only to produce in plenty but to distribute that plenty. Only a bold implementation of the will-to-do is required to open the door to that economy. Give the American people a vision of the freedoms that we might enjoy under a real program of American and world-wide development of resources, and all the opposition of blind men and selfish interests could not prevent its adoption. The people of America will respond if these possibilities are placed before them and if they are shown the way toward practical implementation of the will-to-do. Those who stand for revolutionary change in our economy are numbered in such few thousands as to be insignificant, but those who stand for profound evolutionary changes in the direction of making our economy function and produce the plenty of which we have seen it to be capable are numbered in the millions. . . .

But the keys to post-war planning in this area are the dynamic economy, with expanding production, fair diffusion of the resulting gains, full employment, adequate purchasing power, a balance of security, and adventure.

Democracy and Dynamic Economy

. . . Whether viewed from the material or the ideal point of view, democratic societies are best adapted to the operation and unfolding of the type of civilization in which we live and work. . . .

There are still some who fear democracy cannot plan for peacetime postwar activities. This too is partly enemy propaganda and partly the faintheartedness of those who doubt the capacity of democracy to deal with the general welfare. This too is based upon a complete misunderstanding of the capacity of democratic institutions for constructive action. . . .

[O]ur democracy is more capable than ever of making broad plans of national policy and of local, state, and regional policy as well. We do not stand at the broken end of a worn-out way, but look forward to broad vistas of progress, to higher levels of achievement, to higher standards of material prosperity, and to richer possessions in the world of human values which cannot be measured by money standards.

It is time to outline more sharply a program through which democratic ideals may be more perfectly realized in the affairs of the community in the post-war period. The broad bases of such a program have already been stated in the Four Freedoms and in the Atlantic Charter. . . .

The most vital planning problem in the economic field at the end of the war will be the maintenance of full employment and avoidance of a prolonged depression following a short-lived post-war boom. The economic and social stability of the United States, as of other countries, depends in great measure on our capacity to prevent mass unemployment. But there is no question that full employment in the United States would help other countries after the war in maintaining economic and social stability. Full employment and high national income in the United States means large imports from many lands and high levels of employment in many lands. Internal American prosperity spreads purchasing power throughout the world and tends to promote a high volume of world trade in goods and services. On the other hand, should we experience a slump, it would spell depression for other countries accustomed to sell their commodities and services in our markets. . . .

Neither the United States nor the United Nations can achieve full employment after the war without extensive interchange of the products of world resources. This means that we must consider on what terms world resources will be exchanged. . . .

Since the United States can attain these aims only in cooperation with other nations, it must relate its internal policies to measures facilitating the economic development of other countries. This integration raises many problems which call for decisions on specific as well as general issues. . . .

We are engaged today in a desperate war of survival because the world failed to accept the challenge of a world economy of plenty. This must not happen again. The earth on which we live is indeed the good earth with resources adequate to supply fully the needs of its 2 billion inhabitants, if only this generation can organize the will-to-do. The test is organizational ability and attitudes, not of basic resources. If we can organize and implement our resources and our ideals, we shall witness an unlocking of the latent force of production, a resurgence of the human spirit, a buoyancy that comes from participation in a mighty and constructive undertaking. It is bold and courageous goals not little aims that lift up the human heart. At last in the history of man's upward climb, freedom from want and fear is within his reach.

10.2 President Franklin D. Roosevelt Proposes an Economic Bill of Rights, 1945[2]

In his 1944 State of the Union address, President Franklin Roosevelt called for a "second bill of rights" to ensure all Americans "equality in the pursuit of happiness." The next year, the president again used his State of the Union address to propose what he called an "economic bill of rights." Convinced that the war would soon be won, Roosevelt began to "lay the plans and determine the strategy for the winning of a lasting peace and the establishment of an American standard of living higher than ever before known." The principles elaborated in both the 1944 speech and the 1945 speech excerpted here constituted the outlines of a "Third New Deal" and shaped liberal politics throughout the post–World War II period.

. . . An enduring peace cannot be achieved without a strong America— strong in the social and economic sense as well as in the military sense.

---

2. From Franklin D. Roosevelt, "State of the Union Address," January 6, 1945; available at *The American Presidency Project*, by Gerhard Peters and John T. Wooller, http://www. presidency.ucsb.edu/ws/?pid=16595.

In the State of the Union message last year I set forth what I considered to be an American economic bill of rights.

I said then, and I say now, that these economic truths represent a second bill of rights under which a new basis of security and prosperity can be established for all—regardless of station, race, or creed.

Of these rights the most fundamental, and one on which the fulfillment of the others in large degree depends, is the "right to a useful and remunerative job in the industries or shops or farms or mines of the Nation." In turn, others of the economic rights of American citizenship, such as the right to a decent home, to a good education, to good medical care, to social security, to reasonable farm income, will, if fulfilled, make major contributions to achieving adequate levels of employment.

The Federal Government must see to it that these rights become realities—with the help of States, municipalities, business, labor, and agriculture.

We have had full employment during the war. We have had it because the Government has been ready to buy all the materials of war which the country could produce—and this has amounted to approximately half our present productive capacity.

After the war we must maintain full employment with Government performing its peacetime functions. This means that we must achieve a level of demand and purchasing power by private consumers—farmers, businessmen, workers, professional men, housewives—which is sufficiently high to replace wartime Government demands; and it means also that we must greatly increase our export trade above the prewar level.

Our policy is, of course, to rely as much as possible on private enterprise to provide jobs. But the American people will not accept mass unemployment or mere makeshift work. There will be need for the work of everyone willing and able to work—and that means close to 60,000,000 jobs. . . .

. . . The provision of a decent home for every family is a national necessity, if this country is to be worthy of its greatness—and that task will itself create great employment opportunities. Most of our cities need extensive rebuilding. Much of our farm plant is in a state of disrepair. To make a frontal attack on the problems of housing and urban reconstruction will require thoroughgoing cooperation between industry and labor, and the Federal, State, and local Governments.

An expanded social security program, and adequate health and education programs, must play essential roles in a program designed to support individual productivity and mass purchasing power. I shall communicate further with the Congress on these subjects at a later date.

The millions of productive jobs that a program of this nature could bring are jobs in private enterprise. They are jobs based on the expanded demand for the output of our economy for consumption and investment.

Through a program of this character we can maintain a national income high enough to provide for an orderly retirement of the public debt along with reasonable tax reduction. . . .

. . . The war will leave deep disturbances in the world economy, in our national economy, in many communities, in many families, and in many individuals. It will require determined effort and responsible action of all of us to find our way back to peacetime, and to help others to find their way back to peacetime—a peacetime that holds the values of the past and the promise of the future.

If we attack our problems with determination we shall succeed. And we must succeed. For freedom and peace cannot exist without security. . . .

. . . We Americans of today, together with our allies, are making history—and I hope it will be better history than ever has been made before.

We pray that we may be worthy of the unlimited opportunities that God has given us.

10.3 Robert A. Taft Lays Out the Republican Vision for the Postwar World, 1943[3]

Sometimes known as "Mr. Republican," Ohio Senator Robert A. Taft was one of the best-known, and fiercest, critics of President Roosevelt's foreign and domestic policies. In this 1943 speech to his state's Federation of Republican Women's Organizations, Senator Taft challenges the vision of the "Third New Deal" and postwar planning embraced by the National Resources Planning Board and other New Deal liberals. Taft's conservative vision emphasized private enterprise, state and local control, and limited government spending. An opponent of intervention before the war, Taft remained a fierce critic of the internationalist vision embraced by Roosevelt and his allies during and after that conflict (see Chapters 1 and 12).

Address to the Ohio Federation of Republican Women's Organizations

May 7, 1943
Columbus, Ohio

3. From Robert A. Taft, "Address to the Ohio Federation of Republican Women's Organizations," May 7, 1943, repr. in Clarence E. Wunderlin Jr., ed., *The Papers of Robert A. Taft*, vol. 2, *1939–1944* (Kent, OH: Kent State University Press, 2001): 432–38.

A Republican Program

Republican Women of Ohio:

. . . The Republican Party cannot appeal to the people for responsibility in the midst of a great war without a comprehensive and forward-looking program to meet the conditions which exist. That program cannot be formulated in detail for another year. But in spite of the shortness of time, I wish to state briefly this afternoon my idea of the broad outlines of a Republican program.

The first aim of a Victory Ticket, supported by the Republican Party and I hope by many Democrats and Independents, must be to win the war as completely and as quickly as possible. Regardless of differences as to the wisdom of the President's pre-war policy of active participation in the European war . . . there can be no difference now on the necessity of complete and overwhelming victory in this war. . . . We are fighting, therefore, in order that this country and its people may enjoy peace after the war and in the days to come; in order that we may be left free to work out the destiny of the American Republic. We did not go to war to establish freedom or freedoms throughout the world, except as such a world condition might affect our own liberty. But such freedom will be an inevitable result, at least for a time, of the victory of the liberty-loving nations. . . . Whatever postwar arrangements are worked out, victory in this war will assure peace for many years to come, and it will be long before any other nation goes on a rampage. Furthermore, unless we do win the war and win it completely, we will have little to say about post-war plans.

. . . Our second policy is a necessary corollary of the first. We are in favor of every step necessary or helpful in the winning of the war. In Congress we have granted all the money and all the powers related to such a victory, and we will continue to do so. It is not an easy task, because this administration does not hesitate to use the war as an excuse for demanding powers and appropriations remotely related, if at all, to the war effort. It does not hesitate to use the war to promote New Deal purposes. Republicans in Congress—and we have much more power than we had a year ago—have the duty of drawing the line, of criticizing the requests which are made, of refusing those which are not related directly to the war. We must give the Executive the benefit of the doubt. But, after all, we are fighting to assure our liberties in the future; we should not surrender any such liberties at home except to the extent that is absolutely necessary. . . .

There is a point at which a further draft of men may seriously conflict with the efficient operation of the civilian machine at home. The operation of that machine is equally important as the operation of the Army and Navy. This machine of 125 million people must produce all the food and all the munitions and the supplies for our armed forces and for those of our allies, for our civilians and for many allied peoples. It is a machine infinitely more complicated and difficult to operate, and more likely to stall than the Army. Thirty million families throughout the United States cannot be effectively subjected to military discipline. Compulsion is not the way to get necessary production. . . .

We have had to give power over civilians to fix prices, to control priorities, to ration, and to regulate. We have tried to prescribe proper limitations to those powers, but in the long run the character of the control is determined by the executive departments. In my opinion the executives have been too much inspired by the compulsion theory. They have assumed powers even beyond those granted. Instead of appeals for voluntary action, the theorists in Washington have relied on threats and crackdown. The O.P.A., the Office of Defense Transportation, the Manpower Commission are full of theorists who don't know how an American community thinks or lives. . . . So long as the New Deal controls the executive departments, and its action is inspired by the principles of a planned economy in which every step is regulated by the government, there is nothing we can do in Congress except criticize and hammer against the worst examples of bureaucratic regulation. . . .

The Republican Party proposes after the war to go forward to a better and stronger America under the American constitutional system with just as much liberty and freedom from the government regulation as is possible. The New Deal plan after the war is already written in the reports of the National Resources Planning Board. It provides for continued government regulation, for government ownership of railroads, and the operation of many industries by the government or by corporations in which the government is a partner. It proposes the restoration of all the New Deal agencies, the P.W.A., the W.P.A., the C.C.C., the N.Y.A., except that all of them are to be on a bigger and more elaborate scale. And underlying the entire plan is the theory of unlimited government spending, the theory that deficits are a blessing in disguise. In all these vast reports of the National Resources Planning Board there is not a word said as to how the programs are to be paid for. The argument is used that we have restored prosperity during the war, without any mention of the fact that we are increasing the debt at the rate of sixty billion dollars a year.

The Republican program is to return to the operation of private enterprise; to let the business men run their businesses and the farmers run their farms; to let labor work out its problems with its employers by collective bargaining. The Republican Party is convinced that the system of free industry can restore prosperity. We are convinced that intelligent planning can prevent depressions and unemployment and provide reasonable farm prices, without attempting to regulate every individual and every farmer. We are convinced that unfair competition and monopoly can be prevented without sending government controllers into every store and every plant to regulate profits and direct operations. We are convinced that democracy itself cannot continue to exist unless we permit the states and the cities and schools to run their own affairs. We are convinced that government funds can't be passed out to every group in the population and every state and every school without destroying the independence and the initiative and the morality of our people. The program of the Republican Party is one of progress under the fundamental principles on which American democracy is based—regulation by law and not by the fiats of boards and czars; opportunity to individuals to make a success of their own lives without government interference; state and local control of every matter which can be controlled without national assistance.

. . . Fourth, the Republican Party believes in the principles of social security. . . .

But a social welfare program must recognize two principles: In the long run only those who are working today can support those who are not working today, and government assistance of any kind must come out of the earnings and the standard of living of the workers of the country. Unless we are going to remove all incentive to work, and endanger the whole principle of reward for ability and hard work and education, the burden of the social welfare program cannot go beyond a reasonable expense. Furthermore, if we are going to put a floor under wages, a floor under housing, and a floor under medical care, for those who are unable to earn an adequate sum, we must see that the people who do work, who do save, who do provide their own homes and their own doctors, are better off than the government beneficiaries; otherwise we will remove every incentive to work. We cannot exaggerate the importance of that incentive. On it is based all the progress we have made. On it is based all the differences between the United States and India or China. On it is based the difference between a free democracy and socialism. . . . Whatever our program of social security, it must not destroy the relative position acquired throughout a lifetime of labor by men of varying ability and character and intelligence.

5. Fifth, the Republican Party is in favor of post-war planning in the international field as well as in the United States. We are preparing to meet the problems which will inevitably face this nation after the war, but we don't like the plans which are being made by the National Resources Planning Board and the global thinkers like Henry Wallace. When the war is won we will be one of the victors. We cannot escape the tremendous responsibility of rebuilding the world. Whatever guarantees we assume

or do not assume, we certainly should establish a world in which war is outlawed as far as humanly possible. Undoubtedly we look forward to a number of years of post-war policing before reasonably peace-loving and democratic governments can be set up in the Axis countries. We must deal with tremendously complicated racial problems and economic problems. At Versailles economic problems were almost ignored, and Europe was divided into a great number of small states wholly unable to support themselves. . . .

But the Republican Party believes in protection. We are not free-traders. It is self-evident to me that a general policy of free trade would destroy the standards of living in America. Whether free trade would raise the average of the world as a whole I doubt, but it is obvious to me that it would drag down our own wage level and our own standard of living in this country. Today it is easy for anyone to transport machinery and set up plants in Russia or China or India, and compete with us on a mass-production basis, paying wages one-tenth of what our workmen are accustomed to receive. I do not agree with the view that a foreign market for our manufactured goods except in a few cases is an essential to American prosperity. I cannot see the use of destroying the shoe industry in Columbus in order that we may build more automobiles for export from Detroit. Certainly that export trade is not worthwhile if we must lend to others the money to enable them to buy our goods. Certainly we do not wish to establish an international W.P.A. Our people cannot afford to produce gratis in order to scatter freedom from want throughout the entire world. We cannot restrict the unrestricted importation of agricultural products without reducing our farmers to prices which would mean poverty and hardship. . . .

The level of tariffs should be reasonable, permitting the importation of foreign goods, but compensating for the difference in wage levels and other costs of production. The New Dealers are committed in theory to the lowest possible tariffs. Many of their leaders believe in complete free trade. They find a powerful support in the City of New York, natural because that city has been built up and thrived largely on foreign trade. I believe that we can do far better by assisting other countries to build up their own industries and their own prosperity rather than to operate on the theory that by hook or crook we are going to export American goods to all sections of the world. No outside nation can insure India or China freedom from want. They have never had it, and they probably never will. But we can render them friendly assistance in meeting their own economic problems. They are the only ones who can solve those problems. They cannot solve them by any handout from us. The international trade which will finally result from a reasonable tariff policy is likely to be larger in the end than any we can obtain by the establishment of free trade. . . .

The program that I have proposed is a mere outline. It is subject to infinite revision and the filling in of numerous details, but I believe it offers a basis on which to work. The Republican Party is going forward during the next year confident that the people will turn to it to win the war and establish in the United States the freedoms for which the war is being fought. We are confident of success in the 1944 election because the people know today that a complete reorganization of the government and the infusion of a new spirit will bring the war more quickly to overwhelming victory. We are confident of that success because we stand for those eternal American principles which are woven into life and the thoughts and dreams of ninety per cent of the people who live in the United States.

10.4 Vice President Henry Wallace Plans for a Third New Deal, 1943[4]

Members of President Franklin Roosevelt's administration often disagreed about how to use the power of the federal government to ensure economic security and promote prosperity. Vice President Henry Wallace spoke for the more liberal wing of New Dealers and often pushed Roosevelt to endorse a more interventionist economic agenda. In the first document, a 1943 letter to the president, Wallace lays out his vision for postwar economic and social policy. In the second, a 1944 speech to Democratic supporters, Wallace provides a forceful vision of a "Third New Deal" to protect the rights and economic security of ordinary Americans. Wallace's progressivism and his advocacy of civil rights reform alienated powerful Southern Democrats, and in 1944 he was pushed from the presidential ticket in favor Senator Harry Truman. Wallace returned to national politics in 1948 to unsuccessfully challenge Truman's reelection as the standard-bearer for the new Progressive Party.

February 5, 1943
Henry A. Wallace to Franklin D. Roosevelt

---

4. From "Letter from Wallace to FDR," February 5, 1943, repr. in John Morton Blum, ed., *The Price of Vision: The Diary of Henry A. Wallace, 1942–1946* (Boston, MA: Houghton Mifflin, 1973), 181–82; Wallace, "What America Wants," Address by the Vice President, Los Angeles, Feb. 4, 1944, Henry A. Wallace Papers, University of Iowa. Reprinted by permission, Special Collections, University of Iowa.

Dear Mr. President:

Following your speech to Congress, OWI conducted a poll asking, "Do you think that one of our aims should be to see that everyone in this country has a chance to get a job after the war?" Ninety-nine percent said, "Yes." Of those who said, "Yes," 68 percent said they thought this could actually be done.

Of the 99 percent who said it would be our objective to get a job for everyone after the war, 72 percent said we should start in right now to make plans for this. Twenty-three percent said we should wait until later. Only 4 percent said they didn't know.

I am citing these figures to back up my contention that it is good politics now to ask in the near future for what might be called "lend-lease authorizations on the domestic front." There is opportunity, perhaps, for several more idealistic speeches of a general nature, but it is my impression that the people are now ready and eager for definite action looking toward the assurance of postwar jobs. The problem of demobilizing the army, relocating the war workers, and reconverting the war industries is one of tremendous magnitude and one which cannot be faced by private industry alone. I agree with you that because of shortages of goods there will be a certain amount of hangover prosperity for the first year or two. But both the immediate and ultimate objectives are of such magnitude that we have no time to lose in starting our planning. . . .

Text of Address by Vice President Wallace on the Country's Postwar Needs

On this trip to the West Coast I propose to talk about America Tomorrow. Today I shall speak about what America wants. Later on at San Francisco and Seattle I shall discuss what America can have and how America can get it. We want many different things and some of these are in conflict with others. But let me point out right at the start that the sum total of what we Americans can have is immense. Only a few years ago, when the President said he wanted fifty thousand war planes a year, some people thought he was being visionary. Today we know that the production of a hundred thousand war planes a year is a hard reality. So I tell you we can have twice as much for civilian living after the war as we ever had before the war, and you know that is no dream. There are limits, but they are much bigger than most people even yet realize.

But we cannot have all these things unless we use good sense and good management. If we try to grab too much, all we shall get is another boom and another collapse. That is why we should think clearly about what each of us wants, and then about how our desires can be made to fit into a practical total, and finally how to get that total. This is the practical way of planning, creating and enjoying the common welfare.

The first and most important need has to do with the desires of plain folks who have to work for a living in the factories and the stores, in the schoolhouses and the government offices. More than 50 million of these people with their wives and children have just one basic interest in life—the assurance of a steady job. They would like the assurance of an annual salary or, at any rate, the guarantee of two thousand hours of work a year.

Of course labor wants more than decent wages. It wants to be appreciated, to feel that it is contributing toward making this world a better place in which to live.

The workers of the United States want assurance that they can have jobs when the seven million service men and the ten million war workers, who by their supreme efforts are saving us during this mighty conflict, find it necessary to get back into peacetime work.

They want a plan that will solve the problem when there are more workers than jobs. Nowhere is this situation so acute as right here on the West Coast. When men begin to hunt for jobs the bargaining power of labor begins to weaken and union funds begin to melt away. Workers everywhere know this and therefore are beginning to think in larger terms than merely bargaining for higher wages, shorter hours and better working conditions. They want to have a part in making those decisions, which will determine the future prosperity of the nation. They want to influence government and industry to bring about full use of manpower, full use of resources and full use of technological know-how.

With the United States producing in peace as it has been producing in war, the workers know that they can have opportunities for leisure and culture, and above everything else possibilities for the real education of their children.

Workers want better insurance against sickness, unemployment and old age. They want the Wagner Act, not as a substitute for full employment, but as an insurance against the accidents to which all of us are subject. When post-war contracts are canceled American labor wants work, not a dole. The Wagner Act can never be a substitute for jobs, but combined with jobs it is admirable.

Organized labor has come of age. It has taken its place as a responsible partner of management in the operation of industry and trade. It has accepted responsibility in war for maintaining an increase in production. It has the right to ask for fair and honest treatment from the public.

As a responsible partner, labor wants an opportunity to make creative contributions to industry and to benefit therefrom. During the war hundreds of thousands of workers have submitted ideas for increasing efficiency, enlarging output, saving time and costs, and improving the quality of the product. Labor during the war has enjoyed cooperating with management in doing a real production job, and we must never again let such a rich source of national wealth go untapped. . . .

Some, but not all, big business men want that type of control which will produce big profits. They want to put Wall Street first and the nation second. They want to put property rights first and human rights second. They will fight with unrelenting hatred through press, radio, demagogue and lobbyist every national and State government, which puts human rights above property rights.

To its own conscience this selfish, narrow-visioned branch of big business puts its desires in mild-sounding phrases somewhat as follows: "We must have an economically sound government and a balanced budget. Government spending must be cut down. We must get rid of that 'so and so' in the White House. Then with government out of business and with Wall Street running the country again, we can have what we want—free enterprise. Yes, the free enterprise of old-fashioned America is what we really want."

By free enterprise this type of big business means freedom for freebooters. By free enterprise this type of big business means the privilege of charging monopoly prices without interference by the government; the privilege of putting competitors out of business by unfair methods of competition; the privilege of buying up patents and keeping them out of use; the privilege of setting up Pittsburgh plus price-fixing schemes; the privilege of unloading stocks and bonds on the public through insiders who know their way in and out, up and down, backwards and sideways.

Fortunately, not all big business men ask for these privileges or define free enterprise in the way I have just mentioned. Some of them are as deeply concerned with the problem of full employment as labor itself. They are anxious to see such modification in taxation laws as will place the maximum incentive on that type of business activity which will give full employment. Some of these larger business men have marvelous new inventions which they would like to put into volume production at the earliest possible moment. Such men are oftentimes more interested in increasing production, and thereby serving humanity, than in making money for money's sake, but they know that even from the standpoint of serving humanity it is necessary to make a reasonable profit if this private enterprise economy of ours is to survive. Therefore they want the assurance of large and expanding markets.

The small business man is just as much interested in free enterprise as the big business man, but he means something quite different in his use of the word. Free enterprise to the little business man means the opportunity to compete without fear of monopoly controls of any kind. The small manufacturer wants free access to markets and the assurance that he will not suddenly find himself crushed by some hostile financial power. . . .

Some of the business men who most want to serve the world in the post-war period are probably those who have rather recently graduated from the ranks of the small business men into handling large affairs in the war effort. Because of his unusual capacity, this kind of man has made large sums of money during the war, but has paid nearly all of his profits to the government. He will come out of the war with large plant facilities. He wants to know how to reconvert as fast as possible. His success has often depended largely upon his fine relationship with labor. Appreciating the loyalty of labor, he wants to give his workers jobs in the post-war period, not so much from the standpoint of making money as from the standpoint of doing things both for his workers and for the country. Such men are in some ways the hope of America and of the world. . . .

. . . We all want jobs, health, security, freedom, business opportunity, good education and peace. We can sum this all up in one word and say that what America wants is pursuit of happiness. Each individual American before he dies wants to express all that is in him. He wants to work hard. He wants to play hard. He wants the pleasures of a good home with education for his children. He wants to travel and on occasion to rest and enjoy the finer things of life. The common man thinks he is entitled to the opportunity of earning these things. He wants all the physical resources of the nation transformed by human energy and human knowledge into the good things of life, the sum total of which spells peace and happiness. He knows he cannot have such peace and happiness if the means of earning peace and happiness are denied to any man on the basis of race or creed.

The common man means to get what he is entitled to. Any failure to utilize our resources to the full will cause him to throw over any system which he thinks stands in his way. The impulse of humanity toward full use and full expression is now so intense as to be identical with life itself. We who love democracy must make it politically and economically a capable servant of the irresistible instincts of man and nature toward full use.

All of us want to be needed and appreciated. We want to feel that the world would be a poorer place if we died. We want to enjoy the world, contribute to the world, and be appreciated by the world, each in his own little way. . . .

We have the materials to work with. We have the science and technical skills to direct our work. We have innumerable desires for goods and services that we are able to supply. All we need is good management and harmony, less grabbing for ourselves, and more cooperation for the general welfare. Legitimate self-interest can be realized in no other way. By working together for victory in war we have made a resounding success. By working together for the common good in peace we can get results beyond what most American have dared ever to hope.

10.5 Women Give Up Their War Jobs[5]

World War II had the potential to fundamentally transform the labor market in the United States. It did not. Although government and business had cooperated to recruit women to war industries, they had done so only "for the duration" of the war. As the Women's Bureau of the U.S. Department of Labor reported in 1946, many women workers left the workforce when the war ended. Though some were fired, others left voluntarily and eagerly embraced the roles of wife and mother. Even during the war, the marriage rate and birthrate rose. These trends accelerated in the postwar period, giving way to the famed "baby boom" of the postwar period.

Wartime Increases in Employment

From 1940 to the peak of women's war employment in July 1944, the number of women in the labor force has increased by more than 6 million, or by nearly half the 1940 number. This of course reflects the summer employment of women and schoolgirls in agriculture and other highly seasonal work as well as in war factories. However, more than nine-tenths of these additional women in the labor force were in nonagricultural employment.

By July of the next year, just before the close of the war, there had been a decline in the employment of women, though relatively little increase in unemployment. Some women had left the labor force, but there was not an extremely marked difference between July 1944 and July 1945. Women constituted more than a third of the total civilian labor force both in July 1944 and later (March 1945). In July 1945 they were 35 percent of the civilian workers. . . .

From March 1945 to the end of the year, during the closing months of the war as well as in the postwar period, the participation of women in nonagricultural employment was continually decreasing, as shown by the Census *Monthly Reports*. In January 1946 the number of women in the labor force had declined by nearly 4 million from that in the closing period of the war, July 1945. This is a number nearly one-fifth as great as the entire July 1945 female labor force. Although representing in part a decline from the seasonal peak in agriculture, over half of the reduction occurred in nonagricultural employment. Of the decline of more than 2

---

5. From U.S. Department of Labor, Women's Bureau, *Employment of Women in the Early Postwar Period* (Washington, DC: U.S. Government Printing Office, 1946), 1–2, 5–6, 11–13.

million women in nonagricultural pursuits, just over half came at the close of and immediately after the war, July to September 1945.

The increased unemployment among women was not nearly so great as the employment decline. In January 1946 something over half a million women were unemployed, only 60,000 more than in the previous July. This was a number very much less than the prewar unemployment of women, which amounted to about 1¾ million in March 1940.

After the war, many women left the labor force. However, the total number of women of working age in the population was larger in 1946 than in 1940. Although numbers of women outside the labor force have increased somewhat, larger proportions of the female population may remain a part of the labor force in the postwar period than before the war. In January 1946 over 30 percent of the adult women of the country could be accounted workers. . . .

No complete figures exist as yet on the occupational or industrial distribution of women workers in any period since the war. It may be considered fairly certain that among women workers somewhat smaller proportions in the postwar than during the war period are in manufacturing. Contributing to this conclusion are the following:

> 1. Reports on heavy lay-offs in direct war manufacturing immediately following the end of the war which were considerably heavier for women than for men.—By September 1945 it was reported that 1 out of every 4 women employed in factories in June had been dropped, and all major manufacturing groups had smaller proportions of women in September than in June (except for a very slight increase in the proportion of women in food industries). By December, more than 1 million women had lost factory jobs, more than half of them immediately after the war.
> 2. The trend in placements of women—to be discussed later in this report.
> 3. Notes from many localities indicating types of employment needing workers which emphasize heavy demands for service and for clerical employees.

While the facts just noted indicate a smaller proportion of women in manufacturing since the war than at the war peak, nevertheless, judging from reports of women war workers in various areas on their postwar work intentions and from announced plans for expansion in many industries, somewhat larger proportions of all women workers are likely to be in manufacturing than in 1940.

The experience after the last war was that representative war manufacturing plants, though employing fewer women after the war than at the war peak, nevertheless employed both larger numbers and larger proportions of women than in the prewar period. . . .

Trends in Redistribution of Women War Workers

As has been stated, the female labor force declined by nearly 4 million after the war, though the major part of this decline did not appear as an addition to the rolls of the unemployed. There are no over-all figures to show the types of industries or occupations in which displaced women war workers have found employment. The nearest approximation to such information is in an analysis of all placements made by the U.S. Employment Service, which may be taken as some indication of the situation, though it includes only those placed by this agency, and many workers find jobs through direct contact with employers; moreover, placement includes service to all those who apply to the Employment Service, and reports therefore are not limited in coverage to those specifically displaced from war jobs.

Proportions Women Constituted of Total Postwar Placements and of Prewar Labor Force

It is of interest to compare the proportions women constituted of the 1940 labor force and of late war and postwar placements by the U.S. Employment Service. . . . [W]omen constituted much larger proportions of the nonagricultural placements in March 1944 than of those employed in March 1940. In March 1945 women's proportions among placements had declined somewhat from the previous war year but still were well above the proportion they were of the 1940 employed. In the latter part of 1945, the proportions of women among those placed had declined, but they still constituted much the same part of the total as in 1940 employment and were slightly above 1940 proportions in employment in manufacturing and in government, and to a somewhat greater extent, in service industries.

Distribution of Women in Postwar Placements Compared to Their Distribution in the Prewar and Wartime Labor Force

The most marked change in industrial distribution of women workers during the war was in the great increase in their proportions in manufacturing employment and the almost corresponding decline in their proportions in the various service industries. In the nonagricultural placements of women made in the last 3 months of 1945 through the U.S. Employment Service, the distribution among the various industries was much the same as in the labor force of the war period—much larger proportions were in manufacturing, smaller proportions in the services, than in 1940 employment. . . .

Of the women in the manufacturing labor force in 1940, about 43 percent were employed in textiles and apparel. Many plants in these industries had retained and even increased their labor force during the war, making much the same products as in peacetime; the chief change was that the markets were supplied with war needs instead of the normal ones. In the last 3 months of 1945 these industries accounted for 28 percent of all placements of women in manufacturing through the U.S. Employment Service.

Difficulties in Redistribution of Women War Workers

There are certain distinct difficulties that face women in particular in the redistribution of the labor force in the postwar period. Chief among these difficulties, bearing with special force on women, is the frequent lack of openings for many workers at the levels of skill developed during the war. Some women were not in the labor force before the war. Others have developed higher skills during the war period than before. Because they are new entrants to the labor force or to occupations of certain skills, many of these women do not have prior seniority in the jobs they hold when lay-offs occur. Few of them are entitled to the job preferences afforded veterans. When jobs of the skill levels women have developed in war work are no longer available, the tendency is to refer them back to their earlier types of jobs, which many of them no longer desire. In a sample study made in three cities [Atlanta, Ga., Columbus, Ohio, and Trenton, N.J.] by the U.S. Employment Service, it was found that 40 to 61 percent of the openings for women were in clerical, sales, or service jobs, but only 15 to 18 percent of the women claimants had last worked in these fields. Reports from the field indicate that women do not desire to return, not only to service occupations, but in some instances to manufacturing occupations in which they were formerly engaged. For example, some localities report shortages of women workers in garment and hosiery factories owing to women's lack of desire to return to such jobs.

The jobs available for women tend to pay lower basic rates than did their wartime work. Meanwhile elimination of overtime hours and overtime pay have cut amounts in pay envelopes, making women all the more hesitant to accept new jobs where basic rates are lower than they have been receiving. This tends also to keep women longer unemployed and to throw more women for longer periods on unemployment compensation. At the same time, the restrictions on receipt of unemployment compensation bear with particular hardship on women.

Furthermore, the increased number of older women in the labor force, and the tendency for hiring specifications in some types of clerical and manufacturing work to be placed at relatively low age ranges—facts that already have been discussed—indicate that when the labor market eases a greater number of women than before the war may experience difficulties in obtaining jobs owing to their ages.

10.6 Americans Worry about Postwar Employment Prospects: The Gallup Poll, December 27, 1944[6]

The vast majority of Americans were worried that the end of the war would mean the return of the Great Depression. This 1944 poll indicates the degree to which Americans were worried about unemployment and a new economic downturn. Despite these fears, however, the Depression did not return, and instead the postwar period was marked by unprecedented prosperity and widespread upward mobility.

Interviewing Date 12/1–6/44
Survey #336-K   Question #7

After the war, do you think that everyone who wants a job will be able to get one?

Yes	25%
No	68
No opinion	7

By Sex
Men

Yes	28%
No	66
No opinion	6

Women

Yes	22%
No	71
No opinion	7

---

6. From George Gallup, "Postwar Employment, December 1944, Question #336-K," *The Gallup Poll: Public Opinion, 1935–1971*, vol. 1 (New York: Random House, 1972), 478–79.

By Age
21–29 Years

Yes 23%
No 73
No opinion 4

30–49 Years

Yes 25%
No 68
No opinion 7

50 Years and Over

Yes 26%
No 66
No opinion 8

By Occupation
Business and Professional

Yes 22%
No 74
No opinion 4

White Collar

Yes 25%
No 67
No opinion 8

Farmers

Yes 25%
No 69
No opinion 6

By Education
College

Yes 23%
No 65
No opinion 12

High School

Yes 15%
No 72
No opinion 13

Grade School

Yes 16%

No   66

No opinion   18

10.7 President Roosevelt Promises Veterans a New Bill of Rights, 1944[7]

In late 1943, President Franklin Roosevelt proposed a postwar assistance program to World War II veterans. A bill based on the president's recommendations but drafted by the American Legion was introduced in early 1944 and was signed into law on June 22, 1944. The Servicemen's Readjustment Act of 1944—usually referred to as the GI Bill of Rights—provided returning veterans with an array of new entitlements, including low-cost mortgages, low-interest loans to start a business, and education benefits. The law made such assistance available to all veterans—regardless of economic need or active duty—who had served for at least 120 days and had not been dishonorably discharged. The law not only helped individual servicemen and their families, but also helped to preserve the economic prosperity of the war years into the postwar period by providing a kind of economic stimulus.

This bill, which I have signed today, substantially carries out most of the recommendations made by me in a speech on July 28, 1943, and more specifically in messages to the Congress dated October 27, 1943, and November 23, 1943:

1. It gives servicemen and women the opportunity of resuming their education or technical training after discharge, or of taking a refresher or retrainer course, not only without tuition charge up to $500 per school year, but with the right to receive a monthly living allowance while pursuing their studies.

2. It makes provision for the guarantee by the Federal Government of not to exceed 50 percent of certain loans made to veterans for the purchase or construction of homes, farms, and business properties.

3. It provides for reasonable unemployment allowances payable each week up to a maximum period of one year, to those veterans who are unable to find a job.

---

7. From Franklin D. Roosevelt, "Statement on Signing the G.I. Bill," June 22, 1944; available at *The American Presidency Project,* by Gerhard Peters and John T. Woolley, http://www.presidency.ucsb.edu/ws/?pid=1652.

4. It establishes improved machinery for effective job counseling for veterans and for finding jobs for returning soldiers and sailors.

5. It authorizes the construction of all necessary additional hospital facilities.

6. It strengthens the authority of the Veterans Administration to enable it to discharge its existing and added responsibilities with promptness and efficiency.

With the signing of this bill a well-rounded program of special veterans' benefits is nearly completed. It gives emphatic notice to the men and women in our armed forces that the American people do not intend to let them down.

By prior legislation, the Federal Government has already provided for the armed forces of this war: adequate dependency allowances; mustering-out pay; generous hospitalization, medical care, and vocational rehabilitation and training; liberal pensions in case of death or disability in military service; substantial war risk life insurance, and guaranty of premiums on commercial policies during service; protection of civil rights and suspension of enforcement of certain civil liabilities during service; emergency maternal care for wives of enlisted men; and reemployment rights for returning veterans.

This bill therefore and the former legislation provide the special benefits which are due to the members of our armed forces—for they "have been compelled to make greater economic sacrifice and every other kind of sacrifice than the rest of us, and are entitled to definite action to help take care of their special problems." While further study and experience may suggest some changes and improvements, the Congress is to be congratulated on the prompt action it has taken.

There still remains one recommendation which I made on November 23, 1943, which I trust that the Congress will soon adopt—the extension of social security credits under the Federal Old-Age and Survivors' Insurance Law to all servicemen and women for the period of their service.

I trust that the Congress will also soon provide similar opportunities for postwar education and unemployment insurance to the members of the merchant marine, who have risked their lives time and again during this war for the welfare of their country.

But apart from these special benefits which fulfill the special needs of veterans, there is still much to be done.

As I stated in my message to the Congress of November 23, 1943,

"What our servicemen and women want, more than anything else, is the assurance of satisfactory employment upon their return to civil life. The first task after the war is to provide employment for them and for our demobilized workers. . . . The goal after the war should be the maximum utilization of our human and material resources."

As a related problem the Congress has had under consideration the serious problem of economic reconversion and readjustment after the war, so that private industry will be able to provide jobs for the largest possible number. This time we have wisely begun to make plans in advance of the day of peace, in full confidence that our war workers will remain at their essential war jobs as long as necessary until the fighting is over.

The executive branch of the Government has taken, and is taking, whatever steps it can, until legislation is enacted. I am glad to learn that the Congress has agreed on a bill to facilitate the prompt settlement of terminated contracts. I hope that the Congress will also take prompt action, when it reconvenes, on necessary legislation which is now pending to facilitate the development of unified programs for the demobilization of civilian war workers, for their reemployment in peacetime pursuits, and for provision, in cooperation with the States, of appropriate unemployment benefits during the transition from war to peace. I hope also that the Congress, upon its return, will take prompt action on the pending legislation to facilitate the orderly disposition of surplus property.

A sound postwar economy is a major present responsibility.

10.8 Black Veterans Debate the Impact of the GI Bill, 1945[8]

The GI Bill played a key role in constructing the postwar middle class. Millions of Americans took advantage of the law to further their educations, buy homes, start businesses, or obtain vocational training. However, the benefits of the bill were not equally distributed. Because the law worked through private institutions, it often reproduced and even reinforced existing patterns of racial discrimination in the education, labor, and housing markets. African Americans debated the impact of the bill. While some saw the law as an important, albeit imperfect "opening wedge" that might one day provide the black community with important benefits and opportunities, others worried that the law would only widen the gap between the black and white communities. The documents reproduced here demonstrate the terms of that debate. Colonel Campbell Johnson, who served as the racial relations director for the Selective Service, celebrated the law's "color-blindness" and explained its benefits. On the other hand, Charles Hurd recognized the "loophole" in the law that allowed for "different treatment between white and Negro veterans."

---

8. From Col. Campbell Johnson, "The Unforgotten Man," *Opportunity: A Journal of Negro Life*, Winter 1945; Charles Hurd, "Democracy Challenged," *Opportunity: A Journal of Negro Life*, Spring 1945.

The Unforgotten Man

More than a million young Negro men and women have been enlisted and inducted into the armed forces of the United States since May, 1940. They will represent almost a tenth of the returning veterans of World War II and most of them will be entitled to share in the generous veterans' benefits which have been provided by a grateful nation for its heroes of history's most significant war.

One fact that is outstanding with reference to these returning veterans of World War II is that they will not be "forgotten men." When the Selective Training and Service Act was passed in 1940, provision was made not only for the selection of men for training and service but also for returning them to their jobs in civil life. . . .

. . . The Serviceman's Readjustment Act of 1944 and popularly known as the "G.I. Bill of Rights," became law on June 22, 1944. It provides educational aid; assistance in job placement; readjustment allowances during periods of unemployment; and loan guarantees for the purchase, repair, or construction of homes and farms and for the purchase of business property and of farm and business equipment, machines, and tools. In addition, the Servicemen's Readjustment Act extends the benefits of the Disabled Veterans Act to include eligible persons who served in the armed forces on or after September 16, 1940.

It is agreed that never before in history has such an inclusive program been provided by a nation for the heroes of any war. It is a remarkable circumstance, too, in connection with this legislation that it has been passed before the end of the war. . . .

. . . [Under the provision of the law] the private employer who fails or refuses to grant the veteran his reemployment rights as set forth in the Selective Training and Service Act of 1940 as amended may be sued by the veteran himself in the United States District Court for the district in which his former employer maintains a place of business. The veteran may employ his own attorney or he may request the United States Attorney or comparable official to represent him without cost.

A veteran who is restored to a position in the employ of the Federal Government or a private employer is entitled to certain additional benefits. He is considered as having been on leave of absence or on furlough during his period of military service and is restored in employment without loss of seniority. In computing seniority, the veteran is credited with the time he served in the armed forces. The law provides also that he shall be entitled to insurance or other benefits made available by the employer to employees on leave or furlough as of the date the veteran left the job, and he may not be discharged from his job without cause within one year after his restoration.

Experience has shown that military service frequently provides an occupational background that can prove useful after the war. Nine out of every ten soldiers are specialists, and the mechanical, scientific, and technical training which they have received in the armed forces is practical preparation for employment in civilian life. Many veterans will prefer to obtain work at their new skills rather than return to the type of job they had been performing prior to their military training. . . .

Veterans may qualify also for government guaranty up to 50 per cent on loans not exceeding $2,000 for purchase, repair, or construction of homes; purchase or improvement of farms or farm machinery, implement or equipment; and purchase of business property, supplies, equipment, tools, or machinery. If the veteran is eligible and certain conditions are met with regard to the loan, the Veterans Administration is authorized to guarantee loans to veterans on approved applications made to persons, firms, associations, and corporations and to governmental agencies and corporations, either State or Federal. . . .

A summary of all the benefits which a veteran of this war may receive under the various pieces of veteran legislation shows a surprising number of aids. While it is entirely possible that of the millions of returning veterans not one will individually be the recipient of them all, the idea that this could happen is interesting. It should be borne in mind, however, that it is the intent of the people of our Nation that every returning veteran should have all of these benefits to which he may be entitled by reason of physical or vocational handicap or length and quality of service.

Many agencies, both governmental and private, are preparing to use their resources to guarantee that our returning veterans shall know and take advantage of the benefits due them. The Negro veteran, along with all others, will profit by the institutions and agencies upon which he habitually depends for information and guidance, bending their best efforts to assure that he not only is informed but also is given assistance in obtaining those benefits to which he is entitled.

Democracy Challenged

By Charles Hurd

War has created upsets at home almost as drastic, although without the same touch of tragedy, as for soldiers overseas. Among these upsets is the obvious one involved in transplanting millions of persons, including a very large percentage of Negroes, from their familiar surroundings into new ones. Many of these persons are incapable of reaching decisions about their own future, simply because they do not have the facts on which to base decisions. Already, there are indications of grave tensions. . . .

There is the basic argument, officially denied but constantly recurring, that the Army and Navy, on one hand, are not giving an even break to Negro soldiers and sailors and, on the other, that they are not absorbing them in the proportion of Negroes to the whole population. This has been the cause of misunderstanding and bad feeling that can do much harm unless it is checked by reiteration of the facts, if they are found to controvert the argument.

When we switch to the postwar picture, the old bugaboo arises as to questions over equality of opportunity as between Negro veterans and white veterans; between the futures of the two broad racial groups in industrial and economic opportunity. Many of the arguments will be, as they always have been, fostered by extremists on both sides. The only foreseeable offset for them is publicity for the facts. And where the facts are unpleasant, publicity will contribute to correction of them.

It is notable that neither the "G. I. Bill of Rights," the Selective Service Act, nor Public Law N. 16, which lays down the rights and benefits of disabled veterans, contains a single loophole for different treatment as between white and Negro veterans. Where these laws provide specifically for governmental responsibility, every effort is being made to administer them without bias. The problem faced in the future by veterans, however, is the degree to which civilian agencies and civilian facilities can measure up to the promise made by the Government.

The Selective Service Act guarantees to every veteran, with 90 days or more service and a discharge other than dishonorable, reinstatement into the job he held before the war or one of comparable standing if the job was on permanent basis, if the employer still is in business and if the veteran is able to perform the duties of the job.

That is quite clear, except a very large number of veterans, white and colored alike, will have no job to which to return, or may not wish to return to the jobs they had. They may also face contentions over questions whether the jobs they left for military service were in fact permanent. . . .

The second potential opening for dissension will come if there are complaints that the United States Employment Service, acting for the Veterans' Administration, appears in any locality to favor white over Negro veterans in assignment to job openings. No general rule on earth can assure proper handling of this point; only community vigilance. And I daresay there are very few newspapers which will not give ample space to any complaints backed by evidence that this equality is not being observed.

As for physical care of veterans, either those disabled in the war or those who in later years may rate treatment for other types of disabilities, the

Veterans' Administration has taken every precaution, I know, to see that proportionate facilities are set aside for Negro veterans so that at no time may lack of proportionate facilities block admission of Negroes. And lest there be any complaint that negroes are sent to undesirable areas or subjected to treatment inferior to white veterans, the Veterans' Administration has designated hospitals to receive them in virtually every State.

The educational problem is a somewhat tougher one, and likely to breed more complaints than any other unless there is, first of all, a reasoned approach to it, and, afterward, a careful reporting of how this program is working out.

All Negro and white veterans have the same educational benefits under the "G. I. Bill of Rights." Every able-bodied veteran not dishonorably discharged who served more than 90 days is eligible for one year of subsidized education, with tuition fees underwritten up to $500 and subsistence allowance of $50 a month for a single man or $75 a month for men with dependents. He may have as much additional education on this subsidized basis as his time on active duty, up to a maximum of three years. Or he may arrange to take his educational grants in the form of apprentice training or attendance part-time at business or technical schools.

Here we face the fact—applicable to a degree to all veterans but particularly to the Negro ones—that the educational subsidy opens the road for further study to a considerably larger proportion of young men than would have considered such plans possible in the pre-war economy.

The first question is whether the facilities exist to handle those who will apply. Will the approximately 50 Negro institutions of higher learning accommodate the numbers of Negroes who will wish to attend them, or will the hundreds of universities and colleges that accept all races as students be able to accommodate those who apply?

The answer is, in effect, thrown on the shoulders of the operating heads of these schools, because the law is specific in stating that educational grants will be made only to those veterans who can prove to school authorities their right to admissibility under the rules and practices of the schools they wish to attend.

Many thousands of veterans are going to be disappointed in their educational plans. It is important that constant watch be kept and reports issued on whether this disappointment is due to general conditions or whether to unreasonable requirements which draw some line between rules laid down for white veterans with educational ambitions and Negro candidates for the same training.

The veteran is, of course, the first object of concern in these problems, but, while secondary to the veteran, the problems of the transplanted civilian raise peculiar fields of study in relation to the Negro. The story here is in line with, but far more puzzling than after the last war, simply because mass migration, grave changes in communities themselves and new viewpoints all have been developed in this war.

When war industries in the north started the search for millions of new workers, they dipped heavily into the reservoir of Negroes who originally worked in agriculture or in the service industries of small communities. The two companion questions arising out of this migration deal first with the problem of finding out how many migrant workers will wish to go back whence they came, and whether, if they elect to stay where they are, what opportunities exist for them to make a living.

As an instance, Henry Kaiser recruited Negroes by the thousands—genuinely welcomed them—as workers at high wages in his shipyards along the northwest coast. An editor friend in Portland, Oregon, told me recently that one result was to increase the Negro population of that city by twenty-four. The increase in population has created multiple problems of housing and other social questions even while the payrolls are being kept at full height.

What will the problem be like when the war production tapers off, when Portland again becomes a relatively non-industrial shipping center in which the normal jobs are principally filled by persons who have always had them and the excess of jobs will be held open exclusively for war veterans, as very likely will occur?

Certainly, the 23 new Negro workers who flocked there for every one originally established in Portland, will wish in the main to keep on enjoying the type of life financed by their war jobs. So will the many thousands of white workers attracted to this operation. But how will they eat? Will they realize the necessity of readjusting their lives to conditions, perhaps return to the agricultural work which many of them left to take these war jobs? . . .

The problem exemplified by Portland is present in scores of cities where single massive war industries have been established, particularly in the Ohio River Valley and the Middle West. Each is essentially a community problem which cannot be solved entirely within the community. I do not believe that Government can solve it either. Here is a broad field for comment and broad exchange of ideas through the agencies such as the Urban Leagues, with sympathetic cooperation on the part of the newspapers—white *and* Negro—in publicizing these ideas. More constructive reporting can be done on both sides.

The problem of Portland is minute when compared to the questions faced by the great industrial cities headed by Chicago and Detroit. In these, more than any other place, plain speaking appears to be in order—challenging speaking by responsible sources that is louder than the noise made by the fringe of persons who would range themselves in unreasoning manner on one side or the other of the "controversy."

If this plain speaking of a constructive nature is not undertaken, the large northern cities which have spawned the greatest industrial opportunity for the Negro may see gulfs created as bad as those which existed a generation or more ago in the most backward sections of the old South. The riots in Detroit last year gave a fair preview of a future in which passions were permitted to over-rule reason. . . .

The New York Times carried a report of the meeting [of the National Urban League] which read. . .

"The Negro leaders urged that Governors of States and Mayors of cities take immediate steps to promote interracial cooperation 'by clearing away barriers that now stand in the way of mutual understanding and respect between the races.' They accepted for themselves and urged upon their white neighbors the task of helping to integrate the Negro into the new communities in which he was now moving.

"They called for opposition on all sides to the spread of segregation and recommended that practical means be taken, community by community, 'to remove this cause of resentment on the part of the Negro.' . . ."

CHAPTER 11

PRESIDENT FRANKLIN D. ROOSEVELT AND ALLIED DIPLOMACY FOR WAR AND PEACE

Military actions in war are merely the means a nation uses to obtain the political ends for which it went to war. Each Axis power in World War II thus waged war to establish or expand its empire and further its ideological aims. Similarly, their opponents sought not only to prevent this by military means but also to establish a postwar world to their liking. Each of the major Allied powers, however, had a different idea of how such a world would look. This made difficult not only any postwar planning but also, as Chapter 3 illustrated, any common military strategy and even the maintenance of the coalition. Where that previous chapter explored Allied conflicts over strategy and their resolution, this chapter explores their serious political differences and their attempted resolution, with special emphasis on Franklin D. Roosevelt's controversial policies.

As explained in Chapter 3, the Allies agreed that Germany had to be defeated before Japan but disagreed as to how to accomplish this goal. They similarly agreed that the overall political objective was to create a world in which Axis aggression and another world war could not occur but disagreed sharply as to what such a world would look like. Although they had all pledged adherence to the broad principles enunciated in a 1941 document known as the Atlantic Charter, they disagreed sharply in their interpretation of those principles and the postwar world they wished to create.

The British desired a return to the international order that had existed before the rise of the Axis powers, one based upon a European balance of power and maintenance of the existing British and other European empires in Africa, Asia, and the Pacific. The Soviets and the Americans disagreed. They believed that this system had led to Fascism and World War II in the first place, and they consequently pressed for alternative systems, each of which conflicted sharply with the other.

Soviet leader Josef Stalin also believed that the prewar system to which Britain wished to return had isolated the Soviet Union because of its Communist ideology and that it had sanctioned the huge loss of territory and population that the Germans had imposed on the Soviets during

World War I and that the Allies had ratified after the war. By the terms of first the 1918 treaty with Germany and then the Versailles treaties that officially ended the war, the former Russian Empire lost some of the most valuable lands on its western borders—territory that went to Rumania and the re-created states of Poland, Finland, Estonia, Latvia, and Lithuania. Stalin regained much of this territory as a result of the 1939 Nazi-Soviet Pact and his 1939–1940 war with Finland. Hitler quickly conquered this territory when he invaded the Soviet Union in 1941, but throughout the remainder of World War II Stalin demanded its return as part of the Soviet Union. He also pressed for a permanent weakening of Germany and the creation in Eastern Europe of governments "friendly" to the Soviet Union. Britain opposed such moves, which it feared would merely replace the present threat of a hegemonic Germany with an equally threatening hegemonic Soviet Union.

The United States opposed both plans because it believed that either one would simply re-create the system that had led to both world wars in the first place as well as violate the cherished principle of national self-determination—be it in Eastern Europe or in the European colonial empires in Africa, Asia, and the Pacific. Roosevelt thus proposed an alternative and multifaceted vision of the postwar world, which included an end to European colonialism, national self-determination for Asians and Africans as well as Europeans, disarmament of the Axis powers, and the creation of a new League of Nations to accomplish these objectives and maintain world peace. Given the failure of the original League, however, he insisted that real power to enforce the postwar peace would belong to the three major allies and China acting as the "Four Policemen" in order to prevent not just German or Japanese aggression, but any aggression that could trigger another world war.

Such a system would require the Allies to remain unified in the postwar world, despite their differences and disputes with each other. It would also require the American people to accept a major role for their country in the postwar world. To prevent any resurgence domestically of the isolationism of the interwar years and any splits between the Allies while the war was in progress, Roosevelt pressed those Allies to postpone discussion of all controversial postwar issues—especially territorial issues. In their place he favored merely a reassertion of the Atlantic Charter's broad principles on which they all agreed, along with insistence on the total defeat and unconditional surrender of the Axis powers. Despite their official concurrence, Churchill and Stalin consistently pressed for the detailed political discussions that Roosevelt opposed.

In late 1943, the president finally agreed to preliminary postwar discussions that continued throughout 1944. These resulted in a series of important agreements about a new postwar League of Nations at the Dumbarton Oaks Conference, a postwar economic order at the Bretton Woods Conference, and an Anglo-Soviet spheres of influence agreement in the Balkans at a Churchill-Stalin meeting in Moscow. Then in February of 1945, Roosevelt, Churchill, and Stalin met in the Russian Crimean resort of Yalta to ratify these accords and try to reach agreement on remaining postwar issues, as well as plan for final military victory over Germany and Japan. While they succeeded in doing so, their postwar agreements began to break down very soon after they were signed—a breakdown that led to bitter accusations by all three. Then on April 12 Roosevelt died of a massive stroke. What he would have done in this diplomatic crisis had he lived was and remains one of the great "what-ifs" of World War II history.

Roosevelt's consistent efforts to compromise Allied differences and postpone postwar discussions raise a series of issues that have long divided historians. Why did he pursue these policies, and were they wise or would alternative policies have been better? Was he foolish to believe he could cooperate with Stalin in the postwar world—or that China under Chiang Kai-shek could be one of his "Four Policemen"? Were the accords he signed at Yalta the best he could have achieved as his defenders maintain, or a naïve and cowardly sellout of American principles and other peoples as critics have charged?

* * * *

11.1 The Atlantic Charter States Allied War Aims, 1941[1]

Four months before Pearl Harbor, in August of 1941, Roosevelt met with Churchill off the coast of Newfoundland. At the end of this meeting they issued the Atlantic Charter, a combined statement of broad, idealistic war aims. Reproduced here are those war aims as enunciated in the charter.

The President of the United States of America and the Prime Minister, Mr. Churchill, representing His Majesty's Government in the United Kingdom, being met together, deem it right to make known certain common principles in the national policies of their respective countries on which they base their hopes for a better future for the world.

---

1. From State Department, *Bulletin* 5 (Washington, DC: U.S. Government Printing Office, 1942), 125–26.

First, their countries seek no aggrandizement, territorial or other;

Second, they desire to see no territorial changes that do not accord with the freely expressed wishes of the peoples concerned;

Third, they respect the right of all peoples to choose the form of government under which they will live; and they wish to see sovereign rights and self-government restored to those who have been forcibly deprived of them;

Fourth, they will endeavor, with due respect for their existing obligations, to further the enjoyment by all States, great or small, victor or vanquished, of access, on equal terms, to the trade and to the raw materials of the world which are needed for their economic prosperity;

Fifth, they desire to bring about the fullest collaboration between all nations in the economic field with the object of securing, for all, improved labor standards, economic advancement, and social security;

Sixth, after the final destruction of the Nazi tyranny, they hope to see established a peace which will afford to all nations the means of dwelling in safety within their own boundaries, and which will afford assurance that all the men in all the lands may live out their lives in freedom from fear and want;

Seventh, such a peace should enable all men to traverse the high seas and oceans without hindrance;

Eighth, they believe that all of the nations of the world, for realistic as well as spiritual reasons, must come to the abandonment of the use of force. Since no future peace can be maintained if land, sea, or air armaments continue to be employed by nations which threaten, or may threaten, aggression outside of their frontiers, they believe, pending the establishment of a wider and permanent system of general security, that the disarmament of such nations is essential. They will likewise aid and encourage all other practicable measures which will lighten for peace-loving peoples the crushing burden of armaments.

Franklin D. Roosevelt
Winston S. Churchill

11.2 Josef Stalin Demands Territorial Settlements, 1941[2]

Despite formal adherence to the Atlantic Charter, in mid-December of 1941 Stalin made clear to visiting British Foreign Secretary Anthony Eden his territorial demands in Eastern Europe as well as his views on

---

2. From U.S. Department of State, *Foreign Relations of the United States, 1942*, vol. 3 (Washington, DC: U.S. Government Printing Office, 1961), 499–500; and Oleg Rzheshevsky, *War and Diplomacy: The Making of the Grand Alliance: Documents from Stalin's Archives Edited with a Commentary* (Amsterdam: Harwood Academic Publishers, 1996), 28–33.

the future of Germany and the rest of Europe. Reproduced here are excerpts from both the British and the Soviet versions of these Eden-Stalin meetings. The "Curzon Line" mentioned in the British version refers to a proposed 1919 eastern boundary of Poland that largely coincided with the boundary established in the 1939 Nazi-Soviet Pact and in existence from 1939–1941.

British Foreign Secretary Anthony Eden's Summary of His Conversations with Stalin

At my first conversation with M. Stalin, M. Stalin set out in some detail what he considered should be the postwar territorial frontiers in Europe; and in particular his ideas regarding the treatment of Germany. He proposed the restoration of Austria as an independent state, the detachment of the Rhineland from Prussia as an independent state or protectorate, and possibly the constitution of an independent state of Bavaria. He also proposed that East Prussia should be transferred to Poland and the Sudetenland returned to Czechoslovakia. He suggested that Yugoslavia should be restored and even receive certain additional territories from Italy, that Albania should be reconstituted as an independent state, and that Turkey should receive the Dodecanese, with possibly readjustments in favour of Greece as regards islands in the Aegean important to Greece. Turkey might also receive certain districts in Bulgaria, and possibly also in Northern Syria.

In general the occupied countries, including Czechoslovakia and Greece, should be restored to their prewar frontiers, and Mr. Stalin was prepared to support any special arrangements for securing bases, et cetera, for the United Kingdom in Western European countries, e.g., France, Belgium, the Netherlands, Norway, and Denmark. As regards the special interests of the Soviet Union, Stalin desired the restoration of the position in 1941, prior to the German attack, in respect of the Baltic States, Finland, and Bessarabia. The "Curzon Line" should form the basis for the future Soviet-Polish frontier, and Rumania should give special facilities for bases, et cetera, to the Soviet Union, receiving compensation from territory now occupied by Hungary.

In the course of this first conversation, Stalin generally agreed with the principle of restitution in kind by Germany to the occupied countries, more particularly in regard to machine tools, et cetera, and ruled out money reparations as undesirable. He showed interest in a postwar military alliance between the "democratic countries," and stated that the Soviet Union had no objection to certain countries of Europe entering into a federal relationship, if they so desired.

In the second conversation, M. Stalin pressed for the immediate recognition by His Majesty's Government of the future frontiers of the
USSR, more particularly in regard to the inclusion within the USSR of
the Baltic States and the restoration of the 1941 Finnish-Soviet frontier.
He made the conclusion of any Anglo-Soviet agreement dependent on
agreement on this point. I, for my part, explained to M. Stalin that in view
of our prior undertakings to the United States Government it was quite
impossible for His Majesty's Government to commit themselves at this
stage to any postwar frontiers in Europe, although I undertook to consult
His Majesty's Government in the United Kingdom, the United States
Government, and His Majesty's Governments in the Dominions on my
return. . . .

The Soviet Minutes

The Second Meeting. 17 December, 12.00 p.m.

> Present: Comrades Stalin, Molotov and Maisky on the
> Soviet Side; Eden, Cripps and Cadogan on the
> British Side (Comrade Maisky Interprets)

Upon opening the meeting Eden began with the question of whether
Comrade Stalin had seen the results of the morning's work on the texts of
the agreements? . . .

Comrade Stalin said that the results were certainly interesting, but that
he was much more interested in the question of the USSR's future frontiers. Had Eden not received a reply to this question from the British
Government?

Eden answered that he had not and had not even tried to. The
Prime Minister was on a voyage at present, on the ocean, and he could
not communicate with him on the question raised by Comrade Stalin.
*[Rzheshevsky: Eden reported earlier that Churchill had left for the USA to
meet Roosevelt in connection with the development of events in the Pacific.]*
In London, there was nobody who might give the decisive answer to this
question with due authority and in the name of the British Government.
Eden could only repeat now what he had said yesterday, namely, that on
his return to London he would place the question of the USSR western
frontiers before the Government and consult with the United States on
the same question.

Further communications on this matter would have to be conducted through normal diplomatic channels.

Comrade Stalin objected that the question of Soviet frontiers (irrespective of the general question of the frontiers in Central and Western Europe) was of exceptional importance to us. The Soviet Government was especially interested in it because, in particular, it was precisely the question of the Baltic States and Finland that had been the stumbling-block in the negotiations in 1939 on the pact of mutual assistance under Chamberlain's Government....

Comrade Stalin then asked if special permission was required from the British Government to settle the question of the Baltic States? This question was axiomatic. The USSR is waging a fierce struggle against Hitlerite Germany. It is making heavy sacrifices, losing hundreds of thousands of people in the common fight together with Great Britain, its ally. It is bearing the brunt of the war on it shoulders. Is a decision of the British Government still needed to recognise the Soviet western frontier? Is not this question axiomatic? ...

Eden again repeated the motivation of refusal stated above with slight variations.

Comrade Stalin then asked, where might such a formulation of the question lead Britain? Perhaps tomorrow Britain will declare that she does not recognise the Ukraine as part of the USSR.

Eden replied that there was an obvious misunderstanding here. Britain did not recognise only the changes of frontiers that have taken place during the war. The Ukraine had been part of the USSR before the war. Therefore the Premier's declaration as mentioned above could not in any way refer to the Ukraine.

Comrade Stalin replied that the position taken by Eden did not differ essentially from the position Chamberlain's Government had taken in its time on the question of the Baltic States. Comrade Stalin was greatly surprised at this circumstance and, if it was really the case, it would apparently be very difficult to come to terms and conclude the treaties.

Eden expressed regret at this and again returned to his argument, this time emphasizing the need for preliminary consultations with America on the question of the USSR's western frontier. In conclusion he pointed out the difference that, in his view, exists between the state of affairs in 1939 and in 1941. At that time the British Government recognised the Baltic countries as independent States. Today it does not recognise their independent existence and, therefore, the actual situation has radically changed.

Comrade Stalin noted that a highly ridiculous situation had come about....

Eden repeated his former argument and added only that the Atlantic Charter did not admit a change of a State's status without the consent of its population. And in this particular case this provision in the Atlantic Charter might possibly be considered as applicable.

Comrade Stalin responded that if Eden did not change his position, the signature of the treaties would have to be postponed.

Comrade Stalin replied that the whole war between the USSR and Germany started because of the USSR's western frontier including, in particular, the Baltic States. He would like to know whether Britain, our ally, was ready to back us up in the restoration of these frontiers. . . .

Comrade Stalin replied that . . . he absolutely could not understand the position taken by the British Government. Presumably, one ally must support another ally. Should someone come to him and say that it was necessary to separate the Irish Free State from the British Empire, he would send him packing. If Britain wished to have air [and] naval bases in Belgium and Holland he would certainly render her all manner of assistance. That is the way an ally should behave. If Britain did not find it possible to take such a stand, then it would be better to postpone the signature of the treaties and hold to the pact of mutual assistance concluded between the two countries in July. . . .

Comrade Stalin replied that he certainly did not want to ask Eden for the impossible. He well understood the limits of his authority, and he did not address him, but the British Government through him. An involuntary impression was created that the Atlantic Charter was directed not against the people who were striving for global supremacy but against the USSR.

Eden started to dispute this inference resolutely, arguing that the question of Soviet frontiers was in no sense out of keeping with the Atlantic Charter. In view of the points he had already made, however, Eden simply did not have the power to recognise the Soviet western frontier immediately. This only requires time, a measure of postponement.

Comrade Stalin remarked that when Britain was giving her promises to America we were not yet allies. . . .

Comrade Molotov expressed surprise at Eden's persistent defence of his position. We are talking about common military goals, common struggle, but in one of the most important military goals, our western frontier, we cannot derive support from Great Britain. Is this really normal?

11.3 The Allies Announce the Formation of the Grand Alliance and Declare Their War Aims: The Declaration by the United Nations[3]

On January 1, 1942, the Allied powers publicly announced in the Declaration by the United Nations reproduced here the formation of what became known as the Grand Alliance. Note its terms and its connection to the Atlantic Charter. Note also the official name of the alliance, which became the name of the new postwar international organization as well.

January 1, 1942

A Joint Declaration by the United States of America, the United Kingdom of Great Britain and Northern Ireland, the Union of Soviet Socialist Republics, China, Australia, Belgium, Canada, Costa Rica, Cuba, Czechoslovakia, Dominican Republic, El Salvador, Greece, Guatemala, Haiti, Honduras, India, Luxembourg, Netherlands, New Zealand, Nicaragua, Norway, Panama, Poland, South Africa, Yugoslavia

The Governments signatory hereto,

Having subscribed to a common program of purposes and principles embodied in the Joint Declaration of the President of the United States of America and the Prime Minister of Great Britain dated August 14, 1941, known as the Atlantic Charter,

Being convinced that complete victory over their enemies is essential to defend life, liberty, independence and religious freedom, and to preserve human rights and justice in their own lands as well as in other lands, and that they are now engaged in a common struggle against savage and brutal forces seeking to subjugate the world,

Declare:

(1) Each Government pledges itself to employ its full resources, military or economic, against those members of the Tripartite Pact and its adherents with which such government is at war.

---

3. From U.S. Department of State, *Foreign Relations of the United States: The Conferences at Washington, 1941–1942 and Casablanca, 1943* (Washington, DC: U.S. Government Printing Office, 1968), 375.

(2) Each Government pledges itself to cooperate with the Governments signatory hereto and not to make a separate armistice or peace with the enemies.

The foregoing declaration may be adhered to by other nations which are, or which may be, rendering material assistance and contributions in the struggle for victory over Hitlerism.

11.4 President Roosevelt Enunciates the Unconditional Surrender Policy, 1943[4]

Rather than accede to any territorial agreements while the war was in progress, Roosevelt, during a January 24, 1943, press conference at the end of his meeting with Churchill in Casablanca, enunciated unconditional surrender as Allied policy. Note in particular his definition in the last sentence of what this policy meant.

Casablanca, January 24, 1943

. . . I think we have all had it in our hearts and heads before, but I don't think that it has ever been put down on paper by the Prime Minister and myself, and that is the determination that peace can come to the world only by the total elimination of German and Japanese war power.

Some of you Britishers know the old story—we had a General called U. S. Grant. His name was Ulysses Simpson Grant, but in my, and the Prime Minister's, early days he was called "Unconditional Surrender" Grant. The elimination of German, Japanese, and Italian war power means the unconditional surrender by Germany, Italy, and Japan. That means a reasonable assurance of future world peace. It does not mean the destruction of the population of Germany, Italy, or Japan, but it does mean the destruction of the philosophies in those countries which are based on conquest and the subjugation of other people.

4. From U.S. Department of State, *Foreign Relations of the United States: The Conferences at Washington, 1941–1942, and Casablanca, 1943* (Washington, DC: U.S. Government Printing Office, 1968), 726–27.

11.5 The Allies Agree on Postwar Policies: The Moscow Declaration on General Security and the Cairo Declaration, 1943[5]

Reached at the Anglo-Soviet-American Foreign Ministers' Conference held in Moscow in October 1943, the Declaration on General Security reproduced here was the first formal Allied agreement on postwar policies.

While this Moscow conference dealt primarily with Germany, the ensuing November meeting of Churchill and Roosevelt with Chiang Kai-shek in Cairo dealt primarily with the Far East and resulted in the Cairo Declaration, also reproduced here. How do these public declarations relate to previous documents in this chapter?

The Governments of the United States of America, the United Kingdom, the Soviet Union, and China:

united in the determination, in accordance with the Declaration by the United Nations of January 1, 1942, and subsequent declarations, to continue hostilities against those Axis powers with which they respectively are at war until such powers have laid down their arms on the basis of unconditional surrender;

conscious of their responsibility to secure the liberation of themselves and the peoples allied with them from the menace of aggression; recognizing the necessity of ensuring a rapid and orderly transition from war to peace and of establishing and maintaining international peace and security with the least diversion of the world's human and economic resources for armaments; jointly declare:

1. That their united action, pledged for the prosecution of the war against their respective enemies, will be continued for the organization and maintenance of peace and security.

2. That those of them at war with a common enemy will act together in all matters relating to the surrender and disarmament of that enemy.

3. That they will take all measures deemed by them to be necessary to provide against any violation of the terms imposed upon the enemy.

4. That they recognize the necessity of establishing at the earliest practicable date a general international organization, based on the principle of the sovereign equality of all peace-loving states, and open to membership

---

5. From U.S. Department of State, *Foreign Relations of the United States, 1943*, vol. 1 (Washington, DC: U.S. Government Printing Office, 1963), 755–56; and *The Conferences at Cairo and Tehran, 1943* (Washington, DC: U.S. Government Printing Office, 1961), 448–49.

by all such states, large and small, for the maintenance of international peace and security.

5. That for the purpose of maintaining international peace and security pending the re-establishment of law and order and the inauguration of a system of general security, they will consult with one another and as occasion requires with other members of the United Nations with a view to joint action on behalf of the community of nations.

6. That after the termination of hostilities they will not employ their military forces within the territories of other states except for the purposes envisaged in this declaration and after joint consultation.

7. That they will confer and co-operate with one another and with other members of the United Nations to bring about a practicable general agreement with respect to the regulation of armaments in the post-war period.

The Cairo Declaration, 1943

[. . .]

Press Communiqué

President Roosevelt, Generalissimo Chiang Kai-Shek and Prime Minister Churchill, together with their respective military and diplomatic advisers, have completed a conference in North Africa. The following general statement was issued:

"The several military missions have agreed upon future military operations against Japan. The three great Allies expressed their resolve to bring unrelenting pressure against their brutal enemies by sea, land, and air. This pressure is already rising.

"The three great Allies are fighting this war to restrain and punish the aggression of Japan. They covet no gain for themselves and have no thought of territorial expansion. It is their purpose that Japan shall be stripped of all the islands in the Pacific which she has seized or occupied since the beginning of the first World War in 1914, and that all the territories Japan has stolen from the Chinese, such as Manchuria, Formosa, and the Pescadores, shall be restored to the Republic of China. Japan will also be expelled from all other territories which she has taken by violence and greed. The aforesaid three great powers, mindful of the enslavement of the people of Korea, are determined that in due course Korea shall become free and independent.

"With these objects in view the three Allies, in harmony with those of the United Nations at war with Japan, will continue to persevere in the serious and prolonged operations necessary to procure the unconditional surrender of Japan."

11.6 President Roosevelt Informs His Allies of His Postwar Plans, 1942 and 1943[6]

Roosevelt expressed more detailed views about the postwar world during his May–June 1942 conversations with visiting Soviet Foreign Minister Vyacheslav Molotov in Washington and again during his November 1943 conversations with Churchill and Stalin at the Tehran Conference. To what extent did his 1942 views change by late 1943 and to what extent did they remain the same? To what extent did Churchill and Stalin agree or disagree with the president?

May 29, 1942

While serving cocktails, the President discussed at length certain basic considerations on post-war organization. Mr. Churchill (he said) had expressed some idea of reestablishing a post-war international organization which was in effect a revived League of Nations. The President had given Mr. Churchill his own opinion that such an organization would be impractical, because too many nations would be involved. The President conceived it the duty of the four major United Nations (Britain, U.S., U.S.S.R., and China, provided the last achieves a unified central government, opposite which there was still a question-mark) to act as the policemen of the world. The first step was general disarmament. But the four major nations would maintain sufficient armed forces to impose peace, together with inspection privileges which would guard against the sort of clandestine rearmament in which Germany had notoriously engaged during the pre-war years. If any nation menaced the peace, it could be blockaded and then if still recalcitrant, bombed. The President added that which concerned him was the establishment of a peace which would last 25 years, at least the lifetime of the present generation. He and Mr. Stalin were over 60, Mr. Molotov 53; his aim was thus peace in our time. He thought that all other nations save the

---

6. From U.S. Department of State, *Foreign Relations of the United States, 1942*, vol. 3 (Washington, DC: U.S. Government Printing Office, 1961), 568–69; and U.S. Department of State, *Foreign Relations of the United States: The Conference at Cairo and Tehran, 1943* (Washington, DC: U.S. Government Printing Office, 1961), 509–11, 530–32.

Big Four should be disarmed (Germany, Japan, France, Spain, Belgium, Netherlands, Scandinavia, Turkey, Rumania, Hungary, Poland, Czechoslovakia, etc.).

Mr. Molotov remarked that this might be a bitter blow to the prestige of Poland and Turkey. "The Turks," he added, "are an extremely pretentious people." He also inquired about the reestablishment of France as a great power. The President replied that might perhaps be possible within 10 or 20 years. He added that other nations might eventually be accepted progressively at various times among the guarantors of peace whenever the original guarantors were satisfied of their reliability. This might be peace by dictation, but his hope was that it might be so administered that the peoples of the previous aggressor nations might eventually come to see that they have infinitely more to gain from permanent peace than from periodically recurrent wars. . . .

November 28, 1943

Marshal Stalin then raised the question of the future of France. He described in considerable length the reasons why, in his opinion, France deserved no considerate treatment from the Allies and, above all, had no right to retain her former empire. He said that the entire French ruling class was rotten to the core and had delivered over France to the Germans and that, in fact, France was now actively helping our enemies. He therefore felt that it would be not only unjust but dangerous to leave in French hands any important strategic points after the war.

The President replied that he in part agreed with Marshal Stalin. That was why this afternoon he had said to Marshal Stalin that it was necessary to eliminate in the future government of France anybody over forty years old and particularly anybody who had formed part of the French Government. He mentioned specifically the question of New Caledonia and Dakar, the first of which he said represented a threat to Australia and New Zealand and, therefore, should be placed under the trusteeship of the United Nations. In regard to Dakar, the President said he was speaking for twenty-one American nations when he said that Dakar in unsure hands was a direct threat to the Americas.

Mr. Churchill at this point intervened to say that Great Britain did not desire and did not expect to acquire any additional territory out of this war, but since the four great victorious nations—the United States, the Soviet Union, Great Britain, and China—will be responsible for the future peace of the world, it was obviously necessary that certain strategic points throughout the world should be under the [*their?*] control. . . .

The conversation then turned to the question of the treatment to be accorded Nazi Germany.

The President said that, in his opinion, it was very important not to leave in the German mind the concept of the Reich and that the very word should be stricken from the language.

Marshal Stalin replied that it was not enough to eliminate the word, but the very Reich itself must be rendered impotent ever again to plunge the world into war. He said that unless the victorious Allies retained in their hands the strategic position necessary to prevent any recrudescence of German militarism, they would have failed in their duty.

In the detailed discussion between the President, Marshal Stalin, and Churchill that followed, Marshal Stalin took the lead, constantly emphasizing that the measures for the control of Germany and her disarmament were insufficient to prevent the rebirth of German militarism and appeared to favor even stronger measures. He, however, did not specify what he actually had in mind except that he appeared to favor the dismemberment of Germany.

Marshal Stalin particularly mentioned that Poland should extend to the Oder and stated definitely that the Russians would help the Poles to obtain a frontier on the Oder.

The President then said he would be interested in the question of assuring the approaches to the Baltic Sea and had in mind some form of trusteeship with perhaps an international state in the vicinity of the Kiel Canal to insure free navigation in both directions through the approaches. Due to some error of the Soviet translator Marshal Stalin apparently thought that the President was referring to the question of the Baltic States. On the basis of this understanding, he replied categorically that the Baltic States had by an expression of the will of the people voted to join the Soviet Union and that this question was not therefore one for discussion. Following the clearing up of the misapprehension, he, however, expressed himself favorably in regard to the question of insuring free navigation to and from the Baltic Sea.

The President, returning to the question of certain outlying possessions, said he was interested in the possibility of a sovereignty fashioned in a collective body such as the United Nations; a concept which had never been developed in past history. . . .

November 29, 1943

The President then said the question of a post-war organization to preserve peace had not been fully explained and dealt with and he would like to discuss with the Marshal the prospect of some organization based on the United Nations.

The President then outlined the following general plan:

(1) There would be a large organization composed of some 35 members of the United Nations which would meet periodically at different places, discuss and make recommendations to a smaller body.

Marshal Stalin inquired whether this organization was to be world-wide or European, to which the President replied, world-wide.

The President continued that there would be set up an executive committee composed of the Soviet Union, the United States, United Kingdom, and China, together with two additional European states, one South American, one Near East, one Far Eastern country, and one British Dominion. He mentioned that Mr. Churchill did not like this proposal for the reason that the British Empire only had two votes. This Executive Committee would deal with all non-military questions such as agriculture, food, health, and economic questions, as well as the setting up of an International Committee. This Committee would likewise meet in various places.

Marshal Stalin inquired whether this body would have the right to make decisions binding on the nations of the world.

The President replied, yes and no. It could make recommendations for settling disputes with the hope that the nations concerned would be guided thereby, but that, for example, he did not believe the Congress of the United States would accept as binding a decision of such a body. The President then turned to the third organization which he termed "The Four Policemen," namely, the Soviet Union, United States, Great Britain, and China. This organization would have the power to deal immediately with any threat to the peace and any sudden emergency which requires this action. He went on to say that in 1935, when Italy attacked Ethiopia, the only machinery in existence was the League of Nations. He personally had begged France to close the Suez Canal, but they instead referred it to the League which disputed the question and in the end did nothing. The result was that the Italian Armies went through the Suez Canal and destroyed Ethiopia. The President pointed out that had the machinery of the Four Policemen, which he had in mind, been in existence, it would have been possible to close the Suez Canal. The President then summarized briefly the idea that he had in mind. . . .

. . . The President added that he saw two methods of dealing with possible threats to the peace. In one case if the threat arose from a revolution or developments in a small country, it might be possible to apply the quarantine method, closing the frontiers of the countries in question and imposing embargoes. In the second case, if the threat was more serious, the four powers, acting as policemen, would send an ultimatum to the nation in question and if refused, [it] would result in the immediate bombardment and possible invasion of that country.

11.7 The Allies Agree to a Postwar International Organization: The Dumbarton Oaks Agreements, 1944[7]

From late August to early October of 1944, representatives of the major Allied powers met at the Dumbarton Oaks estate in Washington and reached agreement, reproduced here, on the formation of the new postwar international organization that would become the United Nations in mid-1945. Compare the contents of this agreement with the more general views expressed in the preceding 1941–1943 documents reproduced in this chapter.

Proposals for the Establishment of a General International Organization

There should be established an international organization under the title of The United Nations, the Charter of which should contain provisions necessary to give effect to the proposals which follow.

Chapter I.—Purposes

The purposes of the Organization should be:

1. To maintain international peace and security; and to that end to take effective collective measures for the prevention and removal of threats to the peace and the suppression of acts of aggression or other breaches of the peace, and to bring about by peaceful means adjustment or settlement of international disputes which may lead to a breach of the peace;

2. To develop friendly relations among nations and to take other appropriate measures to strengthen universal peace;

3. To achieve international cooperation in the solution of international economic, social, and other humanitarian problems; and

4. To afford a center for harmonizing the actions of nations in the achievements of these common ends.

---

7. From U.S. Department of State, *Foreign Relations of the United States, 1944*, vol. 1 (Washington, DC: U.S. Government Printing Office, 1966), 890–91.

Chapter II.—Principles

In pursuit of the purpose mentioned in Chapter I the Organization and its members should act in accordance with the following principles:

1. The Organization is based on the principle of the sovereign equality of all peace-loving states.

2. All members of the Organization undertake, in order to ensure to all of them the rights and benefits resulting from membership in the Organization, to fulfill the obligations assumed by them in accordance with the Charter.

3. All members of the Organization shall settle their disputes by peaceful means in such a manner that international peace and security are not endangered.

4. All members of the Organization shall refrain in their international relations from the threat or use of force in any manner inconsistent with the purposes of the Organization.

5. All members of the Organization shall give every assistance to the Organization in any action undertaken by it in accordance with the provisions of the Charter.

6. All members of the Organization shall refrain from giving assistance to any state against which preventative or enforcement action is being undertaken by the Organization.

The Organization should ensure that states not members of the Organization act in accordance with these principles so far as may be necessary for the maintenance of international peace and security.

Chapter III.—Membership

1. Membership of the Organization should be open to all peace-loving states.

Chapter IV.—Principal Organs

1. The Organization should have as its principal organs:
   a. A General Assembly;
   b. A Security Council;
   c. An international court of justice; and
   d. A Secretariat.

2. The Organization should have such subsidiary agencies as may be found necessary.

11.8 Churchill and Stalin Divide Eastern Europe, 1944[8]

In October of 1944, Churchill flew to Moscow to discuss with Stalin the future of Eastern Europe. Reproduced here is Churchill's version of one of these meetings, during which they reached agreement on future spheres of influence in the Balkans.

The moment was apt for business, so I [Churchill] said, "Let us settle about our affairs in the Balkans. Your armies are in Rumania and Bulgaria. We have interests, missions, and agents there. Don't let us get at cross-purposes in small ways. So far as Britain and Russia are concerned, how would it do for you to have ninety per cent predominance in Rumania, for us to have ninety per cent of the say in Greece, and go fifty-fifty about Yugoslavia?" While this was being translated I wrote out on a half-sheet of paper:

Rumania	
Russia	90%
The others	10%
Greece	
Great Britain (in accord with U.S.A.)	90%
Russia	10%
Yugoslavia	50–50%
Hungary	50–50%
Bulgaria	
Russia	75%
The others	25%

I pushed this across to Stalin, who had by then heard the translation. There was a slight pause. Then he took his blue pencil and made a large tick upon it, and passed it back to us. It was all settled in no more time than it takes to set down.

Of course, we had long and anxiously considered our point, and were only dealing with immediate war-time arrangements. All larger questions were reserved on both sides for what we then hoped would be a peace table when the war was won.

After this there was a long silence. The pencilled paper lay in the centre of the table. At length I said, "Might it not be thought rather cynical if it seemed

---

8. From Winston S. Churchill, *The Second World War*, vol. 6, *Triumph and Tragedy* (Boston: Houghton Mifflin, 1953), 227–28.

we had disposed of these issues, so fateful to millions of people, in such an offhand manner? Let us burn the paper." "No, you keep it," said Stalin.

11.9 The Allies Reach Postwar Agreements at the Yalta Conference, 1945[9]

In February of 1945 at Yalta on the Crimean Peninsula of the Soviet Union, Churchill, Roosevelt, and Stalin met for a second time and reached a series of agreements regarding the postwar world as well as future military operations against Germany and Japan. These agreements—the most important of which are reproduced here—became quite controversial during the Cold War, when Roosevelt's critics accused him of having naïvely appeased Stalin to the detriment of American interests. Do you think these criticisms fair given the military realities at time? To what extent did these agreements reflect the views and desires of each Allied leader?

The Yalta Protocol of Proceedings, 1945

I. World Organization

It was decided:

1. That a United Nations Conference on the proposed world organization should be summoned for Wednesday, 25th April, 1945, and should be held in the United States of America.

2. The Nations to be invited to this Conference should be:

    a. the United Nations as they existed on the 8th February, 1945; and

    b. such of the Associated Nations as have declared war on the common enemy by 1st March, 1945. (For this purpose the term "Associated Nations" was meant the eight Associated Nations and Turkey.) When the Conference on World Organization is held, the delegates of the United Kingdom and United States of America will support a proposal to admit to original membership two Soviet Socialist Republics, i.e., the Ukraine and White Russia.

3. That the United States Government on behalf of the Three Powers should consult the Government of China and the French Provisional

---

9. From U.S. Department of State, *Foreign Relations of the United States: The Conferences at Malta and Yalta, 1945* (Washington, DC: U.S. Government Printing Office, 1955), 975–82, 984.

Government in regard to decisions taken at the present Conference concerning the proposed World Organization.

4. That the text of the invitation to be issued to all nations which would take part in the United Nations Conference should be as follows:

Invitation

The Government of the United States of America, on behalf of itself and of the Governments of the United Kingdom, the Union of Soviet Socialist Republics, and the Republic of China and the Provisional Government of the French Republic, invite the Government of _____ to send representatives to a Conference of the United Nations to be held on 25th April, 1945, or soon thereafter, at San Francisco in the United States of America to prepare a Charter for a General International Organization for the maintenance of international peace and security.

The above named governments suggest that the Conference consider as affording a basis for such a Charter the Proposals for the Establishment of a General International Organization, which were made public last October as a result of the Dumbarton Oaks Conference, and which have now been supplemented by the following provisions for Section C of Chapter VI:

C. Voting
1. Each member of the Security Council should have one vote.
2. Decisions of the Security Council on procedural matters should be made by an affirmative vote of seven members.
3. Decisions of the Security Council on all other matters should be made by an affirmative vote of seven members including the concurring votes of the permanent members; provided that, in decisions under Chapter VIII, Section A, and under the second sentence of paragraph 1 of Chapter VIII, Section C, a party to a dispute should abstain from voting.

Further information as to arrangements will be transmitted subsequently.

In the event that the Government of _____ desires in advance of the Conference to present views or comments concerning the proposals, the Government of the United States of America will be pleased to transmit such views and comments to the other participating Governments.

Territorial Trusteeship. It was agreed that the five Nations which will have permanent seats on the Security Council should consult each other prior to the United Nations Conference on the question of territorial trusteeship.

The acceptance of this recommendation is subject to its being made clear that territorial trusteeship will only apply to (a) existing mandates of the League of Nations; (b) territories detached from the enemy as a result of the present war; (c) any other territory which might voluntarily be placed under trusteeship; and (d) no discussion of actual territories is contemplated at the forthcoming United Nations Conference or in the preliminary consultations, and it will be a matter for subsequent agreement which territories within the above categories will be placed under trusteeship.

II. Declaration on Liberated Europe

The following declaration has been approved:

> The Premier of the Union of Soviet Socialist Republics, the Prime Minister of the United Kingdom, and the President of the United States of America have consulted with each other in the common interests of the peoples of their countries and those of liberated Europe. They jointly declare their mutual agreement to concert during the temporary period of instability in liberated Europe the policies of their three governments in assisting the peoples of the former Axis satellite states of Europe to solve by democratic means their pressing political and economic problems.
>
> The establishment of order in Europe and the rebuilding of national economic life must be achieved by processes which will enable the liberated peoples to destroy the last vestiges of Nazism and Fascism and to create democratic institutions of their own choice. This is a principle of the Atlantic Charter—the right of all peoples to choose the form of government under which they will live—the restoration of sovereign rights and self-government to those peoples who have been forcibly deprived of them by the aggressor nations.
>
> To foster the conditions in which the liberated peoples may exercise these rights, the three governments will jointly assist the people in any European liberated state or former Axis satellite state in Europe where in their judgment conditions require (a) to establish conditions of internal peace; (b) to carry out emergency measure for the relief of distressed peoples; (c) to form interim governmental authorities broadly representative of all democratic elements in the population and pledged to the earliest possible establishment through free elections of governments responsible to the will of the people; and (d) to facilitate where necessary the holding of such elections.
>
> The three governments will consult the other United Nations and provisional authorities or other governments in Europe when matters of direct interest to them are under consideration.
>
> When, in the opinion of the three governments, conditions in any European liberated state or any former Axis satellite state in Europe make such action necessary, they will immediately consult together on the measures necessary to discharge the joint responsibilities set forth in this declaration.

By this declaration we reaffirm our faith in the principles of the Atlantic Charter, our pledges in the Declaration by the United Nations, and our determination to build in cooperation with other peace-loving nations world order under law, dedicated to peace, security, freedom, and general well-being of all mankind.

In issuing this declaration, the Three Powers express the hope that the Provisional Government of the French Republic may be associated with them in the procedure suggested.

III. Dismemberment of Germany

It was agreed that Article 12 (a) of the Surrender Terms for Germany should be amended as follows:

The United Kingdom, the United States of America, and the Union of Soviet Socialist Republics shall possess supreme authority with respect to Germany. In the exercise of such authority they will take such steps, including the complete disarmament, demilitarization, and dismemberment of Germany as they deem requisite for future peace and security. . . .

IV. Zone of Occupation for the French and Control Council for Germany

It was agreed that a zone in Germany, to be occupied by the French Forces, should be allocated to France. This zone would be formed out of the British and American zones and its extent would be settled by the British and Americans in consultation with the French Provisional Government.

It was also agreed that the French Provisional Government should be invited to become a member of the Allied Control Council of Germany.

V. Reparation

The heads of the three governments agreed as follows:

1. Germany must pay in kind for the losses caused by her to the Allied nations in the course of the war. Reparations are to be received in the first instance by those countries which have borne the main burden of the war, have suffered the heaviest losses, and have organized victory over the enemy.

2. Reparation in kind to be exacted from Germany in three following forms:

   a. Removals within 2 years from the surrender of Germany or the cessation of organized resistance from the national wealth of Germany located on the territory of Germany herself as well as outside her territory (equipment, machine-tools, ships, rolling stock, German investments abroad, shared of industrial, transport, and other enterprises in Germany, etc.), these removals to be carried out chiefly for purpose of destroying the war potential of Germany.

b. Annual deliveries of goods from current production for a period to be fixed.

c. Use of German labor.

3. For the working out on the above principles of a detailed plan for exaction of reparation from Germany, an Allied Reparation Commission will be set up in Moscow. It will consist of three representatives—one from the Union of Soviet Socialist Republics, one from the United Kingdom, and one from the United States of America.

4. With regard to the fixing of the total sum of the reparation as well as the distribution of it among the countries which suffered from the German aggression the Soviet and American delegations agreed as follows:

> The Moscow Reparation Commission should take in its initial studies as a basis for discussion the suggestion of the Soviet Government that the total sum of the reparation in accordance with the points (a) and (b) of the paragraph 2 should be 20 billion dollars and that 50% of it should go to the Union of Soviet Socialist Republics.

The British delegation was of the opinion that pending consideration of the reparation question by the Moscow Reparation Commission no figures of reparation should be mentioned.

The above Soviet-American proposal has been passed to the Moscow Reparation Commission as one of the proposals to be considered by the Commission.

VI. Major War Criminals

The Conference agreed that the question of the major war criminals should be the subject of enquiry by the three Foreign Secretaries for report in due course after the close of the Conference.

VII. Poland

The following Declaration on Poland was agreed by the Conference:

> A new situation has been created in Poland as a result of her complete liberation by the Red Army. This calls for the establishment of a Polish

Provisional Government which can be more broadly based than was possible before the recent liberation of [the] Western part of Poland. The Provisional Government which is now functioning in Poland should therefore be reorganized on a broader democratic basis with the inclusion of democratic leaders from Poland itself and from Poles abroad. This new Government should then be called the Polish Provisional Government of National Unity.

M. Molotov, Mr. Harriman, and Sir A. Clark Kerr are authorized as a commission to consult in the first instance in Moscow with members of the present Provisional Government and with other Polish democratic leaders from within Poland and from abroad, with a view to the reorganization of the present Government along the above lines. This Polish Provisional Government of National Unity shall be pledged to the holding of free and unfettered elections as soon as possible on the basis of universal suffrage and secret ballot. In these elections all democratic and anti-Nazi parties shall have the right to take part and to put forward candidates.

When a Polish Provisional Government of National Unity has been properly formed in conformity with the above, the Government of the U.S.S.R., which now maintains diplomatic relations with the present Provisional Government of Poland, and the Government of the United Kingdom and the Government of the United States of America will establish diplomatic relations with the new Polish Provisional Government of National Unity, and will exchange Ambassadors by whose reports the respective Governments will be kept informed about the situation in Poland.

The three Heads of Government consider that the Eastern frontier of Poland should follow the Curzon Line with digressions from it in some regions of five to eight kilometers in favor of Poland. They recognize that Poland must receive substantial accession of territory in the North and West. They feel that the opinion of the new Polish Provisional Government of National Unity should be sought in due course on the extent of these accessions and that the final delimitation of the Western frontier of Poland should therefore await the Peace Conference.

[Following this declaration, but omitted here for reasons of space, are brief statements on Yugoslavia, the Italo-Yugoslav frontier and Italo-Austrian frontier, Yugoslav-Bulgarian relations, Southeastern Europe, Iran, meetings of the three foreign secretaries, and the Montreux Convention and the Straits.]

The Yalta Agreement on Soviet Entry into the War Against Japan, 1945

The leaders of the three Great Powers—the Soviet Union, the United States of America, and Great Britain—have agreed that in two or three months after Germany has surrendered and the war in Europe has terminated the Soviet Union shall enter into the war against Japan on the side of the Allies on condition that:

1. The *status quo* in Outer-Mongolia (The Mongolian People's Republic) shall be preserved;

2. The former rights of Russia violated by the treacherous attack of Japan in 1904 shall be restored, viz:

> a. the southern part of Sakhalin as well as all the islands adjacent to it shall be returned to the Soviet Union,
>
> b. the commercial port of Dairen shall be internationalized, the preeminent interests of the Soviet Union in this port being safeguarded and the lease of Port Arthur as a naval base of the USSR restored,
>
> c. the Chinese-Eastern Railroad and the South-Manchurian Railroad which provides an outlet to Dairen shall be jointly operated by the establishment of a joint Soviet-Chinese company; it being understood that the preeminent interests of the Soviet Union shall be safeguarded and that China shall retain full sovereignty in Manchuria;

3. The Kurile islands shall be handed over to the Soviet Union.

It is understood, that the agreement concerning Outer-Mongolia and the ports and railroads referred to above will require concurrence of Generalissimo Chiang Kai-shek. The President will take measures in order to obtain this concurrence on advice from Marshal Stalin.

The Heads of the three Great Powers have agreed that these claims of the Soviet Union shall be unquestionably fulfilled after Japan has been defeated.

For its part the Soviet Union expresses its readiness to conclude with the National Government of China a Pact of friendship and alliance between the USSR and China in order to render assistance to China with its armed forces for the purpose of liberating China from the Japanese yoke.

11.10 President Roosevelt Sends Messages to Stalin and Churchill Just before His Death, 1945[10]

Roosevelt died on April 12, 1945, just two months after the Yalta Conference. During this time period serious Allied conflict erupted, as Britain and the United States accused the Soviet Union of violating the Yalta Accords in Poland and the rest of Eastern Europe, while Stalin accused his Western allies of trying to negotiate a separate peace with the Germans in northern Italy. Reproduced here are two of Roosevelt's

---

10. From U.S. Department of State, *Foreign Relations of the United States, 1945* (Washington, DC: U.S. Government Printing Office, 1967–1968), 3:745–46; 5:210.

final messages to Churchill and Stalin that clearly illustrate the difficulty in trying to determine how the president would have behaved toward his wartime partners had he lived.

Roosevelt's Anger with Stalin, [April 4] 1945

I have received with astonishment your message of April 3 containing an allegation that arrangements which were made between Field Marshals [Harold] Alexander and [Albert] Kesselring at Berne [Switzerland] "permitted the Anglo-American troops to advance to the East and the Anglo-Americans promised in return to ease for the Germans the peace terms."

In my previous messages to you in regard to the attempts made in Berne to arrange a conference to discuss a surrender of the German army in Italy I have told you that: (1) No negotiations were held in Berne, (2) The meeting had no political implications whatever, (3) In any surrender of the enemy army in Italy there should be no violation of our agreed principle of unconditional surrender, (4) Soviet officers would be welcomed at any meeting that might be arranged to discuss surrender.

For the advantage of our common war effort against Germany, which today gives excellent promise of an early success in a disintegration of the German armies, I must continue to assume that you have the same high confidence in my truthfulness and reliability that I have always had in yours.

I have also a full appreciation of the effect your gallant army has had in making possible a crossing of the Rhine by the forces under General [Dwight D.] Eisenhower and the effect that your forces will have hereafter on the eventual collapse of the German resistance to our combined attacks.

I have complete confidence in General Eisenhower and know that he certainly would inform me before entering into any agreement with the Germans. He is instructed to demand and will demand unconditional surrender of enemy troops that may be defeated on his front. Our advances on the Western Front are due to military action. Their speed has been attributable mainly to the terrific impact of our air power resulting in destruction of German communications, and to the fact that Eisenhower was able to cripple the bulk of the German forces on the Western Front while they were still west of the Rhine.

I am certain that there were no negotiations in Berne at any time and I feel that your information to that effect must have come from German sources which have made persistent efforts to create dissension between us in order to escape in some measure responsibility for their war crimes. If that was [General Karl] Wolff's purpose in Berne, your message proves that he has had some success.

With a confidence in your belief in my personal reliability and in my determination to bring about, together with you, an unconditional surrender of the Nazis, it is astonishing that a belief seems to have reached the Soviet Government that I have entered into an agreement with the enemy without first obtaining your full agreement.

Finally I would say this, it would be one of the great tragedies of history if at the very moment of the victory, now within our grasp, such distrust, such lack of faith should prejudice the entire undertaking after the colossal losses of life, material and treasure involved.

Frankly I cannot avoid a feeling of bitter resentment toward your informers, whoever they are, for such vile misrepresentations of my actions or those of my trusted subordinates.

Roosevelt's Last Letter to Churchill, [April 11] 1945

I would minimize the general Soviet problem as much as possible because these problems, in one form or another, seem to arise every day and most of them straighten out as in the case of the Berne meeting.

We must be firm, however, and our course thus far is correct.

Chapter 12

The Atomic Bomb and the End of World War II

The German surrender in May of 1945 left the Japanese Empire alone in the struggle with the United States. By this time, Japan was in a hopeless position, and unlikely to win the war. Nevertheless, Japanese forces and Japanese civilians kept fighting, even going so far as to embrace kamikaze and other suicide tactics.

The campaigns for the islands of Iwo Jima and Okinawa seemed to confirm American fears that the Japanese would fight to the death. The Battle of Iwo Jima lasted for five weeks and resulted in 26,000 American casualties. The struggle for Okinawa was even more grueling. Capturing the small island took more than two months and cost the lives of at least 100,000 Japanese troops and 12,500 American ones. The final battles of the Pacific War convinced many Americans—ordinary citizens and political and military leaders alike—that the Japanese were unlikely to surrender any time soon.

The military and diplomatic situation changed dramatically with the successful explosion of an atomic bomb in mid-July 1945. The United States had been working on an atomic bomb since 1939 (see Chapter 7). In 1942, President Roosevelt ordered the atomic program reorganized, expanded, and handed over to the War Department. The Manhattan Project, as it was known, was a massive undertaking. The success of the Trinity test on July 16 held out the promise of a quick end to the war in the Pacific.

Yet answering the scientific and technical question of how to *build* an atomic bomb opened up military, diplomatic, and moral questions about how to *use* it. Many of the scientists who had devoted every waking hour for more than three years to solving the problem of the bomb suddenly began to consider the implications of their creation. One June 1945 report, issued by a group of Manhattan Project scientists and led by James Franck, warned presciently of a nuclear arms race in the postwar period and urged the United States to conduct a noncombat demonstration of the new weapon before using it against Japanese targets. The scientific community was hardly united on this issue, however. The Interim Committee, a body that included policy makers and industrial leaders, as well as scientists, rejected this Franck Committee recommendation and instead endorsed the "direct military use" of the new bomb.

While American policy makers may have disagreed over how to use the new weapon, there was never any doubt that it would and should be used. Secretary Stimson later recalled: "At no time, from 1941 to 1945, did I ever hear it suggested . . . that atomic energy should not be used in the war." President Truman and his advisers likely saw the new weapon as a way to end the war in the Pacific on terms favorable to the United States. The decision to use the new weapon against Japan happened quickly. On July 26, the United States issued the Potsdam Declaration reiterating the demand that Japan submit to an unconditional surrender and warned that if it did not, it would face "prompt and utter destruction." Eleven days later, on August 6, the United States dropped an atomic bomb on the city of Hiroshima, destroying 20 percent of the city's buildings and killing some 100,000 people within hours. President Truman, then on his way home from the Potsdam Conference, told the American people about the bomb and about the effort to build it: "We have spent more than two billion dollars on the greatest scientific gamble in history, and we have won."

Two days later, on August 8, the Soviet Union declared war on Japan and invaded Manchuria. On the next day, August 9, the United States dropped a second atomic bomb on Nagasaki, killing another 75,000 Japanese citizens and wounding 50,000 more. The bombs eventually led to some 130,000 additional deaths from injury and radiation poisoning.

The Japanese Empire surrendered on August 14, five days after the attack on Nagasaki. Most Americans agreed with President Truman's assessment that the bomb had been the "greatest thing in history." Public opinion polls showed widespread support for the use of the bomb—a support rooted in the belief that the bombs had ended the war and spared countless American lives.

Historians, however, have been less sanguine about the bomb and its destruction of two Japanese cities. Indeed, this question has generated considerable disagreement and antipathy among professional historians. For much of the immediate postwar period, historians tended to accept U.S. officials' assurances that the bomb had ended the war and had saved hundreds of thousands of American, Japanese, and Chinese lives. These traditionalists tended to see the bomb as the only alternative to a long and costly invasion of Japan. In the 1960s, a new generation of historians began to reject these assumptions. Some revisionists argued that the bomb had not been necessary to end the war and that the Empire of Japan was on the verge of surrender well before Hiroshima. Others claimed that the Truman administration later exaggerated anticipated casualty figures to defend its actions. Perhaps most damning were revisionist interpretations that argued the bomb had been dropped not to secure American victory against Japan, for which it was not needed, but rather to preclude Soviet entry into the war and acquisition of territory as well as to intimidate Moscow and alter its behavior in Eastern Europe with a demonstration of America's new and awesome power.

It is true that the bomb had diplomatic as well as military implications. The Manhattan Project was so shrouded in secrecy that even Vice President Harry Truman knew nothing of it until he became president after Roosevelt's death in April of 1945. The veil of secrecy applied to international allies as well as enemies. The United States agreed to work with Great Britain to develop a nuclear bomb, but Roosevelt and Churchill ignored warnings that secrecy within the Grand Alliance would lead to a postwar nuclear arms race and decided to keep Stalin in the dark. Thanks to spies inside the Manhattan Project, however, the Soviet leader was all too aware that his allies were building a new super bomb.

The Western Allies' decision to keep atomic secrets from the Soviets soured the relationship with the USSR in the postwar period. Nevertheless, the documentary record does not support the idea that the United States dropped the bomb for the sole purpose of intimidating the Soviets. Rather, American policy makers considered the bomb necessary to end the war quickly, with minimal loss of American lives, and on terms favorable to the United States. Documentary evidence in Japanese and Soviet archives also casts doubt on the revisionists' claim that Japan was prepared to surrender in the summer of 1945.

Yet the traditionalists' assertion that the bomb ended the war and prevented a costly invasion has also come under fire. While the most recent histories agree that the bomb ended the war more quickly than any of the available alternatives would have, these new studies also emphasize the importance of Soviet entry into the Pacific War in the Japanese decision to surrender. These studies thus raise the possibility that the war might have ended before the invasion planned for November 1945. Newer studies have also cast significant doubt on the human cost of such an invasion.

Scholars have also suggested that the same racist dehumanization of the Japanese people that had permitted their internment in the United States made the decision to drop the bomb easier for U.S. policy makers (see Chapter 5, Documents 8 and 9). Others have argued that the earlier embrace of conventional bombing against civilian targets paved the way for the use of nuclear weapons against similar targets. By the last year of the war, the targeting and killing of civilians had become an accepted part of the war, in both the Pacific and European theaters. Allied air campaigns had leveled the German city of Dresden in February of 1945 and Tokyo a month later. All told, the bombing campaigns against these two cities were deadlier than Hiroshima and Nagasaki combined. As historian Gary Hess has concluded, by the end of the war, American officials had become "desensitized to moral considerations. They no longer seemed relevant."

The documents in this chapter raise questions about the use of the bomb and the consequences of that decision. Why did the United States agree to work with Great Britain but not the Soviet Union? What effect might this decision have had on the Grand Alliance? After the bomb had been successfully tested, what options did U.S. policy makers have about its use? Why did they reject alternatives to using the bomb in a combat situation? How did U.S. policy makers understand the consequences of the bomb? What moral questions does the use of atomic power raise? Did the use of the atomic bomb against civilian targets mark a significant departure from earlier practice? Was this truly a historical turning point?

* * * *

12.1 Supreme Court Justice Felix Frankfurter Shares with President Franklin D. Roosevelt Physicist Niels Bohr's Suggestion That the Soviets Be Informed about the Atomic Bomb Project, 1944[1]

Niels Bohr, a Danish-born physicist, fled Denmark in 1943 for Great Britain, where he joined the British nuclear weapons project code-named Tube Alloys. Bohr, whose work on atomic structure and quantum theory had won him the 1922 Nobel Prize in Physics, joined the British mission to the Manhattan Project in 1943. In 1944, Bohr approached Supreme Court Justice Felix Frankfurter with his fear that the decision to keep Stalin in the dark about the atomic project would imperil the wartime alliance and lead to a disastrous postwar arms race between the Soviet Union and the West. In the letter excerpted here Frankfurter relayed these concerns to President Roosevelt. Bohr's warnings fell on deaf ears. By the war's end, the Soviets still had received no official notice of the Manhattan Project.

---

1. From Franklin D. Roosevelt Papers, President's Secretary's Files, Roosevelt Library, Hyde Park, NY; repr. in Michael B. Stoff, Jonathan F. Fanton, and R. Hal Williams, eds., *The Manhattan Project: A Documentary Introduction to the Atomic Age* (New York: McGraw-Hill, 1991), 64–65.

September 8, 1944

Dear Frank:

Here is a letter from my Danish friend [Niels Bohr—letter not reproduced here].

From many long talks with him I gather that there are three solid reasons for believing that knowledge of the pursuit of our project can hardly be kept from Russia: (1) they have very eminent scientists, particularly Peter Kapitza, entirely familiar through past experience with these problems; (2) some leakage, even if not of results and methods, must inevitably have trickled to Russia; (3) Germans have been similarly busy, and knowledge of their endeavors will soon be open to the Russians. Therefore, to open the subject with Russia, without of course making essential disclosures before effective safeguards and sanctions have been secured and assured, would not be giving them anything they do not already—or soon will—substantially have.

In a word, the argument is that appropriate candor would risk very little. Withholding, on the other hand, might have grave consequences. There may be answers to these considerations. I venture to believe, having thought a good deal about it, that in any event these questions are very serious.

My very best wishes for successful days in the tasks immediately ahead.
Affectionately yours,

[Felix Frankfurter, Supreme Court Justice]

12.2 Churchill and President Roosevelt Reject Informing the Soviets, 1944[2]

Roosevelt and Churchill had agreed in 1943 that their two nations would work together to develop an atomic bomb. Their Quebec Agreement of that year also prohibited either nation from using nuclear weapons against the other and required both nations to consent if such weapons were used against a third party or if either wished to share information about the project with a third party. A year later, and only ten days after the Bohr and Frankfurter letters, Roosevelt and Churchill met at the president's home in Hyde Park, New York, after a second conference in Quebec and firmly rejected the Danish

---

2. From U.S. Department of State, *Foreign Relations of the United States: The Conference at Quebec, 1944* (Washington, DC: U.S. Government Printing Office, 1972), 492–93.

physicist's suggestion that Stalin be apprised of the Manhattan Project while agreeing that their own nuclear collaboration should continue after the war had ended.

Aide-Mémoire of Conversation Between the President and the Prime Minister at Hyde Park, September 18, 1944

1. The suggestion that the world should be informed regarding TUBE ALLOYS, with a view to an international agreement regarding its control and use, is not accepted. The matter should continue to be regarded as of the utmost secrecy; but when a "bomb" is finally available, it might perhaps, after mature consideration, be used against the Japanese, who should be warned that this bombardment will be repeated until they surrender.

2. Full collaboration between the United States and the British Government in developing TUBE ALLOYS for military and commercial purposes should continue after the defeat of Japan unless and until terminated by joint agreement.

3. Enquiries should be made regarding the activities of Professor Bohr and steps taken to ensure that he is responsible for no leakage of information, particularly to the Russians.

F[ranklin] D R[oosevelt]   W[inston] S C[hurchill]

12.3 Secretary of War Henry L. Stimson Informs President Harry Truman of the Atomic Bomb Project, April 25, 1945[3]

The Manhattan Project operated under terms of utmost secrecy. Even Harry Truman, who had headed up the Committee to Investigate the National Defense Program before he became vice president, knew nothing about the project. It fell to Secretary of War Henry Stimson to educate Truman about the nuclear bomb project after Roosevelt's death in April of 1945. In the memorandum reprinted here, Stimson predicts that the Manhattan Project will achieve success within four months and raises questions about the wartime use of the new weapon and its postwar regulation. Like Bohr, Stimson worries

---

3. From Stimson Memorandum to Harry Truman, April 25, 1945, Henry Stimson Diary, Manuscripts and Archives, Yale University, available at National Security Archive. http://nsarchive.gwu.edu/NSAEBB/NSAEBB162/3b.pdf.

about the potential for a postwar arms race that would jeopardize "modern civilization." The memorandum therefore recommends the formation of a select committee to make recommendations on these issues.

1. Within four months we shall in all probability have completed the most terrible weapon ever known in human history, one bomb of which could destroy a whole city.

2. Although we have shared its development with the UK, physically the US is at present in the position of controlling the resources with which to construct and use it and no other nation could reach this position for some years.

3. Nevertheless it is practically certain that we could not remain in this position indefinitely.

a. Various segments of its discovery and production are widely known among many scientists in many countries, although few scientists are now acquainted with the whole process which we have developed.

b. Although its construction under present methods requires great scientific and industrial effort and raw materials, which are temporarily mainly within the possession and knowledge of US and UK, it is extremely probable that much easier and cheaper methods of production will be discovered by scientists in the future, together with the use of materials of much wider distribution. As a result, it is extremely probable that the future will make it possible to be constructed by smaller nations or even groups, or at least by a large nation in a much shorter time.

4. As a result, it is indicated that the future may see a time when such a weapon may be constructed in secret and used suddenly and effectively with devastating power by a willful nation or group against an unsuspecting nation or group of much greater size and material power. With its aid even a very powerful unsuspecting nation might be conquered within a very few days by a very much smaller one, although probably the only nation which could enter into production within the next few years is Russia.

5. The world in its present state of moral advancement compared with its technical development would be eventually at the mercy of such a weapon. In other words, modern civilization might be completely destroyed.

6. To approach any world peace organization of any pattern now likely to be considered, without an appreciation by the leaders of our country of the power of this new weapon, would seem to be unrealistic. No system of control heretofore considered would be adequate to control this menace. Both inside any particular country and between the nations of the world,

the control of this weapon will undoubtedly be a matter of the greatest difficulty and would involve such thorough-going rights of inspection and internal controls as we have never heretofore contemplated.

7. Furthermore, in the light of our present position with reference to this weapon, the question of sharing it with other nations and, if so shared, upon what terms, becomes a primary question of our foreign relations. Also our leadership in the war and in the development of this weapon has placed a certain moral responsibility upon us which we cannot shirk without very serious responsibility for any disaster to civilization which it would further.

8. On the other hand, if the problem of the proper use of this weapon can be solved, we would have the opportunity to bring the world into a pattern in which the peace of the world and our civilization can be saved.

9. As stated in General Groves' report, steps are under way looking towards the establishment of a select committee of particular qualifications for recommending action to the Executive and legislative branches of our government when secrecy is no longer in full effect. The committee would also recommend the actions to be taken by the War Department prior to that time in anticipation of the postwar problems. All recommendations would of course be first submitted to the President.

12.4 The Franck Committee Warns of a Nuclear Arms Race and Calls for a Noncombat Demonstration of the Bomb, 1945[4]

In 1945, a group of nuclear scientists appointed by Arthur Compton met in secret to discuss the implications of the Manhattan Project. The committee, led by German-born physicist James Franck, produced a report in June of 1945 recommending the United States not use the atomic bomb against any country but rather conduct a demonstration of the new weapon for international observers. The committee also raised concerns about a postwar arms race and advocated "effective international control of nuclear explosives."

---

4. From Franck, Hughes, Nickson, Rabinowitch, Seaborg, Stearns, and Szilard, "Political and Social Problems," June 11, 1945, Manhattan Engineer District Records, National Archives, Washington, DC; repr. in *Bulletin of the Atomic Scientists* 1 (May 1946), and in Michael B. Stoff, Jonathan F. Fanton, and R. Hal Williams, eds., *The Manhattan Project: A Documentary Introduction to the Atomic Age* (New York: McGraw-Hill, 1991), 140–47.

If no efficient international agreement is achieved, the race for nuclear armaments will be on in earnest not later than the morning after our first demonstration of the existence of nuclear weapons. After this, it might take other nations three or four years to overcome our present head start, and eight or ten years to draw even with us if we continue to do intensive work in this field. . . .

The consequences of nuclear warfare, and the type of measures which would have to be taken to protect a country from total destruction by nuclear bombing, must be as abhorrent to other nations as to the United States. England, France, and the smaller nations of the European continent, with their congeries of people and industries, would be in a particularly desperate situation in the face of such a threat. Russia and China are the only great nations at present which could survive a nuclear attack. However, even though these countries may value human life less than the peoples of Western Europe and America, and even though Russia, in particular, has an immense space over which its vital industries could be dispersed and a government which can order this dispersion the day it is convinced that such a measure is necessary—there is no doubt that Russia will shudder at the possibility of a sudden disintegration of Moscow and Leningrad and of its new industrial cities in the Urals and Siberia. Therefore, only lack of mutual *trust*, and not lack of *desire* for agreement, can stand in the path of an efficient agreement for the prevention of nuclear warfare. The achievement of such an agreement will thus essentially depend on the integrity of intentions and readiness to sacrifice the necessary fraction of one's own sovereignty, by all the parties to the agreement.

From this point of view, the way in which the nuclear weapons now being secretly developed in this country are first revealed to the world appears to be of great, perhaps fateful, importance.

One possible way—which may particularly appeal to those who consider nuclear bombs primarily as a secret weapon developed to help win the present war—is to use them without warning on an appropriately selected object in Japan. It is doubtful whether the first available bombs, of comparatively low efficiency and small size, will be sufficient to break the will or ability of Japan to resist, especially given the fact that the major cities like Tokyo, Nagoya, Osaka, and Kobe already will largely have been reduced to ashes by the slower process of ordinary aerial bombing. Although important tactical results undoubtedly can be achieved by a sudden introduction of nuclear weapons, we nevertheless think that the question of the use of the very first available atomic bombs in the Japanese war should be weighed very carefully, not only by military authorities, but by the highest political leadership of this country. If we consider international agreement on total prevention of nuclear warfare as the paramount objective, and believe that it can be achieved, this kind of introduction of atomic weapons to the world may easily destroy all our chances of success. Russia, and even allied countries which bear less mistrust of our ways and intentions, as well as neutral countries may be deeply shocked. It may be very difficult to persuade the world that a nation which was capable of secretly preparing and suddenly releasing a weapon as indiscriminate as the rocket bomb and a million times more destructive, is to be trusted in its proclaimed desire of having such weapons abolished by international agreement. We have large accumulations of poison gas, but do not use them, and recent polls have shown that public opinion in this country would disapprove of such a use even if it would accelerate the winning of the Far Eastern war. It is true that some irrational element in mass psychology makes gas poisoning more revolting than blasting by explosives, even though gas warfare is in no way more "inhuman" than the war of bombs and bullets. Nevertheless, it is not at all certain that American public opinion, if it could be enlightened as to the effect of atomic explosives, would approve of our own country being the first to introduce such an indiscriminate method of wholesale destruction of civilian life.

Thus, from the "optimistic" point of view—looking forward to an international agreement on the prevention of nuclear warfare—the military advantages and the saving of American lives achieved by the sudden use of atomic bombs against Japan may be outweighed by the ensuing loss of confidence and by a wave of horror and repulsion sweeping over the rest of the world and perhaps even dividing public opinion at home.

From this point of view, a demonstration of the new weapon might best be made before the eyes of representatives of all the United Nations, on the desert or a barren island. The best possible atmosphere for the achievement of an international agreement could be achieved if America could say to the world, "You see what sort of a weapon we had but did not use. We are ready to renounce its use in the future if other nations join us in this renunciation and agree to the establishment of an efficient international control."

After such a demonstration the weapon might perhaps be used against Japan if the sanction of the United Nations (and of public opinion at home) were obtained, perhaps after a preliminary ultimatum to Japan to surrender or at least to evacuate certain regions as an alternative to their total destruction. This may sound fantastic, but in nuclear weapons we have something entirely new in order of magnitude of destructive power, and if we want to capitalize fully on the advantage their possession gives us, we must use new and imaginative methods.

It must be stressed that if one takes the pessimistic point of view and discounts the possibility of an effective international control over nuclear weapons at the present time, then the advisability of an early use of nuclear bombs against Japan becomes even more doubtful—quite independently of any humanitarian considerations. If an international agreement is not concluded immediately after the first demonstration, this will mean a flying start toward an unlimited armaments race. . . .

One may point out that scientists themselves have initiated the development of this "secret weapon" and it is therefore strange that they should be reluctant to try it out on the enemy as soon as it is available. The answer to this question was given above—the compelling reason for creating this weapon with such speed was our fear that Germany had the technical skill necessary to develop such a weapon, and that the German government had no moral restraints regarding its use. . . .

The development of nuclear power not only constitutes an important addition to the technological and military power of the United States, but also creates grave political and economic problems for the future of this country.

Nuclear bombs cannot possibly remain a "secret weapon" at the exclusive disposal of this country for more than a few years. The scientific facts on which their construction is based are well known to scientists of other countries. Unless an effective international control of nuclear explosives is instituted, a race for nuclear armaments is certain to ensue following the first revelation of our possession of nuclear weapons to the world. Within ten years other countries may have nuclear bombs, each of which, weighing less than a ton, could destroy an urban area of more than ten square miles. In the war to which such an armaments race is likely to lead, the United States, with its agglomeration of population and industry in comparatively few metropolitan districts, will be at a disadvantage compared to nations whose population and industry are scattered over large areas.

We believe that these considerations make the use of nuclear bombs for an early unannounced attack against Japan inadvisable. If the United States were to be the first to release this new means of indiscriminate destruction upon mankind, she would sacrifice public support throughout the world, precipitate the race for armaments, and prejudice the possibility of reaching an international agreement on the future control of such weapons.

Much more favorable conditions for the eventual achievement of such an agreement could be created if nuclear bombs were first revealed to the world by a demonstration in an appropriately selected uninhabited area. . . .

To sum up, we urge that the use of nuclear bombs in this war be considered as a problem of long-range national policy rather than of military expediency, and that this policy be directed primarily to the achievement of an agreement permitting an effective international control of the means of nuclear warfare.

The vital importance of such a control for our country is obvious from the fact that the only effective alternative method of protecting this country appears to be a dispersal of our major cities and essential industries.

J. Franck, Chairman
D. J. Hughes
J. J. Nickson
E. Rabinowitch
G. T. Seaborg
J. C. Stearns
L. Szilard

12.5 The Scientific Panel of the Interim Committee Recommends Combat Use of the Bomb against Japan, 1945[5]

In May of 1945, Secretary of War Stimson convened the Interim Committee to advise President Truman on matters pertaining to nuclear energy and weaponry. Made up of prominent political, scientific, and industrial figures, the panel was tasked with making recommendations regarding the wartime and postwar use of nuclear technology. The committee rejected the idea of a technical demonstration and saw no "acceptable alternative to direct military use" of atomic power.

You have asked us to comment on the initial use of the new weapon. This use, in our opinion, should be such as to promote a satisfactory adjustment of our international relations. At the same time, we recognize our

---

5. From Compton, Lawrence, Oppenheimer, and Fermi, "Recommendations on the Immediate Use of Nuclear Weapons, June 16, 1945, Manhattan Engineer District Records, National Archives, Washington, DC; repr. in Michael B. Stoff, Jonathan F. Fanton, and R. Hal Williams, eds., *The Manhattan Project: A Documentary Introduction to the Atomic Age* (New York: McGraw-Hill, 1991), 149–50.

obligation to our nation to use the weapons to help save American lives in the Japanese war.

(1) To accomplish these ends, we recommend that before the weapons are used not only Britain, but also Russia, France, and China be advised that we have made considerable progress in our work on atomic weapons, that these may be ready to use during the present war, and that we would welcome suggestions as to how we can cooperate in making this development contribute to improved international relations.

(2) The opinions of our scientific colleagues on the initial use of these weapons are not unanimous: they range from the proposal of a purely technical demonstration to that of the military application best designed to induce surrender. Those who advocate a purely technical demonstration would wish to outlaw the use of atomic weapons, and have feared that if we use the weapons now our position in future negotiations will be prejudiced. Others emphasize the opportunity of saving American lives by immediate military use, and believe that such use will improve the international prospects, in that they are more concerned with the prevention of war than with the elimination of this specific weapon. We find ourselves closer to these latter views; we can propose no technical demonstration likely to bring an end to the war; we see no acceptable alternative to direct military use.

(3) With regard to these general aspects of the use of atomic energy, it is clear that we, as scientific men, have no proprietary rights. It is true that we are among the few citizens who have had occasion to give thoughtful consideration to these problems during the past few years. We have, however, no claim to special competence in solving the political, social, and military problems which are presented by the advent of atomic power.

12.6 Conventional versus Nuclear Bomb Destruction: Dresden and Hiroshima, 1945

On February 13 and 14, 1945, only months before Hitler committed suicide and Germany surrendered, the Allies dropped 650,000 incendiary bombs on the German city of Dresden. The bombing created a firestorm that engulfed eight square miles and killed some 135,000 men, women, and children. The bombing all but destroyed the city once known as the "Florence of the North." Like the firebombing of Tokyo, which took place a month later and cost at least 85,000 Japanese lives, the attack on Dresden was part of a strategic bombing campaign designed in part to break the public's will to fight.

In August 1945, the United States dropped two atomic bombs, known as Fat Man and Little Boy, on the Japanese cities of Hiroshima and Nagasaki. Together, the two bombings killed at least 129,000 people. In addition to the human toll, the bombs imposed extensive physical damage on both cities. American officials estimated that the Hiroshima bomb destroyed 4.7 square miles of the city; Japanese officials determined that almost 70 percent of the city's buildings had been destroyed and another 6–7 percent damaged.

Allegorie der Gute by Blick von Rathaustrum, 1945. Richard Peter, "Allegorie der Gute," Between September 1945 and December 1945, Deutche Fotohek, Wikimedia Commons, https://upload.wikimedia.org/wikipedia/commons/6/66/Fotothek_df_ps_0000010_Blick_vom_Rathausturm.jpg

Hiroshima Aftermath, cropped version with writing by Paul Tibbets, August 6, 1945. Paul Tibbets, Hiroshima Aftermath, Cropped Version, August 6, 1945, WikiMedia Commons, at http://titan.iwu.edu/~rwilson/hiroshima/rama3.htm.

12.7 Public Opinion Polls Show Strong Support for the Atomic Bomb, August 1945[6]

In August 1945, public opinion expert Hadley Cantril found tremendous public support for the use of the atomic bomb against Hiroshima and Nagasaki. Support for the bomb, which most Americans believed had saved hundreds of thousands of American lives, remained robust four months after the war's end.

(US Aug. 8 '45) Do you approve or disapprove of using the new atomic bomb on Japanese cities? Asked of a cross-section of people who had heard of the bomb. 96% of a national sample is represented.

	Approve	Disapprove	No opinion
United States	85%	10%	5%

---

6. From Hadley Cantril, *Public Opinion, 1935–1946* (Princeton, NJ: Princeton University Press, 1951), 20, 21, 23.

(US Sept. '45) Do you think the United States should try to keep the secret of how to make atomic bombs as long as we can, or do you think we should let some other countries also know how to make them?

	Share	*Keep*	*Miscellaneous or Don't know*
United States	12%	85%	3%

(US Dec. '45) Which of these comes closest to describing how you feel about our use of the atomic bomb?

We should not have used any atomic bombs at all. 4.5%
We should have dropped one first on some unpopulated region,
    to show the Japanese its power, and dropped the second one
    on a city only if they hadn't surrendered after the first one 13.8%
We should have used the two bombs on cities, just as we did 53.5%
We should have quickly used many more of them before
    Japan had a chance to surrender 22.7%
Don't know 5.5%

General Bibliography

Introduction

Hess, Gary R. *The United States at War, 1941–1945.* 3rd ed. Wheeling, IL: Harlan Davidson, 2011.

Kennedy, David M. *Freedom from Fear: The American People in Depression and War, 1929–1945.* New York: Oxford University Press, 1999.

Murray, Williamson, and Allan R. Millett. *A War to Be Won: Fighting the Second World War.* Cambridge, MA: Belknap/Harvard University Press, 2000.

Overy, Richard. *Why the Allies Won.* New York: W. W. Norton, 1995.

Weinberg, Gerhard L. *A World at Arms: A Global History of World War II.* 2nd ed. New York: Cambridge University Press, 2005.

Zeiler, Thomas W. *Annihilation: A Global Military History of World War II.* New York: Oxford University Press, 2011.

Chapter 1: The Yanks Are Coming . . . Again: U.S. Entry into World War II

Dallek, Robert. *Franklin D. Roosevelt and American Foreign Policy, 1932–1945.* New York: Oxford University Press, 1995.

Doenecke, Justus D., and John E. Wilz. *From Isolation to War, 1931–1941.* 4th ed. Malden, MA: Wiley Blackwell, 2015.

Reynolds, David. *The Creation of the Anglo-American Alliance, 1939–1941: A Study in Competitive Cooperation, 1937–1941.* Chapel Hill: University of North Carolina Press, 1981.

———. *From Munich to Pearl Harbor: Roosevelt's America and the Origins of the Second World War.* Chicago: Ivan R. Dee, 2001.

Chapter 2: Over Here: Mobilizing the American People for War

Blum, John M. *V Was for Victory: Politics and American Culture during World War II.* New York: Harvest/HBJ, 1977.

Klein, Murray. *A Call to Arms: Mobilizing America for World War II.* New York: Bloomsbury Press, 2013.

Kryder, Daniel. *Divided Arsenal: Race and the American State during World War II.* Cambridge: Cambridge University Press, 2000.

Sparrow, James T. *The Warfare State: World War II Americans and the Age of Big Government.* New York: Oxford University Press, 2011.

Chapter 3: Creating a Global Allied Strategy to Defeat the Axis Powers

Kimball, Warren F. *Forged in War: Roosevelt, Churchill, and the Second World War.* New York: William Morrow, 1998.

Matloff, Maurice. *Strategic Planning for Coalition Warfare, 1943–1944.* Vol. 6 of *United States Army in World War II: The War Department.* Washington, DC: U.S. Government Printing Office, 1959.

Matloff, Maurice, and Edwin Snell. *Strategic Planning for Coalition Warfare, 1941–1942.* Vol. 3 of *United States Army in World War II: The War Department.* Washington, DC: U.S. Government Printing Office, 1953.

Reynolds, David, Warren F. Kimball, and A. O. Chubarian. *Allies at War: The Soviet, American, and British Experience, 1939–1945.* New York: St. Martin's Press, 1994.

Stoler, Mark A. *Allies in War: Britain and America against the Axis Powers, 1940–1945.* London: Hodder-Arnold, 2005.

Chapter 4: Fighting and Defeating Nazi Germany

Ambrose, Stephen E. *Citizen Soldiers: The U.S. Army from the Normandy Beaches to the Bulge to the Surrender of Germany, June 7, 1944–May 7, 1945.* New York: Simon & Schuster, 1997.

Atkinson, Rick. *An Army at Dawn: The War in North Africa, 1942–1943; The Day of Battle: The War in Sicily and Italy, 1943–1944;* and *The Guns at Last Light: The War in Western Europe: 1944–1945.* The Liberation Trilogy. New York: Henry Holt, 2002, 2007, 2013.

Miller, Donald L. *Masters of the Air: America's Bomber Boys Who Fought the Air War against Nazi Germany.* New York: Simon & Schuster, 2006.

Morison, Samuel Eliot. *The Battle of the Atlantic, 1939–1945.* Vol. 1 of *History of United States Naval Operations in World War II.* New York: Castle Books, 2001. First published 1947 by Little, Brown.

Overy, Richard. *The Bombing War, Europe, 1939–1945.* London: Allen Lane, 2013.

Chapter 5: The War against Japan—and the Japanese

Daniels, Roger. *Prisoners without Trial: Japanese Americans in World War II.* New York: Hill and Wang, 1993.

Dower, John W. *War without Mercy: Race & Power in the Pacific War.* New York: Pantheon Books, 1986.

Iriye, Akira. *Power and Culture: The Japanese-American War, 1941–1945.* Cambridge, MA: Harvard University Press, 1981.

Schaller, Michael. *The U.S. Crusade in China, 1938–1945.* New York: Columbia University Press, 1979.

Spector, Ronald H. *Eagle against the Sun: The American War with Japan*. New York: Free Press/Macmillan, 1985.

Thorne, Christopher. *Allies of a Kind: The United States, Britain, and the War against Japan, 1941–1945*. New York: Oxford University Press, 1978.

Chapter 6: For the Duration: Life and Society on the American Home Front

Erenberg, Lewis A., and Susan E. Hirsch, eds. *The War in American Culture: Society and Consciousness during World War II*. Chicago: University of Chicago Press, 1996.

Kruse, Kevin, and Stephen Tuck, eds. *Fog of War: The Second World War and the Civil Rights Movement*. New York: Oxford University Press, 2012.

Lichtenstein, Nelson. *Labor's War at Home: The CIO in World War II*. Cambridge: Cambridge University Press, 1982.

Takaki, Ronald. *Double Victory: A Multicultural History of America in World War II*. Boston: Little, Brown, 2000.

Terkel, Studs. *"The Good War": An Oral History of World War II*. New York: New Press, 1984.

Chapter 7: The Manhattan Project and Beyond: The Role of Science, Medicine, and Technology in the American War Effort

Hartcup, Gary, and Sir Bernard Lovell. *The Effect of Science on the Second World War*. London: Palgrave Macmillan, 2003.

Kennedy, Paul. *The Engineers of Victory: The Problem Solvers Who Turned the Tide in the Second World War*. New York: Random House, 2013.

Rhodes, Richard. *The Making of the Atomic Bomb: 25th Anniversary Edition*. New York: Simon & Schuster, 2012.

Richards, Pamela Spence. *Scientific Information in Wartime: The Allied-German Rivalry, 1939–1945*. Westport, CT: Greenwood Press, 1994.

Chapter 8: The Intelligence War: Code Breaking, Cryptography, Intelligence Gathering, and Allied Victory

Budiansky, Stephen. *The Battle of Wits: The Complete Story of Codebreaking in World War II*. New York: Free Press, 2000.

Copeland, B. Jack. *Colossus: The Secrets of Bletchley Park's Codebreaking Computers*. New York: Oxford University Press, 2010.

Drea, Edward. *MacArthur's ULTRA: Codebreaking and the War Against Japan, 1942–1945*. Modern War Studies. Lawrence: University Press of Kansas, 1991.

Hastings, Max. *The Secret War: Spies, Ciphers, and Guerillas, 1939–1945*. New York: Harper, 2016.

Hinsley, F. H. *British Intelligence in the Second World War*. 5 vols. London: Her Majesty's Stationery Office, 1979–1990.

Chapter 9: The United States and the Holocaust

Breitman, Richard, and Allan J. Lichtman. *FDR and the Jews*. Cambridge, MA: Belknap/Harvard University Press, 2013.

Neufeld, Michael J., and Michael Berenbaum, eds. *The Bombing of Auschwitz: Should the Allies Have Attempted It?* Lawrence: University Press of Kansas, 2000.

Novick, Peter. *The Holocaust in American Life*. New York: Mariner Books, 2000.

Wyman, David S. *The Abandonment of the Jews: America and the Holocaust, 1941–1945*. New York: New Press, 1984.

Chapter 10: Planning and Preparing for the Peace at Home

Brinkley, Alan. *The End of Reform: New Deal Liberalism in Recession and War*. Repr. ed. New York: Vintage, 1996.

Cohen, Lizabeth. *A Consumers' Republic: The Politics of Mass Consumption in Postwar America*. New York: Alfred A. Knopf, 2003.

Frydl, Kathleen. *The GI Bill*. Cambridge: Cambridge University Press, 2009.

Katznelson, Ira. *When Affirmative Action Was White: An Untold History of Racial Inequality in Twentieth-Century America*. New York: W. W. Norton, 2005.

Mettler, Suzanne. *Soldiers to Citizens: The G.I. Bill and the Making of the Greatest Generation*. New York: Oxford University Press, 2011.

Chapter 11: President Franklin D. Roosevelt and Allied Diplomacy for War and Peace

Dallek, Robert. *Franklin D. Roosevelt and American Foreign Policy, 1932–1945*. New York: Oxford University Press, 1995.

Kimball, Warren F. *The Juggler: Franklin Roosevelt as Wartime Statesman*. Princeton, NJ: Princeton University Press, 1991.

Louis, William Roger. *Imperialism at Bay: The United States and the Decolonization of the British Empire, 1941–1945*. New York: Oxford University Press, 1978.

Smith, Gaddis. *American Diplomacy during the Second World War, 1941–1945*. 2nd ed. New York: Wiley, 1985.

Woolner, David B., Warren F. Kimball, and David Reynolds. *FDR's World: War, Peace, and Legacies*. New York: Palgrave Macmillan, 2008.

Chapter 12: The Atomic Bomb and the End of World War II

Alperowitz, Gar. *Atomic Diplomacy: Hiroshima and Potsdam*. New York: Vintage, 1965, 1985.

Frank, Richard B. *Downfall: The End of the Imperial Japanese Empire*. New York: Random House, 1999.

Hasegawa, Tsuyoshi. *Racing the Enemy: Stalin, Truman, and the Surrender of Japan*. New York: Belknap Press, 2006.

Rotter, Andrew. *Hiroshima: The World's Bomb*. New York: Oxford University Press, 2008.

Walker, J. Samuel. *Prompt and Utter Destruction: Truman and the Use of Atomic Bombs against Japan*. 3rd ed. Chapel Hill: University of North Carolina Press, 2016.